This book contains a descriptive gazetteer of all the secular buildings (including industrial sites) known by their surviving remains to have existed within the Crusader Kingdom of Jerusalem.

The site descriptions take the form of brief notes with full bibliographical references and location maps, accompanied in most cases by photographs and drawings. The gazetteer is preceded by an introduction which analyses the range of building types to be found in the Crusader Kingdom, and is followed by a supplementary gazetteer listing other sites as 'possibles', 'rejects' or 'don't knows'.

This gazetteer has been compiled under the auspices of the British School of Archaeology in Jerusalem, and is published as a companion volume to Dr Pringle's three-volume work *The Churches of the Crusader Kingdom of Jerusalem* (1993–).

# Secular buildings in the Crusader Kingdom of Jerusalem

# Secular buildings in the Crusader Kingdom of Jerusalem

## An archaeological gazetteer

DENYS PRINGLE

CAMBRIDGE
UNIVERSITY PRESS

CAMBRIDGE UNIVERSITY PRESS
Cambridge, New York, Melbourne, Madrid, Cape Town, Singapore, São Paulo, Delhi

Cambridge University Press
The Edinburgh Building, Cambridge CB2 8RU, UK

Published in the United States of America by Cambridge University Press, New York

www.cambridge.org
Information on this title: www.cambridge.org/9780521102636

First published 1997
This digitally printed version 2009

*A catalogue record for this publication is available from the British Library*

*Library of Congress Cataloguing in Publication data*

Pringle, Denys.
Secular buildings in the Crusader Kingdom of Jerusalem: an
archaeological gazetteer / by Denys Pringle.
  p.  cm.
Includes bibliographical references (p.   ) and index.
ISBN 0 521 46010 7
1. Buildings – Jerusalem (Latin Kingdom) – Gazetteers.
2. Jerusalem – Buildings, structures, etc. – Gazetteers.  3. Jerusalem
(Latin Kingdom) – Gazetteers.  I. Title.
D183.P75 1997
720'.95694'09021 – dc20    96-31664 CIP

ISBN 978-0-521-46010-1 hardback
ISBN 978-0-521-10263-6 paperback

# CONTENTS

| | |
|---|---|
| *List of plates* | *page* viii |
| *List of figures* | xiii |
| *List of tables* | xvi |
| *Preface* | xvii |
| *List of abbreviations* | xix |
| **Introduction** | 1 |
| **Addenda** | 111 |
| **Gazetteer** | 15 |
| **Supplementary gazetteer** | 112 |
| Possibles | 112 |
| Rejects | 115 |
| Don't knows | 119 |
| *Bibliography* | 121 |
| *Maps* | 141 |
| *Index of place-names* | 152 |

# PLATES

*The photographs are the author's unless otherwise stated.*

|  |  | page |
|---|---|---|
| I | Acre (**no. 5**): courtyard of a house. | 17 |
| II | Acre (**no. 5**): Burj as-Sultan, from S. | 17 |
| III | Acre (**no. 5**): inner N wall of Crusader city. | 17 |
| IV | Acre (**no. 5**): Khan ash-Shuna, incorporating remains of Pisan market. | 17 |
| V | al-'Affula (**no. 7**): medieval redoubt or tower. | 18 |
| VI | 'Ain al-Haramiya (**no. 11**): vaulted cistern. | 19 |
| VII | 'Ain Duq (**no. 13**): medieval aqueduct. | 19 |
| VIII | Ascalon (**no. 20**): rounded tower belonging to Richard I's refortification (1192). | 21 |
| IX | 'Atlit (**no. 21**): Pilgrims' Castle, from E. | 22 |
| X | Tall al-Badawiya (**no. 24**): basement of tower. | 24 |
| XI | Baisan (**no. 26**): the castle. | 25 |
| XII | Bait 'Itab (**no. 31**): courtyard building. | 27 |
| XIII | Bait 'Itab (**no. 31**): hall-house. | 27 |
| XIV | Bait Jubr at-Tahtani (**no. 33**): tower beside the Jericho road. | 28 |
| XV | Kh. Bait Kika (**no. 34**): barrel-vaulted building. | 28 |
| XVI | Bait Safafa (**no. 37**): interior of tower. | 29 |
| XVII | Kh. Bal'ama (**no. 41**): tower, remains of N wall (photo. from Macalister 1930). | 30 |
| XVIII | Kh. Bal'ama (**no. 41**): vaulted tunnel leading to spring (photo. courtesy of the Israel Antiquities Authority, Neg. no. 25.093). | 30 |
| XIX | Beaufort Castle (**no. 44**): from S (photo. Iain MacIvor, 1963). | 32 |
| XX | Belvoir Castle (**no. 46**): outer SE corner tower, overlooking Jordan Valley. | 33 |

| | | |
|---|---|---|
| XXI | Belvoir Castle (**no. 46**): inner ward, from SE. | 33 |
| XXII | Kh. Bir Zait (**no. 53**): courtyard building, S range. | 34 |
| XXIII | al-Bira (**no. 54**): Crusader *curia* (Khan al-Bira), groin-vaulting enclosing tower. | 35 |
| XXIV | Kh. al-Burj (**no. 58**): tower (photo. courtesy of the Israel Antiquities Authority, Neg. no. 2613). | 37 |
| XXV | Kh. al-Burj, Burj al-Jauz (**no. 61**): main street of Frankish settlement, flanked by houses. | 38 |
| XXVI | Kh. al-Burj (**no. 62**): remains of tower. | 38 |
| XXVII | Burj al-Ahmar (**no. 63**): S wall of tower. | 39 |
| XXVIII | Kh. Burj al-Far'a (**no. 64**): from NW. | 40 |
| XXIX | Kh. Burj as-Sur (**no. 71**): inside NW corner of tower. | 42 |
| XXX | Burj Baitin (**no. 73**): tower from W. | 42 |
| XXXI | Burj Bardawil (**no. 74**): vault 4, known as *al-Baubariya*. | 43 |
| XXXII | Caesarea (**no. 76**): town walls, NE tower. | 44 |
| XXXIII | Caesarea (**no. 76**): town walls, N gate-tower. | 44 |
| XXXIV a-b | Caesarea (**no. 76**): town walls, capitals in N gate-tower. | 44 |
| XXXV | Caesarea (**no. 76**): town walls, interior of E gate. | 45 |
| XXXVI | Caesarea (**no. 76**): courtyard of Fatimid house, reused in Crusader period. | 45 |
| XXXVII | al-Habis (**no. 97**): castle, upper ward looking towards keep. | 49 |
| XXXVIII | al-Habis (**no. 97**): castle, view S from keep. | 49 |
| XXXIX | Tall Hisban (**no. 102**): Mamluk bath-house, overlying village buildings. | 51 |
| XL | Jerusalem (**no. 115**): town walls, NW corner, showing foundations of Tancred's Tower. | 54 |
| XLI | Jerusalem (**no. 115**): Herodian Tower of Hippicus, abutted by NE curtain (*14*) of Citadel. | 55 |
| XLII | Jerusalem (**no. 115**): S front of Hospital, facing David Street. | 55 |
| XLIII | Jerusalem (**no. 115**): Street of Herbs, covered market. | 55 |
| XLIV | Jerusalem (**no. 115**): Crusader shop fronts in Street of Mount Sion. | 56 |
| XLV | Jerusalem (**no. 115**): Crusader fountain head, excavated in front of Damascus Gate in 1980. | 56 |
| XLVI | Jifna (**no. 118**): gateway to courtyard building. | 58 |
| XLVII | Jifna (**no. 118**): courtyard building, E side of courtyard. | 58 |

| | | |
|---|---|---|
| XLVIII | Karak (**no. 124**): castle, from SE. | 60 |
| XLIX | Karak (**no. 124**): castle, E wall, looking N from tower 4. | 60 |
| L | Karak (**no. 124**): Crusader W wall of inner ward, with Ayyubid–Mamluk keep behind. | 60 |
| LI | Karak (**no. 124**): vaulted passage (now underground), running N from chapel. | 60 |
| LII | Kh. al-Karmil (**no. 126**): E wall of tower, from E (photo. *c*.1920, courtesy of the École Biblique et Archéologique Française de Jérusalem, Neg. no. 2755). | 61 |
| LIII | Kh. al-Karmil (**no. 126**): tower, vaulted basement, looking N. | 61 |
| LIV | Khan as-Sawiya (**no. 128**): from SW. | 61 |
| LV | Kh. Kurdana (**no. 133**): water-mill and dam, from SE. | 63 |
| LVI | Kh. Kurdana (**no. 133**): vaulted wheel-chambers with mill room above, from SW with tower behind. | 63 |
| LVII | Kh. Kurdana (**no. 133**): wheel-chamber of water-mill. | 63 |
| LVIII | Kh. Kurdana (**no. 133**): arrow-slit with stirrup base in S wall of tower. | 63 |
| LIX | Kuwaikat (**no. 135**): vault (photo. 1934, courtesy Israel Antiquities Authority, Neg. no. 6926). | 64 |
| LX | Latrun (**no. 136**): S range of inner ward. | 66 |
| LXI | Latrun (**no. 136**): interior of tower (?) to SW of inner ward. | 66 |
| LXII | Kh. al-Lauza (**no. 137**): courtyard building and terraces. | 66 |
| LXIII | Lifta (**no. 138**): barrel-vaulted cistern with house above it. | 66 |
| LXIV | Majdal Yaba (**no. 144**): door to tower. | 69 |
| LXV | Majdal Yaba (**no. 144**): S side of central courtyard. | 69 |
| LXVI | Kh. Manawat (**no. 145**): sugar factory. | 69 |
| LXVII | Kh. Manawat (**no. 145**): rock-cut olive-press. | 69 |
| LXVIII | Kh. al-Manhata (**no. 146**): rock-cut base of tower in quarry. | 70 |
| LXIX | Miʿiliya (**no. 152**): castle, NW tower. | 71 |
| LXX | Miʿiliya (**no. 152**): castle, NE tower. | 71 |
| LXXI | Minat al-Qalʿa (**no. 153**): towers flanking gateway on E. | 72 |
| LXXII | Montfort Castle, Qalʿat al-Qurain (**no. 156**): from E. | 73 |

| | | |
|---|---|---|
| LXXIII | Montfort Castle, Qal'at al-Qurain (**no. 156**): inner ward, looking E from keep. | 75 |
| LXXIV | Montfort Castle, Qal'at al-Qurain (**no. 156**): mill and dam below castle, converted into thirteenth-century hall-house. | 75 |
| LXXV | Montfort Castle, Qal'at al-Qurain (**no. 156**): thirteenth-century hall-house, interior. | 75 |
| LXXVI | Montreal, Shaubak (**no. 157**): castle, from NW. | 76 |
| LXXVII | Montreal, Shaubak (**no. 157**): Frankish and Ayyubid structures inside the castle. | 76 |
| LXXVIII | Qalansuwa (**no. 160**): Crusader hall, doorways to basement and first floor. | 77 |
| LXXIX | Qal'at ad-Damm (**no. 162**): castle, N corner. | 78 |
| LXXX | Qal'at Hunin (**no. 164**): castle, from NW. | 79 |
| LXXXI | Qal'at Jiddin (**no. 165**): N wall of inner ward (photo. courtesy Israel Antiquities Authority, Neg. no. 25.326). | 82 |
| LXXXII | Qal'at Jiddin (**no. 165**): latrine closet in E tower (*A*). | 82 |
| LXXXIII | Qal'at Jiddin (**no. 165**): W tower (*B*), S elevation. | 82 |
| LXXXIV | Qal'at Jiddin (**no. 165**): W tower (*B*), S door and mural stair. | 83 |
| LXXXV | Qaqun (**no. 168**): tower from NE. | 83 |
| LXXXVI | Qasr al-'Atra, *le Chastelez* (**no. 174**): curtain wall on NW side of mound. | 85 |
| LXXXVII | al-Qubaiba (**no. 178**): house 3, showing entrance to basement and stair to upper floor. | 87 |
| LXXXVIII | al-Qubaiba (**no. 178**): wine-press in house 3. | 87 |
| LXXXIX | ar-Ram (**no. 182**): courtyard building, view over courtyard. | 89 |
| XC | ar-Ram (**no. 182**): tower, interior. | 89 |
| XCI | ar-Ram (**no. 182**): courtyard building, outlet from wine-press. | 89 |
| XCII | Kh. Rushmiya (**no. 190**): tower, interior of forebuilding. | 91 |
| XCIII | Safad (**no. 191**): distant view of castle from NE, taken by K.A.C. Creswell *c*.1919 (courtesy of the Israel Antiquities Authority, Neg. no. 167859). | 92 |
| XCIV | Saffuriya (**no. 192**): tower, from SW. | 92 |
| XCV | Sidon (**no. 201**): Land Castle, photographed from S by K.A.C. Creswell, *c*.1919 (photo. from the Creswell Archive, Ashmolean Museum, University of Oxford, Neg. no. C5286) | 94 |

| | | |
|---|---|---|
| XCVI | Sidon (**no. 201**): Sea Castle, interior looking E (photo. Iain MacIvor, 1963). | 95 |
| XCVII | as-Sumairiya (**no. 208**): vaulted range, looking S. | 97 |
| XCVIII | at-Taiyiba (**no. 215**): NE angle of outer enceinte. | 99 |
| XCIX | Tawahin as-Sukkar (**no. 219b**): sugar factory. | 100 |
| C | Tiberias (**no. 222**): vaulted building in town centre. | 102 |
| CI | Tibnin (**no. 223**): castle, from SW (photo. courtesy of the École Biblique et Archéologique Française de Jérusalem, Neg. no. 7172). | 102 |
| CII | at-Tira (**no. 224**): Crusader tower (photo. courtesy of the Israel Antiquities Authority, Neg. no. 34.430). | 102 |
| CIII | Umm at-Taiyiba (**no. 228**): tower interior, S wall of SE bay. | 104 |
| CIV | Umm Khalid (**no. 229**): courtyard building, S range (photo. courtesy of the Israel Antiquities Authority, Neg. no. 13.156). | 104 |
| CV | al-Wu'aira (**no. 230**): rock pinnacle that formerly supported the bridge to the outer gate. | 105 |
| CVI | al-Wu'aira (**no. 230**): NE tower and ravelin. | 106 |
| CVII | al-Wu'aira (**no. 230**): rock-cut E ditch. | 106 |
| CVIII | Yalu (**no. 231**): W wall, with projecting tower. | 107 |
| CIX | Yalu (**no. 231**): mural stair leading to blocked door. | 107 |
| CX | Yazur (**no. 233**): tower, from N. | 108 |
| CXI | Yazur (**no. 233**): tower, E wall. | 108 |
| CXII | Yazur (**no. 233**): tower, E window from inside. | 109 |
| CXIII | Yazur (**no. 233**): tower, opening in vault for stair to upper floor. | 109 |

# FIGURES

|   |   | page |
|---|---|---|
| 1 | Map showing the location of urban settlements in the Kingdom of Jerusalem. | 3 |
| 2 | Plans of towers: (a) Kh. al-Karmil (**no. 126**); (b) Majdal Yaba (**no. 144**); (c) Saffuriya (**no. 192**); (d) Qal'at ad-Damm (**no. 162**); (e) Qarawat Bani Hassan, Burj al-Yaqur (**no. 170**); (f) Umm at-Taiyiba (**no. 228**); (g) Jaba' (**no. 108**). | 7 |
| 3 | Acre (**no. 5**): plan of Crusader structures in the Old City. | 16 |
| 4 | 'Ain Salman al-'Anid (**no. 14**): plan of group of vaulted buildings. | 19 |
| 5 | Arsuf (**no. 19**): town plan. | 20 |
| 6 | Ascalon (**no. 20**): town plan. | 21 |
| 7 | 'Atlit (**no. 21**): plan of the castle and walled *faubourg*. | 22 |
| 8 | 'Atlit: sketch of site, showing location of castle and *faubourg* (**no. 21**), moated tower (**no. 22**), Bait al-Milh (**no. 28**) and Kh. Dustray (**no. 90**). | 23 |
| 9 | 'Atlit (**no. 21**): bath-house in the *faubourg*. | 23 |
| 10 | Tall al-Badawiya (**no. 24**): plan of tower basement. | 24 |
| 11 | Baisan (**no. 26**): plan of the castle. | 25 |
| 12 | Bait 'Itab (**no. 31**): plan of hall-house, later incorporated into courtyard building. | 26 |
| 13 | Bait Jubr at-Tahtani (**no. 33**): plan and section of tower. | 28 |
| 14 | Beaufort Castle (**no. 44**): plan. | 31 |
| 15 | Beirut (**no. 45**): sketch plan of city. | 32 |
| 16 | Belvoir Castle (**no. 46**): plan. | 32 |
| 17 | Kh. Bir Zait (**no. 53**): plan of courtyard building. | 34 |
| 18 | al-Bira (**no. 54**): plan of twelfth-century Frankish 'new town'. | 36 |

| | | |
|---|---|---|
| 19 | al-Burj, Qal'at Tantura (**no. 57**): plan of keep-and-bailey castle. | 37 |
| 20 | Kh. al-Burj, al-Burj al-Jauz (**no. 61**): plan of hall-house. | 38 |
| 21 | Burj al-Ahmar (**no. 63**): plan of castle. | 39 |
| 22 | Burj al-Malih (**no. 66**): plan of defensive enclosure. | 40 |
| 23 | Burj as-Sahl (**no. 70**): plan of courtyard building. | 41 |
| 24 | Burj Bardawil (**no. 74**): plan. | 43 |
| 25 | Caesarea (**no. 76**): plan of city. | 44 |
| 26 | Kh. Dustray (**no. 90**): remains of castle and road station. | 48 |
| 27 | al-Habis (**no. 97**): plan of castle. | 50 |
| 28 | Jerusalem (**no. 115**): plan of the city. | 53 |
| 29 | Jerusalem (**no. 115**): plan of the Citadel (David's Tower). | 54 |
| 30 | al-Jib (**no. 117**): plan of Crusader additions to a building complex of fifth- to eighth-century date. | 57 |
| 31 | Kafr Lam (**no. 121**): plan of early Muslim fort. | 59 |
| 32 | Karak (**no. 124**): plan of the castle. | 59 |
| 33 | Kh. Kurdana (**no. 133**): plan of fortified mill complex. | 62 |
| 34 | Latrun (**no. 136**): plan of inner part of castle. | 65 |
| 35 | Majdal Yaba (**no. 144**): plan of castle. | 68 |
| 36 | Mi'iliya (**no. 152**): plan of inner ward of castle. | 71 |
| 37 | Kh. al-Misqa (**no. 155**): plan and section of vaulted building. | 72 |
| 38 | Montfort Castle (**no. 156**): plan and section of castle. | 73 |
| 39 | Montfort Castle (**no. 156**): plans and sections of mill, later converted into first-floor hall. | 74 |
| 40 | Qalansuwa (**no. 160**): plan of Crusader buildings surviving in village centre. | 77 |
| 41 | Qal'at Abu'l-Hasan (**no. 161**): plan of castle. | 78 |
| 42 | Qal'at ad-Damm (**no. 162**): plan of castle. | 78 |
| 43 | Qal'at Hunin (**no. 164**): plan of castle. | 80 |
| 44 | Qal'at Jiddin (**no. 165**): plan and section of Crusader castle. | 81 |
| 45 | Qaqun (**no. 168**): plans and section of tower. | 84 |
| 46 | al-Qubaiba (**no. 178**): plan of Frankish 'new town'. | 86 |
| 47 | Qula (**no. 180**): plan of tower and vaulted building. | 87 |
| 48 | ar-Ram (**no. 182**): plan of the *curia* of the steward of the canons of the Holy Sepulchre. | 88 |
| 49 | Kh. Rushmiya (**no. 190**): plan of tower with fore-building. | 91 |

| | | |
|---|---|---|
| 50 | Safad (**no. 191**): plan of castle in 1875–6. | 92 |
| 51 | Tall as-Safi (**no. 194**): plan of castle. | 93 |
| 52 | Sidon (**no. 201**): town plan. | 94 |
| 53 | Suba (**no. 207**): plan of castle. | 96 |
| 54 | as-Sumairiya (**no. 208**): plan of courtyard building. | 96 |
| 55 | at-Taiyiba (**no. 215**): plan of Castle of St Elias. | 98 |
| 56 | Tawahin as-Sukkar (**no. 219b**): plan and section through sugar factory. | 100 |
| 57 | Tawahin as-Sukkar (**no. 219b**): plan and section through mill. | 101 |
| 58 | Tyre (**no. 227**): plan of city. | 103 |
| 59 | Umm Khalid (**no. 229**): plan of S range of courtyard building. | 105 |
| 60 | al-Wu'aira (**no. 230**): plan of castle. | 106 |
| 61 | Yalu (**no. 231**): plan of surviving remains of castle. | 107 |
| 62 | Yazur (**no. 233**): plan of tower. | 108 |

# TABLES

|   |                                | *page* |
|---|--------------------------------|--------|
| 1 | Urban settlements              | 4      |
| 2 | The areas enclosed by town walls | 5    |
| 3 | Towers                         | 8      |
| 4 | Hall-houses                    | 12     |

# PREFACE

In January 1988, the Council of the British School of Archaeology in Jerusalem determined to continue the School's tradition of research into the medieval buildings of Palestine, already established by such projects as the architectural survey of medieval Muslim buildings in Jerusalem (see Burgoyne 1976; Burgoyne and Richards 1987) and of the church buildings of the Crusader Kingdom of Jerusalem (Pringle 1982; 1993), by forming a Committee for Medieval and Ottoman Architecture. The Committee's remit has been to promote and coordinate the field survey and publication of the principal surviving medieval buildings of the area. One of its first tasks has therefore been to commission the compilation of lists of buildings that might be worthy of further investigation. The gazetteer of secular buildings in the Crusader Kingdom of Jerusalem published here is compiled within these general terms of reference. However, it is hoped that as well as serving as a guide to future workers in the field, it may also be of value to historians, archaeologists and historical geographers concerned with the building history and topography of the Crusader Kingdom.

I am grateful to Cambridge University Press for agreeing to publish the Gazetteer as a companion volume to *The Churches of the Crusader Kingdom of Jerusalem: A Corpus* (3 vols., 1993–). Indeed, it is in many ways a by-product of that larger, more comprehensive project. Among the many institutions that have contributed directly or indirectly to the additional field work and archive and library research on which the Gazetteer is based I would also like to mention, in addition to the British School of Archaeology in Jerusalem itself: the British Academy, for sponsorship of the Burj al-Ahmar excavation and survey project (1983), the Belmont Castle excavations (1986–8), and the Medieval and Ottoman Architectural Survey (1988–); the Royal Archaeological Institute, for sponsorship of a survey of Crusader castles in 1989; the Israel Antiquities Authority, for the granting of survey permits and of access to the archives of the former Palestine Department of Antiquities (1918–48), housed in the Palestine Archaeological (Rockefeller) Museum, Jerusalem; the Palestine National Authority, for permission to survey a sugar mill in the territory of Jericho (1995); the Department of Antiquities of Jordan; and the Palestine Exploration Fund, for access to their archive collection.

Among those who have assisted me with information about secular buildings, often unpublished, I would also like to thank especially Dr Adrian Boas, Dr Ronnie Ellenblum, Dr Rafael Frankel, Dr John France, Dr Shimon

Gibson, Mr Richard Harper, Dr Adam Johns, Mr Andrew Petersen and Ms Brigitte Porëe.

Credits for illustrations will be found in the lists of figures and plates. However, particular mention should here be made of the assistance in surveying and drawing monuments in the field that I have received from the architects Peter E. Leach (who also drew the maps) and Matthew Pease.

RDP.

*Edinburgh, March 1996*

# ABBREVIATIONS

| | |
|---|---|
| *AI* | Palestine under the Crusaders. *Atlas of Israel*, sheet IX/10, ed. J. Prawer and M. Benvenisti. Jerusalem (1970) |
| Ar. | Arabic |
| BSAJ | British School of Archaeology in Jerusalem |
| *Cart. des Hosp.* | *Cartulaire générale de l'ordre des Hospitaliers de Saint-Jean de Jérusalem (1100–1311)*, ed. J. Delaville le Roulx, 4 vols. Paris (1894–1906) |
| *Churches* | D. Pringle, *The Churches of the Crusader Kingdom of Jerusalem: A Corpus*, 3 vols. (in progress). Cambridge (1993–) |
| Cr. | Crusader |
| diam. | diameter |
| Gr. | Greek |
| H. | Horva(t), meaning 'ruin' (Hebrew) |
| Hebr. | Hebrew |
| *IHC* | *Itinera Hierosolymitana Crucesignatorum (saec. XII–XIII)*, ed. S. de Sandoli, 4 vols. SBF, Coll. maj., vol. XXIV. Jerusalem (1978–84) |
| *Itin. Ric.* | *Itinerarium Peregrinorum et Gesta Regis Ricardi*, in *RS*, vol. XXXVIII.i, London (1864) |
| Kh. | Khirba(t), meaning 'ruin' (Arabic) |
| Med. | Medieval |
| PAM | Palestine Archaeological (Rockefeller) Museum, Archives of the Dept of Antiquities of the Government of Palestine (1918–48) |
| PEF | Palestine Exploration Fund Archives, London |
| *PPTS* | *Palestine Pilgrims' Text Society Library*, 13 vols. London (1890–7) |
| *q.v.* | *quod vide* (denotes cross reference) |
| *RHC Occ* | *Recueil des historiens des croisades. Historiens occidentaux*, 5 vols. Paris (1844–95) |
| *RHC Or* | *Recueil des historieus des croisades. Historiens orientaux*, 5 vols. Paris (1872–1906) |
| *RRH* | *Regesta Regni Hierosolymitani*, ed. R. Röhricht. Innsbruck (1893) |
| *RRH Ad* | *Regesta Regni Hierosolymitani. Additamentum*, ed. R. Röhricht. Innsbruck (1904) |

| RS | *Rerum Britannicarum Medii Aeui Scriptores, or Chronicles and Memorials of Great Britain and Ireland in the Middle Ages* (Rolls Series), 99 vols. London (1858–97) |
| Rus. | Russian |
| SSCLE | Society for the Study of the Crusades and the Latin East |
| SWP | Survey of Western Palestine |

Six- or eight-figure grid references are to the Palestine (or Israel) Grid. In the Gazetteer they are followed by a number in square brackets, which refers to the relevant map at the end of this volume (pp. 141–51).

# INTRODUCTION

## The Scope of the Gazetteer

The Gazetteer represents an attempt to list all the secular buildings (including industrial sites) known by their surviving remains to have existed within the boundaries of the Kingdom of Jerusalem at any time between 1099 and 1291. Each entry consists of a site number and name (with Crusader, Arabic and Hebrew alternatives), a reference to the Palestine (or Israel) Grid, a very brief description of the nature of the surviving or recorded structural remains, and a list of sources. Since the Gazetteer is intended to be archaeologically rather than historically based, references to medieval primary sources are usually omitted unless they provide evidence for dating or important descriptive information about the structures concerned. In compensation for this limitation, it may be noted that in many cases the secondary sources quoted will themselves provide a means of entry into the primary sources; a fairly comprehensive survey of the primary sources relating to castle-building may also be found in the volumes by Paul Deschamps (1934; 1939a). Unlike *Churches*, however, no attempt has been made to include in the Gazetteer a full list of buildings that are known only from documentary sources and of which no archaeological traces remain.

The Gazetteer excludes all religious buildings, since churches are listed and described in detail in *Churches* and the Islamic buildings of medieval and Ottoman Palestine will be covered by another gazetteer, which is being compiled by Andrew Petersen. Among the various Muslim buildings constructed in Palestine at the time of the Kingdom of Jerusalem, however, may be noted in particular: a mosque built in 'Ajjul (Grid ref. 167.159), between Nablus and al-Bira, by Abū'l-Majd Ibn 'Abd al-Jalīl in Ramadan 572 H/June–July AD 1176–7 (PAM: report by S. A. S. Husseini, 3 Jan. 1935; squeeze

nos. 561–2; photo no. 9447; cf. Palestine 1948: 101); and a mosque at Bait Hanun (Grid ref. 106.105), built by the amir Shams al-Dīn Sunqur in 1239 (Sukenik 1946). Muslim cemeteries dating from the Frankish period have been excavated at Kh. Tall ad-Durur (**no. 89**), Tall Mubarak (Grid ref. 1434.2155: Stern 1978: 4–9, pl. 46.15; 1994: 31–3, fig. 7; Tombs 1985: 17–18), Tall Dair 'Alla (**no. 81**), Tall Qiri (Grid ref. 1610.2278: Ben-Tor and Portugali 1987: 5, 7–8), Kh. Tall al-Far'a (**no. R4**), Tall al-Hasi (**no. R5**) and Tantura (**no. 218**). Remains of possible Samaritan synagogues at 'Ain Sarin (Grid. ref. 176.178: Palestine 1948: 89; Kedar 1989: 85, 89–90) and Nablus (see *Churches*, II, *q.v.*) require further investigation.

Field surveys conducted on either side of the Jordan in recent years have begun to document archaeologically, from such evidence as pottery scatters and other surface remains, some hundreds of sites that were evidently occupied or used in the twelfth and thirteenth centuries. Such sites are only included in the Gazetteer if the surviving remains include (or seem likely to include) structures datable to either of those centuries or if they point to industrial activities being undertaken at the site (e.g. sugar production, iron smelting, glass production). The same criteria also apply to archaeological strata devoid of structures that have been identified during excavation.

Where structures do survive, of course, the ethnic identity of the builders is still not always certain. Depending on its location, for instance, a village house identified archaeologically could have been constructed by an indigenous Muslim, Jewish, Samaritan or Christian family, or even by Latin settlers. The justification for inclusion in the Gazetteer is therefore that the area in which the site lay was under nominal Frankish control at the time when the structure was erected. On this basis a number of structures identified as belonging to the 'Ayyubid period' have been included. How-ever, the Ayyubid–Mamluk castles of 'Ajlun, or Qal'at ar-Rabad (Johns 1931; Bowen 1981), Subaiba (Ellen-blum 1989; Amitai 1989; cf. Deschamps 1939a: 144–74), as-Salt (Meistermann 1909: 315; Duncan 1928; de Vaux 1938: 400–1; Johns 1937: 29; Franciscan Fathers 1977: 73; Gavin 1985: fig. 3), Mount Tabor (Battista and Bagatti 1976; see also *Churches*, II, *q.v.*) and Jazirat Fara'un (**no. R9**) must be excluded, as they were not Frankish constructions, despite being built on the edges of the Kingdom in areas that had once been under Frankish control. The Damascene castle at Jarash (Grid ref. 235.188), remains of which could at one time still be seen enclosing the temple of Artemis (Harding 1967: 98), must also be excluded, since it represents an example of Crusader deconstruction, rather than con-struction, carried out by Baldwin II's men in 1121 (William of Tyre, XII, 16); the same applies to the twelfth-century stone-robbing of a Byzantine building identified at Tall al-Akhdar (Grid ref. 1387.2058: Porath 1989a).

Many of the structures included in the Gazetteer are identified as belonging to the Frankish period purely on the basis of their form or their method of construc-tion. In some cases the attribution is not entirely certain and needs to be checked by additional field work and analysis. Ashlar bearing a diagonal dressing and ma-sonry marks may almost always be safely attributed to the Crusader period, though the possibility of reuse has always to be borne in mind. Diagonal tooling and certain types of masonry mark, however, are also found, though not together, on buildings of the Ayyubid period. Rusticated or bossed masonry with smoothly drafted edges is also a characteristic of Crusader buildings, though here again masonry of a broadly similar type was used from the Iron Age to the Mamluk period. Pointed barrel-vaults or groin-vaults, particularly those with transverse arches of ashlar and with smooth fine white plaster applied to the interior surfaces, will often be Frankish, but may also be Ayyubid or Mamluk. Very little is known of the buildings constructed in Palestine in the two centuries immediately preceding the Crusaders' capture of Jerusalem in 1099. There is therefore every possibility that some of the structures attributed to the Crusaders may in fact belong to the periods of Fatimid or Seljuk control; indeed a number of the sites identified as 'Crusading' by the Survey of Western Palestine (and included on that basis in the *Atlas of Israel*'s map of Crusader Palestine) have on further investigation turned out to be Byzantine. (On masonry and construc-tion methods, see Deschamps 1934; Kalayan 1968; Pringle 1981a; Burgoyne and Richards 1987: 88–100; Ellenblum 1992.)

None the less, it is abundantly clear from the study of church buildings and castles, which are often datable through documentary references, that the period of Crusader control in the twelfth century resulted in the construction of buildings, both religious and secular, being undertaken west of the Jordan on a scale un-known since Byzantine and Umayyad times. In con-trast, the interest of Mamluk builders seems to have been focussed mainly on the major cities such as Jerusalem and Gaza, fortresses such as Qal'at Subaiba, 'Ajlun and Karak, and on the network of roads, bridges and khans that assured communications between them and the more important centres of Syria and Egypt. Except in especially favoured areas, such as the sugar-producing region of the Jordan valley and the Ghawr dependent on Karak and in the Jaulan, economic investment in the countryside, and hence building works other than those on a purely village scale, seem to have declined significantly in the areas reconquered from the Crusaders by the Ayyubids and Mamluks in the late twelfth and thirteenth centuries. When doubt exists over the dating of medieval buildings surviving in villages west of the Jordan, the balance of probabili-ties will therefore often favour a Crusader attribution, though in some cases, such as the later additions to the Crusader *curia* at al-Bira, an Ayyubid one may also be possible.

Because of the uncertainty that so often surrounds the precise dating of architecturally undistinguished non-religious medieval buildings in Palestine, the main Gazetteer is followed by a supplementary one, divided into three parts. The first part contains a list of 'poss-ibles' (designated by numbers prefixed by the letter P): these include sites where there is some evidence to suggest that there may be building remains of the Crusader period, but where further archaeological research is needed to provide conclusive proof. The second part lists 'rejects' (designated by the prefix R): these are sites where the identification of Frankish buildings has been suggested at some time in the past, but has since been shown to be erroneous. The Supple-mentary Gazetteer concludes with a list of 'don't knows': these comprise those 'Crusader antiquities sites' that are shown on the Crusader-period map in the *Atlas of Israel*, but whose identification it has proved impossible to confirm or deny.

It should be stressed that the boundaries between the 'definites/probables' in the main Gazetteer and the 'possibles', 'rejects' and 'don't knows' in the Supplementary Gazetteer should not be regarded as fixed, and that certain sites may be expected to migrate from one category to another as archaeological research continues.

## Towns and Cities

There is no easy definition of what constituted an urban as opposed to a rural settlement in the Crusader Kingdom of Jerusalem (see Prawer 1977; 1980; Riley-Smith 1973: 62–98; Benvenisti 1970: 25–8; Pringle 1995a: 69–71). Legally the position is confused by the fact that virtually all Franks who were not clerics or knights were classed as burgesses. Burgess tenure therefore existed in settlements that in terms of their size and economy were no different from villages, while a variety of feudal tenures also existed in the larger cities. The existence of a cathedral church provides no convenient sign of urban status, since the choice of sees was largely, though not entirely, dictated by Byzantine precedent. From the economic point of view, it might be expected that a greater proportion of a town or city's population would have been engaged in economic activities not directly connected with the land; but even here the distinction is blurred, for the inhabitants of a small settlement like al-Bira, numbering some 500–750, included specialist craftsmen, and the agricultural exploitation of the city territories of Acre and Jerusalem by their Frankish inhabitants is well attested.

The size of a settlement's population should have obvious implications for determining its status, but in practice absolute numbers are rarely known. Where a sufficient number of Franks were living, however, there is usually evidence for the existence of a court of burgesses, presided over by a viscount. Some forty such settlements are listed in table 1 (see also fig. 1). To them may be added a further eight 'new towns' established during the Crusader period, which although small and agricultural in character were socially, economically and institutionally towns in the making (Pringle 1995a: 71). The physical size and aspect of these settlements, however, varied enormously (on the physical aspects of Crusader towns and cities, see Benvenisti 1970: 29–209).

In only fourteen towns is there evidence for a circuit of town walls (see table 2). In all but two of these cases (the *faubourg* added to the castle of 'Atlit from *c.*1225 onwards and the Montmusard suburb of Acre which was walled by 1212), the walls already existed before the Crusader conquest and were merely strengthened

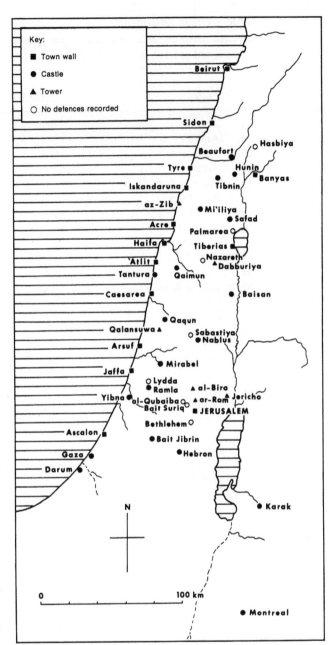

1 Map showing the location of urban settlements in the Kingdom of Jerusalem (see also table 1).

or rebuilt by the Franks. Indeed, most of the documentary evidence for the Frankish construction of town walls dates from after the Third Crusade, when much of it was paid for by Western Crusading leaders. Where remains of Frankish town walls do survive in the Kingdom of Jerusalem, they never stand to their full height. Often they are strengthened with projecting rectangular towers, though a rounded one also occurs at 'Atlit, and rounded and triangular ones at Ascalon.

Table 1 *Urban settlements*

Places listed as having a burgess court and/or viscount

| No. | Place | Cathedral | Church | Tower/castle | Town wall |
|---|---|---|---|---|---|
| 5 | Acre | x | oxx | ox | o |
| 19 | Arsuf | | x | o | o |
| 20 | Ascalon | (x) | xxx | o | o |
| 21 | ʿAtlit | | x | o | o |
| 26 | Baisan | | | o | |
| 32 | Bait Jibrin | | o | o | |
| 42 | Banyas | x | | o | o |
| 44 | Beaufort | | | o | (o) |
| 45 | Beirut | o | xxx | x | x |
| 48 | Bethlehem | o | oo | o | |
| 76 | Caesarea | o | xxx | o | o |
| 80 | Dair al-Balah | | o | x | |
| — | Gaza | | oo | x | (x) |
| — | Haifa | | xxx | x | x |
| 100 | Hasbaya | | | o | |
| 101 | Hebron | o | | o | |
| 106 | Iskandaruna | | o | o | o |
| 110 | Jaffa | | xxx | x | o |
| 114 | Jericho | | x | o | |
| 115 | Jerusalem | o | ooo | o | o |
| 124 | Karak | o | o | o | (x) |
| — | Lydda | o | | x | |
| 144 | Majdal Yaba | | | o | |
| 152 | Miʿiliya | | xx | o | |
| 157 | Montreal | | o | o | |
| 158 | Nablus | | oox | x | |
| — | Nazareth | o | ooo | x | |
| 159 | Qaimun | | o | o | (o) |
| 160 | Qalansuwa | | | o | |
| 164 | Qalʿat Hunin | | | o | |
| 168 | Qaqun | | x | o | |
| — | Ramla | | oo | x | |
| — | Sabastiya | o | o | x | |
| 191 | Safad | | x | o | |
| 201 | Sidon | x | xxx | oo | o |
| 218 | Tantura | | | o | |
| 222 | Tiberias | x | oxx | o | o |
| 223 | Tibnin | | x | o | |
| 227 | Tyre | o | oxx | x | o |
| 235 | Yibna | | o | o | |

Table 1 (*cont.*)

**Other Frankish settlements**

| No. | Place | Church | Tower | Hall/Curia |
|---|---|---|---|---|
| — | Bait Suriq | x | | |
| 54 | al-Bira | o | o-------------------o | |
| 61 | Burj, Kh. al- | | | o |
| 78 | Dabburiya | o | o | |
| — | Palmarea (near Tiberias) | x | | |
| 178 | al-Qubaiba | o | | o |
| 182 | ar-Ram | o | o-------------------o | |
| 237 | az-Zib | | o | |

*Key:*
o = archaeological evidence surviving
x = attested only by documentary evidence

Table 2 *The areas enclosed by town walls*

| No. | Town | Area enclosed in ha. |
|---|---|---|
| 115 | Jerusalem | 86 |
| 5 | Acre | 51.5 < 85.5 |
| 20 | Ascalon | 50 |
| 227 | Tyre | 48 |
| 45 | Beirut | 19 |
| 201 | Sidon | 15 |
| 42 | Banyas | 13 |
| 76 | Caesarea | 10 |
| 21 | 'Atlit | 9 |
| 110 | Jaffa | 7 |
| 19 | Arsuf | 5 |
| 222 | Tiberias | ? |
| — | Haifa | ? |
| 106 | Iskandaruna | ? |

Gates might be either flanked by towers, as at Caesarea (east gate, first phase), Tyre and Jerusalem (St Stephen's Gate), or set within a gate-tower. The three gate-towers on the town walls of 'Atlit were straight-through, and two had portcullises and possibly slit-machicolations in front of their wing-doors. At Caesarea at least two and possibly all three gates were bent, with a slit-machicolation and a portcullis protecting an outer pair of wing-doors, and an inner pair of wing-doors protected by a slit-machicolation. Most walls had an outer ditch, often with a counterscarp wall; and at Ascalon (1244), Arsuf, Jaffa, Caesarea, Acre and Sidon the walls and towers were revetted with a sloping masonry *talus*. Outer walls or barbicans also occur; but although in the medieval West the appear-ance and development of such outworks is unknown before the thirteenth century, in Palestine the Cru-saders encountered multiple systems of defence when they captured Jerusalem in 1099, Acre in 1103, Tyre in 1124 and Ascalon in 1153; further examples are also attested at Sidon in 1126 and Banyas in 1157 (for further discussion of town defences, see Pringle 1995a).

Most major towns had a castle (see table 1), represen-ting the residence of the king, his castellan or the lord of the place. If the town was held by one of the military orders, as was 'Atlit from 1217, Beaufort from 1260 and Sidon from 1260, the castle would also have constituted their local headquarters. In Jerusalem (**no. 115**) and Sidon (Land Castle, **no. 201**), the castle was joined to the town wall, while in Tiberias (**no. 222**) it was located on the lake side, affording its inhabitants the possibility of escape by boat in time of trouble (Razi and Braun 1992: 217). In Ascalon (**no. 20**), Arsuf (**no. 19**), Beirut (**no. 45**), Caesarea (**no. 76**), Sidon (Sea Castle, **no. 201**) and Tyre (**no. 227**), the castle stood at the point where the land wall met the sea. In Bethlehem (**no. 48**), Lydda, Nazareth and Sabastiya, however, the principal lordly residence was that of the bishop, which may or may not have been fortified (see *Churches*, nos. 61, 137, 169, 225). In addition to its Citadel, excavations in Jerusalem have also revealed parts of the adjacent royal palace (**no. 115**). In the smaller new towns, a tower or hall repre-sented the residence of the steward who was given the task of administering the settlement on behalf of the land-owner (see table 1).

Archaeological excavations in recent years have shed light on the medieval urban topography of Acre (**no. 5**), Arsuf (**no. 19**), Banyas (**no. 42**), Caesarea (**no. 76**), Jerusalem (**no. 115**) and Qaimun (**no. 159**), though the results of excavations in Ascalon (**no. 20**), Beirut (**no.**

45), Jaffa (**no. 110**) and Tiberias (**no. 222**) have to date been more disappointing in this respect. Virtually all that we know of the layout of the new towns of al-Qubaiba (**no. 178**) and Kh. al-Burj (**no. 61**) is also derived from excavation.

Among the port cities, man-made harbours are attested at Acre (**no. 5**), Arsuf (**no. 19**), 'Atlit (**no. 19**), Caesarea (**no. 76**), Beirut (**no. 45**), Sidon (**no. 201**) and Tyre (**no. 227**). At Jaffa (**no. 110**), a natural harbour was protected inadequately by an off-shore reef, while at Ascalon (**no. 20**) goods and passengers seem to have been landed on the beach.

Two types of urban house are mentioned in documentary sources. Houses of an oriental type, consisting of rooms set around a central courtyard, below which there was normally a cistern, have been identified archaeologically in Acre (**no. 5**) and Caesarea (**no. 76**). Houses of a south European type, with vaulted shops, store-rooms or commercial premises on the ground floor and several floors of domestic apartments, or solars, above have been recognized in Acre (**no. 5**), Jerusalem (**no. 115**) and Caesarea (**no. 76**), and one with a ground-floor *loggia* in Nablus (**no. 158**). Houses with barrel-vaulted basements containing evidence for agricultural or industrial processes set end-on to the street and with living areas above, have been recorded in the new towns of al-Bira (**no. 54**), al-Qubaiba (**no. 178**) and Kh. al-Burj (**no. 61**). The remains of houses that survive within the protective circuit of castle walls at Mi'iliya (**no. 152**) and Montreal (**no. 157**) have yet to be fully studied.

Covered market streets (*sūq*, pl. *aswāq*) dating from the Crusader period still exist in Acre (**no. 5**) and Jerusalem (**no. 115**), though one that once existed in Nablus (**no. 158**) was destroyed by an earthquake in 1927.

In addition to the urban cemeteries that were associated with churches or chapels (details of which may be found in *Churches*), Christian cemeteries of the Crusader period have also been investigated in 'Atlit (**no. 19**) and Caesarea (**no. 76**).

Examples of urban water supply and drainage, bath-houses, stables, kitchens, bakeries and other industrial activities are listed below.

## Castles

Castles have excited more interest and discussion than any other type of Crusader building, including churches (for general treatments of the subject, see: Rey 1871; Deschamps 1934; 1939a; 1973; Lawrence 1936; 1988;

Smail 1956: 204–4; 1973: 89–122; Fedden and Thomson 1957; Müller-Wiener 1966; Benvenisti 1970: 277–339; Prawer 1972: 295–318; Eydoux 1982; Pringle 1988; 1989; Marshall 1992: 93–144; Kennedy 1994). With a handful of notable exceptions such as Karak, Montreal and Belvoir, however, Crusader castles have survived less well in the Kingdom of Jerusalem proper than in other parts of the Latin East. Two principal reasons may account for this apparent imbalance in the rate of survival. In the first place, not only do the most impressive surviving Crusader castles, such as Crac des Chevaliers and Marqab, date essentially from the thirteenth century, when most of the Kingdom of Jerusalem itself was already in Muslim hands, but they were also repaired and recommissioned after they had fallen to the Mamluks. Secondly, and conversely, most of the castles in the Kingdom of Jerusalem that were not dismantled by Saladin after 1187 were systematically razed by the Mamluks from the 1260s onwards to prevent their being reused by the Latins.

Most of the castles in the Kingdom of Jerusalem of which traces remain therefore date from the twelfth century and are relatively modest works. Their study, however, sheds light not only on the development of military and domestic architecture in that period, but also on the processes of Frankish settlement in the countryside and of the formation of lordships (Pringle 1986a: 12–22; Tibble 1989; Ellenblum 1991; and forthcoming; Kennedy 1994: 21–61).

The most striking feature of Crusader castles is that from the very earliest phase of military conquest they are almost invariably constructed of stone. Earth and timber castles, however, are not entirely unknown. Remains of an early motte have been excavated below the Land Castle in Sidon (**no. 201**); and an eye-witness account of the construction of a motte (*Toronum in sabulo*) surmounted by a timber tower opposite Damietta in the Nile Delta is given by James of Vitry in April 1221 (*Lettres*, VII, lines 174–85, 197 (ed. Huygens, 139–40)).

The simplest and commonest type of castle is that consisting of a masonry tower. More than eighty towers of which there are surviving remains are listed in table 3. Towers could fulfil various functions. At the siege of Antioch (1097–8) they were used in an offensive military role. Later they were used to protect roads at Kh. Dustray (**no. 90**) and Bait Jubr at-Tahtani (**no. 33**), and a mill at Kh. Kurdana (**no. 133**). In Bethany (**no. 47**) and at-Tabgha (**no. 213**) towers served as refuges for isolated monastic communities. Urban towers on the Italian model are also attested in Acre (**no. 5**), and

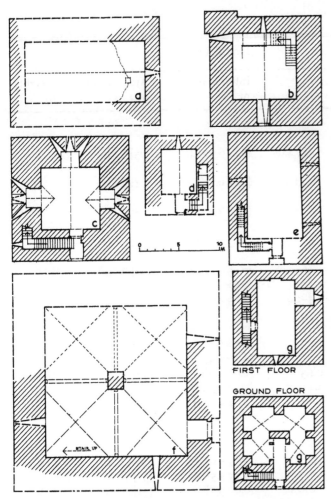

2  Plans of towers: (a) Kh. al-Karmil (**no. 126**); (b) Majdal Yaba (**no. 144**); (c) Saffuriya (**no. 192**); (d) Qal'at ad-Damm (**no. 162**); (e) Qarawat Bani Hassan (Burj al-Yaqur, **no. 170**); (f) Umm at-Taiyiba (**no. 228**); (g) Jaba' (**no. 108**) (drawn by M. Pease).

*église-donjons* at Safitha in the County of Tripoli and possibly at Safad (*Churches*, II, no. 193). The majority of towers, however, seem to have served a residential purpose, containing on their upper floor either a chamber or a solar, dependent on other adjacent domestic buildings, or, in the case of those with an internal floor area exceeding 60–70 m², a principal domestic hall.

With the exception of the thirteenth-century keep at Montfort Castle (**no. 156**), towers are invariably rectangular, with a preference for square, or nearly square, over elongated ground plans (see fig. 2). They seem only rarely to have stood more than two storeys (or about 15 m) high, and in the Kingdom of Jerusalem there is only one recorded instance of a timber floor, at Kh. Kurdana (**no. 133**). The floors are usually barrel-vaulted, though in some cases the basements consist of

pairs of parallel barrel-vaults supported on a spine wall, and in others the basement and upper floors were covered by groin-vaults supported on one or more internal piers. The entrances are almost invariably at ground level and apparently undefended, though in some cases a box-machicolation survives at the wall-head. At Tall al-Badawiya (**no. 24**), however, there was a portcullis; and at Umm at-Taiyiba (**no. 228**) possibly a slit-machicolation. Stairs would often, though not always, be accommodated within the wall thickness. Although there are defensive arrow-slits at Qaqun (**no. 168**) and Kh. Kurdana (**no. 133**), windows were evidently more often intended for admitting air and light than for shooting from (for further discussion of the form and function of Crusader towers, see Pringle 1986a: 15–22; 1994b).

Towers associated with other masonry buildings are found at Kh. Bait Kika (**no. 34**), Kh. Istuna (**no. 107**), Qalansuwa (**no. 160**), Qula (**no. 180**) and az-Zababida (**no. 236**). At al-Burj (Qal'at Tantura, **no. 57**), Kh. al-Burj (**no. 58**), Burj al-Ahmar (**no. 63**), Burj al-Lisana (**no. 65**), Burj Bait Nasif (**no. 72**), Burj Baitin (**no. 73**) and Yazur (**no. 233**), towers were set within an enclosure wall which also contained other buildings. At Kh. Dustray (**no. 90**), which belonged to the Templars, the character of the surrounding structures, which included stables and cisterns, suggests a road station (**no. 90**). In some cases, such as Bait Safafa (**no. 37**), al-Bira (**no. 54**), ar-Ram (**no. 182**) and possibly Kh. Manawat (**no. 145**), the structures surrounding a tower have the character of courtyard buildings, or *maisons fortes* (see below). In other cases, such as Kh. Bal'ama (*Castellum Beleismum*, **no. 41**), Summail (**no. 209**) and possibly 'Ibillin (**no. 103**), a tower formed the central element of a fully defensible castle. Towers with fortified enclosure walls and an outer ditch are found in Baisan (**no. 26**), Kh. al-Burj (*Castrum Ficuum*, **no. 59**) and Qal'at ad-Damm (**no. 162**). At Burj al-Far'a (**no. 64**) a rock-cut ditch also protected the promontory on which the tower stands, while in Caesarea, another promontory castle with a central tower, the rock ditch was filled by the sea (**no. 76**). The structures surrounding the tower at al-Habis (**no. 97**) would also have been defensible, being sited on top of a rocky eminence. More complex castles, with inner and outer wards, could also develop in time from an inner core centred on an early tower; examples include Beaufort (**no. 44**), Latrun (**no. 136**) and Majdal Yaba (*Mirabel*, **no. 144**). At Suba (*Belmont*, **no. 207**) and at-Taiyiba (**no. 215**) on the other hand, the core of the castle has more the character of a *maison forte* (see below).

Table 3. *Towers*

| No. | Name | Ground floor | | First floor | | Storeys | Height |
| | | External dims. m | Wall m | Internal dims. m | Area m 2 | | m |
| --- | --- | --- | --- | --- | --- | --- | --- |
| 5 | Acre (Burj as-Sultan) | *c.*17.5 × *c.*15 | | | | | |
| 7 | 'Affula, al- | 19 × 19 | | | | | |
| 9 | 'Ain al-Habis | 10 × 7.4 | 1.35/2.05 | [6.2/6.5 × 4] | [25] | [2] | |
| 16 | 'Aliya, Kh. | 11 × 11 | | | | | |
| 21 | 'Atlit: suburb | 14.1 × 11.7 | 1.2/1.35 | [12 × 9.3] | [112] | [2] | |
| 22 | 'Atlit, 1.3 km SSW of | | | | | | |
| 24 | Badawiya, Tall al- | 28 × 18.9 | 2.6/5.5 | [22.8 × 8.3] | [189] | [2] | |
| 25 | Ba'ina, al- (?) | | | | | | |
| 26 | Baisan | 17.6 × 17.3 | 3 | [11.5 × 11.3] | [130] | [2] | *c.*12 |
| 28 | Bait al-Milh | | | | | | |
| 33 | Bait Jubr at-Tahtani | *c.*9.5 × 6.6/8.1 | 0.96/2.08 | [7.15/7.5 × 4.3] | [32] | [2] | |
| 34 | Bait Kika, Kh. | *c.*8 × *c.*8 | *c.*1.7 | [4.6 × 4.6] | [21] | ? | |
| 37 | Bait Safafa | 18.2 × 13.7 | 2.5–2.9 | [12.5 × 8.65] | [108] | 2 | 17 |
| 39 | Bait 'Ur al-Fauqa | | | | | | |
| 41 | Bal'ama, Kh. | >8 × >8 | | | | 2 | *c.*14 |
| 44 | Beaufort Castle | *c.*12 × *c.*12 | 2.75 | [6.5 × 6.5] | [42] | 2 | |
| 47 | Bethany | 14.8 × 14.4 | 4 | [6.3 × 6.4] | [44] | ? | |
| 48 | Bethlehem | 18.4 × 16.4 | *c.*4.3 | [9.8 × 7.8] | [76] | 2 | > 11.5 |
| 54 | al-Bira | *c.*16 × *c.*14 | 2.4/2.7 | [10.6 × 9.2] | [98] | [2] | |
| 57 | al-Burj, Qal'at Tantura | 16.4 × 16.4 | 5 | [11.4 × 11.4] | [130] | [2] | |
| 58 | Burj, Kh. al- | | | | | 2 | |
| 59 | Burj, Kh. al- (Castrum Ficuum) | 25 × 20 | | | | | |
| 62 | Burj, Kh. al- (Salome ?) | | | | | | |
| 63 | Burj al-Ahmar | 19.7 × 15.5 | 2.2 | [15.3 × 11.1] | [169] | 2 | *c.*14 |
| 64 | Burj al-Far'a, Kh. | 11.0 × *c.*10.5 | 2.5 | [6 × *c.*5.5] | [33] | 2 | |
| 65 | Burj al-Lisana | *c.*12.75 × 9.7 | 1.8/2.0 | [8.9 × 5.7] | [51] | [2] | |
| 67 | Burj al-Malih (Turris Salinarum) | | | | | | |
| 68 | Burj al-Qibli | | | | | | |
| 69 | Burj ash-Shamali | | | | | | |
| 71 | Burj as-Sur | 15.0 × 11.9 | 3 | 11.0 × 7.9 | 87 | 2 | > 9.5 |
| 72 | Burj Bait Nasif (near) | *c.*10 × 10 | | | | | |
| 73 | Burj Baitin | 11 × 9.5 | | | | | |
| 75 | Burj Misr | *c.*12 × *c.*12 | *c.*2.5 | [*c.*7 × *c.*7] | [49] | 2 | |
| 76 | Caesarea | | | | | | |
| 78 | Dabburiya | | | | | | |
| 85 | Da'uk, Tall | | | | | | |
| 86 | Dhahiriya, Kh, adh- | | | | | | |
| 90 | Dustray, Kh. | *c.*15.5 × *c.*11.0 | 2.4 | [10.7 × 6.2] | [66] | [2] | |
| 97 | al-Habis (al-Aswīt) | *c.*8.4 × *c.*5.3 | *c.*1.0 | [6.4 × 3.3] | [21] | | |
| 100 | Hasbaya | | | | | | |
| 103 | 'Ibillin | | | [10 × 8.8] | [88] | [2] | |
| 107 | Istuna, Kh. | | | | | | |
| 108 | Jaba' | 11.4 × 11.4 | 1.1–3 | 9 × 4.8 | 43 | 3 | > 9 |
| 111 | Jaladiya, Kh. | | | | | | |
| 114 | Jericho | | | | | | |
| 115 | Jerusalem: David's Tower | 20 × 16 | | | | | |
| 115 | Jerusalem: Tancred's Tower | 35 × 35 | | | | | |

Table 3 (*cont.*)

| No. | Name | Ground floor | | First floor | | Storeys | Height |
| | | External dims. m | Wall m | Internal dims. m | Area m 2 | | m |
| --- | --- | --- | --- | --- | --- | --- | --- |
| 120 | Kafr Jinnis | | | | | | |
| 122 | Kafr Sum, Kh. | | | | | | |
| 126 | Karmil, Kh. al- | 18.9 × 12.9/13.2 | 1.95/2.95 | [13 × 7] | [91] | 2 | |
| 129 | Khuljan, Kh. al- | | | | | | |
| 133 | Kurdana, Kh. | c.11 × 9.9 | 1.35/2.2 | [7.3 × 7.2] | [49] | 2 | |
| 136 | Latrun | 14 × 14 | c.3/4 | [8.5 × 6.5] | [55] | > 2 | |
| 139 | Madd ad-Dair | c.16 × c.12.5 | 1.7/2.0 | [12 × 8.5] | [102] | [2] | |
| 144 | Majdal Yaba | 13.9 × 13.0 | 3 | [7.9 × 7] | [55] | [2] | |
| 145 | Manawat, Kh. | 8.9 × > 8 | 1.9/2.6 | | | | |
| 146 | Manhata, Kh. al- | | | | | | |
| 149 | Maslakhit, Kh. | | | | | | |
| 151 | Mazra'a, Kh. al- | | | | | | |
| 156 | Montfort | (20 × 24) | | | | | |
| 158 | Nablus | | | | | | |
| 159 | Qaimun, Tall: A | 12.5 × 9 | 2 | [8.5 × 5] | [42] | [2] | |
| 159 | Qaimun, Tall: B | 22 × 18 | 3 | [16 × 12] | [192] | [2] | |
| 160 | Qalansuwa | 12.05 × 12.05 | c.2–3 | [7 × 7] | [49] | | > 12.3 |
| 162 | Qal'at ad-Damm | 9.3 × 8.5 | 1.4/2.5 | [5.4 × 4.3] | [23] | [2] | |
| 163 | Qal'at ad-Dubba | 10.3 × 8.5 | 1/1.8 | [7.8 × 4.9] | [38] | | |
| 165 | Qal'at Jiddin: A | c.16 × c.15.5 | 3.3/5.4 | [9.6 × 8.5] | [82] | 2 | > 13 |
| 165 | Qal'at Jiddin: A | 16.4 × 16.4 | 2.3 | c.13 × c.13 | 169 | 3 | > 14.8 |
| 166 | Qal'at Rahib | | | | | | |
| 168 | Qaqun | 17.6 × 14.5 | 2.8 | [12.8 × 9.7] | [124] | 2 | > 8.5 |
| 169 | Qaratiya | | | | | | |
| 170 | Qarawat Bani Hassan | 16.0 × 11.3 | 2.2 | [10.5 × 6.8] | [71] | 2 | > 11.6 |
| 171 | Qarhata, Kh. | | | | | | |
| 176 | Qasr ash-Shaikh Raba | 8.85 × 8.85 | | | | | |
| 180 | Qula | c.17 × 12.8 | 3 | [6.8 × 11] | [75] | [2] | |
| 182 | Ram, ar- | 14.3 × 12.7 | 2.1/2.7 | [9.6 × 7.6] | [73] | [2] | |
| 188 | Rujm as-Sayigh | | | | | | |
| 190 | Rushmiya, Kh. | 20.8 × 13.2 | 2.5 | [15.8 × 8.2] | [130] | [2] | |
| 192 | Saffuriya | 15 × 15 | 3.75 | [7.5 × 7.5] | [56] | [2] | > 13 |
| 203 | Sinjil | c.10 × ? | | | | | |
| 209 | Summail | | | | | | |
| 213 | Tabgha, at- | 15.6 × 11.9 | 3/3.3 | [9.5 × 5.8] | [55] | [2] | |
| 215 | Taiyiba, at- | c.15 × c.15 | | | | | |
| 216 | Tall al-Fukhkhar | | | | | | |
| 224 | Tira, at- | c.12 × 11.6 | c.2.2 | [7 × 7.75] | [52] | [2] | |
| 228 | Umm at-Taiyiba | 26.3 × 26.3 | 4.1 | 18.2 × 18.2 | 327 | 2 | |
| 233 | Yazur | 12.8 × 12.6 | 2.8/2.9 | [7.1 × 6.9] | [49] | [2] | |
| 236 | Zababida | 14 × 12.5 | 1.4 | [11.2 × 9.7] | [109] | [2] | |
| 237 | az-Zib | | | | | | |

*Note:* Square brackets indicate estimated figures and dimensions.

Castles of enceinte, in which the principal defensive provision was invested in the outer wall or walls, rather than in a central core, include Burj al-Malih (**no. 66**), Montreal (**no. 157**), Qasr al-ʿAtra (*le Chastelez*, **no. 174**) and Tibnin (**no. 223**). Rectangular or quadrangular castles enclosed by a dry ditch include Hunin (**no. 164**), Iskandaruna (**no. 106**) and Kh. at-Tuquʿ (*Tekoa*, **no. 226**).

Irregular castles sited on spurs or promontories cut off by a ditch include Karak (**no. 124**), Montfort (**no. 156**), Qalʿat Abuʾl-Hasan (**no. 161**), Qalʿat ad-Dubba (**no. 163**), al-Wuʿaira (**no. 230**) and Yalu (*Castellum Arnaldi*, **no. 231**). At Tantura (*Merle*, **no. 218**) and ʿAtlit (**no. 21**) the castle is surrounded on three sides by sea, while in Sidon (Sea Castle, **no. 201**) it is on an island joined to the mainland by an artificial causeway.

Regular rectangular castles with towers at the corners and sometimes also at intervals along the sides are also found. This type of castle is sometimes misleadingly and tautologically referred to by modern commentators as a *castrum*, though a four-towered castle or *quadriburgium* is a more apt description, at any rate for the smaller types. The origin of the type is doubtless Roman or Hellenistic, though more recent examples would have been available for study by the Frankish settlers among the early Muslim fortifications that they found when they arrived in Palestine. Early Muslim forts with trapezoidal plans, solid rounded or rectangular corner towers, gates set between rounded turrets and walls with external pilaster buttresses existed and were reoccupied in the Frankish period at Kafr Lam (**no. 121**) and Minat al-Qalʿa (**no. 153**). The Franks themselves built four-towered castles at Bait Jibrin (**no. 32**), Tall as-Safi (*Blanchegarde*, **no. 194**) and Yibna (*Ibelin*, **no. 235**), though in the latter two cases the evidence comes mainly from William of Tyre rather than from archaeology. St Margaret's Castle on Mount Carmel was also apparently of this type, though it was possibly based on an earlier Muslim fort (**no. 196**). At Miʿiliya (**no. 152**), a twelfth-century *quadriburgium* and its associated settlement and church were enclosed by a polygonal outer enceinte. Fully developed examples of regular concentric castle planning are to be found in the twelfth-century castles of Belvoir (**no. 46**), Dair al-Balah (*Darum*, **no. 80**), and probably al-Fula (*la Feve*, **no. 96**).

Cave castles include ʿAin al-Habis (*Cava de Suet*, **no. 10**), Magharat Fakhr ad-Din (**no. 141**), Tirun an-Niha (*Cave de Tyron*, **no. 225**) and the Templar castle situated on top of Jabal Quruntul overlooking Jericho (**no. 109**). A natural rock castle lacking man-made defences has been identified at Kh. as-Sila (**no. 202**) in Transjordan.

In Hebron the castle (**no. 101**) formed an annexe attached to the Herodian precinct enclosing the tombs of the Patriarchs and the cathedral church of St Abraham (*Churches*, I, no. 100).

Other castle remains of an indeterminate nature have been suggested or identified at Bait Dajan (**no. 29**), Dair Abu Mashʿal (*Belfort*, **no. 79**), Jezreel (**no. 116**), Tall al-Maʿshuqa (**no. 148**), Qaratiya (**no. 169**), Kh. al-Qasr (**no. 173**), Qasr al-Mantara (**no. 175**), Ras al-Qantara (*Sarepta*, **no. 186**), Ras Kikis (**no. 187**), Sidon (Land Castle, **no. 201**), Summail (**no. 209**), Tafila (**no. 214**), Tiberias (**no. 222**) and Shafa ʿAmr (**no. P25**).

Little remains of the castles built in the thirteenth century in the Kingdom of Jerusalem. The most extensive, though inaccessible, is ʿAtlit, built by the Templars on a sea-girt promontory from 1217 onwards and defended on the landward side by a double wall and outer ditch with counterscarp (**no. 21**). The Templars also reconstructed Safad (**no. 191**) to a concentric plan between 1240 and 1260, and from 1260 onwards they rebuilt the Sea Castle in Sidon (**no. 201**) as their order's headquarters in the lordship and added to the defences at Beaufort (**no. 44**). The Teutonic Order built the new castle of Montfort (**no. 156**) between 1226/7 and c.1240 with a D-shaped *donjon* and inner ward enclosed by an outer enceinte. The inner ward of another of their castles, Qalʿat Jiddin (**no. 165**), contains two residential towers and is likewise surrounded by an outer wall. Parts of the Jerusalem Citadel (**no. 115**) and the castle of Arsuf (**no. 19**) may also belong to the thirteenth century.

Military works associated with one or other of the medieval sieges of Acre (1189–91 or 1291) have been excavated at Tall Kaisan (**no. 123**) and Kh. at-Tantur (**no. 217**). Some of the features identified at Tall al-Fukhkhar (**no. 216**) may also be similarly explained.

Among the various defensive features that survive in the castles of the Kingdom of Jerusalem may be noted: indirect or bent entrances at Belvoir (**no. 46**) and ʿAtlit (**no. 21**); portcullises at Latrun (**no. 136**), Qasr al-ʿAtra (*le Chastelez*, **no. 174**) and Sidon (Sea Castle, **no. 201**); posterns at Belvoir (**no. 46**) and Qasr al-ʿAtra (*le Chastelez*, **no. 174**); slit-machicolations above entrances at Belvoir (**no. 46**), Baisan (**no. 26**), al-Baʿina (house, **no. 25**), Bait ʿItab (hall-house, **no. 31**), al-Burj (**no. 57**) and Sidon (Sea Castle, **no. 201**); box-machicolations at Kh. Kurdana (**no. 133**), ʿAtlit (**no. 21**), Montfort (**no. 156**), Sidon (Sea Castle, outer gate, **no. 201**) and in timber at Qalʿat Jiddin (**no. 165**); a *chemin de ronde* leading to a row of arrow-slits inside the wall at Qalʿat Jiddin (**no. 165**), Latrun (**no. 136**) and Safad (**no. 191**); arrow-slits with pointed-arched heads at Belvoir (**no. 46**) and Karak (**no. 124**), with lintelled heads at Mi'iliya (**no. 152**) and Kh. Rushmiya (**no. 190**), with fish-tail bases at Qaqun (**no. 168**) and stirrup bases at Kh. Kurdana (**no. 133**); casemates with triple arrays of arrow-slits at Saffuriya (**no. 192**); crenellations at 'Atlit (**no. 21**); and evidence for a timber bridge at Baisan (**no. 26**).

Castle chapels are attested by surviving remains or documentary evidence at Arsuf (?) (*Churches*, I, no. 12), 'Atlit (**no. 26**), Bait Jibrin (**no. 31**), Beaufort (**no. 41** [non-surviving]), Belvoir (**no. 57**), al-Fula (**no. 90**), Iskandaruna (?) (**no. 102**), Jaffa (**nos. 111–12**), Karak (**no. 130**), Latrun (*Churches*, II, no. 136), Montfort (**no. 146**), Qal'at Jiddin (**no. 180**), Safad (**no. 194**), St Margaret's Castle (**no. 212**), Shaubak/Montreal (**nos. 229–30**), Sidon (**no. 242**), Suba (**no. 247**), Tiberias (**no. 267**), Tibnin (**no. 269**), Tirun an-Niha (**no. 274**), and Wadi Musa/al-Wu'aira (**no. 277**). Halls occur at Beaufort (**no. 44**) and Montfort (**no. 156**).

Cisterns are found in the castles of Beaufort (**no. 44**), Belvoir (**no. 46**), Burj al-Lisana (**no. 65**), Burj al-Malih (**no. 66**), Dair Abu Mash'al (**no. 79**), Karak (**no. 124**), Montfort (**no. 156**), Qasr al-Mantara (**no. 175**), Safad (**no. 191**) and Suba (**no. 207**). There are cisterns under the towers at Bethany (**no. 47**), Kh. Dustray (**no. 90**) and Qaqun (**no. 168**), and in the ditch at Burj al-Far'a (**no. 64**). A cistern operated by a *nuria* is attested at al-Fula in 1169/72 (**no. 96**); and at Montreal a rock-cut tunnel led to a spring (**no. 157**).

A kitchen survives in the castle of Belvoir (**no. 46**) and bread ovens in 'Atlit (**no. 21**) and Karak (**no. 124**). Montfort (**no. 156**) and Suba (**no. 207**) contained wine-presses, and stables are found in Belvoir (**no. 46**), Kh. Dustray (**no. 90**), the Jerusalem Citadel (**no. 115**), Latrun (**no. 136**), Suba (**no. 207**) and Tibnin (**no. 223**). Latrines with chutes are found at Qal'at Jiddin (**no. 165**), Safad (**no. 191**: in a tower of the inner ward, though probably Mamluk) and probably Montfort (**no. 156**). Fragments of sculptural decoration have been recovered from Belvoir (**no. 46**), Latrun (**no. 136**; *Churches*, II, no. 136), Montfort (**no. 156**) and Suba (**no. 207**).

## Other Non- or Semi-Fortified Rural Dwellings

Besides towers and castles, a range of other non- or semi-fortified domestic buildings also survive in the countryside of Palestine. Some of these may be identified as the houses of lesser knights or sergeants, equivalent to the *maisons fortes* or moated manors of the West. The fact that they often appear less easily

defensible than the more obviously castellated structures does not necessarily imply that their owners were of lesser social standing, for some of the halls that they contain are considerably larger than those found in towers (cf. Pringle 1994b: 342, fig. 2). Some rural buildings, however, can more probably be identified as estate centres (*curiae*), occupied by the stewards who administered the lands of absentee secular or ecclesiastical land-owners. Others, such as that in which Ibn Jubayr was entertained in the neighbourhood of Acre in 1184 (*Voyages*, trans. Gaudefroy-Demombynes, II, 354; cf. Pringle 1994a: 49), evidently represent the house of a Muslim or Christian village headman, or *rā'īs*. When no documentary evidence exists, it is often impossible to tell precisely the function of a building from its surviving structure alone. The following typology is therefore based principally on form, rather than on function.

A number of hall-houses, consisting of a first-floor hall set above a vaulted basement, are recorded (see table 4). At Qalansuwa (**no. 160**) a large hall-house, with vaulting at both levels consisting of groin-vaults carried on piers or columns, formed part of a larger complex of structures, the interpretation of which is not altogether clear. A thirteenth-century hall-house situated below the Teutonic Order castle of Montfort (**no. 156**) and incorporating an earlier water-mill had a rib-vaulted hall and an attached tower containing a high rib-vaulted chamber; it may perhaps have been a guest-house, intended for use by high-status visitors to the castle. More usually, however, hall-houses were more simply vaulted, and, except for their elongated shape and larger size, some of them are in effect little different from towers. At Bait 'Itab (**no. 31**) the ground-floor entrance is even defended by a slit-machicolation, though it later seems to have been replaced by a first-floor door more conveniently approached up an external staircase. This change was made possible by the enlargement of the hall-house into a courtyard building. Other hall-houses forming part of courtyard buildings survive at Kh. Bait 'Ainun (**no. 27**), Kh. al-Lauza (**no. 137**), al-Qubaiba (**no. 178**) and possibly at Jifna (**no. 118**); while at Bait Safafa (**no. 37**), the *curiae* of the stewards of the canons of the Holy Sepulchre at al-Bira (**no. 54**) and ar-Ram (**no. 182**), and possibly also at Kh. Manawat (**no. 145**), a courtyard building developed around a residential tower.

Other courtyard buildings have been identified at Kh. 'Adasa (**no. 6**), 'Aqraba (**no. 18**), Kh. al-'Ayadiya (**no. 23**), Kh. al-Baubariya (**no. 43**), Kh. Bir Zait (**no. 53**), Burj as-Sahl (**no. 70**), Dair Yasin (**no. 84**), Kh. Kafr Sum

Table 4. *Hall-houses*

| No. | Name | Ground floor | | | First floor | | | |
|-----|------|--------------|---|---|-------------|---|---|---|
| | | External dims. m | Wall m | | Internal dims. m | Area m 2 | Stories | Height m |
| 14 | 'Ain Salman al-'Anid | 26.9 × 13.8 | 2.8/2.1 | | [23.4 × 8.8] | [206] | 2 | |
| 25 | Ba'ina, al- (?) | | | | | | | |
| 27 | Bait 'Ainun, Kh. | 22.6 × 8.6 | | | | | | |
| 31 | Bait'Itab | 29 × 13.3 | 3.2/2.8 | | [23.1 × 7.5] | [173] | 2 | |
| 53 | Bir Zait, Kh. | 26.4 × 12 | 1.6/2 | | [22.8 × 7.5] | [171] | [2] | |
| 60 | Burj, Kh. al- (Burj Sansan) | 19.5 × 9.75 | 1.8 | | [15.9 × 6.15] | [98] | [2] | |
| 61 | Burj, Kh. al- (Burj al-Jauz) | 27.7 × 10.6 | 2.3 | | [23.1 × 6] | [139] | [2] | |
| 91 | Fahma (?) | 24.6 × 12.5 | 0.85/2.6 | | [22.3 × 7.5] | [167] | [2] | |
| 118 | Jifna (?) | | 2.1/2.4 | | [23.3 × 7.4] | [172] | [2] | |
| 131 | Kidna | 27.5 × 10.6 | [2.3] | | [23 × 6] | [138] | [2] | |
| 137 | Lauza, Kh. al- | | | | 11 × 4.2 | 46 | 2 | |
| 156 | Montfort: guest house | | | | 28 × 7.7/9.5 | 234 | 2 | 13.75 |
| 160 | Qalansuwa | 28/30 × 16.5 | 1.9 | | 25 × 14.2 | [325] | 2 | > 10 |
| 178 | al-Qubaiba | c.25 × 9.2 | 1.2/1.6 | | [22 × 6/6.6] | [137] | [2] | |
| 229 | Umm Khalid | 25.4 × 10 | 1.6 | | [22.2 × 6.7] | [149] | [2] | |

*Note:* Square brackets indicate estimated figures and dimensions.

(no. 122), Kh. al-Kufriya (no. 132), Lifta (no. 138), Kh. al-Manhata (no. 146), Shu'fat (no. 200), as-Sumairiya (no. 208) and possibly Kh. Tabaliya (no. 212). At Umm Khalid (no. 229) and Burj Bardawil (no. 74) the outer walls of the courtyard buildings have projecting solid rectangular buttresses, giving them a semi-fortified appearance, similar to that of the inner ward of the castle of at-Taiyiba (no. 215). The courtyard building at Kh. al-Qu'da (no. 179) also had two projecting towers.

At Burj Bardawil (no. 74) the courtyard building has a fan-shaped annexe containing vaulted buildings constructed downhill to one side of it. In the case of Suba (*Belmont*, no. 207) and at-Taiyiba (no. 215), a courtyard building came to form the core of a concentric castle. Another courtyard building at Kh. 'Iqbala (*Aqua Bella*) just below Suba, however, though clearly an ecclesiastical building, very possibly an infirmary belonging to the Order of St John (*Churches*, I, no. 101; cf. Pringle 1992), may conceivably have been originally built as the *maison forte* of a secular owner (cf. Johnson 1995: 5).

At Kh. al-Misqa (no. 155), a building whose ground floor consisted of a pair of barrel-vaults, side by side, possibly represents a house analogous to those in the 'new town' at al-Qubaiba (no. 178) or tower B at Qal'at Jiddin (no. 165).

Vaulted structures whose functions are not easily discernible have been recorded at Bait 'Irza (no. 30), Bait Jibrin (no. 32), Kh. Bait Tulma (no. 38), Tall Da'uk (no. 85), 'Id al-Minya (no. 104), Kh. Jaryut (no. 113), Kh. al-Khan (no. 127), Khan as-Sawiya (no. 128), Kh. Kusbur (no. 134), Kuwaikat (no. 135), Rantiya (no. 184), Sarafand al-Kharab (no. 197) and Tall al-Fukhkhar (no. 216). Other buildings of indeterminate function exist at 'Ain Siniya (no. 15), Biddu (no. 49), Kh. Dair as-Sida (no. 83), Qal'at Rahib (no. 166), Ramallah (no. 183), ash-Shaikh Sha'ala (no. 198), Sirin (no. 205) and Kh. Su'aida (no. 206).

In 'Amwas (no. 17) a Roman bath-house was adapted for alternative use, apparently as a store-house. Walls and foundations are also recorded at Kh. Bait Mazmil (no. 36), Kh. Burin (no. 55), Kh. Burin (no. 56), al-Mazra'a (no. 150), Rafidiya (no. 181) and Kh. as-Sira (no. 204).

Masonry from destroyed Crusader buildings exists at Qaluniya (no. 167) and Yibna (no. 235), and carved decorative details at 'Aqraba (no. 18), Ras Kikis (no. 187) and Kh. Rumaila (no. 189).

Indigenous village houses of the Frankish period have been excavated at Tall Abu Ghurdan (no. 2), Capernaum (no. 77), Dhiban (no. 87), Kh. Din'ala (no. 88), Kh. Tall ad-Durur (no. 89), Kh. Faris (no. 94), Hebron (no. 101), Tall Hisban (no. 102), Kh. 'Iribbin (no. 105), Kh. Karaza (no. 125), Mairun (no. 143), Kh. Marus (no. 147), Kh. Rumaila (no. 189), Kh. Shama' (no. 199), Kh. Summaqa (no. 210) and Kh. Zuwainita (no.

238). Occupation of a cave house is also attested at Kh. Susiya (**no. 211**).

A rural Christian cemetery, not apparently associated with a church (though possibly, nevertheless), has been recorded at Kh. Balʿama (**no. 41**; see also *Churches*, I, no. 37).

Features associated with rural dwellings, such as wine- and olive-presses, cisterns and pools, are listed in a following section.

## Water Supply and Drainage

Wells are attested at ʿAin at-Tina, near Burj as-Sahl (**no. 70**), and at Summail (**no. 209**); and a Roman well remained in use at Bir Burin (**no. 50**).

Vaulted tunnels led to springs at Kh. Balʿama (**no. 41**) and Suba (**no. 207**), and a rock-cut one at Montreal (Shaubak, **no. 157**). Open cisterns (*birka*, pl. *birāk*) were fed from springs at ʿAin al-Ajab (**no. 8**), Kh. al-Kufriya (**no. 132**), Kh. al-Lauza (**no. 137**) and ʿAin as-Sultan (**no. 12**), the latter being Roman in origin. Other open reservoirs are found at ʿAin Salman al-ʿAnid (**no. 14**), al-Bira (**no. 54**), Dair ʿAmis (**no. 82**), Kh. al-Karmil (**no. 126**), Kh. al-Misqa (**no. 155**), Qalansuwa (**no. 160**), Qiryat Frostig (**no. 177**) and al-Qubaiba (**no. 178**).

Vaulted cisterns are found at ʿAin al-Haramiya (**no. 11**), Kh. Bait Tulma (**no. 38**), Bir Khuwailifa (*Reonde Cisterne*, **no. 52**), Qaluniya (**no. 167**), Qaqun (**no. 168**, reused Byzantine), Qarawat Bani Hassan (**no. 170**, ? Mamluk) and Qiryat Frostig (**no. 177**). One cistern near Lifta (**no. 138**) has remains of a house on top, possibly that of the cistern-keeper; a former cistern-keeper (*cysternarius*) from the village of Kafr ad-Dik, named John the Syrian, is mentioned in a document of 1175 (*RRH*, no. 533; Pringle 1986a: 59). Rock-cut cisterns are found associated with the church of St John in the Woods in ʿAin Karim (*Churches*, I, 45, no. 8), and below the castle of Suba (**no. 207**), where they appear to be Byzantine in origin.

Aqueducts for irrigation and for powering mills are recorded in the oasis of Jericho, at ʿAin as-Sultan (**no. 12**) and ʿAin Duq (**no. 13**); others are found at Kh. Fasayil (**no. 95**), Kh. Jaryut (**no. 113**) and Kh. Manawat (**no. 145**). In Lifta, an aqueduct is associated with a courtyard building and garden terraces (**no. 138**). A water supply system for the Benedictine convent in Bethany consisted of a collection system which fed rainwater into a cistern and thence by means of terracotta pipes down through the convent (*Churches*, I, 133).

Roman aqueducts supplying water to the cities of Caesarea (**no. 76**) and Tyre (Ras al-ʿAin, **no. 185**) were kept in use in Crusader times. Rock-cut cisterns exist below the Frankish houses in the settlement of Kh. al-Burj (**no. 61**) and in Caesarea (**no. 76**). In Jerusalem (**no. 115**), cisterns, aqueducts, rainwater collecting pools and a *nuria* are attested (on water supply in general, see Benvenisti 1970: 263–7).

A bath-house is attested archaeologically in the thirteenth-century Frankish suburb of ʿAtlit (**no. 21**). Ayyubid ones are found in the castles on Mount Tabor (see *Churches*, II, *q.v.*) and on Jazirat Faraʿun (**no. R9**), and a Mamluk one at Tall Hisban (**no. 102**). Documentary sources also mention baths in Crusader Acre (*RRH*, nos. 256, 668, 674, 698, 721, 1200 and 1257), Jaffa (*RRH*, no. 667), Jerusalem (*RRH*, nos. 516 and 576) and Tyre (*RRH*, nos. 665, 691, 1114, 1184 and 1331).

Latrines with chutes evacuating into cess-pits and/or drains are recorded in Abu Ghosh (*Churches*, I, no. 1, p. 15, fig. 4), Acre (**no. 5**), Burj Bardawil (**no. 74**) and Caesarea (**no. 76**), and, as mentioned above, in the castles of Qalʿat Jiddin, Montfort and Safad.

## Agricultural and Industrial Installations

Although the Templar mill at Daʿuk (**no. 85**) does not apparently survive, other horizontal water-mills for milling corn survive with dams at al-Haddar (*Molendina Trium Pontium*, **no. 98**), Kh. Kurdana (**no. 133**), al-Mirr (*Molendina desubter Mirabellum*, **no. 154**) and Montfort (**no. 156**). Those below Montreal (**no. 157**) were stream powered (on water-mills, see Benvenisti 1970: 247–521; Pringle 1986b: 68–71, 78–9).

Sugar-mills survive in Jericho (**nos. 12–13, 114**), at Tall Dair ʿAlla (**no. 81**), al-Faifa al-Gharbiya (**no. 92**), Kh. Fasayil (**no. 95**) and Montreal (**no. 157**), and at three Jordan Valley sites known simply as Tawahin as-Sukkar, or the 'sugar-mills' (**nos. 219a, 220 and 221**). A sugar factory was established inside the castle of Baisan (**no. 26**) in the thirteenth century; and one at Kh. Manawat, with a water-mill fed by an aqueduct, is attested in 1168 (**no. 145**). Factories are also known at Tall Qasila (**no. 172**) and Tawahin as-Sukkar (**no. 219b**). Other structures relating to sugar-production have been identified at Abu Arabi ash-Shamali (**no. 1**), Tall Abu Sarbut (**no. 3**), Tall Fandi al-Janubi (**no. 93**), al-Haditha (**no. 99**), Jaljuliya (**no. 112**), Kh. al-Mahruqat (**no. 142**), as-Safi (**no. 193**), al-Yanuhiya (**no. 232**) and Yesod ha-Maʿala (**no. 234**). The date of foundation of these factories is not always certain, since the period of greatest use, particularly for those in the Jordan Valley, appears to have been in Mamluk times (on sugar-mills and sugar-production generally, see Benvenisti 1970: 253–6; Ashtor 1977).

Installations for extracting salt from sea water are recorded at ʿAtlit (**no. 22**) and Bait al-Milh (**no. 28**). Saltings are also alluded to in the name, Burj al-Malih (*Turris Salinarum*, **no. 67**).

Olive-presses are recorded at Bait Mahsir (**no. 35**), Baituniya (**no. 40**), Kh. Dinʿala (**no. 88**), Qalʿat Rahib (**no. 166**), and Qarawat Bani Hassan (**no. 170**, ? Mamluk). Presses of the rotary kind are specifically attested in the cathedral complex in Bethlehem (*Churches*, I, 153, fig. 46), in the basement below the infirmary hall at Kh. ʿIqbala (*Churches*, I, 245, no. 101), in Jifna, also below a possible hall (**no. 118**), in a courtyard building in Lifta (**no. 138**), and in village houses in al-Qubaiba (**no. 178**). Presses of the screw type, used for the secondary pressing of olives, are found at Kh. Bir Iklil (**no. 51**), al-Qubaiba (**no. 178**) and Kh. Manawat (**no. 145**). In a vault of the Benedictine convent buildings in Bethany and in Lifta (**no. 138**) the timber screws and beams also survive, though the dates of these examples are as yet unknown (on medieval olive-presses in general, see Benvenisti 1970: 257–8; Frankel 1985; 1987b; Frenkel 1987).

Wine-presses exist in the basements of the houses of the Frankish settlements at Kh. al-Burj (**no. 61**) and al-Qubaiba (**no. 178**), and in the courtyard building (*curia*) of another such settlement at ar-Ram (**no. 182**). They are also found in the castles of Montfort and Suba (see above). In the Benedictine convent at Bethany there survives a wine-cellar, with the concave stone supports that once supported the barrels (*Churches*, I, 133, nos. 59–60).

The extraction and smelting of iron ore is attested at Kh. Abu Thawwab (**no. 4**) and Magharat al-Warda (**no. 140**). Stone quarries exist at Kh. al-Lauza (**no. 137**) and

Kh. al-Manhata (**no. 146**). A limekiln has been excavated in Mairun (**no. 143**), and pottery kilns in Acre (**no. 5**). Glass manufacturing is well attested at as-Sumairiya (**no. 208**), and suggested at Tall Sahl as-Sarabat (**no. 195**) and possibly Kh. Kafr Bassa (**no. P17**). Hearths and chimneys that were associated with industrial activities yet to be identified have been found in the basements of some of the houses of the Frankish settlement at Kh. al-Burj (**no. 61**).

Kitchens with a row of rounded stone hearths to support metal cauldrons are recorded in the Benedictine convent at Bethany (*Churches*, I, 133, nos. 59–60) and in Belvoir Castle (**no. 46**). Bakeries with large domed ovens occur in the Hospitaller complex at Abu Ghosh (*Churches*, I, no. 1, fig. 4), in the Benedictine monastery of Mount Tabor (*Churches*, II, nos. 115–16, fig 15), in the castle of Karak (? Ayyubid, **no. 124**), in the *faubourg* of ʿAtlit (**no. 21**)), in excavations in Jaffa (**no. 110**), and in a house basement in al-Qubaiba (**no. 178**). In al-Bira (**no. 54**), a modern bakery established in a medieval house basement may possibly perpetuate an earlier arrangement, as may a number of the bakeries located in medieval vaults in Jerusalem (cf. Cohen 1989: 113–14). Village clay ovens (*tabūn*, pl. *tawabayn*) have been excavated at Kh. Tall ad-Durur (**no. 89**), Kh. Marus (**no. 147**) and Tall Sahl as-Sarabat (**no. 195**), and in post-Crusader village occupation of former Frankish sites such as Burj al-Ahmar (**no. 63**) and the monastery of St Mary of Carmel (*Churches*, II, no. 213).

Frankish road stations are documented at ʿAin al-Haramiya (**no. 11**), Kh. Dustray (**no. 90**) and Qalʿat ad-Dam (**no. 162**), and a stable complex, probably replacing Kh. Dustray, in the *faubourg* of ʿAtlit (**no. 21**). A bridge existed at al-Haddar (*Molendina Trium Pontium*, **no. 98**) and another of Roman date was repaired at Jisr al-Ghajar (**no. 119**).

# GAZETTEER

## 1 ABU ARABI ASH-SHAMALI

2065.2140 [6]

**Sugar-production site**, attested by large quantities of sugar-pot sherds.

Lenzen, Kareem and Thorpe 1987: 316-17 (no. 10).

## 2 ABU GHURDAN, Tall

2087.1781 [6]

near *Tall Dair ʿAlla*

Excavation of **indigenous village**, occupied seventh to fifteenth centuries.

Franken and Kalsbeek 1975; Pringle 1981b; Sauer 1976; Van der Kooij 1993: 342.

## 3 ABU SARBUT, Tall

2072.1788 [6]

Excavated structures relating to **sugar-production** in the Ayyubid and Mamluk periods.

de Haas, LaGro and Steiner 1989; 1992.

## 4 ABU THAWWAB, Khirbat

230-1.1747 [6]

**Iron ore extracting and smelting site**, in use in Ayyubid and Mamluk periods.

Coughenour 1976; Glueck 1951: 225, 238; Gordon 1987: 294 (site 3/3); Pringle 1981b: 49.

## 5 ACRE

1568.2586 [3]

*ʿAkka*; Hebr., *ʿAkko*
(fig. 3; pls. I–IV)

**Port city**, in Frankish hands 1104–87 and capital of the kingdom 1191–1291. The **vaulted basements** of many Crusader buildings, including **houses** of courtyard and S European type, survive as foundations for buildings of the late eighteenth and early nineteenth centuries, allowing much of the **urban topography** that is described and illustrated in contemporary documents and maps to be reconstructed. **Tower** (Burj as-Sultan: *c*.17.5 by *c*.15 m) surviving at NE seaward end of the former Venetian quarter (pl. II).

Benvenisti 1970: 78–113, figs.; Bralevski 1946; Calano 1980; Desimoni 1884; Dichter 1973; 1979a; 1979b; Favreau-Lilie 1982; Jacoby (D) 1977; 1979; 1982; 1989a; 1989b; 1993; Kedar and Stern 1995; Kesten 1962; 1993; Langé 1965: 39–64, figs.; Le Strange 1890: 328–34; Makhouly 1941; Makhouly and Johns 1946; Mariti 1769: II, 61–116; Marmardji 1951: 144–8; Müller-Wiener 1966: 72–4, plan 23, pls. 99–100; Prawer 1953; 1973; 1980: 217–49; Pringle 1993, III; 1994b; Rey 1878; 1883: 451–71, fig.; 1888; Richard 1953; 1966; Riley-Smith 1990: 102–3; Volterra 1989; Winter 1944.

The inner N rampart of Ḍāhir al-ʿUmar (1749–75) encapsulates the inner Crusader **town wall** (pl. III), which with a fronting **ditch** extended further E than the present E wall (rebuilt after 1799). A second Crusader wall was built by 1212, enclosing the first wall on the E and NE and continuing as a **double wall** around the suburb of Montmusard on the N; the only surviving visible trace appears to be the base of a **rounded** tower marking the outer wall's northern seaward termination and a stone bearing the arms of Henry II of Cyprus, which possibly came from the tower that he built in 1286.

3   Acre (**no. 5**): plan of Crusader basement structures surviving in the Old City (after Kesten 1962). Key: (1) Burj al-Khazna, probably incorporating the tower of the Hospital; (2–3) other towers on the inner town wall; (4) Hospital; (5) church of St John the Baptist; (6) mosque of al-Jazzar (1781); (7) modern Greek Orthodox church of St George, on site of Genoese church of St Lawrence; (8) Khan al-Faranj, on foundations of Venetian *fondaco*; (9) Burj as-Sultan (Venetian tower); (10) Crusader vault below present Greek Catholic church of St Andrew; (11) Khan ash-Shuna, on foundations of Pisan square (*platea*); (12) Khan al-ʿUmdan, on foundations of the royal customs house (*Cour de la Chaine*); (13) inner harbour; (14) Tower of the Flies, representing the end of the E harbour mole; (15) site of church of St Andrew.

Alderson 1843; Deschamps 1939a: *passim*; Druks 1984; Frankel 1987a; Jacoby 1993: 91–6; Kedar, forthcoming; Pringle 1995a; Rahmani 1971: 58–9, pl. 8; Rey 1871: 171–2, fig. 43; Rustum 1926; SSCLE 1987: 22–3 (nos. 28–9).

Excavations E of the Turkish walled city have revealed in area D (1973–4) the S end of a large **building**, built of well-dressed *kurkar* faced with marble, which was eventually destroyed by fire (Grid ref. 15760.25859); 340 m further E, in area E, a defensive wall with a *talus*, possibly forming part of the **outer city wall**, was excavated in 1974–6, and just E of it (1979) in area E1 a vaulted room and **pottery kiln**.

Dothan 1973; 1974; 1975b; 1976a: 37, figs. 35, 40; 1976b; 1978: 92–3, pl. vb; 1993a: 23–4; Dothan and Linder 1974; Kedar, forthcoming.

I Acre (**no. 5**): courtyard of a house of the Frankish period.

III Acre (**no. 5**): the inner N city wall, with *talus* and ditch, which formerly separated the old city from the thirteenth-century suburb of Montmusard.

II Acre (**no. 5**): Burj as-Sultan, from S.

IV Acre (**no. 5**): Khan ash-Shuna, incorporating remains of the Pisan square.

**Hospitaller compound**, comprising excavated remains of the hospital, convent and administrative buildings, set around a rectangular courtyard and including on S a large ground-floor **hall** (31 by 15 m internally, walls 2.9 m thick), with eight bays of rib-vaults springing from cylindrical piers, and on W at first-floor level the fragmentary remains of a rib-vaulted **hall** with **latrines** at its N end emptying through a **latrine pit** and a **vaulted drain** into the city ditch; to S, **undercrofts** of St John's church and of the infirmary (*domus infirmorum*).
Goldmann 1959; 1962a; 1962b; 1966; 1967; 1974; 1987; 1993; Pringle 1993: III.

Remains of **double harbour**, the inner defined on S by part-natural part-artificial reef on which the present mole is built, the outer by sunken remains of a mole extending on E from shore to Tower of the Flies.
Abel 1914; Flinder, Linder and Hall 1993; Gertwagen 1989a; Hall, Flinder and Linder 1968; 1989b; Linder 1971; Linder and Leenhardt 1964; Linder and Raban 1965; Link 1956; Raban 1993a.

**Sculpture and architectural fragments**
Barasch 1971: 211–21; Jacoby (Z) 1982b: 124–6, figs. 99–100, 108, 111, 113; Rahmani 1980a: 111–13, pl. XXIV.

*Churches*, III.

# 6 'ADASA, Khirbat

1727.1372 [8]

Syriac, *Adasa*; Cr. *Hadessa*

**Courtyard building**, identified from aerial photographs. The survival of medieval remains suggests that Kh. ʿAdasa, rather than Kh. ʿAddasa (Grid ref. 1704.1392), is to be identified as *Adasa*, mentioned as belonging to the Jacobite church of St Mary Magdalene in Jerusalem in a Syriac text of 1138 (Abel 1967: II, 250), and as *Hadessa*, whose boundary with *Ramathes* (ar-Ram, **no. 182**) was disputed by the Jacobites and the canons of the Holy Sepulchre *c.*1161 (Bresc-Bautier, no. 131; *RRH*, no. 365); this despite the fact that Kh. ʿAddasa is marginally closer to ar-Ram.

Bouillon 1898: 294–5, photo. p. 293; Gibson 1982: 157; Nau 1899: 429; Palestine 1929; 1948: 157; Pictorial Archive n.d.: film strip I, frames 75–6; Prawer 1980: 132 n.124; Prawer and Benvenisti 1970.

v al-ʿAffula (**no. 7**): medieval redoubt or tower, built using Roman sarcophagi.

# 7 al-ʿAFFULA

1775.2240 [5]

Hebr. ʿAfula
(pl. v)

**Fortified redoubt** (or **tower**?), 19 m square and > 5.5 m high, built on rise in centre of former village. The lower four courses are of rough blocks with largish pinnings, the upper course of Roman sarcophagi filled with mortared rubble (cf. Saffuriya, **no. 192**). Pottery from the interior suggests occupation in the twelfth and thirteenth centuries, though the date of construction is uncertain. (At one time this site was confused with al-Fula/*la Feve*, **no. 96**.)

Dothan 1955; 1975c: 36; 1993b; Hoade 1978: 574, 674–5; Israel 1964: 1387; Palestine 1948: 33; Pringle 1981b: 49; Sukenik 1948: 69–70, figs. 1.k, 10–11, pl. xxv.

# 8 ʿAIN AL-AJAB

1622.1393 [8]

Open **cistern**, associated with spring.

Bagatti 1947: 192, 195–7, 223, fig. 39; 1979: 95, fig. 34; Baldi 1973: 164; Hoade 1978: 586.

# 9 ʿAIN AL-HABIS

1624.1304 [8]

*Desert of St John*

Barrel-vaulted base of **tower** (10 m E–W by 7.4 m N–S, walls 1.35–2.05 m thick) built into hill side, with stairs to vanished upper floor leading off to left of door in S wall; converted into chapel (of St Elizabeth), probably after *c.*1480.

Bagatti 1948: 14–17, pl. 2; 1983: 20, pl. 1; Petrozzi 1971: 146; Pringle 1993: I, 24–6, fig. 8, pl. XII; 1994b.

# 10 ʿAIN AL-HABIS

2282.2365 [6]

Cr. *Cava de Suet, praesidium . . . in regione Suita/ Suhite*; Med. Ar. *Habis Jaldak*

**Cave castle**, established by 1109 in remains of Byzantine monastic *laura* in cliffs on S side of the Yarmuq gorge. Except for Muslim occupations in 1111–13, 1118 and 1182, in Frankish hands until just before 1187 (cf. William of Tyre, XVIII, 21 (1158); XXII, 16 (1182)).

Deschamps 1933: 47–57; 1934: 26, 77; 1935; 1939a: ii, vii, 9, 59, 99–116, 211–13, 215, 220, 222, 238, pl. XIII; 1943: 99–100; Eydoux 1982: 234; Johns 1937: 30; Kennedy 1994: 7, 40, 52–4; Mittmann 1970: 20–2; Nicolle 1988; 1989; Pringle 1993: I, 26; Schumacher 1917: 164–8, pls. XIIb, XIII–XIV; 1926: 532–3, pls. LXXXA, LXXXI–LXXXIII.

# 11 ʿAIN AL-HARAMIYA

1740.1561 [8]

*Spring of the Brigands/Templars*; Med. Ar. *Birkat al-Dāwiyya* (Pool of the Templars)
(pl. VI)

Groin-vaulted **cistern**, apparently associated with a former Templar **road station** at which Saladin spent the night of 14 October 1192 (Imād al-Dīn (trans. Massé, 397); Abū Shāmā (*RHC Or*, v, 87)).

VI  'Ain al-Haramiya (**no. 11**): vaulted cistern, beside the Jerusalem–Nablus road.

Abel 1934: 371; Conder and Kitchener 1881: II, 302; Guérin 1874: II, 36; Guide Bleu 1932: 545; Hoade 1978: 546; Palestine 1948: 103; Pringle 1985a: 147, fig. 1; 1994a: 52, fig. 3, pl. III; Robinson 1841: III, 76.

# 12 'AIN AS-SULTAN

### 1921.1419 [9]

*Elisha's Spring*; Cr. *Fons Helysei*

Natural spring feeding rounded masonry **pool** of Roman date, used in the twelfth century for irrigation and **water-mills** (Belard of Ascoli, IV (*IHC*, II, 46)).

Dorrell 1993; Palestine 1929: 250; 1948: 122; Schiller 1979: 280–1.

# 13 'AIN DUQ

### 1902.1445 [9]

Cr. *Jardinz Abraham, Campi Abraham, Abrahe Ortus* (pl. VII)

Repair of **aqueduct** carried on masonry arch (now fallen) across a wadi supplying water for irrigation and **sugar mills**.

Augustinović 1951: 141–2; Benvenisti 1970: 263–5, photo.; Conder and Kitchener 1881: III, 206–7; Hamilton 1959: 5–6, fig. 1, pl. I; Mann 1979; Meinardus 1969: 327; Rey 1883: 386.

# 14 'AIN SALMAN AL-'ANID

### 1627.1410 [8]

*Kh. Salman*
(fig. 4)

VII  'Ain Duq (**no. 13**): medieval aqueduct.

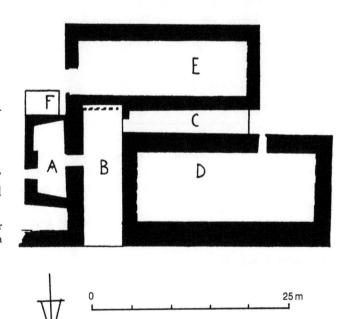

4  'Ain Salman al-'Anid (**no. 14**): group of vaulted buildings (from Bagatti 1947: fig. 45).

Group of **vaulted buildings**, including two-storey **hall** (26.9 by 13.8 m, walls 2.1/2.8 m) on N, with enclosure wall. **Reservoir** (10.65 by 5.7 m), 50 m to SE, fed by spring.

Bagatti 1947: 78, 192, 219–20, 237, fig. 45, pls. 39.98, 40.100; Ellenblum 1992: 177; Finkelstein and Magen 1993: 144, 28* (no. 147); Schick 1867.

## 15 'AIN SINIYA

1718.1532 [8]

Cr. *Valdecurs, Aineseins* (?), *Ainesens* (?)

Identification of 'a **small Crusading fort**' by Conder and Kitchener remains unverified. Usually identified as *Aineseins* (or *Ainesens*), one of twenty-one *casalia* granted by Godfrey of Bouillon to the Holy Sepulchre (Bresc-Bautier, no. 26; *RRH*, no. 74), though C.N. Johns (1939) suggests that may have been 'Ain Shams (see Kh. Rumaila, **no. 189**).

Bagatti 1979: 110–11; Conder and Kitchener 1881: II, 291; Palestine 1948: 104; Pringle 1994a: 50.

## 16 'ALIYA, Khirbat

174.269 [3]

Remains of **tower** (11 m square), built of well-dressed stones without draft (date uncertain).

Conder and Kitchener 1881: I, 170; Guérin 1880: II, 62; Israel 1964: 1358; Palestine 1929: 66; 1948: 7; Pringle 1994b.

## 17 'AMWAS

1492.1385 [8]

Cr. *Emaus, Emmaus*
Roman bath-house, adapted in Crusader period with insertion of timber mezzanine floor, possibly for use as a **store-house**; converted into Muslim sanctuary in the fourteenth century.

Gichon 1987: 55; 1993b. On the site, see also: Pringle 1993: I, 52–3; Vincent 1903; Vincent and Abel 1932.

*Churches*, I, no. 10.

## 18 'AQRABA

1825.1705 [6]

Fortified **courtyard building** (*al-Hisn*) at highest point

of village, NW of mosque, consisting of rectangular courtyard between two parallel rows of vaults, entered on E through arched gate flanked by projecting towers. Mosque contains Crusader capitals on fluted marble columns, flanking the *miḥrāb* (1947).

PAM: Reports by Anon. (15 Feb. 1937) and S.A.S. Husseini (14 June 1947).
Conder and Kitchener 1881: II, 386, 389; Palestine 1929; 1948: 116.

## 19 ARSUF

1329.1781 [5]

Cr. *Arsur*; Hebr. *Tel Arshaf*
(fig. 5)
**Town walls** with outer rock-cut ditch and (on S) external buttresses, enclosing three sides of an area about 120/160 m E–W by 345 m N–S, with sea cliffs on W; early Islamic in origin, these were repaired in Crusader period, when roughly built *talus* was also added on S. In NW corner, **castle** of irregular concentric plan with projecting rounded towers, built on rounded hillock and surrounded by rock-cut ditch to landward, commands the **harbour** (34 by 94 m), defined by two artificial moles and a breakwater. The town was in Crusader hands 1101–87 and 1191–1265; from *c*.1163 it was the centre of an independent lordship, before its sale to the Hospitallers in 1261.

Abel 1914; 1967: II, 247; Bagatti 1979: 182–4, fig. 71; Benvenisti 1970: 130–5, figs.; Conder and Kitchener 1881: II, 135; 137–40, plan; Deschamps 1934: 15, 18, 66, 74, 79, 131; 1939a: 5, 8, 23 n.5, 79, 124–5, 166, 215, 224 n.4; Eydoux 1982: 268; Grossmann 1991; Guérin 1874: II, 375–82; Hanauer 1896; Israel 1964: 1425; Johns 1937: 23; Langé 1965: 28, 32, 35, 70, 84–5, 100, 178, figs. 2, 6, 12, 42; Le Strange 1890: 399; Mariti 1769: II, 317–20; Marmardji 1951: 7; Palestine 1929; 1948: 77; Pococke 1743: II, 51; Porath 1989b; Pringle 1993: I, 59–61, fig. 18, pl. XXXI; 1995: 94, fig. 11; Rey 1883: 24, 153, 415–16.

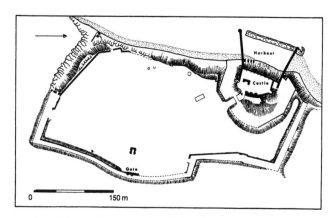

5  Arsuf (**no. 19**): town plan (after Conder and Kitchener 1881).

**Excavations** have so far revealed more about the early Islamic town than its Crusader successor, though work on S wall in 1990 revealed evidence of Crusader repair and of the Mamluk destruction of 1265.

Perkins 1951: 86–7, fig. 11; Roll 1991; Roll and Ayalon 1977; 1982; 1985; 1987; 1989; 1993; Wolff 1994: 514–15, fig. 44.

*Churches*, I, nos. 11–12.

# 20 ASCALON

1071.1191 [7]

'*Asqalan*; Cr. *Ascalon*; Hebr. *Ashqelon*
(fig. 6; pl. VIII)

Remains of **town walls**, describing a semi-circle 1.5 km long to landward with a sea wall on W. A barbican on E protected one of the four gates. The walls incorporate late Roman and early Islamic elements, including a tower mentioned in a Fatimid building inscription of 1150; but their latest phase, attributable to Richard I of England (1192), is characterized by narrow courses of smoothly dressed ashlar with a poured lime concrete core and through-columns, set on a battered plinth with horizontal offsets at 1.2–1.9 m intervals; it includes at least fourteen towers, varying in shape from rectangular to rounded or triangular. **Castle** of Richard of Cornwall (1241) built in NW corner, of concentric design with walls incorporating through-columns, a rock-cut ditch on S and E, and a masonry *talus* fronting the town wall on N; a lintel and a marble slab, both bearing arms of Sir Hugh Wake (two bars and three roundels in chief), evidently belong to this phase of refortification. **Vaulted building** near S gate. Ascalon was in Frankish hands 1153–87, 1192, 1239–47.

Abel 1912; Avi-Yonah and Eph'al 1975; Bagatti 1971c; Benvenisti 1970: 114–30, 228, figs.; Conder and Kitchener 1881: III, 237–47, plan; Deschamps 1934: 61–3; 1939a: 9–11, 13, 15, 17–18, 22, 40, 153–4, 178, 192, 232, 236–9; Eydoux 1982: 64, 188–90; Guérin 1857; 1868: II, 135–49, 161–71; Guthe 1879; Hammond 1995; Hartmann and Lewis 1960; Johns 1937: 29; Kedar and Kaufman 1975; Kedar and Mook 1978; Langé 1965: 67–71, 178–9; Le Strange 1890: 400–3; Mackenzie 1913; Marmardji 1951: 140–3; Marshall 1992: 101–4, fig. 5, pls. 4–5; Ory 1975: 11, pl. I; Prawer 1958; Pringle 1984a; 1993: I, 61–2, fig. 19; 1995a: 84–5, fig. 4, pls. 1–4; Rey 1871: 205–10, fig. 52, pl. XIX; Roberts 1842b: III, 46–9, pl. 68; Sharon 1994; 1995; Stager 1991.

**Excavations** have so far shed little light on the internal topography of the medieval city.

Abel 1921; Garstang 1921a; 1921b; 1922a; 1922b; 1924a; Phythian-Adams 1921; 1923; Stager 1993: 112; Stager and Esse 1986; 1987.

*Churches*, I, nos. 14–24.

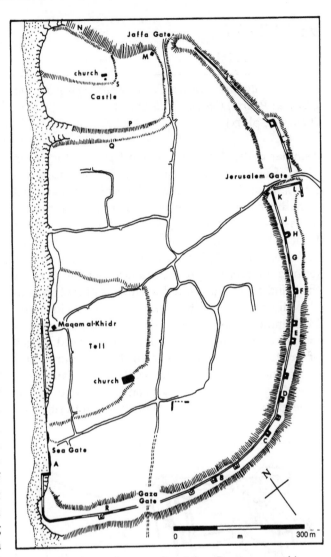

6   Ascalon (**no. 20**): town plan (after Garstang 1921b).

VIII   Ascalon (**no. 20**): rounded tower (*H*), built with through-columns, added to the town walls as part of Richard I's refortification in 1192.

# 21 'ATLIT

1440.2345 [5]

'*Athlith, Pilgrims' Castle*; Cr. *Castrum Peregrinorum, Chastiau Pelerin, Castrum Filii Dei*
(figs. 7–9; pl. IX)

Templar **castle**, built on a sea-girt promontory from 1217/18 onwards, to which a defended **faubourg** was later added; abandoned 1291. The castle was detached from the mainland by concentric defences, comprising a sea-level rock-cut ditch with counterscarp wall in front of two massive walls: an inner wall, 12 m thick and over 30 m high, flanked by two rectangular towers (27 by 21 m, projecting 6–16 m); and an outer wall, 6.5 m thick and 16 m high, with three towers placed so as to allow the defenders of the inner wall a clear field of fire. Main entrance way led between the two walls; posterns in sides of outer towers. The defences enclosed ranges of vaulted halls and a polygonal chapel set around a single inner courtyard. The **wall of the faubourg**, extending 645 m on E and 230 m on S, survives to 7.25 m in height, with a ditch and counterscarp in front; three

IX '*Atlit* (**no. 21**): Pilgrims' Castle, from the E.

gates (two on E, one on S) set in gate-towers and defended by portcullises and (assumed) slit-machicolations, with timber bridges over ditch; also a postern on E. Faubourg contained a **bath-house** and **bakery** (fig. 9), church, **stables** and a free-standing **tower** (14.1 by 11.7 m) with groin-vaulted basement, which was later incorporated into SE corner of the outer defences. **Harbour** to S of castle. Walled **cemetery** to NE, containing at least 1,700 graves covered by monolithic, plastered rubble or whitewashed ashlar grave slabs.

PAM: Excavation archive, 1931–6.
PEF: C.N. Johns papers.

d'Arvieux 1735: II, 12–13; Benvenisti 1970: 175–85, 259–60, 283, 287, 289–90, 345, fig., photos; Biran 1966; Conder 1874: 13; Conder and Kitchener 1881: I, 281, 293–301, figs.; Deschamps 1934: 45, 71–2, 79, 84–5, 88, 91, 94–5, 131, 138, 226–7, 229, 279, fig. 14, pl. XII; 1939a: v, 1, 16, 23 n.5, 24–33, 137, 140, 196, 215, 237, 239, figs. 2–3, pls. XCIII–XCVI; Drake 1873: 99–104, figs.; Eydoux 1982: 167–71, 242; Guérin 1874: II, 285–93; Hartmann 1960; Irby and Mangles 1861: 59–60; Israel 1964: 1379; Jacoby (Z) 1982b: 124, figs. 102–3; Johns 1932; 1934a; 1934b; 1935; 1936a; 1937: 27; 1947; 1975; Kennedy 1994: 124–7, colour pl. 4, fig. 16; King 1946: 30–7; Langé 1965: 31–2, 60, 108, 120–6, 181–2, figs. 6, 43, 66–73, 76; Lawrence 1988: xxxi, xxxii, xxxiii, xxxix, 71, 74n., 131, fig. 49; Linder 1971; McCown 1931: 18, fig. 1; Mariti 1769: II, 293–6; Meistermann 1936: 474–5, fig.; von Mülinen 1908a: 171–86, figs. 71–6; Müller-Wiener 1966: 71–2, plan 22, pl. 98; Ory 1975: 14; Palestine 1929: 12; 1948: 26; Pearlman and Yannai 1964: 125–30; Pococke 1743: II.i, 57; Prawer 1972: 312–18, plan; Pringle 1993: I, 69–71, fig. 23; 1994b; 1995a: 91–2, fig. 9; 1995b: 174, fig.; Raban and Linder 1993; Rey 1871: 93–100, fig. 28, pls. X–XI; Ronen and Olami 1978: 36–49, 12*–13*; Rothschild 1938: 44; Smail 1973: 114–19, figs. 17–18, pls. 21–3.

*Churches*, I, nos. 26–7.

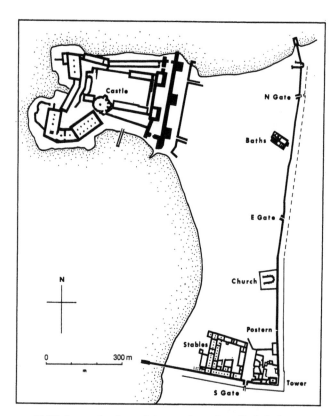

7 '*Atlit* (**no. 21**): plan of the castle and walled *faubourg* (after Johns 1947).

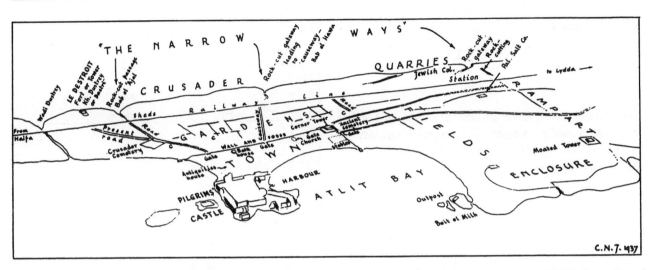

8  'Atlit: sketch of site, showing location of castle and *faubourg* (**no. 21**), moated tower (**no. 22**), Bait al-Milh (**no. 28**) and Kh. Dustray (**no. 90**) (from Johns 1947: fig. 1).

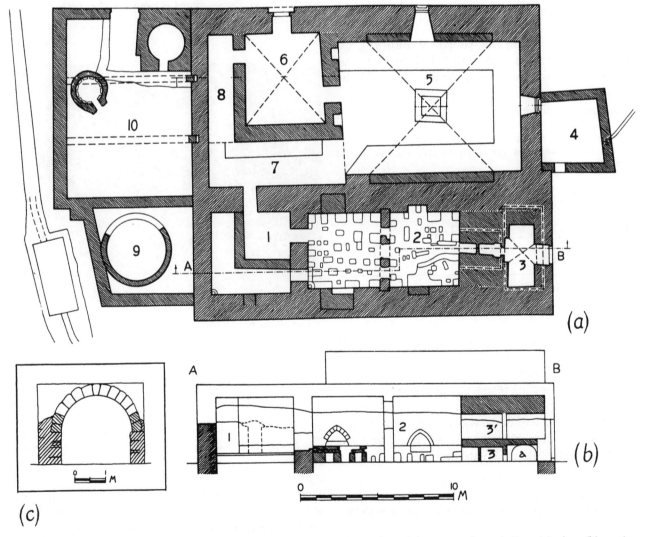

9  'Atlit (**no. 21**): bath-house (1–8) and bakery (9–10) in the *faubourg* (from Johns 1947: fig. 31). Key: (a) plan; (b) section A–B; (c) section through oven 9.

# 22 'ATLIT

(1.3 km SSW of) 1436.2332 [5]

(Fig. 8)

Remains of **moated tower** situated at W seaward end of stone-faced **earth rampart** defining S boundary of lands and **saltings** dependent on 'Atlit Castle.

PEF: C.N. Johns papers.

Johns 1947: 72, fig. 1; 1975: fig. p. 131 (nos. 10–11).

# 23 'AYADIYA, Khirbat al-

1648.2576 [3]

Cr. *la Hadia*; Med. Ar. *al-Ghayadah*; Hebr. *H. Uza*

Foundations of rectangular **courtyard building** excavated just S of main road in 1991. In February 1254, some of the village land of *la Hadia* was being held by Roland Antelmus (*RRH*, no. 1212).

Information: N. Getzov and R. Frankel.

Barag 1979: 204 (no. 16); Ben-Tor 1966; Beyer 1945: 208–10; Frankel 1988: 261, 271–2; Israel 1964: 1372; Palestine 1929; 1948: 20; Pringle 1981b: 53; 1994a: 49.

# 24 BADAWIYA, Tall al-

1743.2445 [3]

*Kh. Ibdawiya*; Hebr. *Tel Hannaton*
(fig. 10; pl. x)

**Tower** (28.0 by 18.9 m), of which only the buried ground floor survives; gate on S (2.95 m wide) with two wing-doors preceded by a portcullis slot, opening through an intersecting rear-arch into a barrel-vaulted room (22.8 by about 8.3 m), ventilated by six vertical rectangular shafts within the walls; door at E end of N wall leads to stair in N wall to vanished upper floor.

PAM: Reports by R.W. Hamilton (3 May 1935) and A.K. Dajani (13 Sept. 1947).

Garstang 1922a: 12; Gertwagen 1987; 1988; 1989c; 1993; Guérin 1880: I, 490–1; Israel 1964: 1379; Palestine 1948: 25; Pringle 1994b: 340, fig. 5b.

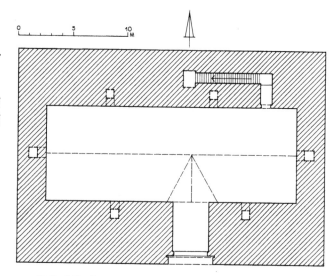

10   Tall al-Badawiya (**no. 24**): plan of tower basement (drawn by M. Pease, after Gertwagen 1989c, with amendments).

x Tall al-Badawiya (**no. 24**): basement of tower, looking W.

# 25 al-BA'INA

1756.2595 [3]

Cr. *Saint Jorge Labane/de la Baene, casale S. Georgii, Sangeor*

Two modern village houses have pointed-arched doorways, one with a defensive slit-machicolation similar to twelfth-century examples at Bait 'Itab (**no. 31**) and

al-Burj (Qal'at Tantura, **no. 57**), suggesting that it may have formed part of a **hall-house** or **tower**. Al-Ba'ina was the *caput* of an independent lordship, held in the twelfth century by Henry of Milly, passing in 1182 to Joscelin III of Courtenay (*RRH*, nos. 588, 614) and by 1249 to the Teutonic Order (*RRH*, nos. 934, 974, 1175).
Bagatti 1971a: 187, figs. 142–3; Pringle 1993: I, 80–1.

*Churches*, I, nos. 28–9.

# 26 BAISAN

1975.2116 [6]

Cr. *Bethsan, Bessan, Beisan*; Hebr. *Bet She'an*
(fig. 11; pl. XI)

**Tower** (17.6 by 17.3 m, walls 3 m thick, est. height about 12 m), built of reused finely jointed rusticated limestone blocks including material from Roman theatre, now incorporated into the 'Old Serail', some 400 m SSE of the theatre; excavations and clearance since 1988 show it to have been of two storeys, the lower covered by a pair of barrel-vaults; ground-floor entrance on N, with slit-machicolation in front of recessed door. Tower surrounded by rectangular wall (dated Umayyad by excavator), with projecting rectangular towers at SE and SW corners, and with outer ditch and counterscarp wall; gate on N reached by timber bridge carried on masonry pier. Barrel-vault (restored) built against inside of N wall. This, rather than the Byzantine fortification on Tall al-Hisn, was evidently the **castle** (*praesidium*) in whose defences the inhabitants had little faith in 1183 (William of Tyre, XXII, 27 (26)); it was restored by Saladin in November 1192 ('Imad al-Dīn (trans. Massé, 397)). Northern part of castle made into **sugar factory** in the late thirteenth century (Mamluk period); other buildings of Ayyubid period excavated 100 m to E.
PEF: C.N. Johns, Field Notebooks 1943–6 (20 April 1945), 1946–7 (Aug. 1946).
Information: J. Seligman, Israel Antiquities Authority.

Abel 1912: 421–3; Ben-Dor 1943: 9, 20–1; Boaz 1990; Deschamps 1939a: 3, 5, 22–3, 63, 100, 105 n.1, 119, 122, 180, 236; Gaudefroy-Demombynes 1923: 64–5; Gertwagen 1992a; 1992b; Gertwagen and Finkelstein 1992; Johns 1937: 24; Kennedy 1994: 39, 40, fig. 12, pl. 12; Pringle 1993: I, 93; 1994b; Seligman 1994; 1995; Yeivin *et al.* 1988: 38, 43, fig. 5.

*Churches*, I, p. 93.

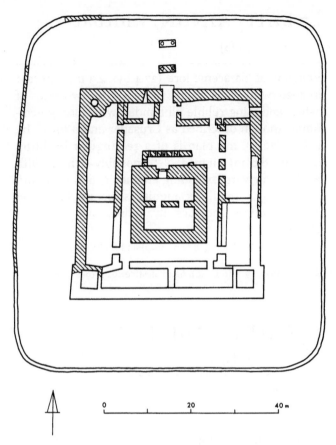

11  Baisan (**no. 26**): plan of the castle (after Seligman 1994).

XI Baisan (**no. 26**): castle, from W.

## 27 BAIT ʿAINUN, Khirbat

1621.1078 [8]

Remains of 'Saracenic fort' (27.4 by 22.9 m) reported in 1920, with walls built 1 m thick with two faces of ashlar enclosing rubble fill bonded with through-columns; though described as Crusader and a tower by J. Ory (1927), the plan is of a **rectangular building** (22.6 by 8.6 m) aligned N–S, possibly a **hall**, with walled courtyard extending another 17.6 m on E and containing a small rectangular structure in its SE corner. Pottery includes Byzantine, medieval and Ottoman.

PAM: Reports by Anon. (18 Nov. 1920) and J. Ory (1927).

Kochavi 1972: 57–8 (no. 118), fig.; Palestine 1929; 1948: 188.

## 28 BAIT AL-MILH

1436.2338 [5]

*Salt Island*
(fig. 8)

Remains of outlying **tower**, associated with ʿAtlit Castle, and **installations for salt production**, including tanks and channels cut in rock.

Conder and Kitchener 1881: I, 300; Johns 1947: 72, figs. 1–2; 1975: fig. p. 131 (no. 9); von Mülinen 1908a: 269–70; Ronen and Olami 1978: 57–8, 15* (no. 99), figs. p. 58.

## 29 BAIT DAJAN

1339.1563 [7]

*Cr. Casellum Maen/Medium, Bedeian* (1335)

'Fragment of ancient building in el Qalʿa' (1948) may possibly be part of the **castle** destroyed by Saladin in September 1191, refortified by Richard I in October 1191 and destroyed again by Saladin in August 1192 (*Itin. Ric.*, IV, 23; IV, 29–30; Bahāʾ al-Dīn (*PPTS*, XIII, 373)). *Bedeian* described by James of Verona (1335) as *castrum dirutum*.

Abel 1927a; 1967: II, 269; Bagatti 1979: 176–7; Conder and Kitchener 1881: II, 251; Guide Bleu 1932: 556; Hoade 1978: 611; Israel 1964: 1429; James of Verona 1335: 181; Johns 1937: 26; Khalidi 1992: 226–8; Langé 1965: 94, 180, fig. 43; Palestine 1948: 81.

## 30 BAIT ʿIRZA, Khirbat

1677.1268 [8]

**Groin-vaults**, supposedly Crusader.

Conder and Kitchener 1881: III, 83; Palestine 1929: 15; 1948: 167.

## 31 BAIT ʿITAB

1551.1268 [8]

*Cr. Bethaatap, Beitatap, Bethahatap*
(fig. 12; pls. XII–XIII)

First-floor **hall-house** (29 by 13.3 m), with ground-floor entrance, defended by slit-machicolation and door with draw-bar, leading into vaulted basement and to

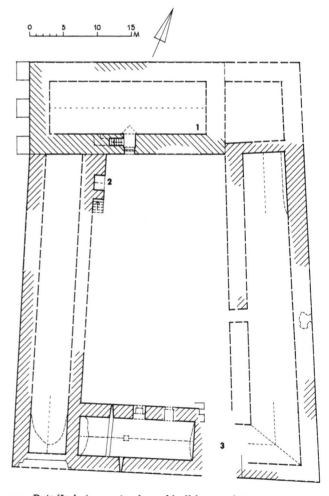

12   Bait ʿItab (**no. 31**): plan of hall-house, later incorporated into courtyard building or *maison forte*. Key: (1) hall-house; (2) stair to first-floor door to hall, added in secondary phase; (3) possible site of entrance to courtyard (drawn by M. Pease, BSAJ Survey 1989).

stair to vanished upper floor inside wall to left. Later incorporated into N range of a **courtyard building** (40/45.7 m E–W by 59 m N–S), with four vaulted ranges around central court and entrance on S; in this phase, hall provided with first-floor entrance and external stair from courtyard. Village sold to the Holy Sepulchre with four others by John Gothman in 1161, to pay for his ransom from the Muslims (Bresc-Bautier, nos. 87–8; *RRH*, nos. 368–9).

PAM: Reports by D.C. Baramki (25 June 1942, 8 July 1944).

Conder and Kitchener 1881: III, 22–4, 83; Ellenblum 1992: 179; Guérin 1868: II, 381–3; III, 321; Hoade 1978: 598; Khalidi 1992: 274–5; Palestine 1929; 1948: 163; Pringle 1991a: 87–8 (no. 1); Rey 1883: 379; Robinson 1841: II, 338–9.

XII  Bait 'Itab (**no. 31**): courtyard building, from SE, looking towards the hall-house.

XIII  Bait 'Itab (**no. 31**): hall-house, showing basement door to right and remains of external stair to first-floor hall to left.

## 32 BAIT JIBRIN

1400.1129 [8]

Cr. *Bethgibelin, Beit Gibelin, Bersabea, Gybelin, Ybelin Hospitalariorum*; Hebr. *Bet Guvrin*

**Concentric castle**: inner ward some 50 m square, with gate on S and at each corner a projecting rectangular tower, of which the SE one was later partly demolished to make way for a church; gate towards W end of S wall; remains of outer wall with *talus* and projecting tower on N. **Barrel-vaulted structure** (later used as village mosque) to SE. Castle built *c*.1134 and granted to Hospitallers in 1136; held until 1187, and 1240–4.

PAM: Report by C.N. Johns (15 Sept. 1945).

Bagatti 1972: 117–18, 123–7, figs. 5–8; Benvenisti 1970: 185–8, figs.; Clermont-Ganneau 1896: I, 25; Conder 1875: 139–41; Conder and Kitchener 1881: III, 268–71, figs., pl.; Deschamps 1934: 18, 55 n.4, 56, 85, 97; 1939a: 10–11, 13, 21–2, 179, 236; Ellenblum 1992: 179; Eydoux 1982: 160, 188; Guérin 1868: II, 307–9; Johns 1937: 24; Kennedy 1994: 31, 32, 58, 145; Kloner 1983a; 1985; 1987; 1993: 201; Kloner and Chen 1983; Langé 1965: 67, 92, 104, 143, 179, figs. 43, 76, 82–4; Lawrence 1988: xxxv; Ory 1975: 26–7; Pringle 1993: I, 95–101; Roberts 1842b: IV, 20–1, pl. 82; de Sandoli 1974: 263.

*Churches*, I, nos. 31–2.

## 33 BAIT JUBR AT-TAHTANI

1905.1396 [9]

(fig. 13; pl. XIV)

Quadrangular **tower** (about 9.5 by 6.6/8.1 m) on scarped rock spur beside the Jerusalem–Jericho road; barrel-vaulted ground floor with stair inside wall, lit by splayed, lintelled embrasure; possibly Templar.

Augustinović 1951: 58–60, figs. 13, 45; Benvenisti 1970: 325; Conder and Kitchener 1881: III, 190–91; Kennedy 1994: 55; Palestine 1929: 16; 1948: 190; Pringle 1991a: 88 (no. 2); 1993: I, 101–2; 1994b: 337, table; 1994c: 162–6, figs. 16.11–14; Roberts 1842b: III, pl. 61.

## 34 BAIT KIKA, Khirbat

1690.1353 [8]

*Kh. Maqiqa*; Cr. *Belrit Kykay*; Hebr. *Ramot*
(pl. XV)

Base of medieval **tower** (about 8 m square, walls about

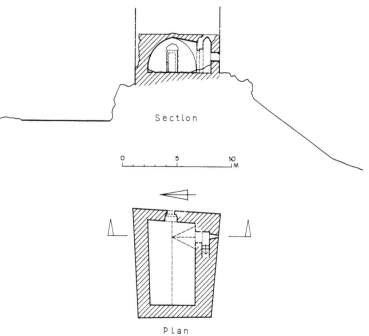

Section

13   Bait Jubr at-Tahtani (**no. 33**): plan and section of tower (drawn by M. Pease, BSAJ Survey 1989).

XIV   Bait Jubr at-Tahtani (**no. 33**): tower standing beside the Jericho road at the point where it emerges from the Wadi Qilt into the plain of the Jordan.

1.7 m thick), annexed to elliptical **barrel-vault** (about 6.5 m by > 15 m). Village returned to Christians in 1241 (Matthew Paris, *Chron. Maj.* (*RS*, LVII.iv, 142)).

Bagatti 1947: 229, fig. 46 (D22); Palestine 1929; 1948: 154; Pringle 1994b.

xv   Kh. Bait Kika (**no. 34**): barrel-vaulted building (April 1979).

## 35 BAIT MAHSIR
### 153.133 [8]

Hebr. *Bet Meʿir*

At NW of village, large medieval **barrel-vault** known as *al-Badd* (the oil-press) (about 35 by 10 m, walls about 2.3 m thick), with three round openings in ceiling, containing two disused **oil-presses**; some stones with diagonal dressing. Recorded in 1947, but apparently now destroyed.

PAM: Reports by S.A.S. Husseini (17, 19 Feb. 1947).
Israel 1964: Khalidi 1992: 275–7; 1459; Palestine 1948: 151.

## 36 BAIT MAZMIL, Khirbat
### 166.130 [8]

**Foundations** of walls, with pottery attesting twelfth-century occupation. Presumed now destroyed.
Bagatti 1948: 15–16; Palestine 1929; 1948: 156; Pringle 1981b: 53.

## 37 BAIT SAFAFA
### 1690.1281 [8]

Cr. *Bethafava, Bethsaphace*
(pl. XVI)

**Tower** (*al-Burj*) (18.2 m NW–SE by 13.7 m NE–SW, walls 2.5–2.9 m thick), standing (in 1937) 17 m high

xvi Bait Safafa (**no. 37**): interior of tower, looking S, showing partially collapsed inserted mezzanine vault.

with floor levels at 8 and 15 m respectively, and an inserted mezzanine carried on a rounded barrel-vault at 3.9 m. Recessed and rebated ground-floor door on NW led into barrel-vaulted basement (12.5 by 8.65 m), enclosing mouth of **cistern**; from here, stair built against NE and NW walls ascended to similarly vaulted first floor (now gone), from which another led up to roof. The tower had a secondary **vault** (*Bubalia*) built against its SW face, and stood at the centre of a **rectangular enclosure**, with a *talus* on NW, SW and SE, a possible gate on NE, and remains of another **vault** at E corner. Village granted to the Hospitallers by Baldwin I before September 1110 (*RRH*, no. 57; cf. no. 293); returned to Franks in 1241 (Matthew Paris, *Chron. Maj.* (*RS*, LVII.iv, 143)).

PAM: Reports by D.C. Baramki (16 Jan. 1941, 13 June 1941).
PEF: C.N. Johns, Field Notes (6 June 1937).
Bagatti 1983: 23; Guide Bleu 1932: 553; Hoade 1978: 599; Johns 1937: 24; Kochavi 1972: 36 (no. 3); Israel 1964: 1469; Palestine 1948: 166; Pringle 1994b.

## 38 BAIT TULMA, Khirbat

1663.1346 [8]

*Kh. 'Ain Tulma; Cr. Tolma; Hebr. H. Bet Telem, H. 'En Telem*

**Vaulted cistern** (15 by 13.4 m, 4.9 m deep, walls 1.7–1.9 m thick), with rusticated quoins. Other **vaulted buildings** near by.

PAM: Report by S.A.S. Husseini (16 July 1934).

Bagatti 1947: 192, 231–2, 236, 237, pl. 37.93; Ellenblum 1992: 177; Finkelstein and Magen 1993: 226, 45* (no. 302); Israel 1964: 1460; Palestine 1948: 154.

## 39 BAIT 'UR AL-FAUQA

1608.1436 [8]

Cr. *Bethoron Superior, Vetus Bethor*

**Tower** (*al-Burj*). Village (described as a *gastina*, but with *villani*) given to Orthodox monastery of St Sabas by Queen Melisende, and sold to Holy Sepulchre in 1163/4 (Bresc-Bautier, no. 133; *RRH*, no. 409).

Bagatti 1979: 106, pl. 40.1; Benvenisti 1970: 19, 233, 311, 314, fig. p. 232; Ellenblum 1992: 179; Finkelstein and Magen 1993: 49, 142, 16*, 28* (nos. 28, 143); Palestine 1948: 111; Pringle 1994b.

## 40 BAITUNIYA

1662.1436 [8]

Cr. *Beitiumen, Urniet*

Large **vaulted building** (*Badd al-Balad*, or 'oil-press of the village'), incorporated into later village houses. Village granted to the Holy Sepulchre by Godfrey of Bouillon (Bresc-Bautier, no. 26; *RRH*, no. 74).

PAM: Report by S.A.S. Husseini (12 April 1941).
Abel 1931: 141–2; Benvenisti 1970: 233, 258; Finkelstein and Magen 1993: 70, 19* (no. 61); Palestine 1929: 19; 1948: 111; Pringle 1994a: 50.

## 41 BAL'AMA, Khirbat

1776.2058 [5]

Cr. *Castellum Beleismum, Chastiau St Job*
(pls. XVII–XVIII)

**Castle**, comprising remains of two-storey vaulted **tower** ( > 8 m square) on hill top, standing at centre of S wall of rectangular **enclosure** (about 60 m E–W by about 40 m N–S), with ranges of rooms along E and W sides. A **vaulted tunnel**, some 30–40 m long, 3 m wide and 4.2 m high, apparently led from the castle to a spring ('Ain as-Sinjib, or Sinjil) at the foot of the hill. Inhumation **graves in stone-lined cists** together with a **stone carved with a Latin cross** in relief (possibly fallen from above) uncovered near tunnel mouth in 1972. The castle existed by 1156 (*RRH*, no. 321) and was in Hospitaller hands by 1187 (Ernoul (ed. de Mas Latrie, 153)).

xvii   Kh. Bal'ama (**no. 41**): tower, remains of N wall showing outline of first-floor vault, as illustrated by Macalister (1930).

xviii   Kh. Bal'ama (**no. 41**): vaulted tunnel leading to spring.

PAM: Reports by P.L.O. Guy (1926), N. Makhouly (1927–42), S.A.S. Husseini (1941) and C.N. Johns (3 Nov. 1941).
PEF: C.N. Johns Papers, Field Notebook 1940–1 (22 Nov. 1941); draft report (3 Nov. 1941).

Abel 1967: II, 357; Bagatti 1979: 137–8, pl. 49.2; Beyer 1940: 185, 193–5; Conder and Kitchener 1881: II, 51–2; Guérin 1874: I, 339–41; Hoade 1978: 569; Johns 1937: 14; Kochavi 1972: 210 (no. 18); Macalister 1930: 205, photo opp. p. 206; Macalister and Masterman 1907: 129; Palestine 1929: 22; 1948: 55; Phythian-Adams 1922; Pringle 1993, I: 106–7, pl. LXXI; 1994b; Schumacher 1910; Yeivin 1973.

*Churches*, I, no. 37.

# 42 BANYAS

## 2150 2947 [4]

Cr. *Belinas, Paneas*

**Town walls**, with projecting rectangular towers and gate-tower on S, enclosing a roughly rectangular area (about 250 by about 220 m, or 13 ha); ditch and counterscarp wall on E, stream beds on S and W. Walls appear to be mostly Ayyubid and Mamluk, though they probably follow the trace of the double enceinte repaired by Baldwin III in 1157 (William of Tyre, XVIII, 13). Other Crusader structures revealed by excavation include remains of castle (?) in NW part of walled town (area C), incorporating rebuilt Roman vaults. Banyas was in Crusader hands in 1128–32 and 1140–64.

Ben-Dov 1978; Benvenisti 1970: 147–54, figs.; Conder and Kitchener 1881: I, 110–12; Deschamps 1939a: 3–10, 14, 108 n.1, 119, 123 n.3, 126, 128, 130, 132, 138, 144–74, 178, 184 nn.4–5, 189, 214–16, 226; 1943: 103; Eydoux 1982: 147–9; Graboïs 1970; 1987; Guérin 1880: II, 308–23; Guide Bleu 1932: 380–2; Hartal, Ma'oz and Tzaferis 1985; Johns 1937: 24; Kitchener 1877: 172–3; Ma'oz 1993; Pringle 1993: I, 108; 1995a: 92–3; Rey 1883: 473; Tzaferis and Avner 1990a; 1990b; 1991; Tzaferis and Israeli 1993; Tzaferis and Muttat 1988; Tzaferis, Peleg and Ma'oz 1989; Van Berchem 1903.

*Churches*, I, no. 38.

# 43 BAUBARIYA, Khirbat al-

## 1664.1863 [5]

Kh. al-Babriya

**Courtyard building**, consisting of two barrel-vaults (11.2 by 18.5 m, and 9.5 by about 17.2 m), set to either side of a courtyard 11 m wide.

Benvenisti 1982: 144 (no. 5), figs. 10–11; Ellenblum 1992: 179; Kochavi 1972: 222 (no. 126); Palestine 1948: 64.

# 44 BEAUFORT CASTLE

1999.3032 [4]

*Qal'at ash-Shaqif Arnun; Cr. Beaufort, Belfort*
(fig. 14; pl. XIX)

Large **castle** incorporating both Frankish and Muslim (Ayyubid, Mamluk and Ottoman) work, in Frankish hands 1139–90 and 1240–68, and held by the Templars from 1260. Roughly triangular in plan (about 150 m N–S by < 100 m E–W), occupying a rocky ridge on W edge of the Litani gorge, with a rock-cut ditch containing **cisterns** on S and NW, and a lower ward on E. From the outer gate on S, a path zig-zagged back and up to enter the upper ward through a barbican at its S end. Both wards were filled with more than one level of vaulted structures, which in the upper ward enclosed a two-storey twelfth-century **tower keep** (about 12 m square, walls 2.75 m thick), representing the earliest Crusader phase. A two-bayed groin-vaulted **hall** with elaborate Gothic portal which stands E of it probably dates after 1260. Remains of **faubourg** to S of castle, defended on W by traces of walls (late ?) with two rounded towers and containing rectangular outwork attributed to Templars (1260).

Boase 1967: 66–7; Conder and Kitchener 1881: I, 128–33, figs., pls.; Deschamps 1934: 29–30, 82, 92–3, 97, 136 n.2, 196 n.2, 228–9, 276; 1939a: 176–208, pls. LIII–LXXV; Enlart 1925: II, 42–3; Eydoux 1982: 153–7; Fedden 1950: pl. p. 65; Fedden and Thomson 1957: 30, pl. 7; Guérin 1880: II, 522–5; Guide Bleu 1932: 415–19, fig.; 1975: 225–7, fig.; Heyck 1900: figs. 131–2; Johns 1937: 23; Kennedy 1994: 41–4, 127–8, pls. 13–14, fig. 3; Lawrence 1988: xxx, 46, 58, 65, 126, figs. 42–43a; Müller-Wiener 1966: 62–3, plan 15, pl. 84; Pringle 1993: I, 110; 1994b; Rey 1871: 127–39, fig. 40, pl. XIII; Smail 1956: 218, 221–3, 226, 227, fig. 2, pls. IIIab.

*Churches*, I, no. 41.

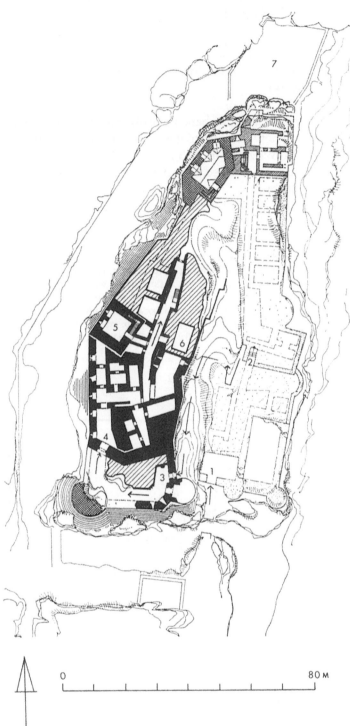

14 Beaufort Castle (**no. 44**): plan. Crusader work shown in black, Muslim work (1190–1240) cross-hatched. Key: (1) outer gate; (2) gate in lower ward; (3) gate to barbican; (4) gate to inner ward; (5) keep or *donjon*; (6) substructure of Templar hall; (7) cistern (after Müller-Wiener 1966: plan 15).

XIX  Beaufort Castle (**no. 44**): from the S (in 1963).

# 45 BEIRUT

196.365 [2]

*Bairut; Cr. Baruth, Berytum, Beritum; Fr. Beyrouth*
(fig. 15)

City in Crusader hands 1110–87 and 1197–1291. Nothing now survives of the Crusaders' **town walls** (370
m E–W by 570 m N–S), **castle-palace** (1205–11) and
**harbour**, described by earlier writers (e.g. Wilbrand of
Oldenburg, I,5 (ed. Laurent, 166–67; *IHC*, III, 204–6)),
though **excavations** have shed some light on the medieval (and earlier) topography.

Boase 1967: 65; Collinet 1925; Davie 1987; Deschamps 1934: 15, 18, 59,
66, 69–70, 71 n.1, 74, 85, 87 n.4, 97 n.3, 106 n.1, 123, 128, 138; 1939a: 9,
15, 29, 147, 187, 196, 213, 216, 224 n.4, 232–3, 237–9; Dussaud 1927:
58–63; Elisséeff 1960; Forest and Forest 1982; Jidejian 1973: 82–91;
Lauffray 1945: pl. II; Le Strange 1890: 408–10; du Mesnil du Buisson
1921; Pringle 1993: I, 111–12, fig. 36; 1994b: 338–9; 1995a: 87–8, fig. 6;
Rey 1871: 173–4, fig. 44; 1883: 521–4; Saidah 1969: 137–9, fig.

*Churches*, I, nos. 42–55.

# 46 BELVOIR CASTLE

1992.2224 [6]

*Kaukab al-Hawa; Cr. Belvoir, Coquet; Hebr. Kokhav ha-
Yarden*
(fig. 16; pls. xx–xxi)

Hospitaller **castle** of rectangular concentric plan, occupied 1168–89 and then by the Ayyubids until 1219;
excavated by Israel Department of Antiquities 1963–8.
The outer enceinte (100 m N–S by 110 m E–W), with
projecting rectangular towers, some with posterns
leading into rock-cut outer ditch, surrounds an inner
ward (50 by 50 m), with four square corner-towers and
a projecting gate-tower on W containing a bent entrance with slit-machicolations over the gates. The
outer gate, on SE, had wing-doors, a slit-machicolation
and enfilading arrow-slits. The inner ward contained
**kitchen** and **stables** on ground floor and chapel on first
floor over gate. **Vaulted cisterns**.

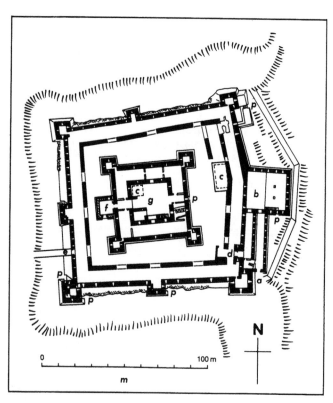

15  Beirut (**no. 45**): sketch plan of city (after du Mesnil du
Buisson 1921: fig. 3).

16  Belvoir Castle (**no. 46**): plan. Key: (a) outer gate; (b)
barbican; (c) cisterns; (d) inner gate; (e) west gate; (f)
gatehouse to inner ward (with chapel over); (g) inner
ward; (p) postern gates (after Ben-Dov 1975b).

xx  Belvoir Castle (**no. 46**): outer SE corner tower, overlooking the Jordan Valley.

xxi  Belvoir Castle (**no. 46**): inner ward, seen from SE.

PEF: C.N. Johns papers, report (3 Dec. 1945), plan (3 Oct. 1943).
Bagatti 1971a: 191–6, figs. 242–7; Ben-Dov 1969; 1972; 1975a; 1975b; 1993a; Ben-Dov and Minzker 1968; Benvenisti 1970: 281–2, 297, 289–90, 294–300, 375–6, figs.; Biller 1989; Biran 1967; 1968; Bouillon 1898: 378–80; Conder 1874: 179–80; Conder and Kitchener 1881: II, 85, 117–19, fig.; Deschamps 1934: 28, 54–5, 85; 1939a: 14, 17, 121–3, 134, 137, 178, 236, fig. 10; 1943: 98; Drake 1875: 29–30; Ellenblum 1992: 173, 182; Eydoux 1982: 224–5; Gal 1991: 53, 35* (no. 60); Guérin 1880: I, 129–32; Israel 1964: 1400; Johns 1937: 23; Kennedy 1994: 58–61, pls. 20–1, colour pl. 1, fig. 5; Khalidi 1992: 52–3; Langé 1965: 29, 31, 92, 100–4, 115, 179, figs. 43, 49–53; Lawrence 1988: xxxiv–xxxv, xxxviii, xxxix, 3n., 65, 66, 128, 135, fig. 47; Minnis and Bader 1988; Palestine 1929: 52; 1948: 44; Prawer 1967; 1972: 300–7, figs.; Pringle 1989: 22–3, fig.; 1993: I, 120–2, fig. 40; and forthcoming (a); Rey 1883: 436–7; Smail 1956: 102, 104 n., 151, 207–8, 231, 235, fig. 5; 1973: 87, 100–2, fig. 12, pl. 9.

Unprovenanced **sculptural fragments** (some of them apparently from chapel).
Barasch 1971: 187–207, figs. 46–7; Jacoby (Z) 1982b: 123–4, 125, figs. 96–7; SSCLE 1987: 22 (no. 26).

*Churches*, I, no. 57.

# 47 BETHANY
1743.1309 [8]

*al-'Azariya; Cr. Bethania, S. Lazarus*

**Tower** (14.8 by 14.4 m, walls 4 m thick), with ground floor raised above rock-cut **cistern**; entered through door and stair in E wall. Built for protection of the nuns of Bethany by Queen Melisende in 1144 (William of Tyre, xv, 26).
Pringle 1983a: 170–2, fig. 7; 1989: 20; 1993: I, 123, 134, fig. 44, pls. LXXXII–LXXXIII; 1994b: 337, table; Saller 1957: 108–9, fig. 23, pl. 59b.

*Churches*, I, nos. 59–60.

# 48 BETHLEHEM
1697.1235 [8]

*Bait Lahm; Cr. Bethleem, Bethlehem*

**Tower** (18.4 by 16.4 m, walls about 4.3 m thick) at SE corner of defensive enceinte surrounding the complex of buildings associated with the church of the Nativity. Rebuilt in the twelfth century, probably on a sixth-century base, with ground-floor door and stair to upper storeys inside N wall. Possibly residence of Latin bishop.
Amico 1620a: 6, plan (no. 19); Bagatti 1952: 226–7, fig. 58, pl. 7; Hamilton 1947: 17, 84; Pringle 1993: I, 150–2, fig. 46, pl. XCVI; 1994b: 342, table.

*Churches*, I, nos. 61–3.

# 49 BIDDU
1641.1378 [8]

**Buildings**, including one (19.3 m long) on site of wely of Shaikh Abu Talal, similar in construction to those in al-Qubaiba (**no. 178**) and identified as a church by Bagatti.

Bagatti 1947: 186–7, 192, 215–16, 221–2, 224; Baldi 1973: 160; Finkelstein and Magen 1993: 220, 43* (no. 287); Hoade 1978: 577; Pringle 1993: I, 160.

## 50 BIR BURIN

1534.2028 [5]

Hebr. *Be'er Borin*

Masonry **well** of Roman period; associated pottery suggests use in Frankish and Mamluk periods.

Israel 1964: 1409; Ne'eman 1990: 60, 41* (no. 56); Palestine 1929; 1948: 53.

## 51 BIR IKLIL, Khirbat

1685.2651 [3]

*Kalil, Kh. Iklil;* Cr. *Clil, Clie;* Med. Ar. *Iklil;* Hebr. *H. Kalil*

**Olive-press.**

Information: R. Frankel.
Barag 1979: 205–6 (no. 42); Beyer 1945: 187; Frankel 1988: 263; Israel 1964: 1358; Palestine 1948: 6.

## 52 BIR KHUWAILIFA

1360.0887 [10]

Cr. *Reonde Cisterne, Rotunda Cisterna*

**Cistern** in use in Crusader period at which Richard I intercepted a Muslim caravan in June 1192 (*Itin. Ric.*, VI, 4; al-Harawī (trans. Sourdel-Thomine, 30)).

Abel 1967: II, 465; Conder and Kitchener 1881: III, 391; Guérin 1868: II, 357; Israel 1964: 1483; Johns 1937: 36; Kloner 1983b; Palestine 1948: 203.

## 53 BIR ZAIT, Khirbat

1682.1535 [8]

(fig. 17; pl. XXII)

**Courtyard building** (about 35 m E–W by 37 m N–S) with barrel-vaulted ranges on E, S and W sides of a courtyard containing a **cistern.**

PAM: Report by D.C. Baramki (15 July 1947).

Abel 1928: 50–1; Benvenisti 1970: 237, photo.; Conder and Kitchener 1881: II, 329; Ellenblum 1992: 180; Guérin 1868: III, 34; Kochavi 1972: 173–4 (no. 72), figs.; Palestine 1929: 83; 1948: 102; Pringle 1986a: 19–20, fig. 6; 1994a: 49–50; de Vaux 1946: 262.

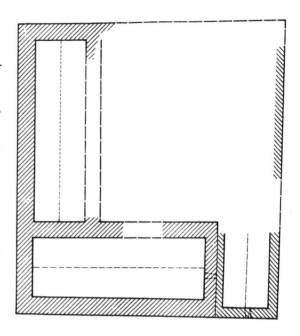

Phase A
Phase B

0  5  10  15 M

17  Kh. Bir Zait (**no. 53**): plan of courtyard building (drawn by P.E. Leach, BSAJ Survey 1982).

XXII  Kh. Bir Zait (**no. 53**): courtyard building, S range, looking E.

# 54 al-BIRA

1705.1459 [8]

Cr. *Birra, Castrum Maome/Mahomaria, Magna Mahomaria, Mahomeria major, Mahumeria*
(fig. 18; pl. XXIII)

**New town**, with remains of barrel-vaulted houses set end on to main street running NE–SW, with church at upper N end and **castle** or **courthouse** (*curia*) at lower end; the latter consisted of a **tower** (about 14 by about 16 m, walls 2.4–2.7 m thick), with basement of two parallel barrel-vaults, set at centre of walled enclosure (about 45 m E–W by about 60 m N–S), with *talus* on W, the space NE of tower being infilled later with groin-vaults. **Pools** (*birak*) to S fed from spring. Al-Bira was granted to the Holy Sepulchre by Godfrey of Bouillon (Bresc-Bautier, no. 26; *RRH*, no. 74); the Frankish settlement was established by the canons by the 1120s, the tower being referred to in 1124 (Fulcher of Chartres, III, 33; William of Tyre, XIII, 12) and the church in 1128 (Bresc-Bautier, no. 6; *RRH*, no. 124).

Abel 1924b: 383, fig. 4; 1926a; 1934: 371–2; 1967: II, 263; Bagatti 1979: 20–4, fig. 5, pl. 4.1–2; Benvenisti 1970: 223–4; Conder and Kitchener 1881: III, 8–9, 88–9; Deschamps 1934: 83 n.3; Ellenblum 1992: 180; Finkelstein and Magen 1993: 163, 32* (no. 178); Goujon 1670: 93–4; Guérin 1868: III, 7–13; Hanauer 1903: 79–80; Johns 1937: 30; Kennedy 1994: 33; Kootwyk 1619: 331–2; Le Strange 1890: 423; Palestine 1929: 24; 1948: 114; Prawer 1980: 126–35; Pringle 1985; 1993: I, 161; 1994a: 43–5; 1994b: 337, table; Robinson 1841: II, 130–33; III: 76; de Saulcy 1853: I, 108; Tobler 1853: II, 494–501.

*Churches*, I, no. 66.

XXIII   al-Bira (**no. 54**): Crusader *curia* (Khan al-Bira), groin-vaulting enclosing the corner of the tower, looking NW. (The blocking wall is that of a modern house.)

# 55 BURIN, Khirbat

1487.1909 [5]

Cr. *Burin, Buria, Casal neuf*; Med. Ar. *Būrīn*

**Foundations** of extensive rectilinear structures of indeterminate date, with surface pottery indicating occupation from Roman–Byzantine period to fourteenth century and later. Hugh of *Buria* mentioned in 1207 (*RRH*, nos.818–19); by 1253, village belonged to the archbishop of Caesarea (*RRH*, no.1210), and in 1265 to the Mamluks.
PAM: Reports by P.L.O. Guy (1926) and N. Makhouly (19 Nov. 1934).

Conder and Kitchener 1881: II, 178; Guérin 1874: II, 349–50; Israel 1964: 1411; Palestine 1929: 25; 1948: 57; Pringle 1986a: 28–9, 76–7 (no. 3).

# 56 BURIN, Khirbat

1535.2034 [5]

Hebr. *H. Borin*

Remains of large **structure** built of dressed *kurkar* blocks; Crusader-period surface pottery.
Israel 1964: 1409; Ne'eman 1990: 57–8, 40* (no. 52).

# 57 al-BURJ

1520.1455 [8]

*Qal'at Tantura, al-Habis*; Cr. *Gith, Git, Tarenta (?), Tharenta (?)*; Hebr. *H. Tittora*
(fig. 19)

Remains of **tower** (*al-Habis*) (about 16.45 m square, walls 5 m thick), with door on E defended by slit-machicolation and draw-bar leading into N end of basement; vaulted stair (1.03 m wide) to right of entrance passage led up inside wall to now-vanished first floor; surrounded by **enclosure** wall (about 52 m N–S by about 54 m E–W, 1.95 m thick), containing remains of other **vaulted structures**. Possibly identifiable as the **castle** of *T(h)arenta*, which fell to the Muslims in 1187 (*Gesta Henrici II* (*RS*, XLIX.ii, 24); Kedar 1982: 122).

PAM: Report by J. Ory (25 Jan. 1929).
PEF: C.N. Johns Papers, Field Notebook 1940–1 (14 Oct. 1940).

Bagatti 1979: 108; Benvenisti 1970: 314, 338; Clermont-Ganneau 1896: II, 98; Conder and Kitchener 1881: III, 15, 110; Guérin 1868: I, 337; Hoade 1978: 538; Kedar 1982: 117–18; Khalidi 1992: 371–2; Palestine 1933: 18; 1948: 107; Pringle 1991a: 88 (no. 3); 1994b; Robinson 1841: III, 57; Vincent and Abel 1932: 368.

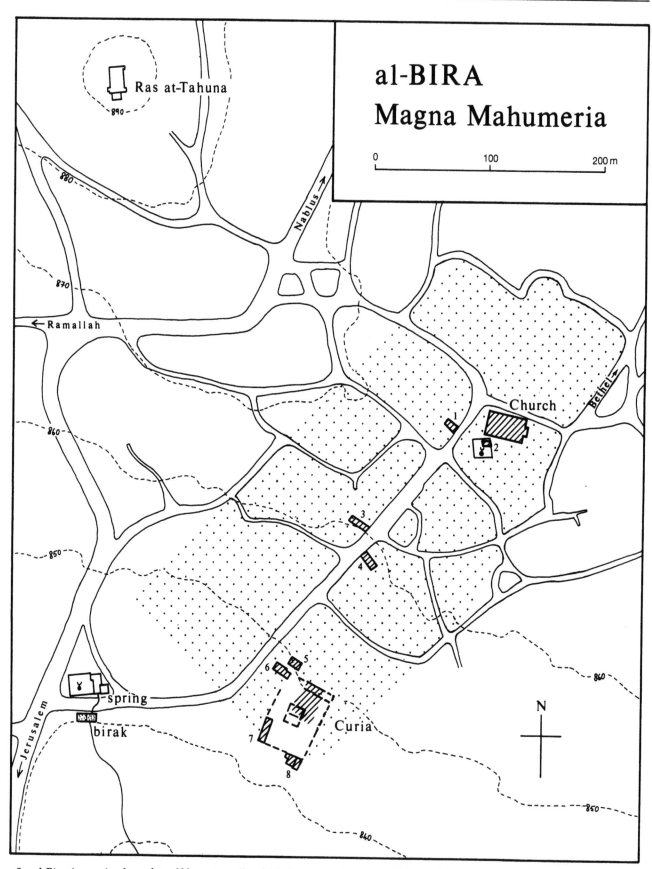

18 al-Bira (**no. 54**): plan of twelfth-century Frankish 'new town' as revealed in the street plan of the 1930s, showing location of recorded houses (1–8). Stippling indicates suggested area of the settlement.

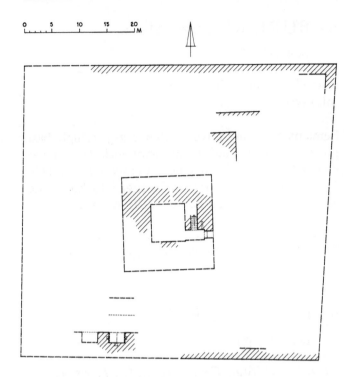

19   al-Burj, Qal'at Tantura (**no. 57**): plan of keep-and-bailey castle (drawn by M. Pease, BSAJ Survey 1989, with additions from notes by C.N. Johns, 1940).

# 58 BURJ, Khirbat al-

1738.1614 [8]

(pl. xxiv)

Large **tower**, with barrel-vaulted ground floor (6.5 m high), entered through door with draw-bar at S end of E

xxiv   Kh. al-Burj (**no. 58**): tower, photographed from the E in 1937.

wall, which also gives access to stair up to right. Tower stands at centre of rectangular **walled enclosure**, with ashlar surviving on N and S and traces of outwork at SE corner; remains of building SW of tower, parallel to S wall.

PAM: Report (9 May 1937).

Conder and Kitchener 1881: II, 307; Guérin 1874: II, 32; Guide Bleu 1932: 545; Kochavi 1972: 169 (no. 41); Palestine 1929: 26; 1948: 97; Pringle 1994a: 46; 1994b.

# 59 BURJ, Khirbat al-

1412.0944 [10]

*Qal'at al-Burj, Burj al-Bayyara, Castle of Figs*; Cr. *Castrum Ficuum, Fiyr, Le Fier*
**Castle**, comprising a **tower** (25 by 20 m) with battered base, standing at centre of a rectangular **enclosure** with truncated E corner (about 52 by 45 m, > 4 m high on NW), surrounded by rock-cut ditch (15 m wide on SE). Raided by Richard I in May 1192 (*Itin. Ric.*, V, 41).

PAM: Reports by R.W. Hamilton (1941) and C.N. Johns (17 April 1941).
Beyer and Alt 1953; Conder and Kitchener 1881: III, 274; Ellenblum 1992: 180; Guérin 1868: II, 258–9; Israel 1964: 1487; Kedar 1982: 118–19 (1993: ch. X, addendum); Kloner 1983b; Kochavi 1972: 72 (no. 203), photo; Palestine 1929: 85; 1948: 206; Prawer 1975: II, 93 n.30; Pringle 1986a: 15, 18; 1994b.

# 60 BURJ, Khirbat al-

1529.1226 [8]

*Burj Sansan*

**Vaulted building**, described as a **tower** (19.5 by 9.75 m, walls 1.8 m thick), constructed with drafted masonry; the dimensions, however, suggest rather a **hall-house** or some other type of structure.

Conder and Kitchener 1881: III, 91; Israel 1964: 1467; Palestine 1929: 26; 1948: 165.

# 61 BURJ, Khirbat al-

1678.1368 [8]

*Burj al-Jauz, Kh. al-Kurum*; Hebr. *Ramot*
(fig. 20; pl. xxv)

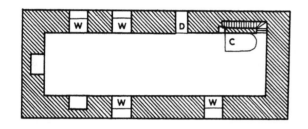

20  Kh. al-Burj, al-Burj al-Jauz (**no. 61**): plan of hall-house (after Conder and Kitchener 1881: III, 110). Key: (c) cistern; (D) door; (W) window.

xxv  Kh. al-Burj, Burj al-Jauz (**no. 61**): main street of Frankish settlement, flanked by houses, looking NW, with site of hall-house on hillock to far left.

**Vault** (10.6 by 27.2 m, walls 2.3 m thick), apparently a **hall-house**, aligned N–S, with door near centre of E wall and stair to vanished upper floor within wall at SE corner; basement lit by four pointed-arched windows; **cistern** below. Downhill to SE, **Frankish village settlement** (excavated 1992–4), consisting of barrel-vaulted houses set end-on to the Jerusalem road and containing **wine-presses** on ground floor; some have rock-cut **cisterns** beneath, and some have **hearths** and chimney flues in wall.

Information: A. Boas and R. Ellenblum.
Bagatti 1947: 208, 229, fig. 46 (C22); Benvenisti 1970: 363; Conder and Kitchener 1881: III, 110, fig.; Palestine 1929: 85; 1948: 153; Tobler 1853: II, 535–8.

# 62 BURJ, Khirbat al-

1696.1483 [8]

near *Kh. Salamiya*; Cr. *Salome*
(pl. XXVI)

Remains of square **tower**, standing 2–3 m high, best preserved on N and E; masonry includes drafted blocks. Probably related to nearby *casale* of *Salome* (Kh. Salamiya), which in 1158/9 belonged to Robert de Retesta (Bresc-Bautier, no. 122; *RRH*, no. 272).

Benvenisti 1970: 338; Finkelstein and Magen 1993: 74–5, 20* (no. 71); Kochavi 1972: 177 (no. 88); Palestine 1929: 85; 1948: 110; Pringle 1994a: 46; 1994b. Cf. Abel 1967: II, 293–4.

# 63 BURJ AL-AHMAR

1455.1917 [5]

*Kh. al-Burj al-'Atut, The Red Tower*; Cr. *Turris Latinae, Turriclee, Tourre-Rouge, Turris Rubea*; Hebr. *H. Burgata*
(fig. 21; pl. XXVII)

Standing S wall and foundations of **tower** (19.7 m N–S by 15.5 m E–W, walls 2.2 m thick and about 14 m high), with ground floor consisting of two parallel barrel-vaults and first floor probably of six bays of groin-vaults, standing at centre of a defensive **enclosure** (about 60 m square, walls 1.7–1.8 m thick) containing levelled remains of other structures. Tower and dependent lands granted to abbey of St Mary Latina by 1158 (*RRH*, no. 331), leased to Hospital c.1187/91 (*RRH Ad*, no. 682a), occupied by Templars by 1236 (*RRH*, no. 1072; *RRH Ad*, no. 1072a) and returned to Hospital by

xxvi  Kh. al-Burj (**no. 62**): remains of tower.

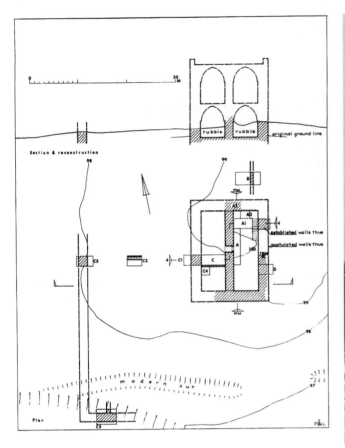

21   Burj al-Ahmar (**no. 63**): plan of castle as revealed by BSAJ excavation in 1983 (drawn by P.E. Leach).

xxvii   Burj al-Ahmar (**no. 63**): S wall of tower, showing remains of vaulting.

agreement in 1248 (*RRH*, nos. 1165, 1356). Excavations (1983) support a likely date of construction of 1110/50 and of destruction by the Mamluks in 1265.

PAM: Reports by K.A.C. Creswell (*c*.1919), J. Ory (20 June 1945), and others (25 Aug. 1922).
PEF: Burj al-Ahmar excavation archive (1993).

Abel 1940a: 41 (no. 13); Bagatti 1979: 135; Benvenisti 1970: 19, 221, 276, 338–9, photo.; Beyer 1936: 43–4; Conder and Kitchener 1881: II, 178; Dar and Mintzker 1987: 213, fig. 11, pls. 52b, 53; Deschamps 1939a: 23; Guérin 1874: II, 349; Israel 1964: 1411; Kennedy 1994: 8, 33–4, 36, 72, 77, pl. 7, fig. 2; Langé 1965: 94, 184, fig. 43; Palestine 1929: 26; 1948: 57; Pringle 1983c; 1983d; 1984b; 1984c; 1984d; 1984e; 1984f; 1986a; 1989: 14–17, figs.; 1994b; Rey 1883: 424; Tibble 1989: 113, 117, 119, 129, 131, 139–42, 151.

# 64 BURJ AL-FAR'A, Khirbat

## 1830.1882 [6]

(pl. xxviii)

**Castle**, consisting of roughly rectangular **enclosure**, possibly with towers at corners, cut off from ridge to W

by rock-cut ditch forming cistern, and enclosing a rectangular two-storey **tower** (11.0 by about 10.5 m, walls 2.5 m thick), built of large rough blocks levelled up with small chips; door (2.1 m high) in tower's SW wall, lintelled with flat relieving arch cut away segmentally on underside, leads through lintelled passage to basement, enclosed by rough-built barrel-vault running NE–SW with lintelled arrow-slits high in end walls and steps to upper floor in W corner.

PAM: Reports by S.A.S. Husseini (28 June 1935), C.N. Johns (March 1935).

Conder and Kitchener 1881: II, 234–5; Guérin 1874: I, 259; Kochavi 1972: 221 (no. 115); Palestine 1929: 26; 1948: 76; Pringle 1989: 17; 1994b.

# 65 BURJ AL-LISANA

## 1748.1562 [8]

*Kh. al-Burj*

XXVIII   Kh. Burj al-Farʻa (**no. 64**): from NW.

Remains of **tower** (about 12.75 m E–W by 9.7 m N–S, walls 1.8–2.0 m thick), standing 2–4 m high, with lintelled door (0.97 m wide, 1.56 m high) on E, made from large reused drafted blocks, leading into collapsed barrel-vaulted ground floor. **Cisterns**. Traces of outer, apparently later, **enclosure**.

Abel 1967: II, 364; Conder and Kitchener 1881: II, 307–9; Drake 1872:

88; Guide Bleu 1932: 545; Kochavi 1972: 171 (no. 57); Palestine 1929: 27; 1948: 103; Pringle 1994a: 46; 1994b.

# 66 BURJ AL-MALIH

## 1932.1927 [6]

*Kh. al-Burj*
(fig. 22)

Oval defensive **enclosure** (98 m E–W by 52 m N–S, wall 2.44–3.0 m thick), on hill with precipitous descents on S and SW; pointed-arched gate on N, opening into courtyard containing **cistern**, with **vaults** ranged around the inner face of the walls. Masonry includes drafted and diagonally dressed ashlar.

PAM: Reports by N. Makhouly (1927), S.A.S. Husseini (28 June 1935).

Abel 1937: 31–2; Benvenisti 1970: 328, photo; Conder and Kitchener 1881: III, 235–6, fig.; Drake 1872: 88; Guérin 1874: I, 278–9; Kochavi 1972: 217 (no. 83), figs.; Palestine 1929: 27; 1948: 75; Rey 1883: 427, 440.

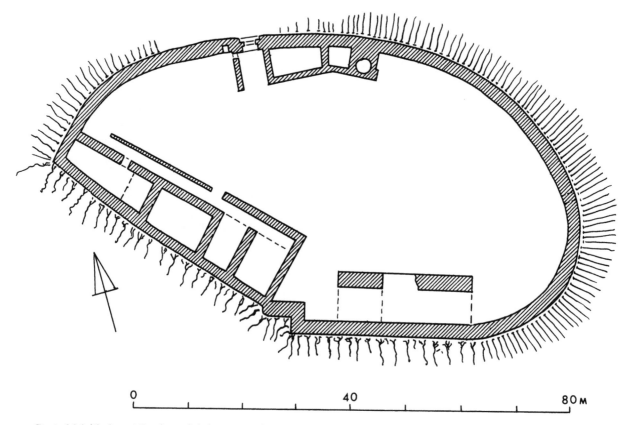

0          40          80 M

22   Burj al-Malih (**no. 66**): plan of defensive enclosure (after plan drawn by C.R. Conder, 2 April 1874 (PEF); cf. Conder and Kitchener 1881: III, 235).

# 67 BURJ AL-MALIH

## 1410.2161 [5]

*Tall al-Malat;* Med. Ar. *al-Malaha, al-Mallūha;* Cr. *Turris Salinarum;* Hebr. *Tel Tanninim.*

Remains of small **tower** on shore, with facing robbed. Given to Hospitallers together with the mound on which it stood by Hugh, lord of Caesarea (*c.*1154–68), and confirmed as theirs in 1182 (*RRH*, no. 619); destroyed by Baybars in 1265 (Ibn al-Furāt *c.*1375: II, 72; al-Maqrīzī *c.*1400b: I.ii, 8).

Benvenisti 1970: 276; Beyer 1936: 29, 62; Conder and Kitchener 1881: II, 33 (*El Helat*); Deschamps 1939: 23; Israel 1964: 1403; Palestine 1948: 46; Prawer 1975: II, 465 n.34; Pringle 1986a: 24–5; 1994b; Riley-Smith 1971: 206; Röhricht 1898: 926 n.2.

# 68 BURJ AL-QIBLI

## 1723.2952 [3]

Remains of a square **tower** of drafted masonry.
Conder and Kitchener 1881: I, 57–8; Pringle 1994b.

# 69 BURJ ASH-SHAMAL

## 1726.2962 [3]

Cr. *le Tor de l'Opital* (?)

**Tower** built of reused drafted masonry and with slightly pointed vaults and arrow-slit.
Conder and Kitchener 1881: I, 48, 58; Guide Bleu 1932: 428; 1975: 238; Prawer and Benvenisti 1970; Pringle 1994b; Smail 1956: 229.

# 70 BURJ AS-SAHL

## 1619.2479 [3]

Hebr. *H. Burgat Mishor*
(fig. 23)

**Courtyard building** (about 50 m square, outer walls about 2.5 m thick), with (?)barrel-vaulted ranges (6.5 m wide internally) on N, W and S sides of courtyard and entrance assumed on E. Rectangular masonry-lined **well** ('Ain at-Tina) to W (3 by 4 m, 17 m deep).
PEF: C.N. Johns Papers, Field Notebook 1946–47 (22 Aug. 1946). PAM: photos 036.427–8.

Israel 1964: 1377; Palestine 1929; 1948: 24.

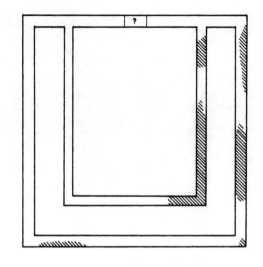

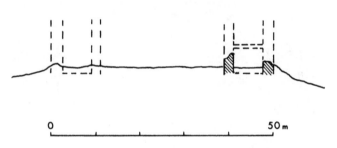

23   Burj as-Sahl (**no. 70**): plan of courtyard building (after C.N. Johns, August 1946).

# 71 BURJ AS-SUR, Khirbat

## 1594.1104 [8]

*Bait Sur;* Cr. *Bethsura, Beithsur*
(pl. XXIX)

**Tower** (15.0 m E–W by 11.9 m N–S, walls 3 m thick at basement level and 2 m above), with W wall standing to 9.5 m and containing rounded-arched opening at first-floor level; internal stair also noted by Conder and Kitchener. *Beithsur* was granted to the Hospital in 1136 by Hugh II, lord of Hebron (*RRH*, no. 164).

Abel 1924b: 210–12, fig. 5; 1967: II, 283; Benvenisti 1970: 221, 276, 325–6, photo; Conder and Kitchener 1881: III, 311–12, 324–5, 374, fig.; Deschamps 1939a: 21; Ellenblum 1992: 180; Guide Bleu 1932: 614; Hoade 1946: 339; 1978: 440; Johns 1937: 25; Kochavi 1972: 54 (no. 97); Meistermann 1936: 348–9, fig.; Palestine 1929: 8; 1948: 179; Pringle 1983a: 171, fig. 7; 1993: I, 23; 1994b.

xxx   Burj Baitin (**no. 73**): tower from W, showing door covered by a lintel.

xxix   Kh. Burj as-Sur (**no. 71**): inside of NW corner of tower, showing possible remains of stair.

# 73 BURJ BAITIN

### 1733.1477 [8]

Cr. *Bethel*
(pl. xxx)

**Tower** (11 m E–W by 9.15 m N–S), at centre of rectangular **enclosure** (36.6 m E–W by 32 m N–S), built on site of Byzantine church and incorporating material from it. Village granted by Balian I of Ibelin to the Premonstratensian canons of St Joseph and St Habakkuk, probably sometime after 1138, and given by them in exchange to the Holy Sepulchre in 1159–60, along with the tower, church and other buildings (Bresc-Bautier, 139–42, nos. 52–3; *RRH*, nos. 368, 360); tower may therefore date any time in the twelfth century before 1159–60.

PAM: Report.

Bagatti 1979: 26–7; Benvenisti 1970: 318–19, fig.; Clermont-Ganneau 1896: II, 283–4; Conder and Kitchener 1881: II, 307; Finkelstein and Magen 1993: 82, 22* (no. 86); Hoade 1978: 543; Kochavi 1972: 178 (no. 91); Palestine 1929; 1948: 113; Pringle 1989: 17; 1993: I: 104, pls. LXVII–LXVIII; 1994a: 48; 1994b; Schneider 1934; Sternberg 1915: 18–19, fig. 3.

*Churches*, I, no. 36.

# 72 BURJ BAIT NASIF

### 1511.1109 [8]

*Kh. al-Burj, Kh. Bait Nasib*; Cr. *Bethenase*; Hebr. *H. Neziv*

**Vaulted building** and **cisterns**. At Kh. Bait Nasib ash-Sharqiya, 500 m to S (Grid ref. 1510.1104), remains of **tower** of uncertain date (about 10 m square), with entrance on W and basement ceiling supported on transverse arch, standing on E side of a rectangular enclosure (about 18/20 m N–S by about 28/30 m E–W) with possible gate on W.

Information: J. France.

Conder and Kitchener 1881: III, 314, 324, 351; Guérin 1868: III, 343–5; Kochavi 1972: 53 (no. 95); Palestine 1929: 75; 1948: 179; Pringle 1994b.

# 74 BURJ BARDAWIL

### 1730.1548 [8]

(fig. 24; pl. xxxi)

## BURJ BARDAWIL

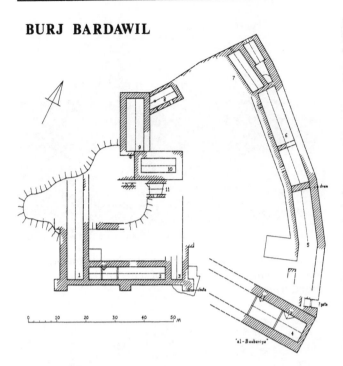

24   Burj Bardawil (**no. 74**): plan (BSAJ/Bir Zeit University Survey 1989).

xxxi   Burj Bardawil (**no. 74**): vault 4, known as *al-Baubariya*, from NE.

**Castle** or semi-fortified **courtyard building** (22 m square), with solid rectangular turrets about 4 m wide projecting 1.95 m from the corners and from mid-way on the sides, and with at least three barrel-vaulted ranges set around a central courtyard; subsequently extended in a fan shape downhill to NE, with a series of barrel-vaults (one known as *al-Baubariya*) defining its perimeter and possibly with gateway on SE.
PAM: Reports by K.A.C. Creswell (*c*.1919), S.A.S. Husseini (6 Feb. 1936).

Benvenisti 1970: 237–8; Conder and Kitchener 1881: II, 306–7, fig.; Deschamps 1939a: 22; Drake 1872: 87–8; Ellenblum 1992: 177, 180; Guérin 1874: II, 36–7; Guide Bleu 1932: 545; Hoade 1978: 546; Johns 1937: 23; Kochavi 1972: 173 (no. 69); Palestine 1929: 26; 1948: 104; Pringle 1989: 20; 1991a: 88–9 (no. 4); 1994a; Smail 1973: 86.

## 75 BURJ MISR

1770.2722 [3]

Hebr. *H. Mezad Abbirim*

**Tower** (about 12 m square, walls about 2.5 m thick), built of massive blocks ( < 3.2 by 1.0 by 1.0 m), with lintelled door opening into vestibule with another door to one side (leading to stair ?). Possibly pre-twelfth century.
PAM: Report by J. Ory (2 June 1921).
Benvenisti 1970: 276; Conder and Kitchener 1881: I, 167; Guérin 1880: II, 69; Palestine 1929: 27; 1948: 4; Pringle 1994b.

## 76 CAESAREA

1401.2120 [5]

*Qaisariya*; Cr. *Caesarea, Cesaire*; Hebr. *H. Qesari* (fig. 25; pls. XXXII–XXXVI)

City occupied by the Crusaders 1101–87 and 1191–1265. **Town walls** (about 450 m N–S by about 240 m E–W), following line of Abbasid/Fatimid defences, achieved final form from Louis IX in May 1252, enclosing three landward sides with sea wall and artificial **harbour** on W; they comprise a wall (height unknown), having in places casemated arrow-slits with sloping sills, fronted by *talus* rising 8 m from bottom of dry ditch (7–8 m wide, 4–6 m deep), with vertical counterscarp wall; fourteen projecting rectangular towers remain, of which one in each side contains a bent entrance, the outer gate in each case consisting of slit-machicolation/portcullis/wing-doors, the inner of wing-doors with or without machicolation. **Castle** ruins on S harbour mole, with **tower-keep** behind wall with rectangular towers, fronted by sea-level rock-cut ditch. **Courtyard houses** excavated SW of E gate (1960–2), one having first floor carried on arches over a street (pl. XXXVI).

Bagatti 1979: 186–94, pls. 61–4; Benvenisti 1970: 135–46; Conder and Kitchener 1881: II, 13–29, figs.; Deschamps 1934: *passim*; 1939: *passim*; Frova, Avi-Yonah and Negev 1975: 282–5, figs.; Guérin 1874: II, 321–39; Hazard 1975; Heyck 1900: figs. 54–5; Holum and Raban 1993: 270–72; Holum *et al.* 1988: 217–35; Israel 1955; Johns 1937: 27; Kedar and Kaufman 1975; Langé 1965: 20–3, 28, 32, 35, 71–85, 108–9,

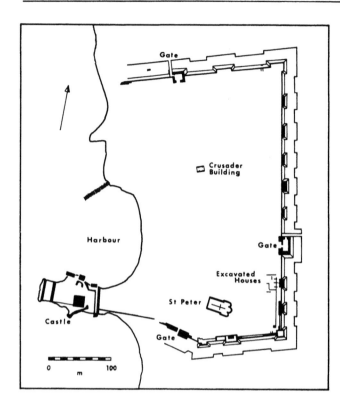

25   Caesarea (**no. 76**): plan of city (after Benvenisti 1970).

xxxiii   Caesarea (**no. 76**): town walls, N gate-tower, showing bent entrance, spring of inner bridge arch and added *talus*.

xxxii   Caesarea (**no. 76**): town walls, N gate-tower, from E.

159, figs. 2, 6, 33–41, 76, 100–2, pl. A; Le Strange 1890: 28–9, 41, 380, 474–5; Mariti 1769: II, 301–16; Marshall 1992: 105–8, fig. 6, pls. 6–7; Müller-Wiener 1966: 74, pls. 101–3; Negev 1960a; 1960b; 1961a; 1961b; 1962; 1963; Negev, Frova and Avi-Yonah 1993: 277–8; Pearlman and Negev 1963; Pearlman and Yannai 1964: 130–45; Porath, Neeman and Badihi 1990; Pringle 1985b; 1993: I, 166, fig. 49; 1995a: 89–91, fig. 8, pls. 5–10; Raban and Holum 1991: 112; Rey 1871: 221–7, figs. 55–6, pl. xxii; 1883: 103, 153, 417, 420; Riley-Smith 1990: 38–9; Ringel 1975: 167–73; Sharon 1978; Weippert 1964: 156–8.

xxxiva-b   Caesarea (**no. 76**): town walls, N gate-tower, capitals supporting rib-vaulting.

xxxv  Caesarea (**no. 76**): town walls, E gate, rib-vaulted interior (restored), looking from outer to inner gate.

xxxvi  Caesarea (**no. 76**): courtyard house, with stairs to upper floor which extended on transverse arches across the street.

**House** in N part of town, with barrel-vaulted basement end-on to street, external stair to first floor on S, and latrine chute in N wall.

Conder and Kitchener 1881: II, 28; Pringle 1993: I, 182–3, fig. 53, pls. CXXIII–CXXV.

To S of cathedral, excavations have revealed two phases of **cemetery** use in the Crusader period, consisting in both cases of inhumations in stone-lined cists, often with evidence for wooden coffins. To W of cathedral platform, the inner part of the inner harbour basin, infilled by the mid eighth century, was overlain by **houses** with courtyards and cisterns, some of which remained in use in the twelfth century while others were filled with rubbish; area nearest to cathedral also used as cemetery in the twelfth and thirteenth centuries.

Raban, Holum and Blakely 1993: 11–51, figs. 13–101; Raban and Stieglitz 1988; Raban *et al.* 1990: 248–9; Wolff 1994: 506–9, figs. 31–3; Yule and Rowsome 1994.

Immediately NE of cathedral, octagonal Byzantine church destroyed by the tenth century and site occupied by **buildings with domestic and commercial-industrial functions**, which continued in use in the twelfth century. Massive foundations indicate large structure, possibly associated with the cathedral, built in the thirteenth century.

Raban, Holum and Blakely 1993: 53–60, fig. 13, 105–27.

**Cemetery** excavated to S of walled city, containing seventy-five burials of the thirteenth century onwards.

Bull 1987: ch. v, p. 8; ch. xv, pp. 47–8; Bull, Krentz, Storvick and Spiro 1990: 80–1, fig. 13; Bull and Tombs 1972; Holland 1973; *Jerusalem Post* (18 July 1972); Raban, Holum and Blakely 1993: 69–70, figs. 139–40; Holum and Raban 1993: 286; Tombs 1985: 18.

**Harbour**, constructed by Herod the Great, greatly reduced in size by the twelfth century, when only the inner basin was in use, enclosed by a **mole** of through-columns on N, and by the **castle mole** on S.

Abel 1914; Fritsch and Bendor 1961; Hohlfelder and Oleson 1980; 1981; Hohlfelder, Oleson, Raban and Vann 1982; 1983; Levine 1975: 13–18; fig. 2; Linder 1971; Linder and Leenhardt 1964; Link 1956: 1–4; MacLeish 1961; Raban 1984; 1986; 1989; 1993b: 290; Raban, Hohfelder, Oleson and Vann 1983; Raban and Linder 1978; Raban and Stieglitz 1988; Raban, Stieglitz and Engert 1989; Raban *et al.* 1990; Stieglitz and Raban 1987.

Repair of Roman **aqueduct**. Water brought into city by bridge over N town ditch.

Reifenberg 1951.

**Sculpture** (unprovenanced).

Jacoby (Z) 1982b: 125–6, figs. 114–15.

*Churches*, I, nos. 68–76.

# 77 CAPERNAUM

2042.2540 [4]

*Talhum*; Hebr. *Kefar Nahum*; Cr. *Capharnaum*

Extensive excavations since 1905 now begin to suggest that the native **village** was not abandoned in the tenth or eleventh century, as was once supposed, but was occupied more or less continuously from the first century BC to the thirteenth century AD, with different areas settled at different times. The twelfth- to thirteenth-century settlement that is described by Burchard of Mount Sion (1283) as 'scarcely seven houses of poor fishermen' (*IHC*, IV, 144) is evidenced archaeologically by coin and pottery finds and **reuse of earlier houses**.

Corbo 1975: 221; Kopp 1949; Loffreda 1972; 1982; 1983; Loffreda and Tzaferis 1993; Orfali 1922; Rahmani 1980b; Spijkerman 1975: 47–8, pl. 3.20; Tzaferis 1982; 1983; 1989.

# 78 DABBURIYA

1852.2331 [6]

Cr. *Buria, Burie, Bures*; Hebr. *Dabereth*

Medieval **tower**, rebuilt by al-Mu'azzam 'Isā (1213) and incorporated into present mosque, may possibly be the successor to that in the **faubourg** undermined by the Muslims in 1182 (William of Tyre, XXII, 15 (14)).

Battista and Bagatti 1976: 167–70; Deschamps 1939a: 59, 122; Guérin 1880: I, 141; Israel 1964: 1394; Palestine 1948: 40; Petrozzi 1976: 276, fig. 65; Pringle 1993: I, 192; 1994b: 337, table; 1995a: 72.

*Churches*, I, no. 81.

# 79 DAIR ABU MASH'AL

1561.1562 [8]

Cr. *Bellifortis* [gen.]

Remains of **wall** built of ashlars with rusticated face and drafted margins, enclosing a rocky platform about 45 m square at highest part of village; rock-cut **cisterns** beneath. Presumed to be part of a twelfth-century **castle**, possibly Hospitaller (cf. *RRH*, no. 433).

Conder and Kitchener 1881: II, 290, 310; Deschamps 1939a: 22–3; Guérin 1874: II, 118–19; Palestine 1929; 1948: 100; Riley-Smith 1967: map 2.

# 80 DAIR AL-BALAH

0883.0917 [10]

Cr. *Darum, Darom*; Med. Ar. *al-Dārūm*

Site of **castle** of four-tower type, with one tower larger than the others, built under Amalric (1162–73) and besieged by Saladin in 1170 (William of Tyre, XX, 19); lost to Saladin in August 1187 and retaken by Richard I in May 1191, by which time there was a *talus* and outer ditch and the number of towers had increased to seventeen, suggesting the addition of an outer wall (*Itin. Ric.*, V, 39; Ambroise, lines 9223–9); dismantled 1192.

Abel 1940b: 67–70; Benvenisti 1970: 281–2; Deschamps 1934; 15, 19, 24, 44, 54 n.1, 55 n.4, 86–8; 1939a: 14–15, 21, 236–7; 1943: 93–4; Eydoux 1982: 252; Johns 1937: 28; Kennedy 1994: 31, 103; Langé 1982: 92, 182, fig. 43; Lawrence 1988: xxxv–xxxvi, xxxviii, 68, 130; Le Strange 1890: 437; Marmardji 1951: 71–2; Prawer 1980: 107–9; Pringle 1993: I, 194–5.

*Churches*, I, no. 82.

# 81 DAIR 'ALLA, Tall

2087.1782 [6]

**Sugar-mill** in village, dating from Ayyubid/Mamluk period and in use until 1967. Tell used as Muslim cemetery in same period.

Khouri 1988b: 54, 69; Van der Kooij 1993: 342; Van der Kooij and Ibrahim 1990: 90, 110.

# 82 DAIR 'AMIS

1816.2896 [4]

Cr. *Dairrhamos, Derreme*

Large basin of great stones and portion of **wall**, apparently of Crusading date. Village identified as belonging to Venice in 1243 (*RRH*, no. 1114).

Conder and Kitchener 1881: I, 114. Cf. Berggötz 1991: 241; Dussaud 1927: 26–7; Guérin 1880: II, 387; Renan 1864: 640.

# 83 DAIR AS-SIDA, Khirbat

1663.1511 [8]

*Dair Sa'ida*

**Building** of well-dressed stones.

Ellenblum 1992: 177; Palestine 1948: 103.

## 84 DAIR YASIN

167.133 [8]

Groin-vaulted **courtyard building** in centre of village (demolished in 1948); possibly Frankish, though Husseini (1938) suggests Mamluk.

PAM: Report by S.A.S. Husseini (14 June 1938).
Abel 1924c: 620; Bagatti 1983: 15; Conder and Kitchener 1881: III, 21; Khalidi 1992: 289–92; Palestine 1948: 155; Tobler 1853: II, 529–30.

## 85 DA'UK, Tall

1616.2530 [3]

*Kh. Da'uk, Khan Da'uk;* Cr. *Doc, Doke, Dochum;* Med. Ar. *Da'ūq, Burj Dahūq*

Khan Da'uk (70 m N–S by 40 m E–W), on tell, contains Frankish **barrel-vault** (35 by 6 m) on N. **Tower** and **mill** of the Templars, referred to in the thirteenth century, do not apparently survive.

Barag 1979: 205 (no. 27); Benvenisti 1970: 249–52; Beyer 1945: 208; Frankel 1980: 200–1; 1988: 261; Israel 1964: 1372; Palestine 1948: 21; Prawer 1975: II, 152 n.47; 454 n.11; Pringle 1986b: 69; 1994b; Prutz 1881: 175; Rey 1883; 481; Riley-Smith 1967: 446, 450; Rothschild 1938: 50; 1949: 63–4, pl. VIII, fig. 2.

## 86 adh-DHAHIRIYA

147.090 [10]

**Tower** (*al-Hisn*), with barrel-vault, rusticated masonry and slit-window(s). However, according to local tradition, which appears to be supported by archaeology, the village was founded by al-Malik al-Ẓāhir Baybars (*c*.1220–77), from whom it takes its name (Abel 1967: II, 421–2).

Ellenblum 1992: 180; Palestine 1929; 1948: 207; Pringle 1994b.

## 87 DHIBAN

2238.1087 [9]

*Dibon;* Med. Ar. *Dhibān, Dhibyān*

Excavated buildings of indigenous **village**, with occupation from Umayyad to Ottoman periods, including fortified building of Umayyad period, reoccupied in Ayyubid–Mamluk times.

Abel 1967: II, 304–5; Franciscan Fathers 1977: 121–3; Harding 1967: 108–9; Le Strange 1890: 438; Pringle 1981b: 51; Sauer 1975; Tushingham 1972; 1993: 351; Winnett and Reed 1964.

## 88 DIN'ALA, Khirbat

1734.2746 [3]

*Kh. Nu'aila;* Cr. *Danehyle, Danehile;* Hebr. *H. Din'ala*

**Village** of Roman period, reoccupied in the twelfth/thirteenth century, when buildings and floors repaired and at least one **oil-press** built or repaired. In 1220, in lordship of *Chastiau de Roi* (*RRH*, no. 934).

Frankel 1985: 112, fig. 4; 1986b; 1988: 263, 269, fig. 1; Israel 1964: 1354; Palestine 1948: 3.

## 89 DURUR, Khirbat Tall ad-

1476.2038 [5]

Hebr. *Tel Zeror*

Double tell with thirteenth- to fourteenth-century village occupation represented by **house walls**, paved courtyard, clay **ovens** (*tawabayn*) and pits on S rise, and contemporary **cemetery** on N one.

Israel 1964: 1408; Kochavi 1993: 1081; Ohata 1966: 2, 23–4, 31–3, pls. I, X; 1967: 6, pls. III, XI–XIII; 1970: 36, 45, pl. I; Palestine 1948: 52; Tombs 1985: 17.

## 90 DUSTRAY, Khirbat

1452.2348 [5]

Cr. *Casel Destreiz, le Destroit, Districtum, Petra Incisa;* Hebr. *H. Qarta*
(figs. 8, 26)

Foundations of **tower** (about 15.5 m E–W by about 11 m N–S, walls 2.4 m thick) on battered rock-cut base containing **cistern**; door with pivot sockets on S, apparently reached by external timber stair; stair to first floor inside N wall. Rock-cut yard (overall about 21 m square) encloses tower on S and E, with **stables** containing rock-cut mangers on E. Other rock-cut features, including **yards**, **reservoirs**, **mangers**, **cisterns**, lie beyond. Built by the Templars as a **road station** in twelfth century; destroyed 1220.

Benvenisti 1970: 176–8, 313; Conder and Kitchener 1881: I, 288, 309–10, fig.; Deschamps 1934; 78; 1939a: 23–5, 29, 32; Guérin 1874: II, 283–5; Israel 1964: 137–9; Johns 1932: 111–13; 1937: 28; 1947: 15–16, 17, 94–8, figs. 6, 38; 1975: 130–2, 137; 1993: 116, fig.; Kennedy 1994: 55, 56–7, 124–5, pl. 44; von Mülinen 1908a: 167–70, fig. 70; Palestine 1929: 91; 1948: 26; Peled and Friedman 1987; Prawer 1975: II, 80, 164; Pringle 1986a: 14, 15, 18; 1994b: 336–7, table; 1994c: 166; Rey 1883: 421; Ronen and Olami 1978; 51–2; 13* (no. 87), figs.; Yeivin 1967: 94–5.

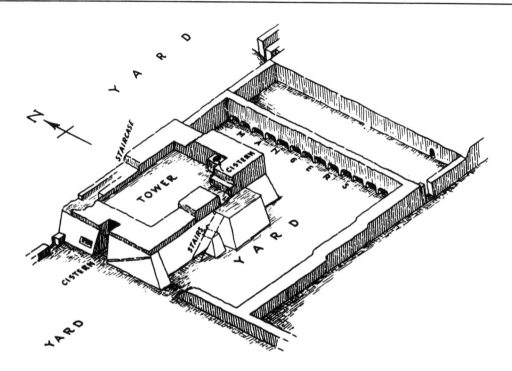

26   Kh. Dustray (**no. 90**): remains of castle and road station (drawn by J. Dikijian, in Johns 1947: fig. 38).

## 91 FAHMA

1666.1988 [5]

*Cr. Fame*

Half-destroyed **vaulted building** (*al-Babriya*), N of church (internally 7.5 m N–S by 22.35 m E–W, walls 2.4 m thick on N, 2.6 m on S, 0.85 m on E, 1.4 m on W), with splayed lintelled opening on S; possibly basement of **hall-house**. Village held by the abbey of St Mary of Mount Sion in 1179 (*RRH*, no. 576).
PAM: Reports by S.A.S. Husseini (14 July 1941) and N. Makhouly (11 June 1946).

Benvenisti 1970: 259; 1982: 137, figs. 4–5; Ellenblum 1992: 180; Palestine 1948: 58; Pringle 1993: I, 205.

*Churches*, I, no. 89.

## 92 al-FAIFA AL-GHARBIYA

194.038 [10]

*Qasr al-Faifa*

**Sugar-mill**; surface pottery mostly of Mamluk period, but including eleventh- to fifteenth-century types.
Khouri 1988b: 111; King *et al.* 1987: 449–50, 457, 459; MacDonald 1992: 258 (site 91), pl. 30; MacDonald *et al.* 1987: 410, fig. 6 (site 91); 1988: 40; Whitcomb 1992: 115, photo 23.

## 93 FANDI AL-JANUBI, Tall

2049.2127 [6]

**Sugar installations**, mostly Mamluk.
Khouri 1988b: 21; Lenzen, Kareem and Thorpe 1987: 315 (no. 2).

## 94 FARIS, Khirbat

219.081 [10]

*Kh. Tadun*

**Village house** and other structures of the twelfth and thirteenth centuries, revealed by excavation.
Johns, McQuitty, Falkner *et al.* 1989; McQuitty 1993a; 1993b; 1994a; 1994b; McQuitty and Falkner 1993.

## 95 FASAYIL, Khirbat

1918.1600 [9]

*Tall/Kh. Fasaʿil; Cr. Phesech, Fasael*

**Aqueduct** and **mill**, presumably for **sugar production**, dating from early Islamic period but possibly still in use in the twelfth century.
Beyer 1940: 189, 201; 1942: 174; Palestine 1948: 120; Porath 1983.

# 96 al-FULA

1789.2243 [5]

Cr. *la Feve, Elful(e), castrum Fabe/Fabbarum*; Hebr. *Kibbutz Merhavya*

Rectangular **castle**, possibly of concentric *quadriburgium* type (about 80/90 m N–S by about 110/120 m E–W), on mound with ditch 30–35 m wide, now represented only by earthworks and fragmentary masonry remains; site of gate with outer hornwork on W; vaulted **cisterns** to W (with *nuria* attested in the twelfth century). Castle first mentioned, in Templar hands, in 1169/72 (Theodoric, XLIV); lost 1187.

Abel 1926c: 194 n.2; Benvenisti 1970: 281–2, 323; Buckingham 1822: II, 381; Conder and Kitchener 1881: II, 82, 101, 116; Deschamps 1934: 28, 85; 1939a: 2, 23, 122–3, 134; 1943: 94–5; Ellenblum 1992: 183; Guérin 1880: I, 110–12; Israel 1964: 1387; Johns 1937: 29; Kedar and Pringle 1985; Kennedy 1994: 55–6, 61, 124; Langé 1965: 20, 26, 35, 92, 178, fig. 43; Palestine 1929: 38; 1948: 33; Rey 1883: 439; de Saulcy 1853: I, 81; 1865: II, 256; Thomson 1876: 478; Wilson 1880a: II, 25–8.

*Churches*, I, nos. 90–91.

# 97 al-HABIS

192.972 [10]

*Petra*; Med. Ar. *al-Aswīt*
(fig. 27; pls. XXXVII–XXXVIII)

**Castle** on rocky height, comprising **tower** (about 8.4 by 5.3 m) on highest point, with surrounding irregular enceinte (max. extent 44 by 16 m); other masonry

XXXVII   al-Habis (**no. 97**): castle, upper ward looking N towards keep.

XXXVIII   al-Habis (**no. 97**): castle, view S from keep.

structures and remains of outer wall on cliff edge downhill (max. extent 115 by 85 m). Presumed to be twelfth-century.

Brooker and Knauf 1988: 186–7; Eydoux 1982: 140–1; Hammond 1970; Horsfield 1938: 5, pls. I–II, V, XI–XII; Johns 1937: 39; Kennedy 1994: 28–30, 33, 121, pls. 4–6; Khouri 1986: 104–6; 1988a: 24–6; Lindner 1985: 45–9; Marino *et al.* 1990a: 4–5; Mayer 1990: 185–7; Pringle 1994b; Zayadine 1985: 164–6, 173, figs. 8, 11.

# 98 al-HADDAR

134.168 [7]

Cr. *Molendina Trium Pontium, Tres Pontes*

Remains of 3 **mills** and **mill dam** on Nahr al-ʿAuja (River Yarqon). Granted to Hospital in 1133 (*RRH*, no. 147). **Bridge** destroyed by Turks in 1917.

PAM: Report by C.N. Johns (19 March 1941).
PEF: C.N. Johns, Field Notebook 1940–1 (19 March 1941).

Benvenisti 1970: 252; Beyer 1951: 180–2, 184–6, 189–90, 192; Clermont-Ganneau 1888: I, 196–7; Conder and Kitchener 1881: II, 251; Israel 1964: 1426; Palestine 1948: 79; *Palestine Gazette*, no. 1087, suppl. 2 (13 Apr. 1941); Pringle 1986b: 69, 78 n.42; Quatremère 1837: I.ii, 253–4.

# 99 al-HADITHA

2025.0781 [10]

**Sugar production site**, indicated by sugar pots and pottery of the twelfth to fifteenth centuries.

Khouri 1988b: 90–1; King *et al.* 1987: 439–42, 453.

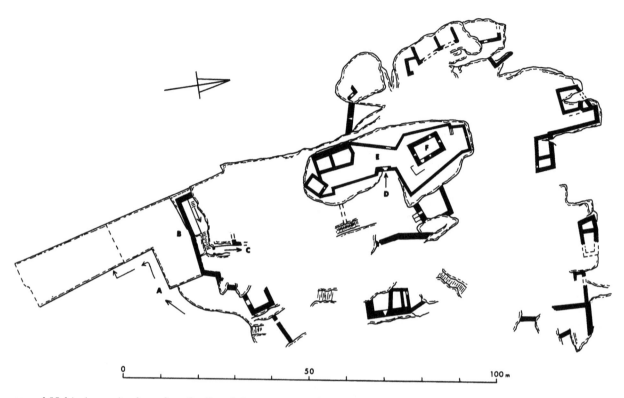

27  al-Habis (**no. 97**): plan of castle. Key: (A) access route from valley; (B) outer gate; (C) entrance gate and ramp; (D) gate to inner ward; (E) inner ward; (F) keep or *donjon* (after Hammond 1970).

## 100 HASBAYA

### 214.312 [2]

Cr. *Assabebe, Hasbeya*

Rectangular **tower** at SE corner of early seventeenth-century castle of the Shihab (Chéhab) family, identified as Frankish by local tradition. Centre of lordship, probably lost by 1148.

Deschamps 1939a: vii; Guide Bleu 1932: 391–2; 1975: 246–7; Johns 1937: 30; Wilson 1880a: II, fig. p. 133. On the lordship, see: Richard 1954; Tibble 1989: 17–21.

## 101 HEBRON

### 1605.1036 [8]

*al-Khalil*; Cr. S. *Abraham, Ebron, Cariatarba*

Fortified **annexe**, identified as the **castle** of the twelfth-century lord of Hebron, added to SW face of the Herodian precinct that enclosed the cathedral church and canons' cloister of St Abraham, to which a crenellated parapet was also added; annexe used in Mamluk times as a caravanserai and madrasa, and in the nineteenth century as barracks; mostly demolished in 1960s.

Conder and Kitchener 1881: III, 307, pl. opp. p. 336; Guérin 1868: III, 217–18; Johns 1937: 37; Kennedy 1994: 22; Pierotti 1869: plan; Pringle 1993: I, 224; Rey 1883: 389–90; Vincent, Mackay and Abel 1923: 163 n.5; Rey 1883: 389–90.

Excavated **village house**, with occupation from Umayyad to Ayyubid period.

Hammond 1965: 268, pl. XIXa.

*Churches*, I, no. 100; II, no. 192 (Tall ar-Rumaida).

## 102 HISBAN, Tall

### 2265.1343 [9]

*Heshbon*; Med. Ar. *Ḥisbān*
(pl. XXXIX)

Although the principal medieval structures, including a bath-house, belong to the Mamluk period (*c.*1260– ), when Hisban was capital of the Balqa' province, excavations show that these overlie **village buildings** of the twelfth and thirteenth centuries.

xxxix   Tall Hisban (**no. 102**): Mamluk bath-house, overlying village buildings.

Abel 1967: II, 348–9; Boraas and Horn 1969: 134, pls. xxii–xxiii; Gaudefroy-Demombynes 1923: 67; Geraty 1975: 585–6, pl. xlviiic; 1993: 629; Johns 1937: 30; Lawlor 1979: 115; Le Strange 1890: 456; Sauer 1973: 50–63, fig. 4; DeVries, forthcoming.

# 103 'IBILLIN

### 1683.2475 [3]

*Cr. Ibillin, Abelina; Hebr. Evlayim*

**Castle**, comprising central **tower** (internally 10 by 8.8 m) with basement of two parallel barrel-vaults, and outer wall with rounded towers of uncertain date (probably eighteenth-century).

Information: R.P. Harper and A. Petersen.

Bagatti 1971a: 142; Beyer 1945: 210; Guérin 1880: I, 420–1; Harper 1992: 79; Hoade 1978: 777; Israel 1964: 1377; Le Strange 1890: 382; Mariti 1769: II, 168; Palestine 1929: 43; 1948: 24; Pringle 1994b.

# 104 'ID AL-MINYA, Khirbat

### 1505.1187 [8]

*Kh. 'Id al-Miya; Hebr. H. 'Adullam*

**Vaulted structure**, possibly Crusader.

Clermont-Ganneau 1896: II, 459; Israel 1964: 1474; Palestine 1929: 64; 1948: 177.

# 105 'IRIBBIN, Khirbat

### 1716.2764 [3]

*Hebr. H. 'Erav*

Reuse of Byzantine church building as **village house**, revealed by excavation.

Ilan 1982; 1988; 1993; Israel 1964: 1354; Palestine 1929: 92; 1948: 3; Pringle 1993: I, 250–1.

# 106 ISKANDARUNA

### 1654.2844 [3]

*Iskandariya; Cr. Scandalion, Scandalium*

**Castle**, described in 1697 as 120 paces square, surrounded by dry ditch, possibly that built by Baldwin I in 1117 (William of Tyre, XI, 30). Traces of **enclosure walls** may also be the **town walls** mentioned by Ibn Jubayr in 1184 (trans. Gaudefroy-Demombynes, III, 356).

Beyer 1945: 205–7, 248; Conder and Kitchener 1881: I, 176; Deschamps 1934: 15, 18; 1939a: 9, 118, 236; Dussaud 1927: 21; Favreau 1977; Guérin 1880: II, 173ff.; Guide Bleu 1932: 434; Johns 1937: 29; Kennedy 1994: 22; Le Strange 1890: 458; Mariti 1769: II, 288–90; Maundrell 1697a: 426; 1697b: 70; Pringle 1993: I, 251; 1995a: 95; Renan 1864: 689, 693, 745.

*Churches*, I, no. 102.

# 107 ISTUNA, Khirbat

### 1802.1598 [8]

*Kh. Kafr Istuna; Cr. Caphastrum*

Remains of **tower** and **vaulted buildings**. In March 1179, village and lands held by abbey of St Mary of Mount Sion (*RRH*, no. 576).

Beyer 1936: 79; 1940: 176, 199; Palestine 1948: 119; Rey 1883: 283, 426.

# 108 JABA'

### 1749.1405 [8]

*Cr. Gabaa, Gebea*
(fig. 2g)

**Tower** (*al-Burj*)(11.4 m square), probably of three storeys and surviving 9 m high; door on S leads into basement, consisting of four groin-vaulted bays carried on large rectangular pilasters and a central pier; stair to left of entrance ascends inside wall to barrel-vaulted first-floor **hall** or **solar** (9 m N–S by 4.8 m E–W), with fireplace in N wall and slit-window in intersecting vaulted casemate to its right; stair continued up inside wall to second floor or roof. Village sold with six others (including *khuraib*) by Aimery of Franclieu, knight of Jerusalem (*fl.* 1171–9), to abbey of St Mary of Mount Sion, before March 1179 (*RRH*, no. 576).

Ellenblum 1992: 181; Finkelstein and Magen 1993: 177–9, 35* (no. 206), colour pl.; Kennedy 1994: 33; Kochavi 1972: 183 (no. 124), figs.; Palestine 1929; 1948: 115; Porter 1867: 179; Pringle 1994b: 342, table, fig. 4g; Rey 1883: 281, 384.

# 109 JABAL QURUNTUL

### 1909.1423 [9]

*Jabal ad-Duq, Tahunat al-Hawa*; Cr. *Docus, castellum Abrahami*

Templar **castle**, established by 1169/72 in the rock-cut caves and cisterns of the former Maccabean fortress of *Doc*, on and around the summit of Jabal Quruntul (Theodoric, XXIX).

Abel 1926b: 530; 1967: II, 375–6; Augustinović 1951: 136–8; Benvenisti 1970: 357–8; Clermont-Ganneau 1896: II, 21; Conder and Kitchener 1881: III, 204–5; Guérin 1874: I, 44; Johns 1937: 36; Palestine 1948: 122; Pringle 1993: I, 253, 257; 1994c: 152–3; Rey 1883: 386.

*Churches,* I, nos. 104–7.

# 110 JAFFA

### 1265.1624 [7]

*Joppa, Yafa*; Cr. *Jaffa, Japhe, Joppe*; Hebr. *Yafo*

**Port town** consisting of walled **castle** or citadel occupying oval hill overlooking natural harbour to N and E, enclosed on E and S by walled **faubourg**. Little survives of the medieval town, though much of the **urban topography** can be reconstructed on the basis of documentary sources and natural features.

Abel 1946; Alderson 1843: pl. 7; Bagatti 1979: 178–9; Deschamps 1939a: 5–6, 15, 17–18, 124, 138, 148, 165–6, 215, 237–8; Enlart 1925: II, 134–6; Kark 1989; Marshall 1992: 139–44; Pringle 1993: I, 264–73, fig. 79; 1995a: 93–4, fig. 10; Roberts 1842b: 64–9, pls. 74–5; Schiller 1980: 211 (photo of harbour, 1870), 213 (photo of land wall, 1877).

Excavations have also revealed fragments of the **sea wall**, built with through-columns, and in the town centre some **vaults** and a thirteenth-century **bread oven**.

Kaplan 1960; 1966: 282; 1967; 1972; 1974; 1975a: 262–3; Kaplan and Kaplan 1976; Shapiro 1978.

*Churches,* I, nos. 109–20.

# 111 JALADIYA, Khirbat

### 126.122 [7]

Cr. *Geladia, Geliadia*

Block of a **tower** built in masonry similar to that of Ascalon, seen by SWP. Village granted to Holy Sepulchre by Amalric, count of Ascalon, in 1160 (*RRH*, no. 356).

Beyer 1942: 185, 186; 1951: 257; Conder and Kitchener 1881: II, 418, 424; Israel 1964: 1443; Khalidi 1992: 113–14; Palestine 1929; 1948: 129.

# 112 JALJULIYA

### 1454.1733 [5]

Cr. *Jorgilia, Jorgilra*

Suggested identification of Crusader **sugar factory** on site of later Ottoman mosque.

Ayalon 1983; Beyer 1936: 50, 81, 85; 1951: 155, 159, 180, 266; Palestine 1948: 85.

# 113 JARYUT, Khirbat

### 1634.1444 [8]

Covered **aqueduct** and **pool**, and **barrel-vaulted buildings**.

Ellenblum 1992: 177; Finkelstein and Magen 1993: 60–1, 18* (no. 46), fig.; Palestine 1929; 1948: 111.

# 114 JERICHO

### 1934.1404 [9]

*ar-Riha*; Cr. *Iericho, Hiericho, Jherico*

Square **tower** (*Burj ar-Riha*) near Russian compound, possibly Frankish in origin, identified from the late fifteenth century as the 'House of Zacchaeus'; now destroyed. Remains of **sugar-mills** beside wadi S of present mosque (information B. Porëe).

Abel 1967: II, 360; Augustinović 1951: 61–3; Baedeker 1876b: 158; Bagatti 1979: 76; Faber 1480–3: II, 42; de Forbin 1819: 94; Meistermann 1936: 377; Pococke 1743: II, 31; Pringle 1993: I, 275–6; 1994b; Roberts 1842b: III, 22–5, pl. 59; Schiller 1979: 177 (photo of 1894); 1980: 181 (photo of 1865).

*Churches,* I, no. 123.

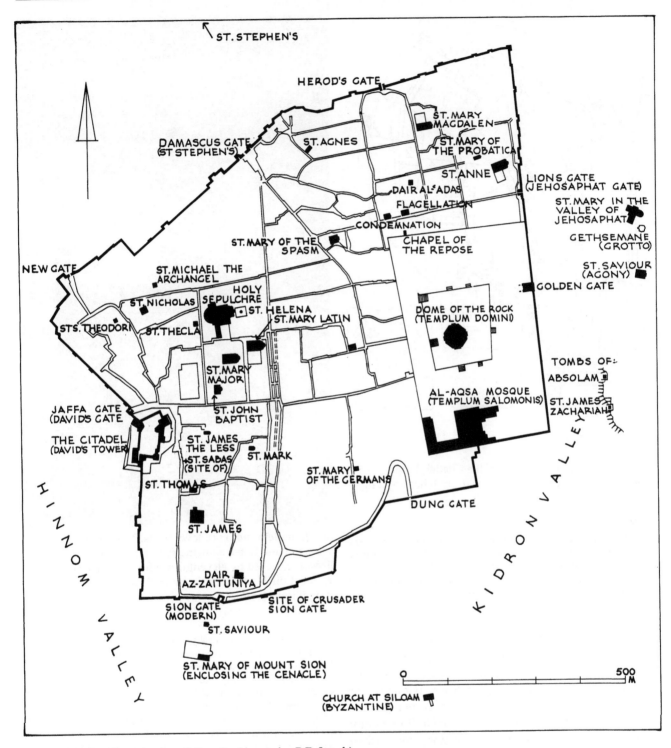

ST. STEPHEN'S

HEROD'S GATE

ST. MARY MAGDALEN

ST. MARY OF THE PROBATICA

DAMASCUS GATE (ST STEPHEN'S)

ST. AGNES

ST. ANNE

LIONS GATE (JEHOSAPHAT GATE)

DAIR AL-ADAS

FLAGELLATION

ST. MARY IN THE VALLEY OF JEHOSAPHAT

CONDEMNATION

GETHSEMANE (GROTTO)

CHAPEL OF THE REPOSE

ST. MARY OF THE SPASM

NEW GATE

ST. SAVIOUR (AGONY)

ST. MICHAEL THE ARCHANGEL

GOLDEN GATE

HOLY SEPULCHRE

ST. NICHOLAS

ST. HELENA

DOME OF THE ROCK (TEMPLUM DOMINI)

STS. THEODORI

ST. MARY LATIN

ST. THECLA

TOMBS OF ABSOLAM

ST. MARY MAJOR

AL-AQSA MOSQUE (TEMPLUM SALOMONIS)

JAFFA GATE (DAVID'S GATE)

ST. JOHN BAPTIST

ST. JAMES ZACHARIAH

THE CITADEL (DAVID'S TOWER)

ST. JAMES THE LESS

ST. SABAS (SITE OF)

ST. MARK

ST. MARY OF THE GERMANS

ST. THOMAS

ST. JAMES

DUNG GATE

HINNOM VALLEY

KIDRON VALLEY

DAIR AZ-ZAITUNIYA

SION GATE (MODERN)

SITE OF CRUSADER SION GATE

ST. SAVIOUR

ST. MARY OF MOUNT SION (ENCLOSING THE CENACLE)

500 M

CHURCH AT SILOAM (BYZANTINE)

28   Jerusalem (**no. 115**): plan of the city (drawn by P.E. Leach).

# 115 JERUSALEM

1720.1316 [8]

al-Quds ash-Sharif; Cr. *Jerusalem, Ierusalem, Hierusalem,*

*Ierosolima;* Hebr. *Yerushalayim*
(figs. 28–9; pls. XL–XLV)

**City** in Crusader hands 1099–1187 and 1229–44.

Abel 1924a; Asali 1989: 130–76; Bahat 1985b; 1988; 1991; 1992;

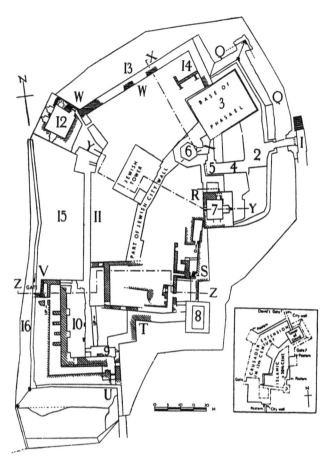

29  Jerusalem (**no. 115**): plan of the Citadel (David's Tower), showing pre-1239 remains (from Johns 1950: fig. 25).

Ben-Dov, Bahat and Rosen-Ayalon 1993; Benvenisti 1970: 35–73; Burgoyne and Richards 1987: 47–9; Gotein 1982; Heydenreich 1965; Johns 1937; Le Strange 1890, 83–223; Prag 1989; Prawer 1952; 1976; 1980: 85–101, 296–314; 1984; 1985; Pringle 1991b; 1993: III; Richard 1965; Riley-Smith 1990: 44–5; Vincent and Abel 1914: 945–73, and *passim*; Yadin 1976.

**Town walls**, rebuilt in 1030s–70s, with forewall (*barbacana*) and ditch around northern part of city between Citadel and Jehoshaphat (E) Gate and on Mount Sion, and with massive **quadrangular tower** (Goliath's or Tancred's Tower, 35 m square) at NW corner (pl. XL). Walls rebuilt by Ayyubids in 1192 (including Mount Sion) and 1202–12 (excluding Mount Sion), demolished by them 1219–20, partially repaired by Crusaders from 1229, dismantled again 1239 or 1244. At St Stephen's Gate, remains of twelfth-century Crusader **gate-tower with bent entrance** in the outer wall in front of Roman N gate. Otherwise scant trace of Crusader defences now visible; foundations of four towers, 23 m square, built astride S wall, appear to be Ayyubid (1202–12).

XL  Jerusalem (**no. 115**): town walls, NW corner (SW of modern New Gate), showing foundations of Tancred's Tower, enclosed by eleventh/twelfth-century wall and rock-cut ditch and overlain by walls of Sulayman the Magnificent (1516).

Avigad 1983: 251–5; Bahat 1985a; 1986; 1987; Bahat and Ben-Ari 1976; Ben-Dov 1982: 338–41; 1983: 65–82; 1987; 1994; Ben-Dov, Bahat and Rosen-Ayalon 1993: 793–6; Benvenisti 1970: 49–52; Broshi 1977; 1987; Broshi and Gibson 1994; Broshi and Tsafrir 1977; Conder 1890; Goldfuss 1984; Hennessy 1968; 1970; Kenyon 1967: 195–6, pls. 76–8; Maeir 1980; Magen 1984; 1988; 1994; Magness 1991; Maier 1993: 62; Margovsky 1971; Prawer 1984; 1985; Pringle 1991b: 106–7; 1995a: 78–81, fig. 2; Schick 1878a; 1889: 216; Sharon 1977; Tsafrir 1990; Vincent 1908: 267–75, pls. I–II; 1913; 1927; Warren and Conder 1884: 235–6, 264–7, 271, 393–7; Wightman 1989; 1994: 259–98; Wilson 1865: 54–6, 73–4, photos 31b–34, pl. XXVII.

**Citadel**, or **David's Tower** (pl. XLI), a castle of irregular plan built S and W of Herod's Tower of Hippicus (or Phasael) astride the city wall, with late Roman, Byzantine, early Islamic, Crusader, Mamluk and Ottoman

XLI   Jerusalem (**no. 115**): Citadel, Herodian Tower of Hippicus, abutted by NE curtain wall (*14*), of which the lower part is Crusader and the upper Mamluk.

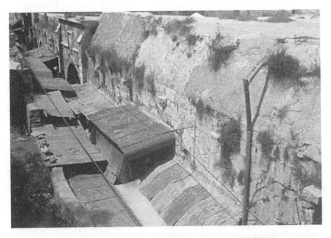

XLII   Jerusalem (**no. 115**): S front of Hospital facing on to David Street, with shops on ground floor and upper floor missing, except for row of corbels that formerly carried an external timber gallery.

XLIII   Jerusalem (**no. 115**): Street of Herbs, covered market attributed to Queen Melisende.

phases; Crusader elements which survived destruction in 1239 are to be found in *talus* around base of Tower of Hippicus (fig. 29: Q–Q), E tower (*7*), E curtain (between *7* and *8*) including stables and postern (*S*), base of SW tower (*10*) also including stables, S postern (*U*), W gateway (*V*), NW curtain (*13*) including lower level of casemated arrow-slits (*W*), and NE curtain (*14*). Other structures excavated W of the Ottoman-period moat in 1990.

Amiran and Eitan 1970a; 1970b; 1976; Benvenisti 1970: 52–3; Geva 1983: 70–1; 1994; Johns 1936b; 1940; 1944; 1950; Reich, Shukron and Billig 1993; Rubin and Jägendorf 1992; Schick 1878b; Sivan and Solar 1984; 1994; Solar and Sivan 1984; Warren and Conder 1884: 167–270; Wilson 1865: 46–8, pls. III.19–21b, XIX.

Excavations in the Armenian Garden, S of Citadel, have revealed part of W **city wall**, including a tower, a barrel-vaulted **cistern** (about 17.5 by about 6 m internally) which possibly underlay S range of **royal palace**, and a large building, possibly a khan, of the Ayyubid period (dated 1212/14–1219/27).

Bahat 1971; Bahat and Broshi 1972; 1976: 56; Ben-Dov, Bahat and Rosen-Ayalon 1993: 797, 800; Broshi 1972; Kenyon 1963: 20–1, pl. xb; 1967: 196, pls. 91–2; Tushingham 1985.

**Muristan (or Hospital) area**, S of Holy Sepulchre, recorded before destruction in 1890s, included remains of churches of St Mary Latin and St Mary Magdalene (or St Mary Parva/Majora), vaulted basements of Hospital buildings, and still surviving row of vaulted **shops** fronting David Street on S with corbels indicating former first-floor timber gallery (pl. XLII).

PEF: Reports and drawings by C. Schick.

Benvenisti 1970: 58–62; Hanauer 1903; Kenyon 1962: 86–8, pl. XXIV; 1967: 194–5; pl. 70; Schick 1873; 1889; 1894; 1902; Warren and Conder 1884: 254–61; Wilson and Warren 1871: 210–12.

xLIV Jerusalem (**no. 115**): Crusader shop fronts in Street of Mount Sion (originally with solars above), later incorporated into a covered market and recently restored.

xLV Jerusalem (**no. 115**): Crusader fountain head, excavated in front of Damascus Gate in 1980. The spout bears a masonry mark representing a key (type 16–22).

Excavations in the Jewish and Maghribi Quarters and on Ophel, S of the Temple Mount (Haram ash-Sharif), have shed light on the **town wall** and Templars' **postern**.

Avigad 1978; 1983: 247–55; Ben-Dov 1982: 343–53; Crowfoot 1945: 77–81, 97–101, pls. x–xv, plan; Glücksmann and Kool 1995; Mazar 1975: 274–9.

Excavations in suburb N of St Stephen's Gate have recorded remains of St Stephen's church, Hospitallers' **pilgrim hospice** (*Asnerie*), and other **buildings**.

Schick 1879; 1890; Vincent 1924; Warren and Conder 1884: 383–92.

**Covered markets**, partly dating from the time of Queen Melisende (Bresc-Bautier, no. 36 [1152]), **shops** and

**houses**. The latter include both traditional oriental urban courtyard houses, and European types with vaulted shops or store-rooms below several floors of domestic rooms (solars) (pls. xLIII–xLIV).

Avigad 1983: 248; Ben-Dov, Bahat and Rosen-Ayalon 1993: 796; Benvenisti 1970: 55–6; Clermont-Ganneau 1896: I, 116–26; Margalit 1993; Pringle 1991b: 110–11; 1995b: 169–70, fig.; de Sandoli 1974: 151–3; Schick 1897; Warren and Conder 1884: 428.

**Water supply**, including cisterns, aqueducts, Pool of Germanus (*Birkat as-Sultan*) in the Hinnom Valley, and a documented water-wheel below Siloam.

Benvenisti 1970: 56–8; Schick 1898; Warren and Conder 1884: 371, 375–6; Wilson 1865: 77–88, pl. VII.

*Churches*, III.

# 116 JEZREEL

## 1811.2182 [6]

*Zir'in*; Cr. *Gezrael, Iezrael, Parvum Gerinum, Zarain*; Hebr. *Tel Yizra'el*

**Vaulted building** and other **structures**, apparently forming part of a **castle** which by the 1180s belonged to the Templars (Raph of Diss (*RS*, LXVIII.ii, 28)). The tower mentioned by nineteenth-century writers appears to be Ottoman.

Abel 1967: II, 364–5; Benvenisti 1970: 19, 220, 276, 313, 345; Beyer 1945: 232; Conder and Kitchener 1881: II, 88; Israel 1964: 1413; Khalidi 1992: 339–40; Palestine 1929: 264; 1948: 67; Petrozzi 1976: 348–61, figs. 87–93; Pringle 1993: I, 276–7; Rey 1883: 440; Ussishkin and Woodhead 1992; 1994: fig. 1; Wilson 1880a: II, 27–8; 1880b: II, 27–8.

*Churches*, I, no. 124.

# 117 al-JIB

## 1676.1396 [8]

*Gibeon*; Cr. *Gabaon*
(fig. 30)

Additions made in the twelfth century to a complex of fifth- to eighth-century buildings, to form a large **courtyard building** (about 75 m N–S by > 50 m E–W), with vaulted ranges around a central courtyard.

PAM: Report by D.C. Baramki (12 Aug. 1941).

Bagatti 1975; Benvenisti 1970: 19, 233; Conder and Kitchener 1881: III, 100; Finkelstein and Magen 1993: 236, 46* (no. 315); Guérin 1868: I, 385; Palestine 1929: 49; 1944: 1270; 1948: 152; Pringle 1983a: 142–60,

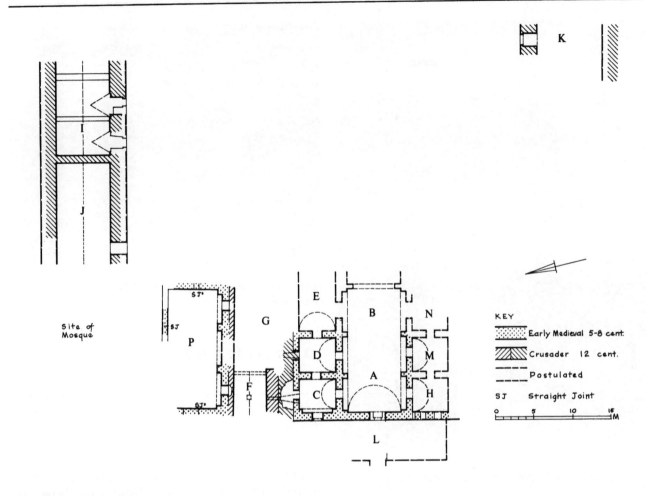

30   al-Jib (**no. 117**): plan of Crusader additions to a building complex of the fifth to eighth centuries (drawn by P.E. Leach, BSAJ Survey 1982).

figs. 1–5, pls. xvi–xviiia; 1993: i, 279; Robinson 1841: ii, 136.

*Churches*, i, p. 279.

# 118 JIFNA

1705.1522 [8]

Cr. *Jafenia* (?)
(pls. xlvi–xlvii)

**Courtyard building** (*al-Burj*) (about 30 m E–W by about 37 m N–S overall), partly overlain by modern houses. Lintelled gate on E has a shallow relieving arch with damaged croix-pattée on keystone set in a pointed-arched recess concealing slit-machicolation (rebuilt after collapse in 1942). Remains of non-projecting tower (*al-Qurnaifa*) at NW corner. On N, building butts on to a vault (*al-Baubariya*) (internally 23.3 by 7.4 m, walls 2.1–2.4 m thick), containing **rotary olive-press** (diam. 2.4 m); this may possibly be the basement of a **hall-house**.

PEF: C.N. Johns, Field Notebook 1941–2 (March 1942).

Abel 1967: ii, 401; Bagatti 1971b; 1979: 112–13; Benvenisti 1970: 234, 238–40, figs.; 1982, 147, figs. 16–18; Deschamps 1939a: 22; Ellenblum 1992: 182; Guérin 1868: iii, 28; Johns 1937: 31; Kochavi 1972: 174–5 (no. 73), figs.; Palestine 1929: 48; 1948: 104; Pringle 1993: i, 279–80; 1994a: 48–9; Robinson 1841: iii, 78; Smail 1973: 86.

*Churches*, i, no. 125.

# 119 JISR AL-GHAJAR

2086.2941 [4]

**Repair of Roman bridge**, attributed to 'Arab' and Crusader periods.
Hai 1983.

XLVII   Jifna (**no. 118**): courtyard building, E side of courtyard.

## 121 KAFR LAM

1440.2269 [5]

*Kafr Lab*; Cr. *Cafarlet, Capharleth, Kafarletum*; Hebr. *Habonim*
(fig. 31)

Trapezoidal **early Muslim fort** (57 m N/42.5 m S by 51 m N–S) with walls (1.5–2.3 m thick) strengthened by external buttresses (1.4 m square) and solid cylindrical corner turrets; pointed-arched gate (2.77 m wide) on S between half-round turrets, with evidence for narrowing and lowering in Frankish period. In 1213, Kafr Lam was sold by the lord of Caesarea to the Hospitallers, who transferred it to the Templars by 1255 (*RRH*, nos. 866, 1233; cf. nos. 768, 1319).

PAM: Reports and photos (1921– ).

Benvenisti 1970: 281–2, 288, 329–31, figs.; Conder and Kitchener 1881: II, 3–4, 29–30; Deschamps 1939a: 23; El'ad 1982; Guérin 1874: II, 302; Hoade 1978: 660; Israel 1964: 1384; Johns 1937: 25; 1947: 26; Kennedy 1994: 18; Khalidi 1992: 170; Langé 1965: 180, fig. 43; von Mülinen 1908a: 210–12, figs. 92–3; Palestine 1948: 30; Pringle 1991a: 89 (no. 6).

## 122 KAFR SUM, Khirbat

1588.1265 [8]

Cr. *Caphason*

Barrel-vaulted complex (**courtyard building**) on hilltop, associated with rock-cut cisterns and remains of

XLVI   Jifna (**no. 118**): gateway to courtyard building.

## 120 KAFR JINNIS

1412.1560 [8]

*al-Kanisa*; Cr. *casellum S. Abacuc, saint Abaccu de Cantie, s. Abacuch de Quantie, s. Abacuc de Cansie*

**Ruins**, possibly of a **tower** associated with the Premonstratensian abbey of St Habakkuk, founded between 1138 and *c*.1150. Site now represented by nothing more than a low mound (1981).

PAM: Reports by Anon. (29 July 1933) and J. Ory (1927, 6–10 Dec. 1935, 7 June 1945).
PEF: C.N. Johns, Field Notebook 1940–1 (Jan. 1941).

Abel 1927b: 393, fig. 1; Bagatti 1979: 174; Conder and Kitchener 1881: II, 265; Guérin 1874: II, 392; Guide Bleu 1932: 551; Hoade 1978: 599–600; Israel 1964: 1435; Johns 1937: 22; Palestine 1929: 51, 197; 1948: 98; Pringle 1993: I, 283–5, pl. CXCVI; 1994b.

*Churches*, I, no. 127.

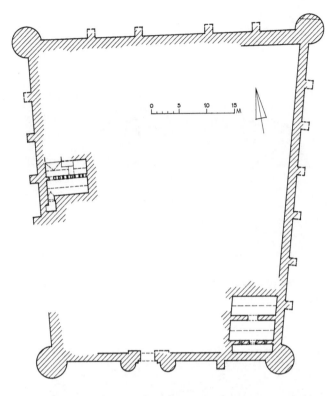

31 Kafr Lam (**no. 121**): plan of early Muslim fort (drawn by M. Pease, BSAJ Survey 1989).

**enclosure wall** in drafted ashlar. Barrel-vaulted **tower** to SE, later made into *Maqam ash-Shaikh Musafar*.

Conder and Kitchener 1881: III, 25; Israel 1964: 1466; Palestine 1948: 163.

## 123 KAISAN, Tall

### 1645.2532 [3]

*Napoleon's Hill*; Cr. *Tolonum Rohardi de Chabor, Turon Dame Joiette*; Hebr. *Tel Qison*

Structural phases and finds revealed by excavation, possibly relating to **military activity** of 1180s–90s or 1280s–90s.

Humbert and Nodet 1979: 447, pl. XIXb; cf. Barag 1979: 205; Beyer 1945: 202; Conder and Kitchener 1881: I, 207, 352; Frankel 1988: 261, 272, fig. 1; Fulco 1975: 239 (no. 43); Israel 1964: 1372; Palestine 1929: 243; 1948: 21.

## 124 KARAK

### 2170.0660 [10]

Cr. *Crac, le Crac de Montreal, Cracum Montis regalis, Petra*

*Deserti, Civitas Petracensis*; Med. Ar. *Karak al-Shawbak* (fig. 32; pls. XLVIII–LI)

**Walled town** on irregular rock-scarped plateau (about 850 m N–S by about 750 m E–W); existing medieval defences mostly Ayyubid and Mamluk. **Castle** on promontory to S (220 m N–S by 40/110 m E–W), detached from town by rock-cut ditch (30 m wide), and containing chapel, **vaulted cisterns** and **bread oven**; lower ward, or barbican, on W flank also contains Frankish work. Castle founded by Payen the Butler, lord of Montreal, in 1142 (William of Tyre, XV, 21); finally surrendered to al-Malik al-ʿAdil in November 1188.

Bliss 1895: 217–20; Boase 1967: 69–70, pl.; 1977: 100–1; Brooker and Knauf 1988: 186; Brown 1989a; 1989b; Deschamps 1934: *passim*, pls.

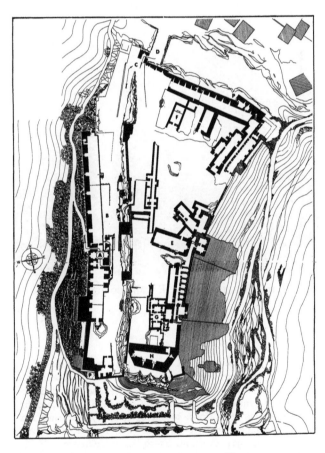

32 Karak (**no. 124**): plan of the castle at basement level. Key: (A) Mamluk gate to outer ward; (B) outer ward, on site of Crusader barbican; (C) site of gate to inner ward; (D) modern entrance from town; (E) twelfth-century chapel; (F) bakery; (G) Ayyubid palace; (H) Ayyubid–Mamluk keep; (J) reservoir; (P) postern gates (after Deschamps 1939a: plan 1).

XLVIII   Karak (**no. 124**): castle, from SE.

L   Karak (**no. 124**): Crusader W wall of inner ward, with Ayyubid–Mamluk keep behind.

XLIX   Karak (**no. 124**): castle, E wall, looking N from tower 4.

LI   Karak (**no. 124**): vaulted passage (now underground), running N from chapel.

IV, XXIC; 1937; 1939a: 80–98, pls. IV–XXVII; 1943: 96; 1964: 44–72, pls. 13–16; DeVries 1991: 280; Dowling 1896; Duncan 1982: 25–6; Eydoux 1982: 142–6; Franciscan Fathers 1977: 130–8, fig.; Gaudefroy-Demombynes 1923: 125–9, 131–4; Guide Bleu 1932: 642–6, fig.; Heyck 1900: figs. 56–9; Hoade 1966: 174, fig. p. 167; Hornstein 1898; Irby and Mangles 1861: 110–12; Johns (CN) 1937: 27–8; Johns (J) 1993; Kennedy 1994: 45–52, pls. 15–19, fig. 4; Lawrence 1988: xxx, 3n., 37, 125–6; Le Strange 1890: 479–80; de Luynes 1871: I, 100ff.; Meistermann 1909: 252–9; 1936: 390; Miller 1991: 89; Müller-Wiener 1966: 47–8, plan 4, pls. 23–7; Musil 1907: I, 45–62, figs. 8–21, 172; Ory 1975: 120; Pringle 1993: I, 286–7, fig. 83; 1995a: 77; Rey 1871: 3, 17, 131–5, 173–4, pl. XIV; de Saulcy 1853: I, 355–84; Smail 1956: 218–22, plan I, pls. I–II; Tristram 1874: 70–97, 105ff., pl. 14; Vincent 1898: 427–8.

*Churches*, I, nos. 129–33.

# 125 KARAZA, Khirbat

2031.2574 [4]

*Chorazin*; Hebr. *Korazin*

**Village buildings** of twelfth to thirteenth centuries.
Israel 1964: 1390; Palestine 1929; 119; 1948: 36; Yeivin 1982.

# 126 KARMIL, Khirbat al-

1627.0922 [10]

Cr. *Carmelus*
(fig. 2a; pls. LII–LIII)

**Tower** (18.90 m N–S by 12.95 m N/13.18 m S, walls 1.95/2.95 m thick) built over narthex of Byzantine church, whose outer walls were buttressed by a masonry *talus* probably in late sixth or seventh century; barrel-vaulted basement, with splayed slit-window on N; first floor now collapsed, but recorded by Rey and Mader as having three casemated arrow-slits on E (pl. LII), two and a door on W, and stair to roof in N wall. Large ancient rectangular **reservoir** (*birka*) to NE, at which King Amalric assembled his army in 1173 (William of Tyre, xx, 28).

PAM: Reports by S.A.S. Husseini (11 Feb. 1945, 28 Jan. 1946).
PEF: C.N. Johns, Field Notebook 1946–7 (18 Jan. 1947).
Bagatti 1983: 91–2, fig. 10, pl. 16; Benvenisti 1970: 266–7, 305–7, photo; Conder 1875: 20; Conder and Kitchener 1881: III, 312, 372–4, fig.; Deschamps 1934: 17, 78, 91; 1939a: 21, 55; Ellenblum 1992: 182; Guérin 1868: III, 166–70; Johns 1937: 25; Keel and Küchler 1982: II, 754–5, fig. 480; Mader 1918: 178–85, fig. 8; Mittmann 1971; Palestine 1929: 52; 1948: 211; Pringle 1983a: 170; 1994b: table, fig. 4a; Rey 1871: 102–4, fig. 30; de Saulcy 1853: II, 103; Schneider 1938; Séjourné 1895: 259–60.

# 127 KHAN, Khirbat al-

1545.1244 [8]

Hebr. *H. Hanot*

**Vaulted buildings**, including one (14 by 10 m) on remains of a Byzantine church next to Roman road from Jerusalem to Eleutheropolis (Bait Jibrin); attributed to 'Ayyubid' and 'Mamluk' periods.

Israel 1964: 1467; Palestine 1948: 164; Shenhav 1986.

# 128 KHAN AS-SAWIYA

1751.1664 [8]

(pl. LIV)

**Vaulted building**, with thick walls and slit-window near one corner, beside the Jerusalem–Nablus road.
Palestine 1948: 96.

LII   Kh. al-Karmil (**no. 126**): E wall of tower, photographed from E (*c.*1920), showing casemates from which the outer facing and embrasures have been robbed.

LIII   Kh. al-Karmil (**no. 126**): tower, vaulted basement, looking N.

LIV   Khan as-Sawiya (**no. 128**): from SW.

# 129 KHULJAN, Khirbat al-

163.206 [5]

*Kh. al-Muntar, Kh. Umm Dar*

Square **tower** of drafted masonry, which SWP identifies as perhaps Crusader.

Conder and Kitchener 1881: II, 61; Palestine 1929: 137; 1948: 54; Pringle 1994b.

# 130 KIBBUTZ SHOMRAT

1608.2620, 1610.2618, 1621.2614 [3]

Three **boundary stones** marked *IANVA* (Genoa) delimiting SW extent of Genoese estate, which in 1255 was centred on *Coketum* (Kuwaikat, Kibbutz Bet ha-Emeq, **no. 135**), where the stones are now preserved.

Frankel 1980; 1986a.

# 131 KIDNA

1403.1172 [8]

Hebr. *Iyye Kidon*

Remains of **fortified building** (27.5 by 10.6 m), possibly a **hall-house**.

Conder and Kitchener 1881: III, 258, 288; Israel 1964: 1471; Khalidi 1992: 218; Palestine 1929: 196; 1948: 173; Warren and Conder 1884: 443.

# 132 KUFRIYA, Khirbat al-

1663.1488 [8]

*Kh. Burj Kufriya (Tower of the Unbelievers)*

**Courtyard-building** (30.5 by 25.1 m) with vaulted ranges on S and W, adjacent to barrel-vault enclosing **spring**, which flows into a **reservoir** (12 m square).

Ellenblum 1991; 1992: 177; Finkelstein and Magen 1993: 70–1, 19* (no. 63); Palestine 1929; 1948: 110.

# 133 KURDANA, Khirbat

1606.2501 [3]

*Tall Kurdana; Cr. Recordana, Recordane; Hebr. Tel Afeq* (fig. 33; pls. LV–LVIII)

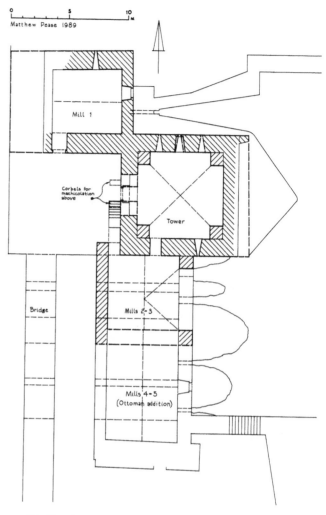

33 Kh. Kurdana (**no. 133**): plan of fortified mill complex, showing two Frankish phases (hatched) and later Ottoman structures (drawn by M. Pease, BSAJ Survey 1989).

**Mill**, with **dam** and two-storey defensive **tower** (about 11 m E–W by 9.9 m N–S). In first phase (late twelfth or thirteenth century), tower had timber lower floor (or mezzanine) carried on stone corbels, one splayed arrow-slit with stirrup base on S, and three on N. In a second phase (probably 1267 onwards), two floors of groin-vaults were inserted springing from corner pilasters, which blocked three of the arrow-slits, the central N one being widened and lengthened in compensation; a large pointed-arched opening (3.3 m wide) on W was defended by a box-machicolation at roof level. Tower flanked on S by two barrel-vaulted wheel-chambers (internally about 2.3 by 7 m) with mill room above, consisting of single barrel-vault (similar in construction to tower vaults) with intersecting open arch on E, and by another wheel-chamber on NW. Another two

LV  Kh. Kurdana (**no. 133**): water-mill and dam, from SE.

LVII  Kh. Kurdana (**no. 133**): water-mill, wheel-chamber for horizontal wheel, showing pivot stone, water inlet (rear left), and hole in vault through which power was transmitted to mill room above.

LVI  Kh. Kurdana (**no. 133**): vaulted wheel-chambers with mill room above, seen from SW, with tower behind.

LVIII  Kh. Kurdana (**no. 133**): arrow-slit with stirrup base in S wall of tower.

wheel-chambers on S and stair to tower roof added in Ottoman period. Village and mills acquired by the Hospitallers by 1154 (*Cart. des Hosp.*, no. 225; *RRH*, no. 293); dispute with Templars over water rights from 1235 settled in 1262 (*Cart. des Hosp.*, nos. 1144, 2107, 2117, 2120, 3032, 3045). Templar chapter met here in 1257/67, suggesting that Kurdana may for a time have been theirs (*Règle du Temple*, §618–19, trans. Upton-Ward, 159). Mill in Hospitaller hands when destroyed by Baybars in May 1267, and, following reconstruction, was to remain in joint Hospitaller-Mamluk ownership under the treaty of 29 May 1267; still in Frankish hands in treaty of 1283 (Holt, *Treaties*, 14, 32–3, 36, 79). Remained in use until 1925.

Barag 1979: 205 (no. 28); Benvenisti 1970: 248–52, 288, pls.; Beyer 1945: 207–8; Frankel 1988: 261, fig. 1; Garstang 1922c; Israel 1964: 1372; Israel: Nature Reserves Authority 1993; Johns 1937: 36; Maisler 1939; Palestine 1929: 125, 244; 1948: 21; Pringle 1986a: 69, pl. XXXI; 1986b: 69 nn.44–5; 1991a: 89 (no. 7); 1994b; Riley-Smith 1967: 446, 450; Rothschild 1938: 50; 1949.

## 134 KUSBUR, Khirbat

### 1570.1117 [8]

**Vaulted buildings**, apparently medieval, on Byzantine foundations, including one with a parabolic vault, well made and plastered (12.2 by 6.1 m, 4.6 m high). Crusader attribution unconfirmed.

PAM: Reports [Kh. Busbur] by Anon. (1 March 1922), D.C. Baramki (17 Sept. 1932).
Palestine 1948: 179.

## 135 KUWAIKAT

### 1642.2640 [3]

Cr. *Coketum, Coquetum*; Med. Ar. *Kawkab*; Hebr. *Kibbutz Bet ha-Emeq* (see also Kibbutz Shomrat, **no. 130**) (pl. LIX)

Rounded ashlar-built **barrel-vault**, described (1934) as all that remained of the Old Khan; possibly part of thirteenth-century Genoese estate centre, though it could be much earlier in date.

PAM: report by N. Makhouly (3 April 1934).

Israel 1964: 1358; Palestine 1948: 6. Cf. Beyer 1945: 207, 213; Khalidi 1992: 21–2.

LIX   Kuwaikat (**no. 135**): vault (photographed in 1934).

## 136 LATRUN

### 1485.1375 [8]

Cr. *Toron des Chevaliers/de los Caballeros, Toronum Militum*; Med. Ar. *al-Natrūn*
(fig. 34; pls. LX–LXI)

Extensive Templar **castle**, beginning as a **tower**, or keep (14 m square, walls 3–4 m thick), with barrel-vaulted basement, enclosed by quadrangular enceinte with *talus* (72 m E–W by 55 m N–S, walls about 3 m thick) and gate with portcullis slot on E; barrel-vaulted ranges extended along N and W sides of enclosure, and groin-vaulted range on S; the remaining area between tower and E gate later infilled with more groin-vaults, supporting now-vanished first floor (possibly including chapel). Parallel to N wall, an outer wall with *talus* (containing *chemin de ronde* in one place), defended by projecting rectangular tower (8.3 m wide, projecting 4.2 m) on NW. Beyond this, traces of polygonal outer ward, following shape of hill, survive downhill on N, SW and ?E, including barrel-vaulted **stables** (*al-baubariya, al-baiqa*) on N, and other vaulted structures on SW. The castle existed by 1169/71 (Benjamin of Tudela (trans. Asher, 87)) and was destroyed in 1191 (*Itin. Ric.*, IV, 23); though nominally held by the Templars 1229–44, there is no trace of thirteenth-century refortification.

PEF: C.N. Johns papers, copies of plans by D. Bellamy (March 1938); Field Notebook 1942–5 (15 Dec. 1945).

Bagatti 1979: 146–8, pl. 54; Barber 1994a: 88, 144, 361; Ben-Dov 1974; 1993b; Benvenisti 1970: 282, 316–18, photo; Beyer 1951: 178; Boase

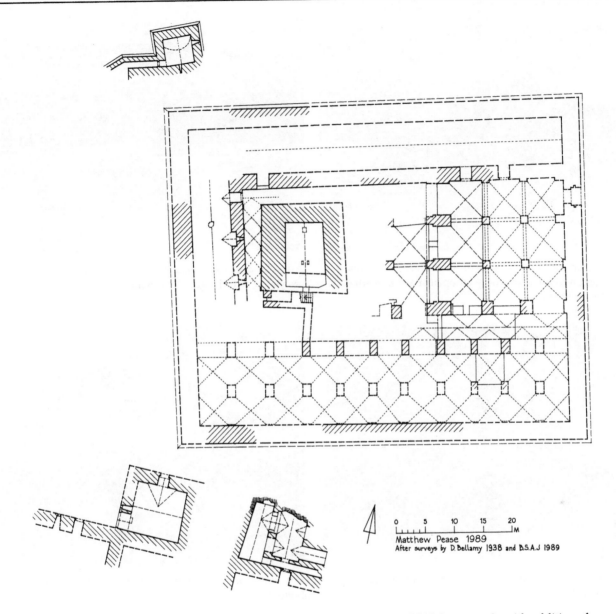

34   Latrun (**no. 136**): plan of the inner part of the castle (drawn by M. Pease, BSAJ Survey 1989 with additions from drawings by D. Bellamy, 1938).

1977: 90–1, 112, pl. XI; van Bruyn 1725: II, 167, 280, pl. opp. p. 239; Conder and Kitchener 1881: III, 15–16, 135; Clermont-Ganneau 1896: I, 492–8; Deschamps 1934; 85; 1939a: 10 n.1, 15, 20; Ellenblum 1992: 182; Guérin 1868: I, 59–60, 309–13; Hoade 1978: 538; Kennedy 1994: 55, 124; Khalidi 1992: 392–3; Langé 1965: 159, 184, fig. 43; Palestine 1929: 199; 1948: 147; Prawer 1975: I, 328, 534, 668; II: 83, 86–7, 90, 94n., 200n., 259, 309n., 310, 409, 442, 524; Pringle 1991a: 89–90 (no. 9); 1993: II, figs. 1–2; 1994b; Prutz 1881: 166, 167.

*Churches*, II, no. 136.

# 137 LAUZA, Khirbat al-

1658.1359 [8]

*Kh. al-Lauz*
(pl. LXII)

**Courtyard building**, terraced into hillside, comprising **hall-house** (11 by 4.2 m internally) uphill on E side with external stair to first floor, large barrel-vaulted grange or byre (21 by 4.8/5.5 m, walls 2.2 m thick) on W, and

LX   Latrun (**no. 136**): S range of inner ward, two bays opening on to what was once an open space immediately S of tower (keep).

LXII   Kh. al-Lauza (**no. 137**): courtyard building, associated with irrigated cultivation terraces.

LXI   Latrun (**no. 136**): interior of a tower (?) to SW of inner ward.

LXIII   Lifta (**no. 138**): barrel-vaulted cistern with house above it.

other structures. Gate on E. Associated with masonry **pool** (capacity 1,200 m³) to SE, fed from spring, which also irrigated terraces to S and E. Remains of **quarry**.

Bagatti 1947: 23, 183, 192, 232–3, 237, fig. 47.96; Conder and Kitchener 1881: III, 119; Ellenblum 1992: 176; Ellenblum, Rubin and Solar 1996; Finkelstein and Magen 1993: 223, 44* (no. 295); Guérin 1868: I, 257; Israel 1964: 1461; Lagrange 1894: 139–40; Palestine 1948: 154; C. Schick, in Zschokke 1865: 62–71.

# 138 LIFTA

### 1686.1338 [8]

Cr. *Clepsta*; Hebr. *Me Neftoah*
(pl. LXIII)

Large **courtyard building** in centre of village consisting of four parallel barrel-vaults with courtyard to S, associated with garden terraces and **aqueduct** from spring; vaults contain large **rotary presses** and a screw-type **olive-press**. Some 500 m NE of village in valley bottom (Grid ref. 1688.1342), barrel-vaulted **cistern** on S side of wadi, with small door (for cleaning) near N end of E wall and remains of cistern-keeper's house above. *Clepsta* was among the villages near Jerusalem ceded to the Franks in 1241 (Matthew Paris, *Chron. Maj.* (*RS*, LVIII.iv, 143)).

Bagatti 1947: 231 n.2; Benvenisti 1970: 19, 233, 257. Cf. Abel 1967: II, 398; Khalidi 1992: 300–3; Tobler 1853: II, 758–60.

## 139 MADD AD-DAIR, Khirbat

1412.1966 [5]

Cr. *Casale Latinae, casale quod fuit Eustachii, Montdidier, Mondisder, Mons Dederi*; Hebr. *Kibbutz Ma'barot, Hafita*

Remains of **tower** (about 16 m N–S by about 12.5 m E–W, walls 1.7–2.0 m thick), with basement consisting of two parallel barrel-vaults (now destroyed). Village given to abbey of St Mary Latin by Eustace Garnier, lord of Caesarea (1105/10–23) (*RRH*, no. 331), later passing with Burj al-Ahmar (**no. 63**) to the Hospitallers and Templars.

Beyer 1936: 43–5; Conder and Kitchener 1881: II, 140; Dar and Mintzker 1987: 210–13, pl. 52a; Israel 1964: 1410; Kennedy 1994: 33, 36; Langé 1965: 94, 184, fig. 43; Palestine 1929: 127; 1948: 56; Pringle 1986a: 37–9, figs. 2–3, 9, pl. VIII; 1994b; Rey 1883: 423.

## 140 MAGHARAT AL-WARDA

2172.1811 [6]

**Iron ore extracting and smelting site**, in use in Ayyubid and Mamluk periods.

Coughenour 1976; 1989; Glueck 1951: 237.

## 141 MAGHARAT FAKHR AD-DIN

203.325 [2]

**Cave fortress** located in cliff face overlooking Wadi Jazzin and consisting of principal passage, about 30 m long, continuing into narrow galleries.

Abdul-Nour and Salamé-Sarkis 1991: 181, no. 10, fig. 1; Guide Bleu 1932: 412.

## 142 MAHRUQAT, Khirbat al-

2058.2000 [6]

**Sugar production site** with twelfth- to fourteenth-century occupation.

Mabry and Palumbo 1988a: 426 (no. 41); 1988b: 278 (no. 41), 296.

## 143 MAIRUN

1914.2653 [4]

Med. Ar. *Mayrūn*; Hebr. *Meiron, Meron, Kefar Meron*

Former Jewish village, comprising remains of third- to fourth-century synagogue and tombs (visited by Jewish pilgrims in thirteenth century), reoccupied between 750 and 1399; **village houses** and **limekiln** (diam. 4–4.7 m) revealed by excavation.

Abel 1967: II, 385; Conder and Kitchener 1881: I, 208; Israel 1964: 1369; Meyers and Barag 1977; Meyers and Hanson 1976; Palestine 1948: 17.

## 144 MAJDAL YABA

1464.1650 [8]

*Majdal Sadiq*; Cr. *Mirabel, Mirabellum*; Hebr. *H. Migdal Afeq*
(figs. 2b and 35; pls. LXIV–LXV)

Complex **castle**, consisting of an early twelfth-century **tower** (1) (13.9 m N–S by 13.0 m E–W, walls 3 m thick), buttressed at SW and NW corners, with door leading into barrel-vaulted basement on E and stair to first floor on W. This stood on W side of a rectangular enclosure (46 m E–W by > 45 m N–S), with barrel- and groin-vaulted ranges on S (2–3), another range on E, and possibly a gate on N. Enclosing this on W, an outer wall with a *talus* extends 65.5 m S from **vaulted building** (5) (14.6 m N–S by > 25 m E–W, walls 2.7 m thick) to SW corner tower (7) (about 8 m square), with rectangular tower (6) (6.5 m wide, projecting 3.1–3.6 m) midway between them. The castle existed by 1152, when it was held against Baldwin III by Manasses of Hierges, husband of Helvis of Ramla (William of Tyre, XVII, 14); between c.1162 and 1171 it became the centre of an independent lordship; it fell to al-'Ādil in July 1187 (*de Expugnatione* (*RS*, LXIV, 229–30)), but was probably not destroyed (*pace Itin. Ric.*, IV, 23), as it is recorded in Ayyubid hands in 1191–2 (*Itin. Ric.*, V, 12; Bahā' al-Dīn (*PPTS*, XIII, 337–8)); abandoned in thirteenth century, and rebuilt in eighteenth to nineteenth centuries.

PAM: Report by J. Ory (1927).

Abel 1927b; Bagatti 1979: 126–9, figs. 52–4, pl. 48; Benvenisti 1970: 194–6, photos; Beyer 1951: 169–72; Chaver 1986, 141–2, photo; Clermont-Ganneau 1896: II, 340–1, fig.; Conder and Kitchener 1881: II, 261, 360–1; Ellenblum 1992: 183; Guérin 1874: II, 132–3; Hoade 1978: 600, 610; Israel 1964: 1433; Johns 1937: 34; Kennedy 1994: 38, pls. 10–11; Khalidi 1992: 396–7; Kochavi and Beit-Arieh 1994: 69–70, 47* (no. 136), figs.; Langé 1965: 94, 184, fig. 43; Palestine 1929: 203; 1948: 91; Pringle 1989: 18–19; 1993: II; 1994b: 340, 342, table, fig. 4b; forthcoming (b); Rey 1883: 412–13; Robinson 1856: 140.

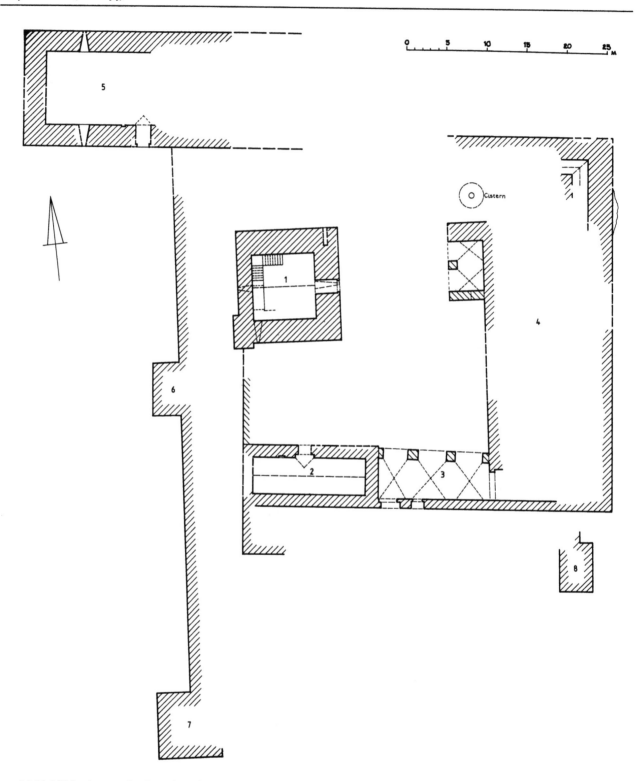

35   Majdal Yaba (**no. 144**): plan of castle (drawn by M. Pease, BSAJ Survey 1988).

LXV   Majdal Yaba (**no. 144**): S side of central courtyard.

LXVI   Kh. Manawat (**no. 145**): sugar factory.

LXIV   Majdal Yaba (**no. 144**): door to tower, with reused Byzantine lintel inscribed: ΜΑΡΤΥΡΙΟΝ ΤΟΥ ΑΓΙΟΥ ΚΗΡΥΚΟΥ (Martyrium of the Holy Kerykos/Cyriacus).

# 145 MANAWAT, Khirbat

1644.2716 [3]

*Kh. Baubriya; Cr. Manueth; Hebr. H. Manot*
(pls. LXVI–LXVII)

LXVII   Kh. Manawat (**no. 145**): rock-cut olive-press.

**Sugar factory**, comprising **aqueduct** and **mill**, adjoining long **building** with ground floor of four groin-vaulted bays, entrance in end wall and stair to vanished first floor in wall to left. **Olive-press** of screw type (pl. LXVII) and **pressing floors** cut in rock close by. **Courtyard building**, incorporating a **tower** (8.9 by >8 m, walls 1.9–2.6 m thick), stood on higher ground to

SE, surrounded by cultivation terraces. Village and sugar factory held in 1168 by Geoffrey le Tor (*RRH*, no. 468); given to Hospital in 1217 (*RRH*, no. 892; cf. no. 1027).

Barag 1979: 203 (no. 4); Benvenisti 1970: 19, 229–30, 259, 276, 333, photo; 1982: 135, fig. 2; Beyer 1945: 197–8, 203, 205, 207–8; Conder and Kitchener 1881: I, 173; Deschamps 1939a: 120; Ellenblum 1992: 183; Frankel 1988: 257–8, 260, fig. 1; Guérin 1880: II, 37–8; Hubatsch 1966: 197, pl. 25; Israel 1964: 1353; Johns 1937: 33; Langé 1965: 92, 184, fig. 43; Palestine 1929: 84; 1948: 2–3; Pringle 1986b: 54.

# 146 MANHATA, Khirbat al-

### 1721.2715 [3]

*Tharthilla* (formerly *Kh. Tharfila*); Cr. *Tarphile, Trefile, Tertille*
(pl. LXVIII)

**Courtyard building, tower** and **stone quarry** for Montfort Castle (**no. 156**).
PAM: Report by N. Makhouly (13 May 1946).

Dean 1927: 28; Frankel 1988: 263, 269–70, fig. 1; Israel 1964: 1355; Palestine 1929: 135; 1948: 4; Peled and Friedman 1987.

# 147 MARUS, Kh

### 1998.2707 [4]

Hebr. *Merot, Marish*

Excavation has revealed remains of fifth-century synagogue building converted into **village houses** in eleventh to fourteenth centuries, with **clay ovens** (*tawabayn*) and external stairs added.
Ilan and Damati 1984; 1985; 1986; 1987a; 1987b; Israel 1964: 1366; Palestine 1929; 1948: 13.

LXVIII   Kh. al-Manhata (**no. 146**): rock-cut base of tower remaining in quarry.

# 148 MA'SHUQA, Tall al-

### 1715.2966 [3]

*Nabi Ma'shuq*; Cr. *la Massoque*

Frankish **masonry** found in reuse, including one **stone incised with a cross of Lorraine**; identified as remains of **castle** built by Baldwin I on outskirts of Tyre in 1107/8 (Ibn al-Qalānisī (trans. Gibb, 82); cf. *RRH*, no. 1286).
Dussaud 1927: 20, 30, 33; Guide Bleu 1932: 416–17; le Lasseur 1922: 4, 12, fig. 6*bis*.

# 149 MASLAKHIT, Khirbat

### 1825.2481 [4]

Cr. *Miscalim*; Hebr. *H. Mislah*

Remains of **tower**, date uncertain.
Frankel 1988: 255, 265; Israel 1964: 1390; Palestine 1948: 36; Pringle 1994b.

# 150 al-MAZRA'A

### 1596.2654 [3]

Med. Ar. *al-Mazra'ah*

Remains of **fortified building** seen by earlier writers identified today with **wall** (about 50 m long) on W side of village centre.
Information: R. Frankel.

Barag 1979: 205 (no. 25); Conder and Kitchener 1881: I, 147; Ellenblum 1992: 183; Frankel 1988: 265; Guérin 1880: II; Hubatsch 1966: 197, pl. 24; Israel 1964: 1356; Palestine 1929: 135; 1948: 5.

# 151 MAZRA'A, Khirbat al-

### 143.222 [5]

Cr. *le Meseraa, casale Rogerii de Chasteillon* (1207); *Casal de Châtillon* (1255); Hebr. *H. Tafat*

Ruins of square vaulted **tower** (presumed now destroyed). Village took its name from former owners, Walter and Roger of Châtillon, and was sold to the Hospital by John Laleman, lord of Caesarea, in April 1255 (*RRH*, no. 1233; cf. no. 818).

C.R. Conder, in Palestine Exploration Fund 1881: 275; Conder and Kitchener 1881: II, 4, 33; Israel 1964: 1385; Palestine 1929: 206; 1948: 31; Pringle 1994b.

# 152 MI'ILIYA

## 1746.2699 [3]

Cr. *Mhalia, Castrum Regis, Chastiau dou Rei, Castellum Novum, Castellum Novum Regis*; Hebr. *Ma'alot*
(fig. 36; pls. LXIX–LXX)

Hilltop **castle** (39.2 m square, walls about 3 m thick) with a projecting rectangular tower at each corner (though SE one now destroyed); towers have splayed lintelled arrow-slits; entrance probably in centre of S wall; traces of internal E range (13 m wide), and possibly of others on N and W, about a central courtyard. Polygonal outer enceinte with sloping face, partly built, partly rock-cut, survives lower down hill, enclosing remains of church and **houses**. Royal castle first mentioned in 1160 (*RRH*, no. 341); perhaps rebuilt by 1179 when it is described as *Castellum Novum* (*RRH*, no. 587; cf. nos. 614, 625, 674); passed to Teutonic Order in 1220 (*RRH*, no. 934; cf. nos. 510, 1120); fell to Baybars 1268/71.

LXIX  Mi'iliya (**no. 152**): castle, NW tower.

LXX  Mi'iliya (**no. 152**): castle, NE tower, S side, showing simple lintelled embrasure.

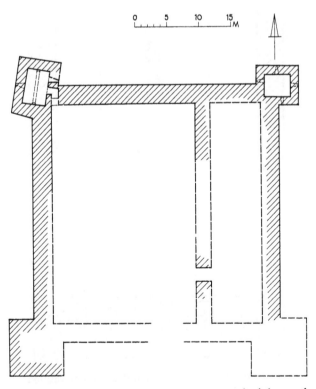

36  Mi'iliya (**no. 152**): plan of the inner ward of the castle (drawn by M. Pease, BSAJ Survey 1989).

Bagatti 1971a: 212–15, figs. 167–8; Benvenisti 1970: 196–8, 281–2, photo.; Beyer 1945: 193–5, 199, 203; Conder and Kitchener 1881: I, 149, 152, 155, 190–1; Deschamps 1939a: 121; Ellenblum 1992: 183; Frankel 1988: 256–7, 263, 265–7; Guérin 1880: II, 60–61; Hoade 1978: 785; Hubatsch 1966: 196–7, pl. 22; Israel 1964: 1358; Johns 1937: 27;

Kennedy 1994: 37–8, 129, 132, pl. 9; Kitchener 1877: 177; Langé 1965: 32, 42, 108, 116, 181, fig. 43; Masterman 1919: 73; Palestine 1929: 200; 1948: 7; Pringle 1986b: 52, 76 n.3; 1991a: 90 (no. 10); 1993, II; 1995a: 74, 75–6; Rey 1883: 478–9.

*Churches*, II, nos. 142–3.

## 153 MINAT AL-QALʿA

1141.1321 [7]

Cr. *Castellum Beroart*; Med. Ar. *Māhūz Azdūd*; Hebr. *H. Ashdod Yam*
(pl. LXXI)

**Early Muslim fort** overlooking sandy beach, with occupation archaeologically attested in tenth to eleventh centuries and possibly in later twelfth century; trapezoidal plan (about 35 m E–W by 55/57 m N–S), with solid rounded corner-turrets on W facing sea and rectangular ones on E; gates in centre of E and W walls, set between shallowly projecting rounded turrets; external wall-face reinforced with rectangular buttresses (1 m broad), spaced 3.5 m apart. Vaulted cells within. E gate was latterly blocked with masonry, and had stairs to wall-head added to either side internally. Frankish reoccupation is assumed on the basis of references in sources and mention in 1169 of Nicolas de Beroard, a knight of Hugh, lord of Ramla (*RRH*, no. 472); however, this has yet to be confirmed archaeologically.

Benvenisti 1970: 281, 288, 326–7; Beyer 1951: 256, 260, 263, 271; Clermont-Ganneau 1896: II, 191; Conder 1875: 157; Conder and Kitchener 1881: II, 426–7; Deschamps 1939a: 22; Elʿad 1982; Guérin 1868: II, 72–3; Johns 1937: 26; Kaplan 1975b; 1993; Kloner 1974; Langé 1965: 32, 108, 120, 181, fig. 43; Lawrence 1988: xxxvi; Le Strange 1890: 22–4, 498; Pipano 1988; Rey 1883: 403, 405; 1884: 344; Smail 1956: 231, 236.

LXXI   Minat al-Qalʿa (**no. 153**): towers flanking gateway on E.

## 154 al-MIRR

1422.1689 [8]

Cr. *Molendina desubter Mirabellum*

**Frankish repair of late Roman/Byzantine mill and dam.** Mills mentioned in 1158/9 (*RRH*, no. 330).

Benvenisti 1970: 252; Beyer 1951: 189–91, 254; Khalidi 1992: 250; Kochavi and Beit-Arieh 1994: 30, 26* (no. 31); Palestine 1948: 91; Pringle 1986b: 69, 78 n.41; Van de Velde 1861: I, 312.

## 155 MISQA, Khirbat al-

1601.1399 [8]

*Khan Misqa*; Cr. *Meschium*
(fig. 37)

**Vaulted building** (18.3 m E–W by 16.8 m N–S), poss-

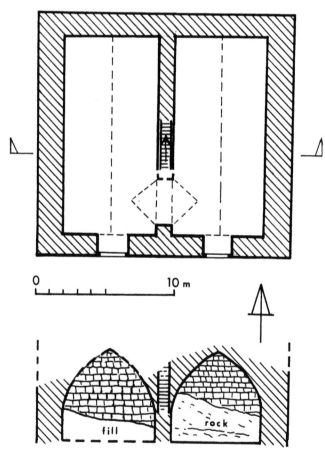

37   Kh. al-Misqa (**no. 155**): plan and section of vaulted building (after Bagatti 1947 and unpublished notes by C.N. Johns, 1943).

ibly basement of a **house** like those at al-Qubaiba (**no. 178**), comprising two parallel barrel-vaults (each 13.9 by 6.5/6.75 m internally), with opening and stair to upper floor in spine wall between them, and two separate entrances on S (pointed-arched, 1.65 m wide, with segmental rear-arches). **Cistern** (18.6 by 9 m) in front. Village granted to abbey of St Mary of Josaphat by Pisellus, viscount of Jerusalem, in 1114 (*RRH*, no. 134; *RRH Ad*, no. 76a).

PEF: C.N. Johns papers [*Kh. el Bureij*] (22 Sept. 1943).

Bagatti 1947; 192, 207, 234, fig. 42, pl. 39.97; Finkelstein and Magen 1993: 211, 41* (no. 265); Palestine 1948: 152.

# 156 MONTFORT CASTLE

## 1715.2722 [3]

*Qal'at al-Qurain, Qal'at al-Qarn*; Cr. *Montfort, Frans Castiaus, Starkenberg* (figs. 38–9; pls. LXXII–LXXV)

Spur **castle**, with D-shaped **donjon** (20 m wide, 24 m

LXXII   Montfort Castle, Qal'at al-Qurain (**no. 156**): from E. The quarry at Kh. al-Manhata (**no. 146**) lies on the ridge to the right.

long) preceded by rock-cut ditch on uphill side and two- to three-storey vaulted inner ward extending about 100 by about 20 m down the promontory and entered through gate-tower with box-machicolation over gate on N; inner ward enclosed by an outer enceinte downhill, with at least two projecting rounded towers and gates on N and E, the former also with a

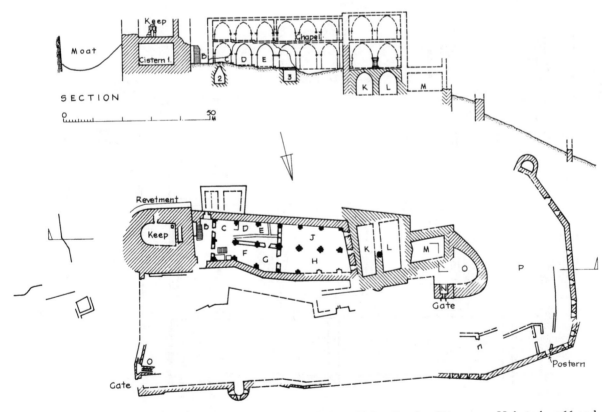

38   Montfort Castle (**no. 156**): plan and section of castle (drawn by P.E. Leach, after Dean 1927, Hubatsch 1966 and Frankel 1993).

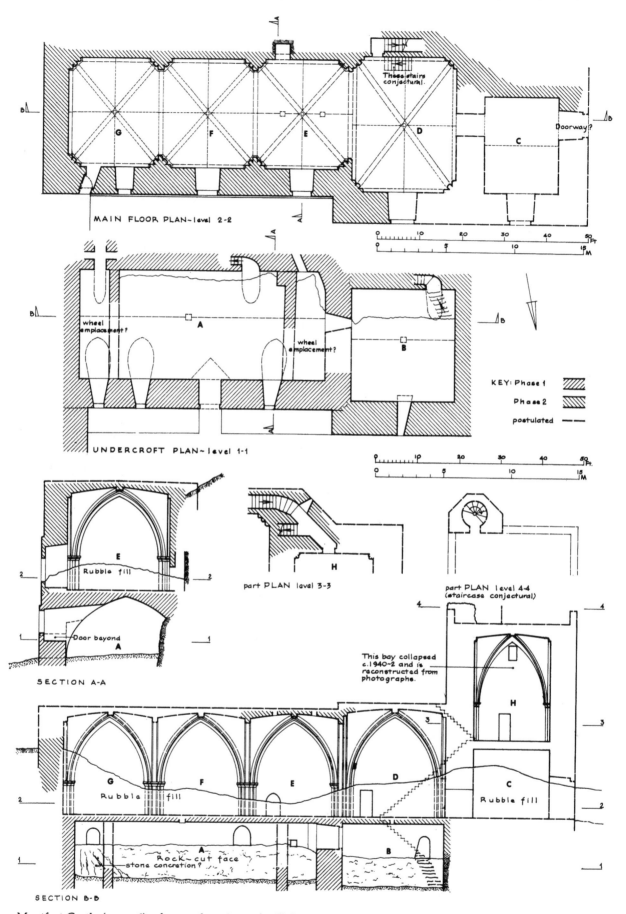

MAIN FLOOR PLAN~level 2-2

These stairs conjectural.

Doorway?

G  F  E  D  C

UNDERCROFT PLAN~level 1-1

wheel emplacement?

A

wheel emplacement?

B

KEY: Phase 1
Phase 2
postulated

SECTION A-A

E

Rubble fill

Door beyond

A

part PLAN level 3-3

H

part PLAN level 4-4
(staircase conjectural)

This bay collapsed
c.1940-2 and is
reconstructed from
photographs.

H

SECTION B-B

G  F  E  D  C

Rubble fill

Rubble fill

A

Rock~cut face
stone concretion?

B

39 Montfort Castle (**no. 156**): plans and sections of mill, later converted into first-floor hall (drawn by P.E. Leach, BSAJ Survey 1982).

LXXIII  Montfort Castle, Qal'at al-Qurain (**no. 156**): inner ward, looking E from keep.

LXXIV  Montfort Castle, Qal'at al-Qurain (**no. 156**): mill with dam across wadi bed below castle, converted into a hall-house in thirteenth century.

LXXV  Montfort Castle, Qal'at al-Qurain (**no. 156**): thirteenth-century hall-house, interior.

box-machicolation. Within the inner ward, a **wine-press** and **cisterns**; finds of **sculpture**, **painted window glass** and **painted masonry** made in 1927 excavations. Below castle on N, a **mill** with **dam** across valley bottom, converted into first-floor **hall** in thirteenth century, possibly for use as a **guest house**. Castle built by Teutonic Order between 1226/7 and *c*.1240; destroyed by Baybars in 1271.

Benvenisti 1970: 289–90, 331–7, 345, fig., photos.; 1977; Beyer 1945: 193, 203, 205; Boase 1971: 181, pls. 121–2; Conder and Kitchener 1881: I, 152, 154, 186–90, pls.; Dean 1927; Deschamps 1934: 81–2, 99; 1939a: 17, 120, 138–9, 225, 237, fig. 11; Eydoux 1982: 183–5; Forstreuter 1967: 41–9, pls. 1–3; Frankel 1988: 265–7; Frankel and Gatzov 1986; Guérin 1880: II, 52–8; Guide Bleu 1943: 504–5, fig.; Hoade 1978: 785–6; von Holst 1981: 39, 221–2, figs. 22–4, 182; Hubatsch 1966; Israel 1964: 1355; Jacoby (Z) 1982b: 124–5, figs. 109–10; Johns 1937: 34; Kennedy 1994: 38, 124, 129–31, fig. 17; Kitchener 1877: 176–7; 1878: 134–5; Langé 1965: 31–2, 42, 60, 108, 112–16, 185, figs. 43, 56–61; Lawrence 1988: xxx, 130n.; Makhouly 1941: 100–1; Makhouly and Johns 1946: 100–2; Mariti 1769: II, 161–2; Marshall 1992: 108–11, fig. 7, pls. 8–9; Masterman 1919: 73–5; 1928; Müller-Wiener 1966: 24, 28, 74–5, pls. 104–5; Palestine 1929: 215; 1948: 4; Pococke 1743: II, 54; Prawer 1972: 308–12, fig.; 1975: II, 180–3, 194, 200, 286n., 356, 470, 472, 475, 484n., 495, 501–2, 524, fig. 3, frontispiece, pl. VI; Pringle 1986b; 1994b; Rangé 1923; 1935a; 1935b; Renan 1864: I, 758–61; Rey 1866: 366; 1871: 143–51, pl. XV; 1883: 491; SSCLE 1987: 15, 22, 23; Thomson 1858: I, 457–9; 1876: 296–8; van de Velde 1861: 195–8.

*Churches*, II, no. 146.

# 157 MONTREAL

2037.9932 [10]

---

*Shaubak*; Cr. *Castrum Saboach, Scobach, Mons Regalis, Mont Real, Monreal*; Med. Ar. *al-Shawbak*
(pls. LXXVI–LXXVII)

LXXVI   Montreal, Shaubak (**no. 157**): castle, from NW.

**Castle** of roughly oval plan, following contours of hill, with at least two concentric enceintes with projecting rectangular towers, enclosing **houses**, church and chapel. Rock-cut passage to spring. Extra-mural suburb and **water-mills** (for sugar and corn) down valley to E. Castle founded by Baldwin I in 1115 (William of Tyre, XI, 26; Fulcher of Chartres, II, 55; Albert of Aachen, XII, 21); surrendered to al-Malik al-ʿĀdil in 1189. Significant Ayyubid and Mamluk additions.

Abel 1967: II, 479–80; Benvenisti 1970: 289, 320, 345; Brooker and Knauf 1988: 185–6; Brown 1988; 1989c; Brünnow and Domaszewski 1904: I, 113–19, figs. 96–104; Deschamps 1934: 15, 21–3, 28 n.3, 91, 93; 1939a: 42–3, 47–8, 54–5, 59, 69–70, 73, 75, pl. I; 1943: 96–7; DeVries 1991: 280, fig. 28; Duncan 1982: 30; Eydoux 1982: 134–6; Franciscan Fathers 1977: 152–3; Hoade 1966: 193–5, fig.; Irby and Mangles 1861: 115–16; Johns 1937: 34; Kammerer 1929: I, 350, 355, 364; II, pls. 131–2; Kennedy 1994: 22, 23–5, 45, 99, 102, 111, pl. 1; Lagrange 1897: 215–17; Langendorf and Zimmerman 1964: 126–43; de Luynes 1871: II, 83–222; Musil 1907: II.i, 2, 22–4, 36, 155, 294–6, 321–4, figs. 169–70; II.ii, 9–10, 221, 236–7; Ory 1975: 237; Pringle 1993: II, fig. 77; 1995a: 74–5; Rey 1871: 273–7; Vincent 1898: 428–9.

*Churches*, II, nos. 229–30.

## 158 NABLUS

1750.1815 [5]

Cr. *Naples, Neapolis*

**Town** without walls, little of whose medieval buildings survived the First World War and the earthquake of 1927. Among those recorded, apart from churches and a hospital (*Jamiʿ al-Masakin*), are the battered base of a large **tower**, presumed to be part of the **castle**, a **house** (*Habs ad-Damm*) with single-bay ground-floor *loggia* and two-light rounded-arched first-floor window, and a **market** (*Khan at-Tujar*, now destroyed).

Abel 1923; 1967: II, 397; Bagatti 1979: 53–5, fig. 16; Benvenisti 1970: 161–5, 276; Beyer 1940: 156–65, 170; Clermont-Ganneau 1896: I, 26; II, 310–22; Enlart 1925: II, 289; Guérin 1874: I, 394, 400; Johns 1937: 34–5; Palestine 1929; 1948: 66; Petrozzi 1973: 225–32, 250–3, 257–60, figs. 76, 84, 91; Pringle 1993: II, fig. 24; 1994b; 1995a: 73.

*Churches*, II, nos. 160–7.

LXXVII   Montreal, Shaubak (**no. 157**): Frankish and Ayyubid structures inside the castle.

## 159 QAIMUN, Tall

1604.2300 [5]

Cr. *Caimun, Caun Mons, Caymont, Mons Cain*; Med. Ar. *al-Qaymūn*; Hebr. *Tel Yoqneʿam*

Excavated remains of **houses**, **tower** (12.5 by 9 m, walls 2 m thick), **tower-keep** or *donjon* (22 by 18 m, walls 3 m thick), and church enclosed by crude **defensive wall**. A **castle** (*munitio*) is attributed to Baldwin I (*RHC Occ*, III, 543n.). Village in hands of abbey of Mount Tabor by 1103 (*RRH*, no. 39), becoming an independent lordship by 1152 (*RRH*, nos. 276, 614); held by Ayyubids 1187–92, passed to Templars by 1262 (*RRH*, no. 1318), and to Mamluks in 1283 (*RRH*, no. 1450).

Avissàr 1995; Ben-Tor 1993: 806; Ben-Tor *et al.* 1987; Ben-Tor, Portugali and Avissàr 1979; Ben-Tor and Rosenthal 1978a; 1978b; Beyer 1945: 240–1; Conder and Kitchener 1881: II, 69–70; Deschamps 1934: 28; Ellenblum 1992: 185; Israel 1964: 1383; Johns 1937: 26; Kennedy 1994: 22; Langé 1965: 181; Palestine 1929: 247; 1948: 29; Prawer 1975: I, 472, 660; II, 61, 78, 80, 99, 152, 524; Pringle 1993: II; 1995a: 78.

*Churches*, II, no. 179.

# 160 QALANSUWA

1485.1878 [5]

Cr. *Calanson*, *Calansue*, *Calanzon*, *Kalensue* (fig. 40; pl. LXXVIII)

Group of buildings around open space in village centre, including: **tower** (*a*) (12.05 m square, surviving

LXXVIII  Qalansuwa (**no. 160**): Crusader hall, doorways to basement and first floor.

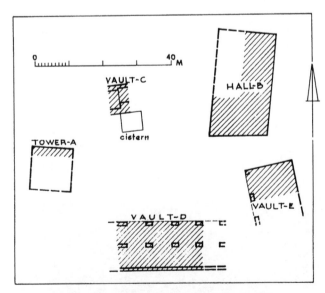

40  Qalansuwa (**no. 160**): plan of Crusader buildings surviving in centre of village (drawn by P.E. Leach, BSAJ Survey 1983).

12.3 m high) to W; first-floor **hall** (*b*) (*c*.16.5 m E–W by 28 m E/30 m W) to E, originally of eight (two by four) groin-vaulted bays (of which two survive as mosque), with principal door on S set in pointed-arched recess with stair to roof leading off from left-hand side of passage, built over similarly vaulted basement with lancet windows and at least two doors; **groin-vaulted ranges** (*d–e*) to S and SE, opening on to central space; and **barrel-vault** (*c*) and **masonry cistern** to N. The village (*castel*) was given to the Hospitallers by the knight Godfrey of Flujeac in 1128 (*RRH Ad*, no. 121a) and, except for 1187–91, remained theirs until taken by Baybars in 1265; however, the lord of Caesarea appears to have retained overlordship, and there is mention of a viscount and lord in 1166 (*RRH*, no. 426) and of Frankish settlers in 1177/87 (*RRH Ad*, no. 554b).

PAM: Reports by K.A.C. Creswell (*c*.1919) and R.W. Hamilton (21 Mar. 1935).

Benvenisti 1970: 15, 19, 173–4, 198, 267, 311, 345; Conder 1874: 15;
1875: 92–3; C.R. Conder, in Palestine Exploration Fund 1881: 277–8;
Conder and Kitchener 1881: II, 165, 199–201, figs.; Deschamps 1939a:
23; Ellenblum 1992: 183; Guérin 1874: II, 350–2; Hoade 1978: 610;
Israel 1964: 1412; Johns 1927: 25; Kennedy 1994: 33, 35, 58, 99; Langé
1965: 94, 180, fig. 43; Meistermann 1936: 469; Ory 1975: 199; Palestine
1929: 214; 1948: 62; Pringle 1986a: 41–58, figs. 10–14, pls. X–XXII; 1989:
17; 1993: II; 1994b; Rey 1883: 420.

# 161 QAL'AT ABU'L-HASAN

189.330 [2]

Cr. *Belhasem*
(fig. 41)

Very ruinous **castle** with two wards and rectangular
towers sited on rock spur (about 100 m N–S by about 30
m E–W) protected on three sides by gorge of the Nahr
al-Awali. Originally Muslim, it was taken by the Franks
in 1128 (William of Tyre, XIII, 25) and held until 1187/8
('Imād al-Dīn (trans. Massé, 76, 99)).

Deschamps 1939a: 221–3, fig. 22, pls. LXXXIII–LXXXVI; 1943: 100, 104;
Guide Bleu 1932: 410; 1975: 224; Le Strange 1890: 475; Prawer 1975: I,
320; Rey 1883: 511.

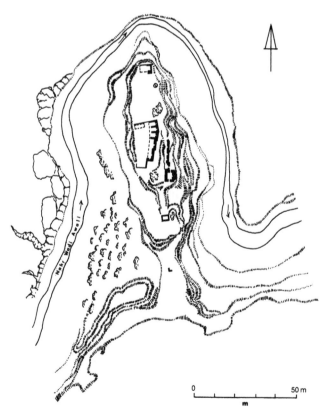

41   Qal'at Abu'l-Hasan (**no. 161**): plan of castle (after P.
Coupel, in Deschamps 1939a: fig. 22).

# 162 QAL'AT AD-DAMM

1841.1361 [8]

*Maldoim, Adumim, Castrum Dumi, Cisterna Rubea, Turris
Rubea, Rouge Cisterne*; Hebr. *Ma'ale Adumim*
(figs. 2d and 42; pl. LXXIX)

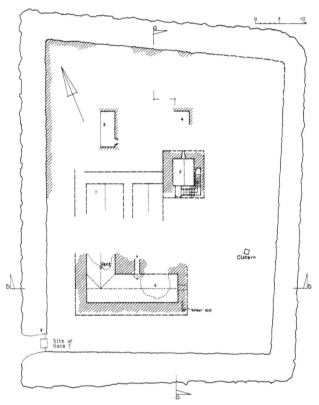

42   Qal'at ad-Damm (**no. 162**): plan of castle (drawn by
M. Pease, BSAJ Survey 1988).

LXXIX   Qal'at ad-Damm (**no. 162**): Templar castle, N
corner showing rock-cut ditch and inner revetment.

Quadrangular **castle** (62 m N/59 m S by 47 m W/50 m E) enclosed by rock-cut ditch (5.6–6.9 m wide), comprising central **tower** (9.3 by 8.5 m) with barrel-vaulted basement and mural stair, and to SW an L-shaped barrelvault with flagged first floor and remains of other vaults. Built by Templars before 1169/72 (Theodoric, XXVIII) to protect Jerusalem–Jericho road, probably on site of late Roman fort serving the same purpose.

Bagatti 1979: 76–9, fig. 25, pls. 23–4; Barber 1994a: 88–9, pl. 1; Benvenisti 1970: 281–2, 324–5, 327, pls.; Conder and Kitchener 1881: III, 172, 207–9, fig.; Ellenblum 1992: 182; Faber 1480–3: II, 68–9; de Forbin 1819: 93; Guide Bleu 1932: 600; Hoade 1946: 356; 1978: 474; Johns 1937: 33; Langé 1965: 94, 184, fig. 43; Mariti 1769: III, 95–8; Palestine 1929: 54; 1948: 190; Pringle 1989: 17; 1993: II; 1994b: 337, table, fig. 4d; 1994c: 153–62, figs. 16.2–10; Rey 1883: 387–8; de Sandoli 1974: 334–5; Sion 1993: 51, fig. 58.

*Churches*, II, no. 251.

# 163 QAL'AT AD-DUBBA

1986.2893 [4]

*Qal'at Dubal*

**Castle** on spur (overall 80 m N–S by 35 m E–W), protected by an oval ditch and incorporating a **tower** (10.3 by 8.5 m) with a bent entrance on W and other structures around a central courtyard; phasing uncertain owing to later (? seventeenth-century) rebuilding.

Conder and Kitchener 1881: I, 122–3, fig.; Enlart 1925: II, 266–7;

Guérin 1880: II, 382; Guide Bleu 1932: 432; Johns 1937: 35; Kitchener 1877: 168; Pringle 1993: II; 1994b; Tibble 1989: 13–14, 20.

# 164 QAL'AT HUNIN

2011.2917 [4]

Cr. *Castellum Novum*, *Chastel Neuf*; Hebr. *H. Mezudat Hunin*
(fig. 43; pl. LXXX)

Rectangular **castle** (about 85 m E–W by about 65/67 m N–S), defended by rock-cut ditch on N, W and S, and by berm and precipice on E; rectangular turret (6.5 m wide, projecting 1.5 m) on E; remains of extensive outer ward on S; little Frankish masonry work left, what remains being mostly Ottoman. Castle belonged to prince of Galilee from 1105/7 and to lord of Toron (Tibnin) from 1115; demolished by Nūr al-Dīn in 1167, rebuilt by Humphrey II of Toron in 1178, lost to Saladin in 1187, destroyed by al-Mu'aẓẓam 'Īsā in 1212, in Frankish hands from 1240, taken and refortified by Baybars in 1266, and extensively rebuilt in the eighteenth century.

Benvenisti 1970: 281–2, 300–3, photo; Conder and Kitchener 1881: I, 87, 123, fig., pl.; Deschamps 1934: 29; 1939a: 14, 17, 119, 126, 128, 130, 134, 146–59, 178, 236, pl. XXXIVa–c; Guide Bleu 1932: 528; Hoade 1978: 771; Israel 1964: 1362; Johns 1937: 27; Kennedy 1994: 42–3; Khalidi 1992: 454–5; Kitchener 1877: 169–70; 1878: 137; Langé 1965: 29, 92, 94, 96–7, 181, figs. 43, 46–8; Lawrence 1988: 3n., 65, 66, 128, 135, figs. 46–46a; Ory 1975: 200; Palestine 1929: 214; 1948: 9; Pringle 1991a: 89 (no. 5); Rey 1993: 478; Robinson 1856: 370–1; Tibble 1989: 13–23, 63, 91, 96–8.

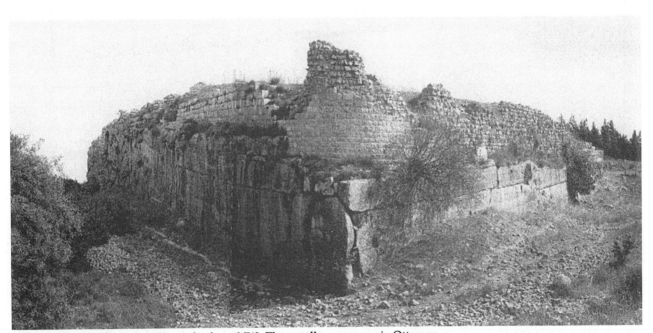

LXXX  Qal'at Hunin (**no. 164**): castle, from NW. The smaller masonry is Ottoman.

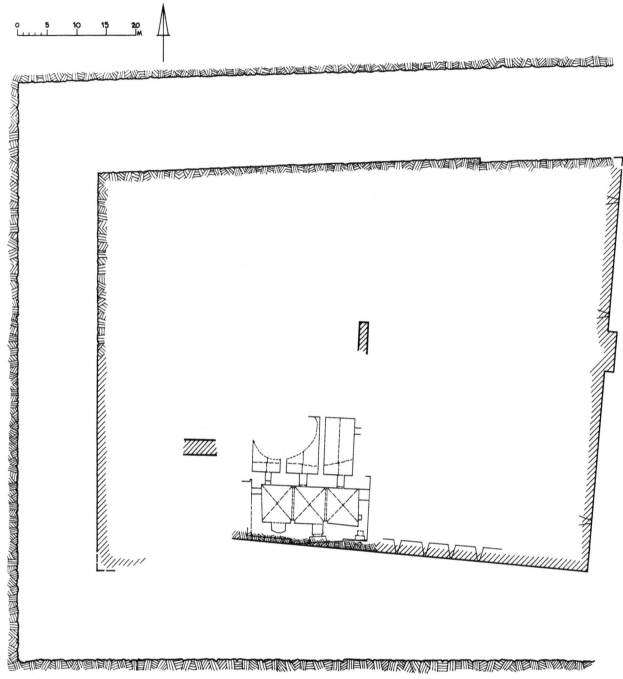

43  Qal'at Hunin (**no. 164**): plan of castle (drawn by M. Pease, BSAJ Survey 1989).

# 165 QAL'AT JIDDIN

1710.2665 [3]

*Kh. Jiddin; Cr. Iudyn, Iudin; Hebr. Mezudat Gadin, Yehi'am*
(fig. 44; pls. LXXXI–LXXXIV)

Remains of **castle**, comprising two **towers** on rocky spur surrounded by high enclosure wall containing *chemins de ronde* leading to embrasures. E tower (*A*) appears earlier (about 15.5 m N–S by about 16 m E–W, walls 3.3–5.4 m thick, surviving 12.5 m high at SW angle): door on W leads into barrel-vaulted basement, with passage to latrine closet (with chute) and stair opening to right; barrel-vaulted first-floor hall or solar

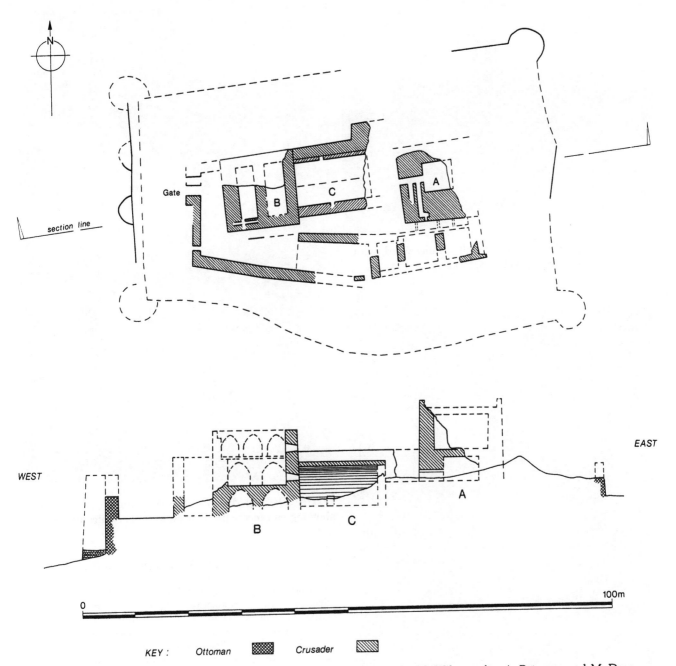

44 Qal'at Jiddin (**no. 165**): plan and section of Crusader castle (drawn by M. Wilson, after A. Petersen and M. Dow, BSAJ Survey 1992).

(about 10 by 7.75/8.5 m), with latrine closet in S wall; stair continues in W wall past barrel-vaulted chamber in S wall to roof. W tower (*B*) or residence (16.4 m square, walls 2.3 m thick) had three storeys, the lower two comprising parallel barrel-vaults, the upper possibly three by three bays of groin-vaults; S wall contains mural stairs, door on first floor with window above opening on to external timber balcony or *hourd*; E wall has embrasures at upper two levels, and chute in NE corner. Space within enclosure subsequently filled with other vaults. Possible remains of outer enceinte with rounded towers flanking gate on W. Castle built by Teutonic Order after 1220, and destroyed by Baybars 1268/71 (Burchard of Mount Sion, IV, 1 (ed. Laurent, 34)); partially rebuilt and again destroyed in eighteenth century.

LXXXI  Qalʿat Jiddin (**no. 165**): N wall of inner ward, with a row of narrow arrow-slits half-way up it.

LXXXIII  Qalʿat Jiddin (**no. 165**): W tower (*B*), S elevation showing entrance with door on to timber balcony above it.

PEF: C.N. Johns, Field Notebook 1940–1 (26 Apr. 1941, 21 May 1941).

Benvenisti 1970: 337; Conder and Kitchener 1881: I, 154, 185; Deschamps 1939a: 121; Frankel 1988: 254, fig. 1; Guérin 1880: II, 24–6; Harper 1992: 79; Hoade 1978: 785; von Holst 1981: 39, figs. 25–6; Hubatsch 1966: 197, pl. 23; Johns 1937: 32; Kennedy 1994: 124, 131, pl. 45; Khalidi 1992: 18–19; Kitchener 1877: 178; 1878: 137; Langé 1965: 32, 42, 108, 116, 184, figs. 43, 62–5; Makhouly 1941: 101–2; Makhouly and Johns 1946: 100, 102–3; Mariti 1769: II, 156–7; Masterman 1919: 72–3; Palestine 1929: 214; 1948: 8; Pringle 1994b; Pringle, Petersen, Dow and Singer 1994; Singer 1991; Thomson 1876: 304–6.

*Churches*, II, no. 180.

LXXXII  Qalʿat Jiddin (**no. 165**): latrine closet in E tower (*A*).

# 166 QALʿAT RAHIB

1800.2755 [4]

Qilaʿ ar-Rahib; Cr. *Raheb*; Hebr. *Mezad Rahav*

by about 22 m, walls 4.7 m thick), built of large roughly rectangular blocks with irregular pinnings and finely cut rusticated quoins with drafted margins; vault built of largish roughly cut voussoirs. Near by, remains of other *vaults* and dispersed blocks of **masonry**, including one inscribed [COLO]NIA.

PAM: Report by R.W. Hamilton (17 May 1940).

Abel 1967: II, 393; Bagatti 1979: 141; Beyer 1942: 180; Clermont-Ganneau 1885: 168; 1896: I, 479–80; Conder and Kitchener 1881: III, 17; Ellenblum 1992: 176–7, 183; Finkelstein and Magen 1993: 221, 44* (no. 291); Israel 1964: 1460; Khalidi 1992: 309–10; Palestine 1929: 215; 1948: 155; de Sandoli 1974: 240, no. 323; Tobler 1853; II, 721–6; Vincent and Abel 1932: 389.

## 168 QAQUN

### 1497.1962 [5]

Cr. *Caco, Cacho*; Hebr. *Yikon*
(fig. 45; pl. LXXXV)

Two-storey **tower** (17.65 m N–S by 14.53 m E–W, walls 2.8 m thick, surviving 8.5 m high), with basement consisting of parallel barrel-vaults with intersections carried on a central column; first floor presumed groin-vaulted, with casemated arrow-slits with sloping fish-tail bases; ceramic pipe from roof to basement inside wall; door and stair presumed to have been in missing W wall and SW corner. Vaulted Byzantine **cistern** reused near by. Castle mentioned in 1123 (Fulcher of Chartres, III, 18, 1; William of Tyre, XII, 21) and apparently still held by lord of Caesarea in 1253 (*RRH*, no. 1210); taken and reforti-

LXXXIV  Qal'at Jiddin (**no. 165**): W tower (*B*), S door and stair inside S wall.

Small square building of large drafted stones, possibly a **tower**, associated with **olive-press** and **vaults**. One of the *casalia* dependent on *Chastiau de Roi* (Mi'iliya), sold to the Teutonic Order in May 1220 (Strehlke, no. 53; *RRH*, no. 934).

Abel 1967: II, 433; Benvenisti 1970: 276; Beyer 1945: 195, 211; Conder and Kitchener 1881: I, 250; Frankel 1988: 264, fig. 1; Israel 1964: 1364; Palestine 1948: 11.

## 167 QALUNIYA

### 1656.1333 [8]

Cr. *Qalonie, Saltus Muratus*; Hebr. *Mevasseret Ziyyon/ Yerushalayim, Moza*

**Barrel-vaulted structure**, probably a **cistern** (about 12

LXXXV  Qaqun (**no. 168**): tower from NE, with fish-tail base arrow-slit in N wall.

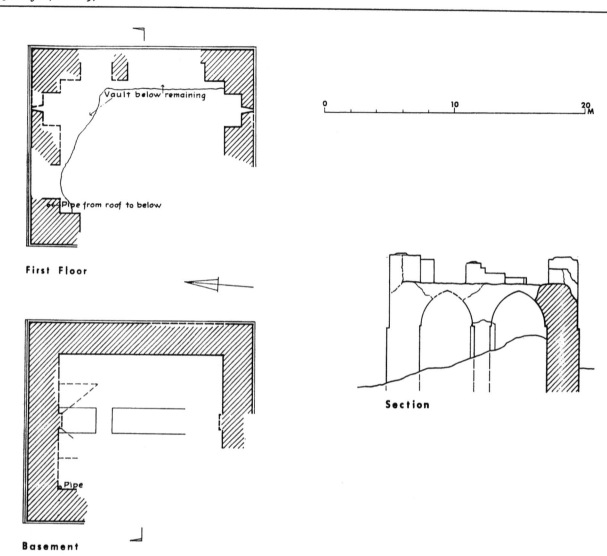

First Floor

Vault below remaining

Pipe from roof to below

Section

Basement

Pipe

45   Qaqun (**no. 168**): plans and section of tower (drawn by P.E. Leach, BSAJ Survey 1983).

fied by Baybars 1265 (Ibn al-Furāt c.1375: II, 101), and unsuccessfully attacked by King Hugh of Cyprus and Prince Edward of England in November 1271 (*Gestes des Chiprois* (ed. Raynaud, 200–1); *Eracles* (*RHC Occ*, II, 461)).

PAM: Report (18 Aug. 1922).

Abel 1940; Bagatti 1979: 185; Benvenisti 1970: 15, 19, 173–4, 198–9, 276, 311, 313; Conder and Kitchener 1881: II, 152–3, 195; Dar and Mintzker 1987: 192–210, figs. 1–10; Deschamps 1939a: 23 n.5; Ellenblum 1992: 189; Guérin 1874: II, 346–8; Israel 1964: 1410; Johns 1937: 25; Kennedy 1994: 35–7, 99, pl. 8; Khalidi 1992: 559–60; Langé 1965: 94, 180, fig. 43; Meistermann 1936: 470; Palestine 1929: 216; 1948: 56; Pringle 1986a: 58–71, figs. 15–18, pls. XXIII–XXX; 1989: 16; 1994b; Rey 1883: 419.

*Churches*, II, no. 182.

# 169 QARATIYA

1239.1169 [7]

Cr. *la Galatie, Galatia, Galatidis*; Med. Ar. *Qaratayyā*; Hebr. *Qeratya*

Remains of **tower** (*Qal'at al-Fanish*) of uncertain date on site of **castle** which fell to Saladin in 1187 and was destroyed in September 1191 ('Imād al-Dīn (trans. Massé, 99); *Itin. Ric.*, IV, 23; *Gesta Henrici II* (*RS*, XLIX.ii, 24)).

Bagatti 1983: 139; Conder 1875: 158; Conder and Kitchener 1881: III, 278; Guérin 1868: II, 124; Israel 1964: 1448; Khalidi 1992: 118–19; Kitchener 1917: 67; Palestine 1929; 1948: 135; Prawer 1975: I, 668; II, 83, 95; Pringle 1994b; Robinson 1841: II, 370.

# 170 QARAWAT BANI HASSAN

## 1595.1705 [5]

(fig. 2e)

**Tower** (*Burj al-Yaqur*) (16.0 by 11.3 m, 11.6 m high, walls 2.2 m thick) of two storeys; basement barrel-vaulted, with stair to first floor leading off from left-hand side of entrance in one of the shorter walls. Other medieval buildings, including **vaulted cistern** and **barrel-vault** containing **olive-press** (*Badd Bunduq*) possibly Mamluk, like the mosque (*Jami' al-'Umari*).

PAM: Report (7 Jan. 1941).

Dar 1986: I, 236, fig. 129, photo. 114; Palestine 1948; 87; Pringle 1994b: table, fig. 4e.

# 171 QARHATA, Khirbat

## 1778.2698 [3]

Hebr. *Mezad Qarha*

Remains of **tower** of drafted masonry.

Benvenisti 1970: 276; Israel 1964: 1358; Palestine 1929: 145; 1948: 7; Pringle 1994b.

# 172 QASILA, Tall

## 1308.1677 [7]

*al-Khirba*; Hebr. *Tel Qasile*

**Sugar factory**, built over remains of ninth- to eleventh-century khan (28 m square).

Ayalon, Gilboa and Harpazi 1989; Ayalon, Gilboa and Shacham 1987; Israel 1964: 1426; Mazar 1986a; 1986b: 9–10, 15, fig. 5; 1989; 1993: 1212; Palestine 1948: 79.

# 173 QASR, Khirbat al-

## 1433.1052 [8]

Hebr. *H. Qazra.*

**Castle** with sloping *talus*.

Conder and Kitchener 1881: III, 283; Israel 1964: 1475; Palestine 1929: 147; 1948: 184.

# 174 QASR AL-'ATRA

## 2090.2677 [4]

Cr. *le Chastelez, Vadum Iacob*; Hebr. *Mezad 'Ateret* (pl. LXXXVI)

**Castle of enceinte** (about 120 m N–S by 29/34 m E–W), on part-natural, part-artificial mound on W bank of River Jordan; irregular in plan, but with roughly rectangular S end defined by rock-cut ditch, and oval outline on N, fronted by shallow ditch and counterscarp bank. **Excavations** (by R. Ellenblum and A. Boas) since 1993 have revealed the trace of the enceinte wall, built in straight sections with lower facing of drafted ashlar blocks largely intact and upper facing robbed. Main gate on S was two-leaved with slots for draw-bar and portcullis; apparently approached from part-natural horn-work to S. Other postern gates on E, W and N, apparently intended to be reached by timber stairs or bridges. No trace of any projecting towers. Castle built between Oct. 1178 and Apr. 1179 and granted to Templars; destroyed methodically by Saladin in Aug. 1179 (William of Tyre, XXI, 25 (26); 29 (30); Ernoul (ed. de Mas Latrie, 52–4); Abū Shāmā (*RHC Or*, IV, 203–9); Ibn al-Athīr (*RHC Or*, I, 635–40); al-Maqrīzī c.1400a: 58–61).

Benvenisti 1970: 281, 303–5; Conder and Kitchener 1881: I, 206; 250–1; Deschamps 1934: 28, 54–5, 83, 85; 1939a: 14, 120, 129–30, 132–3, 240; 1943: 102–3; Eydoux 1982: 163–4, 251; Guérin 1880: I, 341; Israel 1964: 1370; Johns 1937: 27; Kennedy 1994: 57, 106, 110, 113, 117, 140, 141; Kitchener 1877: 167; Kochavi 1972: 269 (no. 75); Langé 1965: 92, 100, 181; Lawrence 1988: 65, 134, 135; Palestine 1929: 217; 1948: 19; Pococke 1743: II, 73; Prawer 1975: I, 555; Roman 1993: 40–1; *The Times*, 2 Sept. 1993.

LXXXVI   Qasr al-'Atra, *le Chastelez* (**no. 174**): curtain wall on NW side of mound, as excavated in 1994.

# 175 QASR AL-MANTARA

186.325 [2]

Cr. *Franche Garde* (?)

**Cisterns**, apparently representing all that remains of a
**castle** overlooking Sidon.
Guide Bleu 1932: 409.

# 176 QASR ASH-SHAIKH RABA

1860.1995 [6]

*Raba* (*Ard al-Qasr*)

**Tower** (8.85 m square), incorporating rusticated masonry with drafted margins, seen by SWP and inferred
to be Crusader; walls completely robbed by 1981.
Traces of a second smaller **tower** NW of village.
Abel 1967: II, 425; Bagatti 1979: 72–3; Conder and Kitchener 1881: II,
243–4; Palestine 1929: 220; 1948: 74; Pringle 1993: II (Raba, *q.v.*).

# 177 QIRYAT FROSTIG

1592.2462 [3]

Round plastered **vaulted cistern** (diam. 3 m) with
square structure (3 by 3 m) on top and remains of **pool**
(6 m square) to N. Another **open cistern** (diam. 6.4 m,
5.5 m deep) to NE.
Ronen and Olami 1983: x, 7 (sites 10–11).

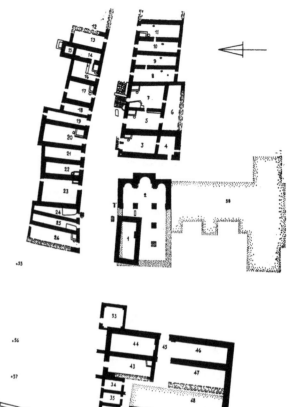

# 178 al-QUBAIBA

1629.1386 [8]

Cr. *Parva Mahomaria, Mahomeriola*
(fig. 46; pls. LXXXVII–LXXXVIII)

**New town** built by the canons of the Holy Sepulchre
before 1164 (Bresc-Bautier, no. 135; *RRH*, no. 400),
comprising a street flanked by **houses**, with vaulted
undercrofts containing agricultural store-rooms and
workshops (e.g. **pressing floors** for wine and oil, **rotary
and screw-type olive-press, bakery**) and living areas
on now-vanished upper floors, a church, a **pool** (*birka*),
and a **courtyard building** (48 by 68 m) enclosing a

46 al-Qubaiba, *Parva Mahumeria* (**no. 178**): plan of the
central area of the Frankish 'new town'. Key: (1)
post-Crusader building; (2) twelfth-century church; (3–33)
Crusader houses and workshops; (34–8) buildings
identified by Bagatti as pre-Crusader; (39–52) Crusader
*curia*, or administrative building, including the steward's
hall (42); (53) modern house; (58) modern Franciscan
convent building (after Bagatti 1947: pl. 42).

first-floor **hall-house** (9.2 by about 25 m internally),
identifiable as the steward's *curia*.

Abel 1926a; Bagatti 1947; Benvenisti 1970: 220, 224–7, 276, 345, fig.,
photos.; Beyer 1942: 179, 180, 198; Clermont-Ganneau 1896: I, 476–8,
figs.; Conder and Kitchener 1881: III, 130–1; Ellenblum 1992: 184;

LXXXVII   al-Qubaiba (**no. 178**): house 3, showing entrance to basement (left) and stair to upper floor (right).

LXXXVIII   al-Qubaiba (**no. 178**): wine press in house 3.

Finkelstein and Magen 1993: 217, 42* (no. 280); Guérin 1868: I, 348–61; 1874: I, 399; Johns 1937: 35; Langé 1965: 155, 185–6, fig. 76; Palestine 1929: 219; 1948: 153; Pringle 1983a: 172–3; 1985a: 163; 1993: II; Riley-Smith 1990: 40–1; de Sandoli 1966; Schick 1901a; 1901b; Smail 1973: 87; Tobler 1853: II, 538–54; Vincent 1931.

*Churches*, II, no. 184.

## 179 QU'DA, Khirbat al-

1701.2722 [3]

Hebr. *H. 'Aqudim*

Fortified **courtyard building** with two towers facing valley to S.

Frankel 1988: 270; Israel 1964: 1355.

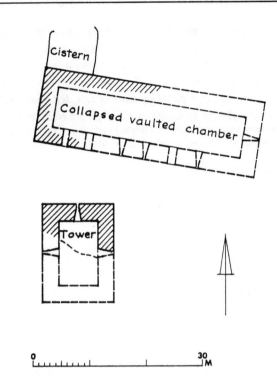

47   Qula (**no. 180**): plan of tower and vaulted building (drawn by P.E. Leach, BSAJ Survey 1983).

## 180 QULA

1459.1605 [8]

Cr. *Cola*
(fig. 47)

Barrel-vaulted base of **tower** (about 17 by 12.8 m, walls 3 m thick), with adjoining **barrel-vaulted structure** (11 by 38 m, walls 2 m thick). The Hospitallers acquired the village from Hugh of Flanders in 1181 (*RRH*, no. 611), and devoted it to the production of foodstuffs for the Jerusalem Hospital (Luttrell 1994: 67).

Abel 1927b: 391, fig. 1; Benvenisti 1970: 227–9, 276, fig.; Conder and Kitchener 1881: II, 297, 358; Deschamps 1939a: 22; Ellenblum 1992: 184; Guérin 1874: II, 390–1; Israel 1964: 1434; Khalidi 1992: 408–9; Kochavi and Beit-Arieh 1994: 112, 74* (no. 285), fig.; Langé 1965: 94, 182, fig. 43; Luttrell 1994: 67; Palestine 1929: 219; 1948: 92; Pringle 1986a: 21–2, fig. 7.

## 181 RAFIDIYA

1724.1811 [5]

Remains of large building complex of medieval date surviving in village. Including **wall** about 16 m long and

2 m thick, built of point-dressed limestone ashlars with masonry marks, apparently reused and showing signs of retouching with flat chisel; side of doorway at E end has angle-roll on outer arris of jambs, hollow chamfer on inner arris of door passage, and spring for rear arch.

Bagatti 1979: 58–9, pl. 17; Guérin 1874: II, 182; Kochavi 1972: 164 (no. 7); Palestine 1929: 221; 1948: 66; Petrozzi 1973: 266–7, fig. 95; Pringle 1993: II, pls. XCIX–C; de Sandoli 1974 (no. 369).

*Churches*, II, no. 185.

## 182 ar-RAM

### 1721.1402 [8]

Cr. *Aram, Rama, Ramatha, Ramathes*
(fig. 48; pls. LXXXIX–XCI)

**Tower** (14.3 by 12.7 m, walls 2.1–2.7 m thick) with barrel-vaulted basement and stair through vault to first floor, subsequently incorporated into a **courtyard building** (57 m E–W by 45 m N–S) with barrel-vaulted ranges set around a central courtyard and later vaulted extensions on W; **wine-press** in SE corner. Identified as the grange (*voltas nostras de Nova Villa*) of the **new town** founded by the canons of the Holy Sepulchre by 1160 (Bresc-Bautier, no. 126).

PAM: Reports by N. Makhouly (1926) and Anon. (following earthquake 1927).

Benvenisti 1970: 19, 233; Bouillon 1898: 291–4, photo.; Conder and Kitchener 1881: III, 13, 155; Ellenblum 1992: 184; Finkelstein and Magen 1993: 168–9, 33* (no. 188), colour pl.; Geikie 1887: II, 170–1; Guérin 1874: I, 200; Kennedy 1994: 33; Prawer 1980: 132–5; Pringle 1983a: 160–74, figs. 6–8, pls. XVIIIb–XXIIa; 1989: 19–21, figs.; 1994b: 337, 342, table; de Saulcy 1853: I, 111–12; Wilson 1880a: I, 214, 218.

*Churches*, II, no. 186.

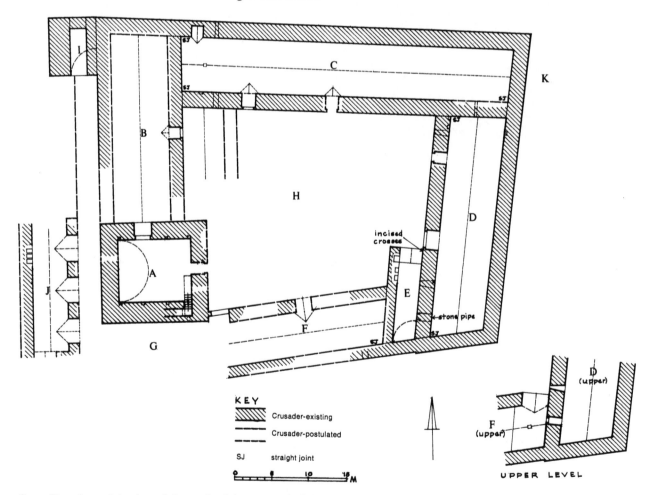

**KEY**

⬛ Crusader-existing

--- Crusader-postulated

SJ  straight joint

**UPPER LEVEL**

48  ar-Ram (**no. 182**): plan of the *curia* of the steward of the canons of the Holy Sepulchre (drawn by P.E. Leach, after BSAJ Survey 1981–2).

LXXXIX    ar-Ram (**no. 182**): courtyard building, view over courtyard from top of tower.

XC    ar-Ram (**no. 182**): tower, interior showing door and stair to first floor.

XCI    ar-Ram (**no. 182**): courtyard building, outlet from wine-pressing floor (*F*) into E vault (*D*).

# 183 RAMALLAH

### 168.145 [8]

Cr. *Ramalie* (?).

Remains of **building** (*al-Burj*), with arched doorway.

Bagatti 1979: 102; Palestine 1944: 1303; 1948: 110; Pringle 1994a: 50.

# 184 RANTIYA

### 1427.1612 [8]

Cr. *Rentie, Rantia, Rentia*; Hebr. *Nofekh*

**Vaulted building** (*al-Baubariya*) (20 m N–S by 10 m E–W, walls 2.3 m thick) with two entrances on E, two slits on E and W, and outer wall on W. Village tithes granted to the Hospital in 1166 (*RRH*, no. 423).

Benvenisti 1982: 144, figs. 14–15; Beyer 1951: 253, 254, 266, 268; Conder and Kitchener 1881: II, 253; Ellenblum 1992: 184; Guérin 1874: II, 391–2; Israel 1964: 1434; Kedar 1982: 117 n.18; Khalidi 1992: 252; Kochavi and Beit-Arieh 1994: 104, 69* (no. 258); Palestine 1948: 92; Prutz 1881: 167.

# 185 RAS AL-'AIN

### 1707.2925 [3]

Cr. *Rasalame, Derina*

Repair of Roman **reservoirs and aqueduct** supplying irrigation system and city of Tyre, described by William of Tyre (XIII, 3; cf. Burchard of Mount Sion (ed. Laurent, 24)) and still in use in the nineteenth century. Village of *Derina*, 'above the great spring from which the aqueduct proceeds', was granted to the Holy Sepulchre in 1125 (Bresc-Bautier, no. 28).

Abel 1967: I, 138, 428, 444, 446; Conder and Kitchener 1881: I, 69–71; Guide Bleu 1932: 432–3, fig.; 1975: 239; Prawer 1980: 146, 160, 179, 197.

# 186 RAS AL-QANTARA

### 177.318 [2]

*Sarepta*; Cr. *Sarphen, Sarepta*

Mound possibly representing site of **castle**.

Abel 1967: II, 449; Guide Bleu 1932: 420; Pringle 1993: II (Sarepta).

*Churches*, II, no. 224.

# 187 RAS KIKIS

### 1761.1793 [5]

On N slope of *Mount Garizim*, near *Tall ar-Ras*; Cr. *Mons Garizim*

Fragmentary remains of **castle**, including **stone carved with fleur-de-lys** (now preserved at W.F. Albright Institute, Jerusalem).

Bagatti 1979: 58; Campbell 1991: 67 (no. 40), figs. 66–7; Guérin 1874: I, 436; Guide Bleu 1932: fig. p. 541; Petrozzi 1973: 220–1, fig. 69; Rey 1883: 428.

# 188 RUJM AS-SAYIGH

### 195.169 [9]

Ruined **tower**, possibly Crusader.

Conder and Kitchener 1881: II, 403; Palestine 1929: 227; 1948: 118.

# 189 RUMAILA, Khirbat

### 1477.1286 [8]

*Tall ar-Rumaila*, W of *'Ain Shams* (village); Cr. *Aineseins* (?), *Bethsames, Bethsame Iudae*; Hebr. *Tel Bet Shemesh*

**Village structures** revealed by excavation on tell to N of abandoned Byzantine monastery, overlain by later cemetery.

Bunimovitz and Lederman 1993: 251; Grant and Wright 1938: pls. XXI–XXII, L; 1939: 86; Hoade 1978: 616; Israel 1964: 1464; Johns 1939; Palestine 1948: 160; Röhricht 1887: 204; Wright 1975: 253.

Stray find of thirteenth-century **capital** decorated with acanthus leaves, miniature columns and four bearded faces.

SSCLE 1987: 19, no. 18.

# 190 RUSHMIYA, Khirbat

### 1502.2439 [3]

Cr. *Francheville* (?); Med. Ar. *Rūshmīya*; Hebr. *H. Rosh Maya* (Haifa-Romena)

(fig. 49; pl. XCII)

**Tower** (20.8 m E–W by 13.2 m N–S, walls 2.5 m thick), with E part of basement groin-vaulted, W part barrel-vaulted; door or window in N wall and chute from

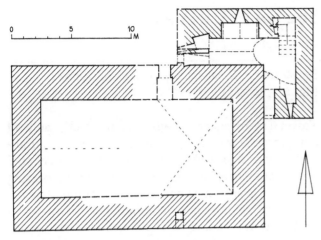

49   Kh. Rushmiya (**no. 190**): plan of tower with fore-building, possibly containing staircase (drawn by M. Pease, BSAJ Survey 1989).

XCII   Kh. Rushmiya (**no. 190**): tower, interior of forebuilding, looking W, showing door, embrasure (restored) and window above.

vanished upper floor in S. Rectangular turret or fore-building (11.2 m E–W by 8.7 m N–S), probably containing a staircase, subsequently added to NE corner,

projecting 3.9 m on E and 4.4 m on N, with door flanked by an arrow-slit in each re-entrant.

Bagatti 1971a: 108; Barag 1979: 209–10 (no. C11); Conder and Kitchener 1881: I, 329–30, fig.; Guérin 1874: II, 249–50; Hoade 1978: 671; Israel 1964: 1375; Kopp 1929: 107–9; von Mülinen 1908a: 32–5, figs. 14–15; Palestine 1929: 228; 1948: 24; Prausnitz 1972; 1974; 1975; Pringle 1991a: 89 (no. 8); 1993: II; 1994b: 340, fig. 5a; Ronen and Olami 1983: xiii, 22–4 (site 34), figs.; Rothschild 1938: 45; Wilson 1880b: II, 150–1.

*Churches*, II, no. 193.

# 191 SAFAD

1965.2638 [4]

Cr. *Saphet*; Hebr. *Zefat*
(fig. 50; pl. XCIII)

Large oval hilltop **castle** of concentric plan (overall 120 m E–W by 280 m N–S), now badly ruined but identified from a description of *c.*1264 and what remains as having had an inner ward, possibly containing a rounded or polygonal chapel or *église-donjon* above a round vaulted **cistern**, enclosed by a wall with seven (apparently rectangular) towers and a *talus* containing a *chemin de ronde*, surrounded in turn by an outer wall with at least six towers (apparently rounded), with an outer ditch and counterscarp. Castle founded 1102, rebuilt 1140 onwards, acquired by Templars 1168, dismantled by al-Muʿaẓẓam ʿĪsā 1218–19, rebuilt by Templars 1240–60 and again by Mamluks after 1266, when a huge cylindrical keep was added.

PAM: Reports by N. Makhouly (21 Sept 1940–11 Sept 1941), municipal engineers (15 Dec. 1926, 17 Oct. 1941), and C.N. Johns (undated).

Anon 1951; Bagatti 1971a: 223–8, figs. 181–4; Bartlett 1851: 209–10, fig. between pp. 208 and 209; Benvenisti 1970: 199–204, fig., photo.; Burckhardt 1822: 317; Conder and Kitchener 1881: I, 248–50, 255–6, plan opp. p. 249; Damati 1985; 1986; 1989; 1990; Dapper 1677: 131–2; Deschamps 1934: 28, 80, 83, 85, 87–8, 92, 100–3, 131, 152 n.2, 229, 269; 1939a: vii, 3, 8, 17, 28, 119, 120, 125, 127, 129–30, 134, 140–2, 159, 164, 178, 186 n.2, 189, 192, 196, 215, 216, 236–9, pl. XXXIV; 1943: 100–1; Dothan 1951; Eydoux 1982: 164–7, 322–3; Favreau-Lilie 1980; Gaudefroy-Demombynes 1923: 118–19; Guérin 1880: II, 419–26; Guide Bleu 1932: 527–8; Isambert 1861: 701; Israel 1964: 1370; Johns 1937: 38; Jowett 1825: 183–4; Kennedy 1994: 128–9; Langé 1965: 26, 29, 31, 42, 92, 94, 96, 186, figs. 43–5; Lawrence 1988: xxxii, xxxiii, xxxix, 65, 66–8, 126, 128, 131, 134, 135, fig. 48; Le Strange 1890: 524–5; Marmardji 1951: 115–17; Masterman 1914; Meistermann 1936: 599–601; Mortet and Deschamps 1911: II, 261–4; Palestine 1929: 213, 229; 1948: 17; Perkins 1951: 87, fig. 12; Pococke 1743: II, 76; Porter 1867: 263–5; Pringle 1985c; 1991a: 90 (no. 11); Rey 1883: 445–6; Robinson 1841: II, 419–22; de Saulcy 1853: II, 517–18; Van Berchem 1902: 413–15; Van Egmond and Heyman 1757: II, 43–5. The text *de Constructione castri Saphet* (*c.*1264) is edited and discussed in: Huygens 1965; 1981; cf. Pringle 1984g; 1985c; trans. Kennedy 1994: 190–8.

*Churches*, II, nos. 193–5.

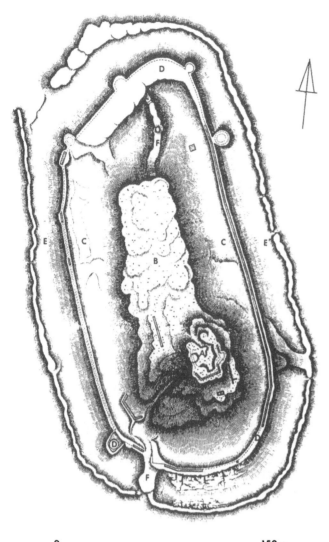

0 ⊢—┴—┴—┴—┴—┤ 150 M

50   Safad (**no. 191**): plan of castle in 1875–6. Key: (A) site of keep; (B) inner ward; (C) inner ditch (*fossata*); (D) outer wall (*antemuralia*); (E) outer ditch (*scama*); (F) probable sites of gates to inner and outer wards (after Conder and Kitchener 1881: I, plan opp. p. 249).

## 192 SAFFURIYA

1765.2399 [5]

*Sepphoris*; Cr. *le Saforie, Sephoris*; Hebr. *Zippori* (fig. 2c; pl. XCIV)

**Tower** (15 m square, walls 3.75 m thick), built of antique *spolia* including sarcophagi with edges drafted in reuse; door (rebuilt in eighteenth century) on S opens into barrel-vaulted basement with intersecting vaults enclosing openings and to left into staircase ascending inside wall; ground floor had casemates on N, E and W, leading to triple arrays of arrow-slits (replaced by plain openings since 1870s); upper part of tower rebuilt in eighteenth century; house added on top around 1900; disfigured by non-historic restoration 1994.

PEF: C.N. Johns, Field Notebook 1946–7 (2 Mar. 1947).

Abel 1967: II, 305–6; Avi-Yonah 1978; Benvenisti 1970: 206–7; Conder and Kitchener 1881: I, 335–8, fig., pl.; Creswell 1959: I, 213; II, 12, fig. 4; Deschamps 1943: 97; Ellenblum 1992: 184; Guérin 1880: I, 369–70; Israel 1964: 1383; Johns 1937: 39; Khalidi 1992: 350–3; Meyers, Netzer and Meyers 1986; 1988: 96; 1992: photos. pp. 4–7; Netzer and Weiss 1993: 13, fig. 19; 1994: 26–7, figs. pp. 14–16, 26, 29; Palestine 1929: 229; 1948: 29; Pococke 1743: II, 62; Pringle 1994b; Rey 1883: 446; Warren 1869: 136–7; Waterman 1937; Weiss 1993.

*Churches*, II, no. 196.

XCIII   Safad (**no. 191**): distant view of castle from NE, taken by K.A.C. Creswell *c*.1919.

XCIV   Saffuriya (**no. 192**): tower, from SW.

# 193 as-SAFI

### 1943.0493 [10]

*ar-Rujum, Kh. Shaikh 'Ali, Kh. as-Safia*

Site associated with **sugar production**, with evidence for occupation in eleventh to fourteenth centuries.

Albright 1924; Khouri 1988b: 105–7; King *et al.* 1987: 448, 456–7; MacDonald 1992: 253 (site 45); MacDonald *et al.* 1987: 410 (site 45); 1988: 39; Mallon 1924: 435; Whitcomb 1992: 115–16, pl. 33–6.

# 194 SAFI, Tall as-

### 1355.1235 [7]

*Tall as-Safiya;* Cr. *Blanchegarde, Blanca Guarda;* Hebr. *Tel Zafit*
(fig. 51)

**Castle** built by King Fulk in 1142 and described by William of Tyre (xv, 25) as having four high towers. Rey's plan (1871) shows a *quadriburgium* (about 50–60 m square) with rectangular towers, enclosing a rectan-

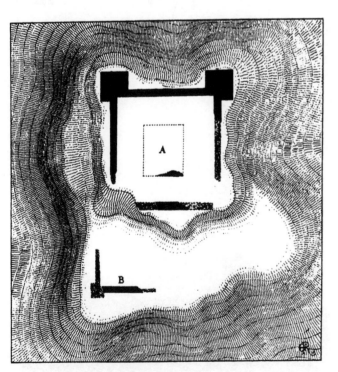

51   Tall as-Safi, *Blanchegarde* (**no. 194**): plan of castle (after Rey 1871: fig. 39).

gular *donjon* and itself preceded by an outer wall on the S. **Excavations** in 1898–1900 failed to confirm this, owing to stone robbing in the intervening period and the existence of a Muslim cemetery which restricted digging; they did, however, uncover a **tower** (about 7.6 by 6.4 m) containing a gate (3 m wide) on N side of site, besides architectural fragments, coins, a ring and pottery indicating Frankish occupation.

Abel 1967: II, 369–70; Benvenisti 1970: 205, 281–2; Bliss 1899; 1900; Bliss and Macalister 1902: 28–43, pl. 7, figs. 10–12; Conder 1878: II, 153; Conder and Kitchener 1881: II, 440; Deschamps 1934: 19, 55 n.4, 56; 1939a: 11–13, 22, 179, 235, fig. 1; Eydoux 1982: 189; Guérin 1868: II, 90; Israel 1964: 1445; Johns 1937: 25; Kennedy (H) 1994: 31, 32; Khalidi 1992: 221–2; Langé 1965: 67, 92, 104, 179–80, fig. 43; Lawrence 1988: xxxv, xxxvii, 68; Macalister 1930: 56–9; Palestine 1948: 131; Pringle 1989: 18; Rey 1871: 123–5, fig. 39; Stern 1993; Vincent 1899: 607–8; Warren and Conder 1884: 442–3.

# 195 SAHL AS-SARABAT, Tall

### 212.135 [9]

Excavated strata of Fatimid and Ayyubid/Mamluk periods, containing clay ovens (*tawabayn*), **plastered floors**, **basins**, **mud-brick and stone walls** and **well** or **cistern**, possibly related to **glass manufacture**.

Khouri 1988b: 80; Suleiman and Betts 1981.

# 196 ST MARGARET'S CASTLE

### 1474.2482 [3]

Cr. *S. Margareta cast(ellum), Cava Templi (castrum)*

Remains of Templar **castle** (Theodoric (1169/72), XXXIX; Röhricht, 'Karten', no. 16 (Matthew Paris, *c.*1252)), destroyed 1821, serving as foundation of lighthouse on the promontory of Mount Carmel above Haifa. Described in fifteenth century as square with corner towers (often confused with monastery of the Carmelites).

Barag 1979: 207–9; Dichter 1979a: 101; Friedman 1971; 1979: 86, 89–90, 120, 143, 152, 199, 207–9, map 4; Johns 1937: 37; Kopp 1929: 95–100; Roberts 1842b: III, pl. 71.

*Churches*, II, no. 212.

# 197 SARAFAND AL-KHARAB

### 131.149 [7]

*Sarafand as-Sughra;* Hebr. *Yad Eli'ezer*

**Vault**, called *al-Babariyya* on 1944 list.

Benvenisti 1982: 151; Khalidi 1992: 412–13; Palestine 1944; 1948: 83.

# 198 ash-SHAIKH SHA'LA

1698.1859 [5]

Large **building** (*al-Baubariya*) 40 m E of wely, with reused lintel bearing Greek inscription dedicating a building to Prophet Elijah.

Bagatti 1979: 70; Palestine 1948: 65.

# 199 SHAMA', Khirbat

1914.2647 [4]

Hebr. *H. Shema'*

Jewish **village occupation** in twelfth to thirteenth centuries revealed by **excavation** (1970–2).

Meyers 1978: 1095; Meyers, Kraabel and Strange 1976: 18–19; Palestine 1929; 1948: 17.

# 200 SHU'FAT

1716.1356 [8]

Cr. *Dersophath*

Rectangular complex in old village centre, possibly a **courtyard building**, incorporating **vaulted structure** (*al-kanisa*) with two pointed-arched windows, doubtfully identified by some as a church.

Abel 1931: 142–3; 1967: II, 372; Bagatti 1979: 13–14; Baldi 1973: 158; Conder and Kitchener 1881: III, 13–14; Guérin 1868: I, 395; Hoade 1978: 529–30; Johns 1937: 28; Meistermann 1936: 487; Pringle 1993: II; de Saulcy 1853: I, 112; Schick 1891: 200; Tobler 1853: II, 889–90.

*Churches*, II, no. 235.

# 201 SIDON

1844.3282 [2]

*Saida*; Cr. *Sagitta, Saget, Saiete, Sayette, Seete, Sidon, Sydon*; Med. Ar. *Saydā*
(fig. 52; pls. xcv–xcvi)

**Port city**, formerly defended by **walls** on S and E and by sea on N and W. At SE angle of town wall, traces remain of **Land Castle** (*Qal'at al-Mu'azzam*), mostly seventeenth century and largely destroyed by archaeologists since 1940s; outer wall with *talus*, ditch and counterscarp probably thirteenth century; excavations also show that castle overlay an early twelfth-century motte

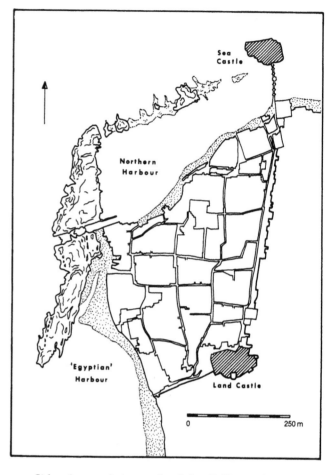

52   Sidon (**no. 201**): town plan (after E. Renan, in Poidebard and Lauffray 1951).

xcv   Sidon (**no. 201**): Land Castle, photographed from S by K.A.C. Creswell, *c*.1919. The standing remains are mostly seventeenth century.

XCVI  Sidon (**no. 201**): Sea Castle, interior looking E towards inner E gate, with chapel on first floor to right.

(7 m high). **Harbour** on N dating in part from Roman–Byzantine period, with **Sea Castle** (*Qal'at al-Bahr*), built 1227–8 and enlarged by Templars from 1260 onwards, defending its N entrance and linked to mainland by causeway and bridge; castle gates defended in different phases by portcullis, and by slit- and box-machicolations. City in Frankish hands 1110–87, Muslim 1187–92, Franco-Muslim condominium 1192–1227, Frankish 1227–49, Muslim 1249–50, Frankish 1250–91.

Abel 1967: II, 461; Anon. 1943: 82–4; 1945: 115–16; 1965: 121; Ben-Dov 1986; Boase 1971: pl. 120; Chéhab 1948: 166; 1950: 112; 1955: 55; Conteneau 1920: 108–24, figs. 20–9, pl. x; 1923: 261–9, figs. 1–4, pl. xxxix; Deschamps 1934: 12, 15, 18, 39, 59, 63–4, 74–5, 78 n.2, 83, 123–4, 131, 138, fig. 15, pls. xiiib and xvi; 1939a: 9, 17–18, 134, 165–7, 222–3, 236–9, figs. 23–4, pls. lxxxvii–xci; Dunand 1939: 79–81; 1940: 118; 1941: 88, 90; 1967: 29–30, 34, pls. i.3 and 5, ii.1–2; Dussaud, Deschamps and Seyrig 1931: pl. 155; Eydoux 1982: 199–205, 251, 253; Guide Bleu 1932: 400–7; 1975: 213–18, fig.; Jidejian 1971: 100–9, pls. 226–30; Johns 1937: 39; Kalayan 1973; Kennedy 1994: 1, 43, 54, 61, 120, 121–4, 129, 142–3, 144, pl. 43, fig. 15; King 1946: 65–70, figs. 17–18; Le Strange 1890: 346–8, 458; Müller-Wiener 1966: 69–71, plans 20–1, pls. 96–7; Pococke 1743: II, 85–7; Poidebard and Lauffray 1951; Pringle 1993: II; 1995a: 88–9, fig. 7; Rey 1871: 153–9, fig. 41, pl. xvi; 1883: 519–20; Roberts 1842b: II, 48–57, pls. 42–5; Saidah 1967: 177; Warren 1870: 326; Warren and Conder 1884: 482–3.

*Churches*, II, nos. 226–45.

## 202 SILA', Khirbat as-

205.020 [10]

Cr. *Celle*; Med. Ar. *al-Sila'*, *al-Sala'*

Natural rock **castle** in Wadi Musa, with surface pottery indicating medieval occupation. Taken by Saladin 1187 ('Imād al-Dīn (trans. Massé, 99)).

Glueck 1970: 197–204; Le Strange 1890: 528; Lindner 1983: 269, fig. 17; Mayer 1990: 177–8; Musil 1907: II.i, 318; Zayadine 1985: 164–6, fig. 9.

## 203 SINJIL

1750.1601 [8]

Cr. *Casale S. Egidii*; Med. Ar. *Sinjil*

Base of **tower** (about 10 m E–W), of which only lower face of S wall survives (1979), built in rusticated blocks with drafted margins. Situated in the royal domain, Sinjil's twelfth-century population included Franks; its lord, Baldwin, issued a charter in 1175 (*RRH*, no. 531).

Benvenisti 1970: 230; Guérin 1874: II, 34–5; Hoade 1978: 547; Johns 1937: 37; Palestine 1929: 231; 1948: 97; Pringle 1993: II; 1994a: 48.

*Churches*, II, no. 146.

## 204 SIRA, Khirbat as-

1862.2255 [6]

Hebr. *H. Zir*

**Buildings** in bossed masonry, described as resembling that of Belvoir Castle.

Conder and Kitchener 1881: II, 124; Israel 1964: 1399; Palestine 1929: 169; 1948: 43.

## 205 SIRIN

1976.2288 [6]

Cr. *Losserin*

**Building** to SW of village. Village sold to Hospital by Simon Cheveron in 1168 (*RRH*, no. 448).

Bagatti 1971a: 283; Beyer 1945: 228, 237, 253; Gal 1991: 26, 22–3* (no. 13); Israel 1964: 1399; Palestine 1929; 1948: 44.

## 206 SU'AIDA, Khirbat

1622.1287 [8]

*Qaryat Sa'ida*; Hebr. *H. Se'adim*

**Vaulted building** on former Byzantine ecclesiastical site.

Clermont-Ganneau 1896: II, 220–2; Conder and Kitchener 1881: III, 134–5; Israel 1964: 1468; Palestine 1929: 216; 1948: 166; Pringle and Leach 1983: 323 n.12.

## 207 SUBA

1620.1324 [8]

Cr. *Belmont*; Hebr. *Zova*
(fig. 53)

Hospitaller **castle** (*c.*1150–91), with rectangular inner ward resembling **courtyard building** with vaulted ranges set around courtyard containing **wine-press**, rock-cut **cisterns** below and solid projecting rectangular turrets flanking narrow entrances on N and E; enclosed by polygonal outer ward lower down hill with scarped *talus* and berm, gatehouse on SE, and **stables** in barrel-vaulted range on ESE. **Architectural fragments** from excavations (1986–8), including capital and part of armorial panel. **Vaulted passage to spring** lower down hill on E.

PAM: Undated report.

Benvenisti 1970: 229; Clermont-Ganneau 1896: I, 480–1, fig. p. 23; Conder and Kitchener 1881: III, 18–19, 157–8; Deschamps 1939a: 15, 20–1; Ellenblum 1992: 185; Guérin 1868: I, 265–78; Harper 1987; 1988; 1989a; 1989b; 1990; Harper and Pringle 1986; 1987; 1988; 1989; Hoade 1978: 601; Johns 1937: 24; Kennedy 1994: 58–9, 61, 113, 145; Khalidi 1992: 317–19; Langé 1965: 94, 179, fig. 43; Mariti 1769: IV, 324–6; Palestine 1929: 231; 1948: 155; Pococke 1743: II, 46–7; Pringle 1989: 21–5, figs.; 1994a: 51; Rey 1883: 378, 383; de Sandoli 1974: 240; Wilson 1880a: I, 201, fig. p. 198; 1880b: II, 81, fig. p. 78; Wolff 1991: 534–5.

*Churches*, II, no. 247.

## 208 as-SUMAIRIYA

1591.2642 [3]

Cr. *Somelaria, la Semerrie*; Med. Ar. *al-Samiriyah al-Bayda*'; Hebr. *Regba*
(fig. 54; pl. XCVII)

**Courtyard building** (60.5 m E–W by 57 m N–S), with ground floor of E range (10.5 by 47 m overall) enclosed by a barrel-vault with five intersecting vaults on its E side springing from rectangular pilasters. Village belonged to the Templars in 1277 (*RRH*, no. 1413).

Barag 1979: 205 (no. 26); Beyer 1945: 208, 212–13; Ellenblum 1992: 185; Guérin 1880: II, 161; Guide Bleu 1932: 506; Khalidi 1992: 30–1; Meyer 1964; Pococke 1743: II, 78; Yogev and Rochman 1985.

**Glass factory** (thirteenth-century) excavated 7 m SE of courtyard building in 1968–9.

Weinberg 1968; 1987.

*Churches*, II, no. 248.

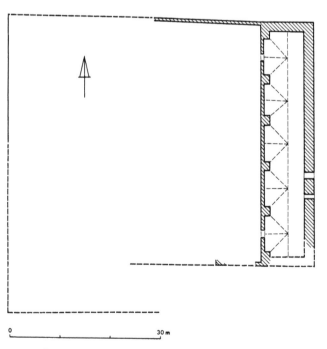

53 Suba (**no. 207**): plan of castle (after drawing by M. Pease, BSAJ excavation 1986–8).

54 as-Sumairiya (**no. 208**): plan of courtyard building (after Meyer 1964).

XCVII    as-Sumairiya (**no. 208**): vaulted range, looking S.

## 209 SUMMAIL

1305.1193 [7]

Remains of medieval **castle** in village (now destroyed), consisting of **tower** enclosed by roughly square enceinte (>30 m E–W) with *talus* and square corner towers. Masonry **well** (*Bir Summail*) to S (Grid ref. 129.117).

Information: A. Petersen.

Conder and Kitchener 1881: II, 413; Israel 1964: 1448–9; Palestine 1948: 135.

## 210 SUMMAQA, Khirbat

1540.2306 [5]

Hebr. *H. Sumaq*

**Excavated structures** and finds (cultural and environmental) relating to **village** occupation of twelfth to fifteenth centuries.

Dar 1984; 1988; 1990: 26; 1993; Horwitz, Tchernov and Dar 1990; Israel 1964: 1381; Palestine 1929; 1948: 28.

## 211 SUSIYA, Khirbat

1598.0905 [10]

Occupation of main hall and small room of **cave house** in twelfth century.

Negev 1984; 1985; Negev and Yeivin 1993. Cf. Palestine 1929; 1948: 209.

## 212 TABALIYA, Khirbat

1696.1272 [8]

Cr. *Tablie, Tyberie*

Ruined **courtyard building** (*Bait Yunan an-Nabi*) (about 31 m square), with vault standing in seventeenth century, entrance on E and cistern (7–8 m square) below court. Identified since late fifteenth century as church of St Habakkuk. Although SWP suggested a Crusading origin, surface finds of pottery and mosaic *tesserae* (in 1943, 1945) led Frs Bagatti and Saller to argue for it being Byzantine, but with medieval occupation; ecclesiastical identification unproven. Village acquired by abbey of St Mary of Mount Sion from Aimery of Franclieu by 1179 (*RRH*, no. 576); returned to Franks in 1241 (Matthew Paris, *Chron. Maj.* (*RS*, LVII.iv, 144); cf. Abel 1967: II, 477).

Bagatti 1983: 27–8; Boniface of Ragusa 1577: 193; van Bruyn 1725: 283ff., fig. 140; Clermont-Ganneau 1896: I, 455; Conder and Kitchener 1881: III, 160–1, fig.; Palestine 1929: 236; 1944: 1322; 1948: 167; Pringle 1993: II; Quaresmi 1626a: II, 457–60; 1626b: 298; Saller 1946: 18–20, fig. 9; Suriano 1485: 134.

## 213 at-TABGHA

2017.2529 [4]

Cr. *Mensa Domini/Ihesus Christi, Tabula, Tabula Domini, la Table Nostre Seignur*; Hebr. *'En Sheva'*

Base of **tower** (11.9 m E–W by 15.6 m N–S, walls 3.0–3.3 m thick), with stair to first floor leading off to left of entrance passage in S wall. Associated with the monastery church of St Peter, or Holy Apostles, which lies a few metres to S.

Hoade 1978: 743, 745; Israel 1964: 1390; Johns 1937: 33–4; Loffreda 1968: 243; 1970: 106–24, figs. 4.E2, 37–42; 1975: fig. 1.7; Palestine 1948: 36; Pringle 1993: II; 1994b.

*Churches*, II, no. 249.

## 214 TAFILA

2074.0278 [10]

Cr. *Taphila, Taphilia, Traphyla*

Probable remains of **castle** below rectangular Ottoman fort. Martin, lord of *Taphilia*, mentioned in 1177 (*RRH*, no. 542).

Abel 1967: II, 487; Brünnow and Domaszewski 1904: I, 109–10; Deschamps 1934: 23; 1943: 96; Duncan 1982: 9; Franciscan Fathers 1977: 149; Hoade 1966: 190; Johns 1937: 40; Kammerer 1929: 355; Lawrence 1939: pl. 103; Mayer 1990: 126, 140, 181, 190, 204–6, 245; Musil 1907: II.i, 317, fig. 166; Prawer 1975: II, 156n.; 1980: 477; Rey 1883: 395.

## 215 at-TAIYIBA

1784.1512 [8]

'*Afra, Castle of St Elias*; Cr. *castiel/castiaus . . . Saint Elyes, Effraon, castrum S. Helyae*
(fig. 55; pl. XCVIII)

**Concentric castle,** having inner ward similar to a courtyard building (about 28 m square), with solid clasping buttresses or turrets at three corners and midway on sides, and possible earlier **tower** (about 15 m square) on SE; gate (1.4 m wide) on E leads through barrel-vault (6.6 m wide) into roughly square open space of same width, from which arches

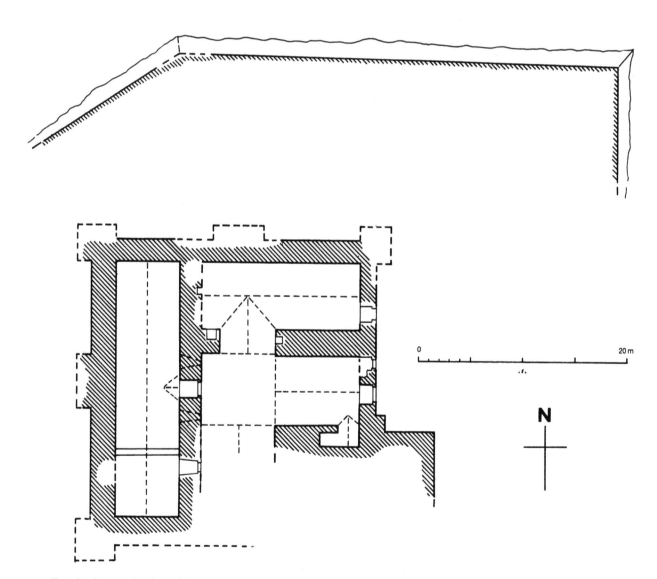

55    at-Taiyiba (**no. 215**): plan of the Castle of St Elias (after drawing by M. Pease, BSAJ Survey 1988).

XCVIII    at-Taiyiba (**no. 215**): NE angle of outer enceinte.

opened into vaults on N and S, and smaller door flanked by windows into barrel-vault running length of building on E; upper storey gone; polygonal outer wall with *talus* surviving on N, NW and NE. Castle granted to Joscelin III of Courtney *c.*1175, reverted to king 1182 (*RRH*, no. 614), granted to William III of Montferrat 1185 (*Ernoul* (ed. de Mas Latrie, 126)), lost 1187.

Abel 1967: II, 402; Bagatti 1979: 33; Benvenisti 1970: 259; 1982: 147–50, figs. 19–20; Conder and Kitchener 1881: II, 370–1, 293; Deschamps 1939a: 22; Ellenblum 1992: 185; Grant 1926: 195, pl. II; Guérin 1868: III, 45; Johns 1937: 28; Kedar 1982: 119; Palestine 1929: 254; 1933: 3; 1948: 105; Pringle 1989: 22, figs. pp. 24–5; 1992a: 148; 1993: II; 1994a: 45–6, fig. 4.

*Churches*, II, no. 250.

# 216 TALL AL-FUKHKHAR

1585.2586 [3]

Cr. *Toron*; Med. Ar. *Tall al-Muṣallīyīn*; Hebr. *Tel ʿAkko*

Mass of fallen masonry at S end of tell, possibly relating to Templars' **tower** mentioned with gardens and vineyard in 1291 (*Gestes des Chiprois*, ed. Raynaud, 243). Elsewhere twelfth- to thirteenth-century activity represented by **pits and drains** revealed in excavation. **Vaulted building** constructed in ashlar at foot of N slope, next to Acre–Safad road.

Dothan 1975a: 86; 1976a: 34; 1993a: 23; Israel 1964: 1372; Palestine 1929: 241; 1948: 20.

# 217 TANTUR, Khirbat at-

1630.2580 [3]

*Jabal at-Tantur*; Med. Ar. *Tall al-ʿAyadīya*; Cr. *Turon de Saladin*; Hebr. *H. Turit*

Site of **Saladin's headquarters** during the siege of Acre 1189–91 (*Eracles* (*RHC Occ*, II, 126–7, 130); ʿImād al-Dīn (trans. Massé, *passim*)); coins from surface collection include one of Henry of Champagne (1192–7), two of Saladin (1174, 1189) and four of Nūr al-Dīn (1146–74). Frankel 1988: 271–2, fig. 1; Israel 1964: 1372; Palestine 1948: 20; Rey 1888: 15–16.

# 218 TANTURA

1422.2246 [5]

*al-Burj*; Cr. *Merle*; Hebr. *Dor*

Remains of **castle** (about 74 m E–W by about 30 m N–S), defended by sea on three sides and by a deep ditch on E. SWP noted a **tower** (6.1 m square, about 12 m high) at one corner in 1870s, but this collapsed in 1895 and may anyway have been a late addition.

Abel 1967: II, 308; Benvenisti 1970: 189; Beyer 1936: 24–7; 1951: 155–7; Buckingham 1822: I, 192; Conder and Kitchener 1881: II, 7–11, figs.; Deschamps 1939a: 23; Foerster 1975: 334; Garstang 1924b: 65, pl. I (p. 64); Guérin 1874: II, 314–15; Israel 1964: 1384; Johns 1937: 34; Khalidi 1992: 193–5; Langé 1965: 184; Palestine 1929: 26, 252; 1948: 31; Pococke 1743: II, 58; Raban 1978: fig. 4; Schumacher 1895; Stern 1985: 24; 1994: 323–8, figs. 230, 233–4; Stern, Ravneh, Kingsley and Raban 1993: 372.

**Cemetery** of thirty-four burials (apparently Muslim) of eighth- to fourteenth-century date excavated near by on site of ruined Byzantine church.

Dauphin 1979a: 236, pl. 29b–c; Stern, Ravneh, Kingsley and Raban 1993: 368.

# 219a/b TAWAHIN AS-SUKKAR

a: 1912.1424, b: 1915.1427 [9]

below *Jabal Quruntul*; Cr. *Jardinz Abraham, Campi Abraham, Abrahe Ortus*
(figs. 56–57; pl. XCIX)

Two **sugar-mills**, powered by water brought by **aqueduct**, from Wadi al-Makkuk, below Jabal Quruntul: (a) has vaulted room to W with Arabic inscription and blason; (b) forms part of factory complex, extending

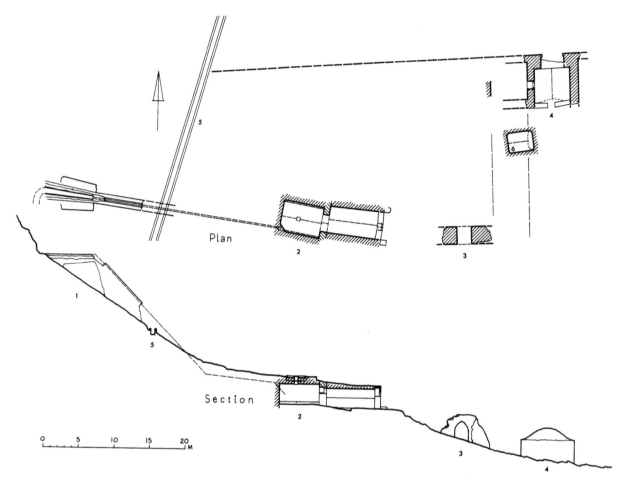

56   Tawahin as-Sukkar (**no. 219b**): plan and section through sugar factory. Key: (1) medieval aqueduct and chute; (2) mill; (3) aqueduct carrying tail-race; (4) gateway to factory; (5) modern aqueduct; (6) cistern (drawn by M. Pease, BSAJ Survey 1995).

XCIX   Tawahin as-Sukkar (**no. 219b**): sugar factory, showing gatehouse (foreground) and aqueduct and mill uphill to left.

over E-facing slope; water supplied from aqueduct down inclined chute to barrel-vaulted mill chamber which contained horizontal wheel (gone) powering mill-stones on floor above; tail race fed a continuation of the aqueduct, represented by solitary standing arch below mill; mill later had barrel-vaulted room added to E; barrel-vaulted gate to factory complex survives to NE, later made into *maqam*; large pile of ash and broken sugar pots downhill outside it. A mill belonging to the Latin monks of *Quarantena* is mentioned in 1116 and 1124 (Bresc-Bautier, no. 94; *RRH*, nos. 82, 104); according to Yāqūt (*c.*1225) Jericho produced the best sugar in the Jordan valley (Le Strange 1890: 396–7).

Abel 1910: 552–4; Augustinović 1951: 118–20; Baedeker 1876: 159; Benvenisti 1970: 254–6, photos.; Conder and Kitchener 1881: III, 221; Mann 1979; Palestine 1929: 253; 1948: 122; Pringle 1993: I, 252; Van Kesteren 1897: 104.

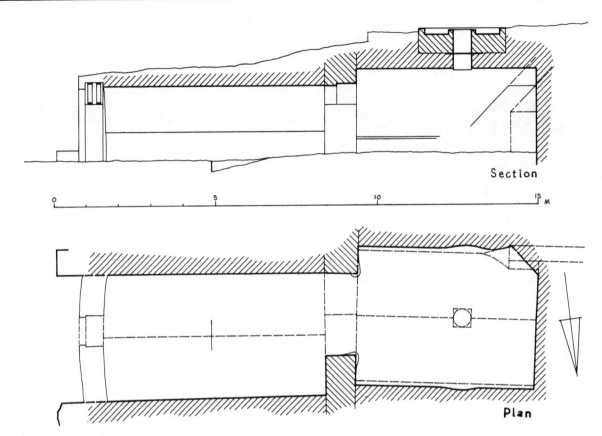

57  Tawahin as-Sukkar (**no. 219b**): plan and section through mill (drawn by M. Pease, BSAJ Survey 1995).

## 220 TAWAHIN AS-SUKKAR

1953.0479 [10]

*Qasr at-Tuba* (150 m SE of *Kh. ash-Shaikh 'Isa*, Byzantine *Zoara*); Cr. *Segor, Palmaria, Palmer*

**Sugar-mills** of Ayyubid and Mamluk periods (twelfth to fifteenth centuries).

Abel 1911: 78–9; 1967: II, 466; Albright 1924: 4–5, pl.; Deschamps 1934: 21 n.2; Frank 1934: 205–7, pl. 8; Glueck 1935: 8–9, fig. 1; Johns 1937: 35; Khouri 1988b: 69, 105–7, pl.; King *et al.* 1987: 446, fig. 4, pl. LXXIV.1–2; Le Strange 1890: 286–92; MacDonald 1992: 249 (site 1), pl. 29; MacDonald *et al.* 1987: 410, pl. LXV.1; 1988: 39–40, fig. 10; Mallon 1924: 432–6, fig. 15; Whitcomb 1992: 114, photo. 25.

## 221 TAWAHIN AS-SUKKAR, Khirbat

2000.0735 [10]

Two groups of **sugar-mills** (eleventh to fifteenth centuries).

Khouri 1988b: 91; King *et al.* 1987: 443, 454–5, 459; Mallon 1924; Whitcomb 1992: 114–15.

## 222 TIBERIAS

2010.2437 [4]

*Tabariya*; Cr. *Tabarie, Tyberias*; Hebr. *Teverya* (pl. c)

Rich deeply stratified **archaeological remains** of the medieval city destroyed largely without record in redevelopment in 1970s–80s. Remains of **castle** survive below the Sea Mosque (*Jami' al-Bahr*), with **barrel-vaults** still standing to W and cutwater-shaped tower formerly projecting into lake on E. The S section of **sea wall** is built on twelfth-century foundations. Other **barrel-vaults** in city centre. City held by Franks 1099–1187, 1241–7.

Abel 1967: II, 483–4; Bernie, Milwright and Simpson 1992: 124–9, figs. 33–5, 38–41; Boase 1977: 105; Conder and Kitchener 1881: I, 362, 366, 371, 420; Dar and Adnan-Bayewitz 1983a; 1983b; Deschamps 1934: 10, 18, 27 n.1, 59, 66, 77, 99 n.1, 122; Dudman 1988; Guide Bleu 1932: 519; Hirschfeld 1992; Hoade 1978: 726–9; Israel 1964: 1393; Johns 1937: 40; Lawrence 1988: 65–6, 134, 135, 136; Le Strange 1890: 338–40; Onn 1991; Palestine 1948: 38–9; Pringle 1993: II; 1995a: 94–5; Razi and Braun 1992; Rey 1883: 447; Roberts 1842b: III, pls. 62, 64–6; Schiller 1981: 168–71; Simpson, Bernie and Milwright 1991.

*Churches*, II, nos. 255–68.

c  Tiberias (**no. 222**): vaulted building in town centre.

## 223 TIBNIN

1888.2889 [4]

Cr. *Toron, Toronum, Tinenin*; Med. Ar. *Tibnin, Thamanin* (pl. CI)

Rounded hilltop **castle**, with projecting rounded and rectangular towers and smooth masonry *talus*, containing vaults and **stables**. Built by Hugh of St Omer *c.*1105, taken by Saladin in 1187, attacked and partly demolished by German Crusaders between Nov. 1197 and Feb. 1198, dismantled by al-Muʿazzam ʿĪsā in 1219/27, rebuilt by Franks in 1229, lost to Baybars in August 1266, and rebuilt in late eighteenth century.

Conder and Kitchener 1881: I, 116, 133–5, 207–8, figs., pl.; Deschamps

CI  Tibnin (**no. 223**): castle, from SW.

1934: 15, 18, 29, 92, pl. XXIa; 1939a: vii, 8–9, 14, 17, 40, 72, 86, 117–43, 164, 166, 178, 187, 189–90, 194, 196, 236, 239, pls. XXXII–XXXIII; 1943: 101–2; 1973: vii, 153; Dussaud, Deschamps and Seyrig 1931: pl. 156; Eydoux 1982: 225–7; Guide Bleu 1932: 430–1; 1975: 238–9; Johns 1937: 40; Kennedy 1994: 40, 55, 121; Kitchener 1877: 169; 1878: 134; le Lasseur 1922: 126–7; Lawrence 1988: 65–6; Prawer 1975: I, 273n., 291n., 294, 306, 555, 558, 559, 637n., 664–5; II, 117, 154, 179, 198–200, 202, 286, 305, 442n., 475, 524; Rey 1871: 141–2; 1883: 499–500; Smail 1956: 210.

*Churches*, II, nos. 269–70.

## 224 at-TIRA

1480.2410 [3]

Cr. *St. Iohan de Tire/Tyr*; Hebr. *Tirat ha-Karmel* (pl. CII)

**Tower** (about 12 m E–W by 11.6 m N–S), with barrel-vaulted basement (7.75 by 7.0 m) lit by pair of long round-headed slit-windows in E wall and one each in N and S; the W wall, which probably contained a ground-floor entrance and (in SW corner) stairs to first floor, was missing. In early Ottoman times, first floor replaced by a house (in 1945 inhabited by Suleiman Mustafa Salman). Remains of another possible **tower**

CII  at-Tira (**no. 224**): Crusader tower, with modern house built on top of it, before its destruction in 1947.

and other **barrel-vaults** surviving to SW suggest that this formed part of a larger rectangular fortified complex, with medieval church of St John to N. All these buildings now apparently destroyed.

PAM: Reports by N. Makhouly (9 May 1932; 5 June 1945).
PEF: C.N. Johns papers, Field Notebook 1945 (24 March).

Barag 1979: 208 (no. H2); Guérin 1874: II, 282–3; Israel 1964: 1375; Johns 1947: 26; Khalidi 1992: 195–8; von Mülinen 1908a: 59–60, figs. 29–30; Palestine 1929: 255; 1948: 23.

*Churches*, II, nos. 272–3.

## 225 TIRUN AN-NIHA

207.331 [2]

*Qal'at an-Niha*; Cr. *Cave de Tyron*; Med. Ar. *Shaqīf Tīrūn*

**Cave castle**, occupied alternately by Franks and Muslims from *c.*1130 until taken by latter in 1253.

Deschamps 1934: 78 n.2; 1939a: ii, viii, 108 n.1, 115, 188, 210–20, 239; 1939b; 1943: 100; Eydoux 1982: 232–4; Guide Bleu 1975: 130; Le Strange 1890: 535; Prawer 1975: I, 320, 333, 434, 605–6; II, 286, 335, 459, 524; Rey 1883: 513; Richard 1991: 9–10; Riley-Smith 1971: II, 204.

*Churches*, II, no. 274.

## 226 TUQU', Khirbat at-

(300 m NE of) 1702.1159 [8]

*Tekoa*: Cr. *Thecua*

Quadrangular hilltop **castle** (41 m N, 48.5 m E, 60.2 m S, 59.6 m W) with walls 2 m thick and > 3.5 m high, and rock-cut ditch on N (about 2.5 m deep, 14–15 m long). Village granted to the Holy Sepulchre by King Fulk in February 1138 (Bresc-Bautier, no. 34; *RRH*, no. 174), but apparently still without defences the following year (cf. William of Tyre, xv, 6).

Bagatti 1983: 64, pl. 11; Benvenisti 1970: 305–6; Ellenblum 1992: 185; Escobar 1976a: 56–7, figs. 1.4, 22–3; 1976b; Gütterling 1921: 35–6; Hirschfeld 1985: 66, 40*, fig. 47 (no. 38); Johns 1937: 40; Palestine 1929; 1948: 182; Pococke 1743: II, 41; Pringle 1993: II, fig. 98; Roger 1664: 212.

*Churches*, II, no. 254.

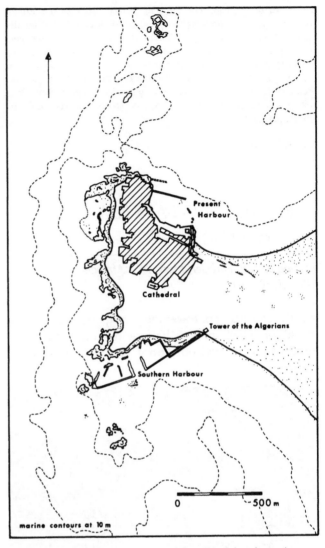

58   Tyre (**no. 227**): plan of city (after Poidebard 1939).

## 227 TYRE

1685.2975 [3]

*Sur*; Cr. *Tyr, Tyrus*
(fig. 58)

**City** held by Crusaders July 1124–May 1291. Sited on promontory, formerly surrounded by double **walls** to seaward, of which traces remain strengthened by through-columns, and by triple walls and sea-level ditch on landward side to E. Site of royal **castle** probably lies near entrance to **harbour** at N end of land wall.

Anon 1965: 112–13; Bikai and Bikai 1987; Chéhab 1975; 1979; Conder and Kitchener 1881: I, 72–81; III, 423–9; Deschamps 1934: 7, 10,

29, 47, 59, 68, 74, 99n., 131, 138, 229, pl. xıa; 1939a: *passim*; Enlart 1925: II, 352–73; Eydoux 1982: 57–65; Great Britain: Naval Intelligence Division 1943a: 323–4; Guérin 1881: II, 180–95; Guide Bleu 1932: 422–7; 1975: 231–7, fig.; Jidejian 1969: 123–41, pls. 132–5; Johns 1937: 40; Lawrence 1988: xxxv–xxxix, 130n.; Le Strange 1890: 19–20, 30, 32, 39, 41, 342–5; Pococke 1743: II, 81–3, pl. IX; Poidebard 1939; Pringle 1993: III; 1995a: 85–7, fig. 5; Rey 1871: 167–9, fig. 42; 1883: 5, 13, 212–13, 215, 500–8; Roberts 1842b: II, 36–43, pls. 37–9.

*Churches*, III.

# 228 UMM AT-TAIYIBA

1920.2283 [6]

*at-Taiyiba*; Cr. *Forbelet*; Med. Ar. *'Afrabala*
(fig. 2f; pl. CIII)

**Castle**, consisting of **tower** (26.3 m square, walls 4.1 m thick) of which only S half of basement survives; groin-vaults carried on central pier (2.12 m square),

with transverse arches springing from moulded consoles; door (2.1 m wide) in E wall of SE bay, lancet windows in each bay and stair against S wall of SW bay. An outer enceinte may be assumed, though no trace now apparent. The castle, probably Hospitaller and dependent on nearby Belvoir, was sacked by Saladin in 1183 (William of Tyre, XII, 27 (26)) and occupied by the Muslims besieging Belvoir in 1187–8 ('Imād al-Dīn (trans. Massé, 81–2, cf. 99); Abū Shāmā (*RHC Or*, IV, 345, cf. 303)).

Abel 1937: 31–9, pl. V; 1967: II, 403; Benvenisti 1982: 137, fig. 3; Conder and Kitchener 1881: II, 87, 126–7; Ellenblum 1992: 185; Gal 1991: 47–9, 33* (no. 53); Guérin 1880: I, 126–7; Israel 1964: 1400; Johns 1937: 29; Kennedy 1994: 33; Palestine 1929: 254; 1948: 44; Pringle 1991a: 90 (no. 12); 1994b: 340, table, fig. 4f.

# 229 UMM KHALID

1375.1929 [5]

*Mukhalid*; Cr. *Castellare Rogerii Longobardi*; Hebr. *Nathanya*
(fig. 59; pl. CIV)

Barrel-vaulted S range (22.2 by 6.7 m internally) and truncated S end of E range (6.4 m wide internally) of **courtyard building** (about 33 m E–W), with solid projecting turret (3.44 m square) at SE corner. Mentioned in 1135 (*RRH*, no. 159); mostly destroyed *c.*1948 and partly excavated 1985–6.

PAM: Report and plan by J.C.B. Richmond (September 1946).
Bagatti 1979: 184–5; Benvenisti 1970: 276; Beyer 1936: 44–5; Buckin-

CIII   Umm at-Taiyiba (**no. 228**): tower interior, S wall of SE bay (the stairs in the picture are modern).

CIV   Umm Khalid (**no. 229**): courtyard building, S range, from S.

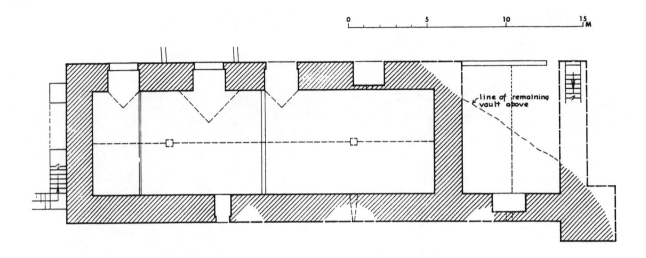

0   5   10   15
M

59   Umm Khalid (**no. 229**): plan of S range of courtyard building (drawn by P.E. Leach, after survey by J.C.B. Richmond, 1946).

gham 1822: I, 218; Conder and Kitchener 1881: II, 142–3; Israel 1964: 1410; Kennedy 1994: 35, 36; Khalidi 1992: 562–3; Langé 1965: 94, 180, fig. 43; Levy 1988; Palestine 1929: 208; 1948: 56; Porath 1986a; 1986b; 1987; Pringle 1986a: 9, 13, 14, 18–20, 39, 73–5, figs. 2–3, 19, pls. XXXII–XXXIII; 1989: 17; Reich 1983: 110–11, figs. 20–3; Wilson 1880a: III, 113.

## 230 al-WUʿAIRA

194.972 [1]

Cr. *Castellum Vallis Moysis, li Vaux Moysi*
(fig. 60; pls. CV–CVII)

**Castle** of roughly trapezoidal shape (about 90 m N–S by about 60/80 m E–W), on rocky site surrounded by ravines, of which that on E has been artificially deepened leaving rock pinnacle to support bridge to barbican and gate at SE corner; walls include rectangular towers; outworks to N and S along ravines; chapel. Frankish castle probably built by Baldwin II in 1127/31, replacing a Muslim one taken in 1107 (Albert of Aachen, X, 28–30); first mentioned 1144 (William of Tyre, XVI, 6); granted to Philip of Milly, lord of Montreal, in 1161 (*RRH*, no. 366); lost to Saladin in 1188.

Beretti 1987; Brooker and Knauf 1988: 186, pl. 14; Brown 1987; 1989d; Brünnow and Domaszewski 1904: I, 415–18, figs. 470–4; Deschamps 1934: 22–3, 276 n.1; 1939a: 9, 38–9, 47–8, 74; DeVries 1991: 280; Eydoux 1982: 139–40; Hoade 1966: 196; Horsfield 1938: 14, pls. XL–XLI; Johns 1937: 41; Kammerer 1929: 5, 350–2, figs. 26, 553, 565; Kennedy (ABW) 1925: 15, 35–6, 37, fig. 50; Kennedy (H) 1994: 24–7, 30, 45, pls. 2–3, fig. 1; Khouri 1986: 145–7, fig.; 1988a: 36–40; Langendorf and Zimmermann 1964: 139–43, pl. IV; Lindner 1985: 93–4; Marino 1993; Marino *et al.* 1990a: 5–10; 1990b; Mayer 1990: 29–30, 97–9, 129–30, 188–91,

CV   al-Wuʿaira (**no. 230**): rock pinnacle that formerly supported the bridge to the outer gate.

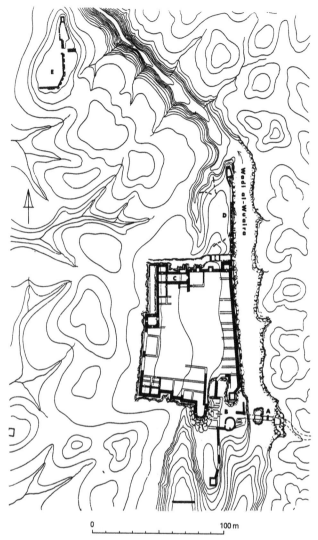

cvII   al-Wuʿaira (**no. 230**): rock-cut E ditch, looking N from outer gate.

60   al-Wuʿaira (**no. 230**): plan of castle. Key: (a) outer bridge and gate; (b) barbican; (c) chapel; (d) ravelin; (e) outwork overlooking wadi (after Musil 1907).

279–80; Musil 1907: II, 65–70, figs. 20–33; Pringle 1989: 18; 1993: II; Rey 1883: 398; Runciman 1951: II, 230 n.1; Savignac 1903; Vannini 1990; Vincent 1898: 430–4, figs.; Zayadine 1985: 164–6, fig. 10.

*Churches*, II, nos. 177–8.

# 231 YALU

1525.1388 [8]

Cr. *Castellum Arnaldi/Arnulfi, Chastel Arnoul/Arnold/ Hernaut*
(fig. 61; pls. cvIII–cIx)

**Spur castle** on N–S promontory, with roughly rectangular plan (about 50 m N–S by 36 m S/about 44 m N), badly ruined, with rectangular tower on W (5 m wide, projecting 2.5 m); vaults and stairs abutting S wall, which possibly contained gate at E end. Royal castle

cvI   al-Wuʿaira (**no. 230**): NE tower and ravelin.

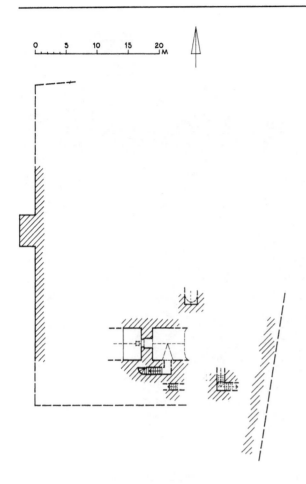

61    Yalu (**no. 231**): plan of surviving remains of castle (drawn by M. Pease, BSAJ Survey 1988).

CIX    Yalu (**no. 231**): mural stair leading to blocked door, now underground.

taken and destroyed by Muslims October 1106 (Albert of Aachen, x, 10–14), rebuilt in winter of 1132–3 (William of Tyre, xIV, 8), in Templar hands by 1179 (*RRH*, no. 572), fell to Saladin 1187 (*Gesta Henrici II* (*RS*, xLIX.ii, 22)).

Abel 1967: II, 240–1; Benvenisti 1970: 281–2, 314–16, photo.; Clermont-Ganneau 1896: II, 91–3; Conder and Kitchener 1881: III, 19; Deschamps 1939a: 9–10, 20; Guérin 1868: III, 290; Hoade 1978: 538; Johns 1937: 26; Kennedy 1994: 31, 32, 55; Kochavi 1972: 236 (no. 231); Pringle 1989: 17; 1991a: 90–1 (no. 13); Runciman 1951: II, 90–1.

# 232 al-YANUHIYA

159.267 [3]

Cr. *Lanahie, Lanoye, Lanahiam, Noie*; Med. Ar. *al-Yānuḥīyah*

### Sugar production site.

Barag 1979: 204 (no. 23); Frankel 1988: 263, 268, fig. 1; Guérin 1880: II, 44–5; Meyer 1978: 23–4; Palestine 1948: 5.

CVIII    Yalu (**no. 231**): W wall, with projecting rectangular tower.

## 233 YAZUR

1317.1592 [7]

Cr. *Casellum de Planis, Casel des Plains, Casale/Casellum Balneorum, Casellum de Templo*; Hebr. *'Azor*
(fig. 62; pls. CX–CXIII)

**Castle**, consisting of **tower** (12.8 by 12.6 m, walls 2.8–2.9 m thick) with barrel-vaulted basement and stair opening though vault; traces of irregular **enclosure walls**

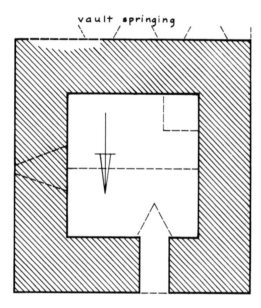

62   Yazur (**no. 233**): plan of tower (drawn by P.E. Leach, BSAJ Survey 1981).

CX   Yazur (**no. 233**): tower, from N.

CXI   Yazur (**no. 233**): tower, E wall, showing round-headed slit-window and springings of secondary vaulted structures.

around edge of hilltop to NW. Fortified by Templars in October 1191 and dismantled by Saladin in August 1192 (*Itin. Ric.*, IV, 29; Bahā' al-Dīn (*PPTS*, XIII, 165–6)).

Abel 1927a; 1967: II, 258; Benvenisti 1970: 168, 259, 276, 313; 1982: 144, figs. 12–13; Deschamps 1934: 79; 1939a: 15, 20 n.2; 1943: 94 (no. 6); Ellenblum 1992: 179; Guérin 1868: I, 26–9; Hoade 1978: 611; Israel 1964: 1429; Johns 1937: 26; Khalidi 1992: 261–2; Langé 1965: 94, 180, fig. 43; Palestine 1929: 262; 1948: 81; Pringle 1983a: 159, 170, fig. 7; 1989: 16–17, photo.; 1993: II.

*Churches*, II, no. 279.

## 234 YESOD HA-MA'ALA

2071.2737 [4]

Near Cr. *Mallaha* (204.277) and *Lacus Meleha*

Excavation has revealed stone-built channels and three plastered basins associated with sugar pots, interpreted as **sugar-producing installations**. Pottery and a

CXII   Yazur (**no. 233**): tower, E window from inside, showing antique column used as transom below rear-arch.

CXIII   Yazur (**no. 233**): tower, opening in vault for timber stair to upper floor.

Cypriot coin suggest thirteenth- to fourteenth-century date, thus probably post-dating the fall of nearby Qal'at Hunin (**no. 164**) and Safad (**no. 191**) to Baybars (1266).

Biran 1993; Biran and Shoham 1987; Palestine 1929; 1948: 14. Cf. Khalidi 1992: 472.

## 235 YIBNA

1261.1416 [7]

Cr. *Ibelin, Ybelin, Gibelim*; Hebr. *Yavne*

Remains of **castle**, built on hilltop in 1141 'of very strong masonry with deep foundations and four towers' (William of Tyre, xv, 24); excavation required to determine plan, which from description appears to have been a *quadriburgium*.

Abel 1924: 202, fig. 1; 1967: II, 352–3; Benvenisti 1970: 207–9, 281–2; Conder and Kitchener 1881: II, 414, 441; Deschamps 1934: 18, 25, 44, 55 n.4, 56; Eydoux 1982: 188–9; Heyck 1900: fig. 70; Hoade 1978: 652; Israel 1964: 1431; Johns 1937: 41; Kennedy 1994: 31, 32, 120; Khalidi

1992: 421–3; Langé 1965: 32, 67, 92, 104, 159, 183–4; Lawrence 1988: xxxv, xxxvi, 68; Ory 1975: 269; Palestine 1929: 262; 1948: 83; Pringle 1989: 14; 1993: II; Smail 1956: 211, 230, 235; 1973: 99–100; Warren and Conder 1884: 443.

Large quantity of Crusader **masonry**, presumably from castle (or church), reused in bridge built by Sultan Baybars 1272/3 and in mausoleum of Abū Hurayra (1293).

Clermont-Ganneau 1896: II, 167–84; Conder and Kitchener 1881: II, 442–3; Mayer and Pinkerfeld 1950: 20–4, figs. 1–11.

*Churches*, II, no. 280.

## 236 az-ZABABIDA

1808.1991 [6]

*Zababda*

**Tower** (14 m E–W by 12.5 m N–S, walls 1.4 m thick), called *al-Baubariya*, with ground floor of seven barrel-vaulted compartments with door on W (and possibly on E), built of large bossed drafted blocks; upper floor gone. **Barrel-vault**, possibly Crusader, against N side.

PAM: Reports by S.A.S. Husseini (2 July 1941) and N. Makhouly (20 Dec. 1946).

Bagatti 1971: 316; Benvenisti 1982: 142, figs. 8–9; Ellenblum 1992: 185; Hoade 1978: 572; Palestine 1948: 74; Petrozzi 1973: 145–8, fig. 32.

# 237 az-ZIB

1598.2728 [3]

Cr. *Casel Imbert, casale Huberti de Paci, Casale Lamberti, Castellum Ziph, Qasale Imbert/Siph*; Hebr. *Akhziv*

Site of Crusader **new town**, founded by Baldwin III in 1146/53 (Strehlke, no. 1; *RRH*, no. 281) on lands of village that had earlier (1104/8–18) belonged to Hubert

of Paceo. **Street plan** and remains of **tower** formerly discernible in Arab village, now mostly destroyed.

Abel 1967: II, 237; Benvenisti 1970: 220–3, plan; Conder and Kitchener 1881: I, 152–3, 155, 193; Frankel 1988: 257, 264, fig. 1; Guérin 1868: II, 164–5; Hubatsch 1966: 197, pl. 26; Johns 1937: 26; Khalidi 1992: 35–7; Palestine 1929: 264; 1948: 1; Prawer 1980: 140–2; Pringle 1993: II.

*Churches*, II, no. 282.

# 238 ZUWAINITA, Khirbat

1708.2695 [3]

Cr. *Zoenita*; Hebr. *H. Bet Zeneita*

**Village buildings** revealed by excavation.

Information: N. Getzov and R. Frankel (1995).
Israel 1964: 1358; Palestine 1929; 1948: 7.

# ADDENDA

## 239 BAIT MIZZA, Khirbat

### 1651.1348

Hebr. *H. Ha-Moza* (*Mevassaret Yerushalayim*)

**Complex of barrel-vaulted buildings**

Information: A. Boas.
Guérin 1868: I, 262–3; Israel 1964: 1460, Palestine 1929; 1948: 154.

## 240 BIR NABALA

### 1686.1394

**Remains of vaults**

Finkelstein and Magen 1993: 47* (no. 318); Fischer, Isaac and Roll 1996: 141 (no. 35); Guérin 1868: I, 393; Palestine 1948: 152

## 241 BURJ AT-TUT

### (?)1682.1334

Three parallel **barrel-vaults**, side by side, now destroyed. Possibly the same as Kh. ʿAin at-Tut (**no. P1**).
Conder and Kitchener 1881: III, 91; Fischer, Isaac and Roll 1996: 143–4 (no. 39); Schick 1893: 136.

## 242 FARRAJ, Khirbat

### 1691.1374

*Kh. al-Biyar*

**Cistern** (10.7 by 17.8 m, walls 1.7 m thick) on N side of road between Bait Hanina and Nabi Samwil, part rock-cut, part ashlar built, feeding **aqueduct** on S.
Bagatti 1947: 228 n.5; Fischer, Isaac and Roll 1996: 141–2 (no. 36), fig. 10, pl. 87; Kochavi 1972: 186 (no. 144); Palestine 1948: 153.

## 243 HAR HAZOFIM

### 1703.1346

*Jerusalem*

**Tower** or **hall-house** (12 m E–W by 19 m N–S, walls 1.7–2.5 m thick), with door in N wall opening into basement and to ascending mural stair to right of passage; door flanked externally by two barrel-vaulted rooms, before which extended a walled courtyard with outer gate on N. Site excavated 1984 and 1993–4; destroyed September 1994.

Information: A. Boas.
Mazor 1984a; 1984b.

# SUPPLEMENTARY GAZETTEER

## Possibles

Without being able to visit every site where remains of the Frankish period have been claimed, suggested or appear possible on the grounds of published descriptions, it is difficult to draw a firm line between 'probables' (let alone 'definites') on the one hand, and 'possibles' on the other. Sometimes even a site visit will not resolve the question, particularly when an original identification was made long ago and the character of the site has now changed. In order that possible Frankish sites should not be discarded without the opportunity for further consideration, the following supplementary gazetteer lists those where Frankish building remains have been claimed, suggested or may possibly exist, but where further investigation is required to determine whether or not the identification is sustainable. As in the main gazetteer, the constraints of space mean that the principal criterion for inclusion here is the survival of physical remains. Sites where the existence of Frankish buildings is known only from documentary sources and where no archaeological trace has been recorded in modern times are therefore excluded; this does not necessarily mean, of course, that such evidence does not exist, nor that it may not one day be brought to light by further archaeological investigation.

## P1 'AIN AT-TUT, Khirbat

### 1663.1326 [8]

Complex of vaulted buildings of uncertain date (see also **no. 241**).

Palestine 1929; 1948: 155; Israel 1964: 1461.

## P2 'AIN FARA

### 1788.1378 [8]

Cr. *Farafronte*

Some of the buildings of the Byzantine-period village associated with the laura of St Chariton might have been occupied in medieval times, though evidence is lacking and it seems as likely that the place was already deserted when it was mentioned in 1179 (*RRH*, no. 576).

Abel 1967: II, 242; Bagatti 1971d; 1979: 15, pl. 1, fig. 1; Finkelstein and Magen 1993: 400–6, 68* (no. 527), figs., plan; Palestine 1929; 1948: 158.

## P3 'AIN SAMIYA

### 1817.1550 [8]

*Kh. Samiya*

Possible Frankish buildings (information: R. Ellenblum).

Kochavi 1972: 173 (no. 66); Palestine 1929; 1948: 119.

## P4 'AMMAM

### 238.151 [9]

Cr. *Ahamant, Haman*

Remains of watch tower (at least 8.1 m high), built of *spolia* on site of early Islamic citadel, with plain lintelled arrow-slits and mural stair to roof. An Ayyubid date after 1187 is now favoured on archaeological grounds;

the location of the Crusader castle is therefore uncertain. In July 1161 'Amman was held by Philip of Milly, lord of Nablus, along with Karak and Montreal, but passed to the Templars when Philip joined the order in 1166 (Strehlke, no. 3; Delaville le Roulx, 'Chartes', 184).

Deschamps 1933: 42–7; 1939a: 48; Duncan 1982: 3; Johns 1937: 36; Northedge 1983; Northedge *et al.* 1993; Wood 1993.

# P5 AQABA

### 1498.8816 [10]

Cr. *Aila, Elim*; Med. Ar. *Ayla*; Hebr. *'Elat*

Excavations show that the early Muslim fort was abandoned *c.*1100 and replaced by another, 1 km to S. The latter is credited to al-Nāṣir Muḥammad (*c.*1320), but was added to under Sultan Qansawh al-Ghawnī (1501–16). The fact that the Frankish castle of 1116–70 cannot now be identified with the early Muslim fort, on account of lack of twelfth-century finds from it, raises the possibility that the Mamluk fort may have been built on its foundations.

Deschamps 1934: 20–3; 1939a: 2, 9, 37, 39 n.1, 44, 49, 53–4, 58 n.1, 59–62; Glidden 1952; Harding 1967: 142–4, pl. 18b; Johns 1937: 28; Khouri 1988b: 135–44, pls.; Khouri and Whitcomb 1988: 13, 33–4; Mayer 1990: 52–3; Roberts 1842b: v, 56–7, pl. 122; Whitcomb 1987a; 1987b; 1988; 1989; Woolley and Lawrence 1936: 141–6.

# P6 BADD AL-BURJ, Khirbat

### 1674.1566 [8]

*Burj Bardawil*

Possible Frankish building (information: R. Ellenblum).

Palestine 1929; 1948: 102.

# P7 BAIT SAILA, Khirbat

### 1645.1427 [8]

*Bait Sila*

Possible Frankish building (information: R. Ellenblum).

Finkelstein and Magen 1993: 63, 18* (no. 50); Palestine 1929; 1948: 112.

# P8 BARZA

### 1796.2692 [3]

Cr. *Berzei, Berzey*; Hebr. *H. Barzayit*

R. Frankel reports thirteenth-century remains.

Frankel 1988: 264, 270 (no. 9), fig. 1; Israel 1964: 1359; Palestine 1948: 7; Rey 1883: 475.

# P9 BIRKAT AL-FAKHT

### 1956.2144 [6]

Medieval vaulted cistern (6 m square) and barrel-vault.

Israel 1964: 1414; Palestine 1948: 68.

# P10 BURAIJ, Khirbat al-

### 1584.1409 [8]

*al-Burj*

Remains of buildings of similar construction to those of al-Qubaiba, though incorporating reused material, and of masonry cistern; on medieval road between Bait Nuba and al-Qubaiba.

Bagatti 1947: 173, 208, 234, fig. 46 (B12); Guérin 1868: I, 348; Palestine 1929; 1948: 109; de Saulcy 1865: I, 87; C. Schick, in Buselli 1886: IV, 386.

# P11 BURJ AL-HASKA

### 1587.1081 [8]

*Burj Haska*

Tower.

Kochavi 1972: 55 (no. 108); Palestine 1929; 1948: 186.

# P12 DAIR AL-MAHRUQ

### 167.132 [8]

*al-Burj*

Remains of several vaulted buildings between Dair Yasin and Qiryat Moshe. Now presumed to be destroyed.

Guérin 1868: I, 395; Palestine 1929: 32; 1948: 155.

# P13 DAIR AL-MIR

### 1538.1629 [8]

*Kh. al-'Amir*

Vaulted courtyard building, ruined walls and cistern, associated with Byzantine and medieval pottery.

Kochavi 1972: 232 (no. 207), figs.; Palestine 1948: 93.

# P14 JAUQ, Khirbat al-

### 1779.2723 [3]

Hebr. *H. Gov*

Foundations of walls and some drafted masonry, attributed to Crusaders by SWP on uncertain grounds.

Conder and Kitchener 1881: I, 177; Israel 1964: 1355; Palestine 1929: 112; 1948: 4.

# P15 al-JUNAID

### 1708.1812 [5]

Ruins of 'fort', facing robbed. Arabic inscriptions in wely.

Kochavi 1972: 164 (no. 6); Guérin 1874: II, 182; Palestine 1929; 1948: 66.

# P16 JUWAR AN-NUKHL, Khirbat

### 17 .30 [3]

Scatter of masonry including well-cut stones, identified by SWP as 'probably Crusading'.

Conder and Kitchener 1881: I, 49, 66.

# P17 KAFR BASSA, Khirbat

### 1521.2054 [5]

Lumps of glass and slag together with pottery of the Frankish and Mamluk periods recovered from surface collection. It remains uncertain whether the debris of glass working is medieval or from an earlier period.

Israel 1964: 1409; Ne'eman 1990: 44–5, 35* (no. 33); Palestine 1929; 1948: 53.

# P18 KAFR MURR, Khirbat

### 1714.1491 [8]

*Kh. Murara*

Foundations of buildings, which SWP state 'may most probably belong to the Crusading period'.

Conder and Kitchener 1881: II, 354; Palestine 1929: 138; 1948: 112; Pringle 1994a: 50.

# P19 NAHF

### 1799.2600 [3]

Cr. *Nef*

Medieval building.

Conder and Kitchener 1881: I, 203, 208, 255; Israel 1964: 1360; Palestine 1929; 1948: 8.

# P20 NIHA

### 1872.2974 [4]

Cr. *Niha, Nyha*

Described by SWP as 'probably a Crusading village' on account of 'large well-dressed stones scattered about', but referred to as a *gastina* (*khirba*) in 1260 and 1269 (*RRH*, nos. 1286, 1366).

Conder and Kitchener 1881: I, 93, 137; Prutz 1881: 176.

# P21 QASR AZ-ZUWAIRA

### 1830.0622 [10]

Hebr. *Mezad Zohar* (*Lower Zohar*)

Find of coin of Amalric I raises the possibility that this fifth- to seventh-century fort was reoccupied by the Franks in the twelfth century as protection for the road between Hebron and Karak. However, similar claims for Umm Baghag (**no. R21**) and Rujm az-Zuwaira (Upper Zohar: **no. R16**) have been disproved by excavation.

Gichon 1975: 153; 1993a: 119 n.3; Guide Bleu 1932: 669.

# P22 QIBYA

## 151.153 [8]

Possible Frankish building (information: R. Ellenblum).
Palestine 1948: 100.

# P23 RAS AD-DIYAR, Khirbat

## 1855.1776 [6]

500 m W of *Bait Dajan*

Foundations of a 'ruined fort' have yielded late Roman, Byzantine and some Crusader-period pottery from surface collection.
Bull and Campbell 1968: 28–9 (no. 15); Palestine 1929; 1948: 115.

# P24 SHABATIN, Khirbat

## 154.152 [8]

Possible Frankish building (information: R. Ellenblum).
Palestine 1929; 1948: 100.

# P25 SHAFA ʿAMR

## 1663.2457 [3]

Cr. *le Saffran, Safran, Sapharanum, Castrum Zafetanum, Saphar castrum, Cafram*; Med. Ar. *Shafraʿamm*; Hebr. *Shefarʿam*

Remains of twelfth-century Templar castle probably incorporated into fortress built by Ḍāhir al-ʿUmar in 1761, though no trace of it has yet been positively identified.
Conder and Kitchener 1881: I, 272; Guérin 1880: I, 410–11; Ory 1975: 229, pl. XVIII; Pringle 1993: II.

*Churches*, II, nos. 227–8.

# P26 YANUN, Khirbat

## 1837.1724 [6]

Possible Frankish building (information: R. Ellenblum).
Palestine 1929; 1948: 116.

# P27 YARIN

## 1721.2790 [3]

Tower or fortlet on hill top surrounded by enclosure wall built of large ashlar masonry; date uncertain. Byzantine church remains to SE.

Conder and Kitchener 1881: I, 258–60; Guide Bleu 1932: 435–6; Prawer and Benvenisti 1970.

# P28 ZAHRAN, Khirbat az-

## 1579.1911 [5]

Diagonally dressed masonry, of uncertain date.
PAM: Report by S.A.S. Husseini (27 Aug. 1941).

Kochavi 1972: 218 (no. 88); Palestine 1929: 193; 1948: 58; Pringle 1986a: 12, 13, 14, 22, 75–6.

# Rejects

This section of the supplementary gazetteer lists sites where the existence of Frankish building remains has at some time or other been claimed, but where subsequent research shows the claim to be unjustified. As with the list of possibles, inclusion in this list does not necessarily imply in every case that no building of the Frankish period ever existed on the site, nor that remains of such may not one day come to light. It simply means that a Frankish identification is not supported by the evidence at present available.

# R1 'AIN ARIK

### 1635.1460

Syriac *Beth 'Arīq*

Village belonging to the Jacobite church of St Mary Magdalene, Jerusalem, in 1138. Visible surviving ancient structures appear to be all Byzantine.

Abel 1967: II, 249–50; Bagatti 1979: 105, pl. 39.2; Conder and Kitchener 1881: III, 7; Guérin 1874: II, 46–7; Palestine 1948: 110.

# R2 al-BASSA

### 1637.2757

Cr. *le Bace, Lebassa*; Med. Ar. *al-Basah*; Hebr. *Shelomi*

Described by SWP as probably a Crusading village and identified by *AI* as a Crusader antiquities site. Excavations have shown the remains to be those of an ecclesiastical farm of the fifth to eighth centuries; although pottery indicates continuing village occupation through the Middle Ages, no buildings of the Crusader period have yet been identified. A capital bearing a cross, once thought to be Crusader, also appears to be Byzantine.

*Crusader identification:* Conder and Kitchener 1881: I, 145, 167; PAM: photo. 7939 (capital); Prawer and Benvenisti 1970. *Site and excavations:* Bagatti 1971a: 180–2; Dauphin 1979b; Israel 1964: 1352; Palestine 1929: 20; 1948: 1.

# R3 DAIR SURUR

### 159.186

Identified by *AI* as a Crusader antiquities site. The ruins, however, appear to be Byzantine and comprise a complex of buildings, with possibly one or more churches, surrounded by a defensive wall.

Bagatti 1979: 34, 132; Clermont-Ganneau 1896: II, 337; Conder and Kitchener 1881: II, 180–5; Palestine 1929: 34; 1948: 62.

# R4 FAR'A, Khirbat Tall al-

### 1823.1881

Limestone cross, attributed to Crusader period but more probably Byzantine. Tell covered by Muslim cemetery in thirteenth to fourteenth centuries.

Palestine 1929; 1948: 76; SSCLE 1987: 24 (no. II); de Vaux *et al.* 1993: 440.

# R5 HASI, Tall al-

### 1244.1063

Med. Ar. *al-Ḥasī*; Hebr. *Tel Hesi*

Mentioned as a camp site of Richard I in 1192 (Bahā' al-Dīn (*PPTS*, XIII, 337–8, 343, 345)) and identified by *AI* as a Crusader antiquities site. But excavations show that the tell was abandoned after the early Islamic period and used thereafter as a cemetery.

Amiran and Worrell 1976: 520; Dahlberg and O'Connell 1989: 131–6; Eakins 1993; Fargo 1993: 634; Israel 1964: 1453; Palestine 1929; 1948: 142; Tombs 1985.

# R6 HERODIUM

### 1729.1193

*Herodion, Kh. Jabal Firdaus*

Identified by *AI* as a Crusader antiquities site; but excavations show no structural phase later than the seventh century.

Foerster 1976; Netzer 1981; Palestine 1929; 1948: 182.

# R7 IRBID, Khirbat

### 1955.2467

Cr. *Arbel*; Hebr. *H. Arbel*

Identified by *AI* as a Crusader antiquities site. Investigation shows the structure to be Mamluk, overlying remains of a fourth century synagogue that was rebuilt in the sixth century and destroyed in the eighth century.

Conder and Kitchener 1881: I, 366–7; Ilan 1989; Israel 1964: 1392; Palestine 1929: 108; 1948: 38.

# R8 ISDUD

### 1171–82.1288–97

Cr. *Azot*; Med. Ar. *Azdūd, Yazdūd*, Hebr. *Tel Ashdod*

Identified by *AI* as a Crusader antiquities site. The buildings, including a mosque, well (dated by an Arabic inscription to AD 1269) and foundations of a khan, appear to be all Mamluk or later, though Irby and Mangles noted that one room of the latter had seemingly been used at some time as a Christian chapel.

Clermont-Ganneau 1896: II, 186, 191, 247; Conder and Kitchener 1881: II, 409; Dothan 1964; Guérin 1868: II, 409; Irby and Mangles 1861: 56; Israel 1964: 1440; Le Strange 1890: 405; Mayer 1934; Palestine 1929; 1948: 126.

## R9 JAZIRAT FARA'UN

### 1360.8751

*al-Quraiya, Pharaoh's Island*; Cr. *Isle de Graye*

Castle with irregular plan (100 m N–S by 24 m E–W overall) and projecting rectangular towers, on hillock at N end of island, containing extensive remains of domestic buildings and small bath-house; built of irregular pieces of granite, with some limestone for doors, windows and quoins, and palm logs for lintels and thresholds. At one time thought to contain Frankish work, but clearance and restoration in early 1980s now makes it seem more likely that the castle is entirely an Ayyubid foundation. Seen by Thietmar in 1217 (XVII, 6–8 (ed. Laurent, 40)).

al-Alfī 1986; Benvenisti 1970: 319–24, figs.; Brooker and Knauf 1988: 187, pl. 15; Deschamps 1934: 23; 1939a: 37 n.1, 44, pl. III; Eydoux 1982: 136–8; Flinder 1977; 1989; Johns 1937: 30; Kennedy 1994: 30; de Laborde 1830: 48–9, pls. 26–7; Musil 1907: II, 260, 305; Pringle 1993: I, 274–5; Rey 1883: 395, 399; Roberts 1842b: v, 14–17, pl. 105; Rothenberg 1961: 86–92, 185–9, figs. 12, 16, pls. 12, 40, 43, 45–6, 48; Savignac 1913; 1936: 257–8, pl. XII; Woolley and Lawrence 1936: 145–6, pl. III.2.

## R10 KAFR KAMA

### 1916.2363

Cr. *Kapharchemme, Capharkeme*

Identified by *AI* as a Crusader antiquities site. Excavations in 1961–3, however, have shown the remains to be those of a double Byzantine church of the early sixth century.

Bagatti 1971a: 274–80, figs. 227–34; Israel 1964: 1395; Ovadiah 1970: 98–9 (nos. 90–1); Palestine 1929; 1948: 41; Saarisalo and Palva 1966.

## R11 MALKAT'HA, Khirbat

### 1516.1208

Hebr. *H. Malka*

Ruined walls of buildings, identified as possibly Crusader by SWP (followed by *AI*), but now appearing more likely to be a Byzantine ecclesiastical site.

Bagatti 1983: 135, fig. 23.1; Conder and Kitchener 1881: III, 120; Israel 1964: 1468; Palestine 1929: 129; 1948: 165.

## R12 NABI BULUS, Khirbat an-

### 1755.1760

Vault below *qubba* suggested Crusader by SWP (followed by *AI*). More probably Byzantine.

Bagatti 1983: 131; Conder and Kitchener 1881: III, 123; Israel 1964: 1464; Ovadiah and Gomez de Silva 1984: 142 (no. 34); Palestine 1929: 140; 1948: 161.

## R13 QAL'AT MARUN

### 191.278

Cr. *Maron*

The existing castle is Ottoman, despite contrary claims. As a rear-fief of Tibnin (*Toron*), however, it is likely that *Maron* would have had a castle of some kind in the twelfth century.

Beyer 1945: 199; 1951: 281; Conder and Kitchener 1881: I, 202, 251; Dussaud 1927: 30; Guide Bleu 1975: 238; Rey 1883: 488–9; Tibble 1989: 89, 91–2, 97–8.

## R14 QASR BARDAWIL

### 2198.2475

*al-Bardawil*

Defended triangular spur (about 110 m N–S by about 90 m on N) on outcrop of rock with ravine on E and cliffs rising above gentler slope on W; mass of collapsed unmortared masonry (about 10 m high), apparently representing remains of casemate enclosure wall, containing oval and rectangular chambers, closes level approach from N, and is preceded by very faint trace of a ditch. Identified by Deschamps and others as a castle built by Baldwin I in 1105 and destroyed by Toghtekin, atabeg of Damascus, in December the same year (Ibn al-Qalānisī (trans. Gibb, 72)). However, more recent survey suggests the occupation to be principally Middle Bronze Age II.

*Crusader identification:* Deschamps 1933: 47–8; 1934: 26; 1939a: 100–1, pls.; Kennedy 1994: 40, 52; Prawer 1975: I, 273, 278; Runciman 1951: II, 95; Schumacher 1888: 215–16; Tibble 1989: 85, 165. *MBA II identification:* Kochavi 1972: 286 (no. 171).

# R15 QASTAL

### 1637.1336

---

Cr. *Belveer, Beauverium*; Hebr. *Ma'oz Ziyyon*

Village belonging to Hospital by *c.*1168 (*RRH*, no. 458); listed among castles supposedly destroyed by al-'Ādil in 1191–2 (*Itin. Ric.*, IV, 23). No trace remains of any Frankish structures, despite contrary claims.

Beyer 1942: 180; Conder and Kitchener 1881: III, 18; Johns 1937: 36; Khalidi 1992: 310–12.

# R16 RUJM AZ-ZUWAIRA

### 1730.0715

---

*Zuwaira al-Fauqa*; Hebr. *Mizpe Zohar* (*Upper Zohar*)

Frankish occupation of this fifth- to seventh-century Byzantine fort was at one time assumed; but no evidence of such was found when the interior of the fort was excavated.

*Crusader identification:* Conder 1897a: map [*Soara*]; Johns 1937: 41; Rey 1871: 104. *Excavation:* Harper 1986; 1987: 219–20.

# R17 SAILUN

### 1775.1625

---

*Shiloh*; Cr. *Seylon*; Med. Ar. *Saylūn*

SWP (followed by *AI*) considered some masonry in the village to be of Crusading date. But, although its mosques were visited by Muslim and Jewish pilgrims in the twelfth and thirteenth centuries (al-Harawī (trans. Sourdel-Thomine, 61–2); Le Strange 1890: 466, 477, 527; Prawer 1988: 180, 219, 232) and in 1227 it belonged (in theory) to the church of Bethlehem (*RRH*, no. 983), extensive archaeological excavations have failed to reveal any structural remains of the period. Coin and pottery finds suggest the site may have been abandoned in the ninth century, reoccupied perhaps only after 1187, and again deserted after 1350, possibly as a result of the plague.

Conder and Kitchener 1881: II, 367–8; Palestine 1929: 229; 1948: 97. *On the excavations:* Anderson 1985: 18; Kempinski 1978; Kjaer 1927; 1930; 1931.

# R18 as-SAMU'

### 1564.0895

---

Cr. *Samoe, Semoa*; Hebr. *Eshtemoa*

What was at one time identified as remains of a Crusader tower or citadel has been shown by excavation to be part of a contemporary building attached to a fourth-century synagogue; the latter was later converted into a mosque (at the time of Saladin, according to local tradition), and both structures had more recently been occupied by village housing.

*Crusader identification:* Benvenisti 1970: 305–7; Beyer 1942: 188; Conder 1875: 21; Conder and Kitchener 1881: III, 412–13; Deschamps 1934: 19; Johns 1937: 39; Prawer and Benvenisti 1970; Rey 1871: 104; 1883: 391. *On the excavations:* Barag 1976; Mayer and Reifenberg 1940; Yeivin 1981; 1993.

# R19 SUHMATA

### 1787.2679

---

Cr. *Samueth, Samahete*; Hebr. *Zomet Hosen*

Described by SWP (followed by *AI*) as probably a Crusading village. Excavations show the remains to be those of a Byzantine church.

Bagatti 1971a: 202–6, fig. 157–62; Conder and Kitchener 1881: I, 149, 192; Guérin 1874: II, 74; Israel 1964: 1359; Makhouly and Avi-Yonah 1934; Palestine 1929: 236; 1948: 7.

# R20 UMM AR-RAS ASH-SHAMALIYA, Khirbat

### 1521.1212

---

Hebr. *H. Bet Bad*

Identified by *AI* as a site of Crusader antiquities. Descriptions show it to be a Byzantine church site, with inscriptions in Syriac and Greek.

Avi-Yonah 1934: 45–6; Bagatti 1983: 133–5, fig. 20.6, pl. 19; Israel 1964: 1468; Palestine 1929; 1948: 165.

# R21 UMM BAGHAG

185.067

Hebr. *'En Boqeq*

Byzantine fort of fifth to seventh centuries. A coin of
Amalric I, excavated from a late deposit, could have
been dropped at any time from the twelfth century
onwards and cannot be taken as evidence for Frankish
occupation.

Gichon 1993a: 50–1 (table 4/1), 428.

# 'Don't knows'

There follows, finally, a list of all those Crusader
antiquities sites identified by the *Atlas of Israel* and not
treated above (or in *Churches*) for which insufficient
evidence has been found to allow the existence of
surviving Frankish buildings to be either confirmed or
rejected.

166.262 Abu Sinan (Cr. *Busenen*).
171.173 Dair, Kh. al- (Cr. *Deira*).
178.272 Fasil Danyal, Kh. (Hebr. *H. Pazelet*;
       incorrectly identified by *AI* as Cr.
       *Danehyle*).

164.267 al-Ghabasiya (Cr. *Cabecie, le Ghabezie*).
124.109 Judaida, Kh. (Cr. *Elgedeide*).
165.262 Kafr Yasif (Cr. *Cafresi, Cafriasif*).
172.164 Lubban Sharqiya (Cr. *Lubanum*).
190.242 Lubiya (Cr. *Lubia*; Hebr. *Lavi*).
175.261 Makhuz, Kh. (Cr. *Mahus*; Hebr. *H. Mahoz*).
160.276 Mushairifa, Kh. al- (*at-Taba'iq*; Cr. *Meserefe*;
       Hebr. *Misrefot Yam, Tel Rosh ha-Niqra*).
136.108 al-Qubaiba (Cr. *Deirelcobebe*; Hebr. *H. Kefar
       Lakhish*).
177.243 Ruma, Kh. al- (Cr. *Roma, Rome*; Hebr. *H.
       Ruma*).

# BIBLIOGRAPHY

**Abbreviations**

| | |
|---|---|
| AASOR | Annual of the American Schools of Oriental Research |
| ADAJ | *Annual of the Department of Antiquities of Jordan* |
| AI | Palestine under the Crusaders. *Atlas of Israel*, sheet IX/10, ed. J. Prawer and M. Benvenisti. Jerusalem (1970) |
| AJA | *American Journal of Archaeology* |
| AOL | *Archives de l'Orient latin*, 2 vols. Paris (1881–4) |
| BAIAS | *Bulletin of the Anglo-Israel Archaeological Society* |
| BAR | British Archaeological Reports |
| BASOR | *Bulletin of the American Schools of Oriental Research* |
| BJPES | *Bulletin of the Jewish Palestine Exploration Society* |
| BMB | *Bulletin du Musée de Beyrouth* |
| Cart. des Hosp. | *Cartulaire générale de l'ordre des Hospitaliers de Saint-Jean de Jérusalem (1100–1311)*, ed. J. Delaville le Roulx, 4 vols. Paris (1894–1906) |
| CCCM | *Corpus Christianorum, Continuatio Mediaevalis* (Turnhout 1966– ) |
| Churches | *The Churches of the Crusader Kingdom of Jerusalem: A Corpus*, 3 vols. (in progress). Cambridge (1993– ) |
| CNI | *Christian News from Israel* |
| DRHC | *Documents relatifs à l'histoire des croisades*. Paris (1946– ) |
| EAEHL | *Encyclopedia of Archaeological Excavations in the Holy Land*, ed. M. Avi-Yonah and E. Stern, 4 vols. Jerusalem (1975–8) |
| EI | *Encyclopaedia of Islam* |
| ESI | *Excavations and Surveys in Israel* |
| IEJ | *Israel Exploration Journal* |
| IHC | *Itinera Hierosolymitana Crucesignatorum (saec. XII–XIII)*, ed. S. de Sandoli, 4 vols. SBF, Coll. maj., vol. XXIV. Jerusalem (1978–84) |
| Itin. Ric. | *Itinerarium Peregrinorum et Gesta Regis Ricardi*, in *RS*, vol. XXXVIII.i. London (1864). Trans. in *Chronicles of the Crusades*, Bohn's Antiquarian Library, pp. 54–339. London (1848). |
| JA | *Journal asiatique* |
| JPOS | *Journal of the Palestine Oriental Society* |
| LA | *Liber Annuus Studii Biblici Franciscani* |
| NEAEHL | *The New Encyclopedia of Archaeological Excavations in the Holy Land*, ed. E. Stern, 4 vols. Jerusalem (1993). |
| PAM | Palestine Archaeological (Rockefeller) Museum, Archives of the Dept of Antiquities of the Government of Palestine (1918–48) |
| PEF | Palestine Exploration Fund Archives, London |
| PE(F)Q(S) | *Palestine Exploration (Fund) Quarterly (Statement)* |
| PPTS | *Palestine Pilgrims' Text Society Library*, 13 vols. London (1890–7) |
| QDAP | *Quarterly of the Department of Antiquities in Palestine* |
| RB | *Revue biblique* |
| RHC Occ | *Recueil des historiens des croisades. Historiens occidentaux*, 5 vols. Paris (1844–95) |
| RHC Or | *Recueil des historiens des croisades. Historiens orientaux*, 5 vols. Paris (1872–1906) |
| ROL | *Revue de l'Orient latin* |
| RRH | *Regesta Regni Hierosolymitani*, ed. R. Röhricht. Innsbruck (1893) |
| RRH Ad | *Regesta Regni Hierosolymitani. Additamentum*, ed. R. Röhricht. Innsbruck (1904) |
| RS | *Rerum Britannicarum Medii Aeui Scriptores, or Chronicles and Memorials of Great Britain and Ireland in the Middle Ages* (Rolls Series), 99 vols. London (1858–97) |
| SBF, Coll. maj. | Studium Biblicum Franciscanum, Collectio maior. Jerusalem (1941– ) |

| | |
|---|---|
| SBF, Coll. min. | Studium Biblicum Franciscanum, Collectio minor. Jerusalem (1961– ) |
| TS | *La Terra Santa* |
| ZDPV | *Zeitschrift des Deutschen Palästina-Vereins* |

## Sources before c.1291

Abū Shāmā. *Le livre des deux jardins*, in *RHC Or*, vols. IV–V.

Albert of Aachen. *Liber Christianae Expeditionis pro Emundatione Sanctae Hierosolimitanae Ecclesiae*, in *RHC Occ*, vol. IV.

Ambroise. *L'Estoire de la guerre Sainte (1190–1192)*, ed. and trans. G. Paris, Paris (1897). *The Crusade of Richard Lion-Heart*, trans. M. J. Hubert, Columbia University Records of Civilization, Sources and Studies, vol. XXXIV, New York (1941).

Benjamin of Tudela. *The Itinerary of Benjamin of Tudela*, ed. (Hebr.) and trans. M.N. Adler, London (1907). Trans. Asher, in T. Wright, *Early Travels in Palestine*, London (1848), pp. 63–126.

Bresc-Bautier, G. (ed.). *Le Cartulaire du chapitre du Saint-Sépulcre de Jérusalem*, in *DRHC*, vol. XV.

Burchard of Mount Sion. *Descriptio Terrae Sanctae*, ed. J.C.M. Laurent, *Peregrinatores Medii Aeui Quatuor*, Leipzig (1864), pp. 1–100. In *PPTS*, vol. XII. In *IHC*, vol. IV, pp. 119–219.

Delaville le Roulx, J. (ed.). 'Chartes de Terre Sainte', in *ROL*, 11 (1905–8), 181–91.

*Eracles* = *L'Estoire d'Eracles empereur et la conquête de la Terre d'Outremer*, in *RHC Occ*, vols. I–II.

Ernoul. *Chronique d'Ernoul et de Bernard le Trésorier*, ed. L. de Mas Latrie, Paris (1871).

*de Expugnatione Terrae Sanctae Libellus*, in *RS*, vol. LXVI, pp. 209–62. Extracts in *IHC*, vol. III, pp. 109–19.

Fulcher of Chartres. *Gesta Peregrinantium Francorum cum Armis Hierusalem Pergentium*, in *RHC Occ*, vol. III. Ed. H. Hagenmeyer, *Historia Hierosolymitana (1095–1127)*, Heidelberg (1913). Trans. F.R. Ryan, *A History of the Expedition to Jerusalem, 1095–1127*, Knoxville (1969).

*Gesta Henrici II et Ricardi I* (wrongly attributed to Benedict of Peterborough), in *RS*, vol. XLIX, 2 vols.

*Les Gestes des Chiprois*, ed. G. Raynaud, Publications de la Société de l'orient latin, Série historique, vol. V, Geneva (1887).

al-Harawī al-Mawṣilī. *Guide des lieux de pèlerinage*, ed. and Fr. trans. J. Sourdel-Thomine, Damascus (1957).

Holt, P.M. *Treaties = Early Mamluk Diplomacy (1260–1290): Treaties of Baybars and Qalāwūn with Christian Rulers*, Islamic History and Civilization, Studies and Texts, vol. XII. Leiden/New York/Cologne (1995).

Ibn al-Qalānisī. *The Damascus Chronicle of the Crusades*, trans. H.A.R. Gibb. London (1932).

Ibn Jubayr. *Voyages*, trans. M. Gaudefroy-Demombynes, 3 vols., in *DRHC*, vols. IV–VI.

'Imād al-Dīn al-Iṣfahānī. *Conquête de la Syrie et de la Palestine par Saladin*, trans. H. Massé, in *DRHC*, vol. X.

James of Vitry. *Lettres de Jacques de Vitry (1160/1170–1240), évêque de Saint-Jean-d'Acre*, ed. R.B.C. Huygens. Leiden (1960).

Matthew Paris. *Chronica Majora*, in *RS*, vol. LVII, 7 vols.

Ralph of Coggeshall. *Chronicon Anglicanum*, in *RS*, vol. LXVI, pp. 1–208.

Ralph of Diss. *Opera Historica*, in *RS*, vol. LXVIII, 2 vols.

*La Règle du Temple*, ed. H. de Curzon, Société de Paris, vol. CCXXVIII, Paris (1896). Trans. J. Upton-Ward, *The Rule of the Templars*, Studies in the History of Religion, vol. IV, Woodbridge (1992).

Röhricht, R. 'Karten und Pläne zur Palästinakunde aus dem 7. bis 16. Jahrhundert', in *ZDPV* 14 (1891), 8–11, 87–92, 137–41; 15 (1892), 34–9, 185–8; 18 (1895), 173–82.

Strehlke, E. (ed.). *Tabulae Ordinis Theutonici*. Berlin (1869). Reprinted Toronto (1975).

Theodoric (Theodericus). *Libellus de Locis Sanctis*, ed. R.B.C. Huygens, in *CCCM*, vol. CXXXIX, pp. 143–97. In *PPTS*, vol. V.

Wilbrand of Oldenburg, *Peregrinatio*, ed. J.C.M. Laurent, *Peregrinatores Medii Aeui Quatuor*, Leipzig (1864), pp. 159–91. In *IHC*, vol. III, pp. 195–249.

William of Tyre, *Chronicon*, ed. R.B.C. Huygens, in *CCCM*, vols. LXIII–LXIIIa, Turnholt (1986). Trans. E.A. Babcock and A.C. Krey, *A History of Deeds Done Beyond the Sea*, 2 vols., Records of Civilization, Sources and Studies, vol. XXXV, New York (1943).

## Sources after c.1291

Abdul-Nour, H. and Salamé-Sarkis (1991). Troglodytisme médiéval au Liban: premières données. *Berytus*, 39: 177–87.

Abel, F.M. (1910). Exploration de la vallée du Jourdain. *RB*, 7: 532–56.

(1911). *Une croisière autour de la Mer Morte*. Paris.

(1912). Exploration de la vallée du Jourdain. *RB*, 9: 402–23.

(1914). Le littoral palestinien et ses ports. *RB*, 11: 556–90.

(1921). Chronique. Les fouilles d'Ascalon. *RB*, 30: 102–6.

(1923). Chronique, IV. – Naplouse. Essai de topographie. *RB*, 32: 120–32, figs. 6–9, pl. IV.

(1924a). L'état de la cité de Jérusalem au XIIe siècle. In C.R. Ashbee (ed.), *Jerusalem 1920–1922: Being the Records of the Pro-Jerusalem Council during the First Two Years of the Civil Administration*, pp. 32–40. London.

(1924b). Topographie des campagnes machabéennes (suite). *RB*, 33: 201–17, 371–87.

(1924c). Review of H. Goussen, *Über georgische Drucke und Handelschriften* (München-Gladbach, 1923). *RB*, 33: 611–23.

(1926a). Les deux « Mahomerie » el-Bireh, el-Qoubeibeh. *RB*, 35: 272–83.

(1926b). Topographie des campagnes machabéennes (suite). *RB*, 35: 206–22, 510–33.

(1926c). Chronique. Lettre d'un templier trouvée récemment à Jérusalem. *RB*, 35: 288–95.

(1927a). Yazour et Beit Dedjan ou le Chastel des Plains et le

Chastel de Maen. *RB*, 36: 83–9.

(1927b). Mirabel et la tour d'Aphek. *RB*, 36: 390–400.

(1928). Notes sur les environs de Bir-Zeit. *JPOS*, 8: 49–55.

(1931). 'Aṭṭārah et Naṣbeh au moyen âge. *JPOS*, 11: 141–3.

(1934). La question gabaonite et l'Onomasticon. *RB*, 43: 347–73.

(1937). 'Afrabalā-Forbelet et l''Ophra de Gédéon. *JPOS*, 17: 31–44, pl. v.

(1940a). La liste des donations de Baîbars en Palestine d'après la charte de 663 H. (1265). *JPOS*, 19: 38–44.

(1940b). Les confins de la Palestine et de l'Egypte sous les Ptolémées (suite). *RB*, 49: 55–75, 224–39, pls. VII–VIII.

(1946). Jaffa au moyen-âge. *JPOS*, 20.1: 6–28.

(1967). *Géographie de la Palestine*, 3rd edition, 2 vols. Paris.

Albright, W.F. (1924). The Archaeological Results of an Expedition to Moab and the Dead Sea. *BASOR*, 14: 2–12.

Alderson, R.C. (1843). *Notes on Acre and some of the Coastal Defences of Syria*. Papers on Subjects Connected with the Duties of the Corps of Royal Engineers, vol. VI. London.

al-Alfî, A.M.S. (1986). *Sinai Monuments: Island of Pharaoun: Citadel of Salah al-Din*. Cairo.

Amico, B. (1620a). *Trattato delle piante e immagini de Sacri Edifizi di Terra Santa*. Rome (1609), repr. Florence.

(1620b). *Plans of the Sacred Edifices of the Holy Land*, trans. T. Bellorini and E. Hoade, with preface and notes by B. Bagatti. SBF, Coll. maj., vol. X. Jerusalem (1953).

Amiran, R. and A. Eitan (1970a). Excavations in the Court-yard of the Citadel, Jerusalem, 1968–1969 (Preliminary Report). *IEJ*, 20: 9–17, pls. 5–8.

(1970b). Excavations in the Jerusalem Citadel. *Qadmoniot*, 3: 64–6. [in Hebr.]

(1976). Excavations in the Jerusalem Citadel. In Y. Yadin (ed.), *Jerusalem Revealed: Archaeology in the Holy City 1968–1974*, pp. 52–4. Jerusalem.

Amiran, R. and J.E. Worrell (1976). Hesi, Tel. In *EAEHL*, vol. II, pp. 514–20.

Amitai, R. (1989). Notes on the Ayyūbid Inscriptions at al-Ṣubayba (Qal'at Nimrūd). *Dumbarton Oaks Papers*, 43: 113–19.

Anderson, F.G. (1985). *Shiloh: The Danish Excavations at Tall Sailūn, Palestine in 1926, 1929, 1932 and 1963, II. The Remains from the Hellenistic to Mamlūk Periods*. National Museum of Denmark, Archaeological-Historical Series, vol. XXIII. Copenhagen.

Anon. (1943). Chronique. *BMB*, 6 (1942–3): 81–7.

(1945). Chronique. *BMB*, 7 (1944–5): 109–20.

(1951). Notes and News. *IEJ*, 1 (1950–1): 121–4, 247–52.

(1965). Chronique. *BMB*, 18: 111–25.

d'Arvieux, L. (1735). *Mémoires du chevalier d'Arvieux*, 6 vols. Paris.

Asali, K.J. (1989) (ed.). *Jerusalem in History*. Buckhurst Hill.

Ashtor, E. (1977). Levantine Sugar Industry in the Later Middle Ages – An Example of Technological Decline. *Israel Oriental Studies*, 7: 226–80. Reprinted in *Technology, Industry and Trade: The Levant versus Europe, 1250–1500*. Variorum Collected Studies, vol. CCCLXXII, ch. III. London (1982).

Augustinović, A. (1951). *Gerico e dintorni. Guida*. Jerusalem.

Avigad, N. (1978). Jerusalem, the Jewish Quarter of the Old City, 1977. In Notes and News, *IEJ*, 28: 200–1.

(1983). *Discovering Jerusalem*. Jerusalem.

Avissàr, M. (1995). Tel Yoqne'am. The Crusader Acropolis. *Hadashot Arkheologiot*, 103: 36–7, fig. 36. [in Hebr.]

Avi-Yonah, M. (1934). Mosaic Pavements in Palestine. *QDAP*, 3 (1933–4): 26–73.

(1978). Sepphoris. In *EAEHL*, vol. IV, pp. 1051–5.

Avi-Yonah, M. and Y. Eph'al (1975). Ashkelon. In *EAEHL*, vol. I, pp. 121–30.

Ayalon, E. (1983). Sugar Factory or Mill at Jaljuliya. *Israel – Land and Nature*, 8: 122–3.

Ayalon, E., E. Gilboa and S. Harpazi (1989). A Public Building of the Early Arabic Period and Crusader Remains at Tel Qasile – the 12th–13th seasons. *Israel – People and Land: Eretz Israel Museum Yearbook*, new series, 5–6 (1987–9): 9–22; 11*. [in Hebr. with Eng. summary]

Ayalon, E., E. Gilboa and T. Shacham (1987). A Public Building of the Early Islamic Period at Tell Qasile. *Israel – People and Land: Eretz Israel Museum Yearbook*, new series, 4: 35–52; 7*–8*. [in Hebr. with Eng. summary]

Baedeker, K. (1876a). *Palestine and Syria: Handbook for Travellers*. Leipzig/London.

(1876b). *Jerusalem and its Surroundings: Handbook for Travellers* (Partial reprint of Baedeker 1876a). Freiburg/Jerusalem (1973).

Bagatti, B. (1947). *I monumenti di Emmaus el-Qubeibeh e dei dintorni. Resultato degli scavi e sopraluoghi negli anni 1873, 1887–90, 1900–2, 1940–44*. SBF, Coll. maj., vol. IV. Jerusalem.

(1948). *Il Santuario della Visitazione ad 'Ain Karim (Montana Judaeae): Esplorazione archeologica e ripristino*. SBF, Coll. maj., vol. V. Jerusalem.

(1952). *Gli antichi edifici sacri di Betlemme*. SBF, Coll. maj., vol. IX. Jerusalem.

(1971a). *Antichi villaggi cristiani di Galilea*. SBF, Coll. min., vol. XIII. Jerusalem.

(1971b). Gifna. Villaggio cristiano di Giudea. *TS*, 47: 247–56.

(1971c). Il cristianesimo ad Ascalon. *TS*, 47: 22–30.

(1971d). Il villaggio bizantino e la laura. In G. Lombardi, *La Tomba di Rahel. H. Farah – W. Farah presso Anatot. La sua relazione con la Bibbia e la questione della Tomba di Rahel*. SBF, Coll. min., vol. XI, pp. 152–72. Jerusalem.

(1972). Il cristianesimo ad Eleuteropoli (Beit Gebrin). *LA*, 22: 109–29.

(1975). L'edicifio ecclesiastico di el-Gib (Gibeon). *LA*, 25: 54–72, pls. 29–40.

(1979). *Antichi villaggi cristiani di Samaria*. SBF, Coll. min., vol. XIX. Jerusalem.

(1983). *Antichi villaggi cristiani della Giudea e del Neghev*. SBF, Coll. min., vol. XXIV. Jerusalem.

Bahat, D. (1971). Jérusalem: Jardin arménien. In Chronique archéologique, *RB*, 78: 598–9.

(1985a). Jerusalem. Dung Gate. *ESI*, 4: 54.

(1985b). New Discoveries in Jerusalem. *BAIAS* (1984–5): 50–3.

(1986). Les portes de Jérusalem selon Mukaddasi. Nouvelle identification. *RB*, 93: 429–35.

(1987). Sanuto's Map and the Walls of Jerusalem in the Thirteenth Century. *Eretz-Israel*, 19: 295–8, 83*. [in Hebr. with Eng. summary]

(1988). Nouvelles découvertes concernants les croisés à Jérusalem. In E.M. Laperrousaz (ed.), *Archéologie, art et histoire de la Palestine*, pp. 197–204. Paris.

(1991). Topography and Archaeology, Crusader Period, Ayyubid Period. In J. Prawer and H. Ben-Shammai (eds.), *The History of Jerusalem (1099–1250)*, pp. 68–134. Jerusalem. [in Hebr.]

(1992). 'The Topography and Toponomy of Crusader Jerusalem.' Unpublished Ph.D. thesis, Hebrew University of Jerusalem. [in Hebr.]

Bahat, D. and M.B. Ben-Ari (1976). Excavations at Tancred's Tower. In Yadin 1976: 109–10.

Bahat, D. and M. Broshi (1972). Jerusalem, Old City, the Armenian Garden. In Notes and News, *IEJ*, 22: 171–82, pl. 34b.

(1976). Excavations in the Armenian Garden. In Yadin 1976: 55–6.

Baldi, D. (1973). *Guida di Terra Santa*. Jerusalem.

Barag, D. (1976). Eshtemoa. In *EAEHL*, vol. II, pp. 386–8. Jerusalem.

(1979). A New Source Concerning the Ultimate Borders of the Latin Kingdom of Jerusalem. *IEJ*, 29: 197–217.

Barasch, M. (1971). *Crusader Figural Sculpture in the Holy Land: Twelfth Century Examples from Acre, Nazareth and Belvoir Castle*. Jerusalem.

Barber, M. (1994a). *The New Knighthood: A History of the Order of the Temple*. Cambridge.

(1994b) (ed.). *The Military Orders: Fighting for the Faith and Caring for the Sick*. Aldershot.

Bartlett, W.H. (1851). *Footsteps of Our Lord and His Apostles in Syria, Greece and Italy*. London.

Battista, A. and B. Bagatti (1976). *La fortezza saracena del Monte Tabor (A.H. 609–15: A.D. 1212–18)*. SBF, Coll. min., vol. XVIII. Jerusalem.

Ben-Dor, I. (1943). *Guide to Beisan*. Jerusalem.

Ben-Dov, M. (1969). The Excavations at the Crusader Fortress of Kokhav-Hayarden (Belvoir). *Qadmoniot*, 2.1: 22–7. [in Hebr.]

(1972). The Crusader Castle of Belvoir. *CNI*, 23.1: 26–8.

(1974). The Fortress of Latrun. *Qadmoniot*, 7.3–4: 117–20. [in Hebr.]

(1975a). Crusader Fortresses in Eretz-Israel. *Qadmoniot*, 8.4: 102–13. [in Hebr.]

(1975b). Belvoir (Kokhav Hayarden, Kaukab el Hawa). In *EAEHL*, vol. I, pp. 179–84.

(1976). Crusader Castles in Israel. *CNI*, 25: 216.

(1978). Banias – A Medieval Fortress Town. *Qadmoniot*, 11.1: 29–33. [in Hebr.]

(1982). *In the Shadow of the Temple: The Discovery of Ancient Jerusalem*, trans. I. Friedman. Jerusalem.

(1983). *Jerusalem's Fortifications: The City Walls, the Gates and the Temple Mount*. Tel Aviv. [in Hebr.]

(1986). The Sea Fort and the Land Fort at Sidon. *Qadmoniot*, 19.3–4: 113–19. [in Hebr.]

(1987). The Mediaeval 'Tanners' Gate' and the 'Moors' Gate' in Ottoman Times. *Qadmoniot*, 20.3–4: 115–19. [in Hebr.]

(1993a). Belvoir (Kokhav ha-Yarden). In *NEAEHL*, vol. I, pp. 182–6.

(1993b). Latrun. In *NEAEHL*, vol. III, pp. 911–13.

(1994). Excavations and Architectural Survey of the Archaeological Remains along the Southern Wall of the Jerusalem Old City. In H. Geva (ed.), *Ancient Jerusalem Revealed*, pp. 311–20. Jerusalem.

Ben-Dov, M., D. Bahat and M. Rosen-Ayalon (1993). Jerusalem: Early Arab to Ayyubid Periods. In *NEAEHL*, vol. II, pp. 786–800.

Ben-Dov, M. and Y. Minzker (1968). Kokhav Ha-Yarden (Belvoir). In Chronique archéologique, *RB*, 75: 419–20, pl. LI.

Ben-Tor, A. (1966). Excavations at Horvat 'Usa. *'Atiqot*, Hebrew series, 3: 1–24, 1*–2*, pls. I–IV. [in Hebr. with Eng. summary]

(1993). Jokneam. In *NEAEHL*, vol. III, pp. 805–11.

Ben-Tor, A. *et al.* (1987). A Regional Study of Tel Yoqne'am and its Vicinity. *Qadmoniot*, 20.1–2: 2–17. [in Hebr.]

Ben-Tor, A. and Y. Portugali (1987). *Tell Qiri: A Village in the Jezreel Valley. Report of the Archaeological Excavations 1975–1977*. Qedem, vol. XXIV. Jerusalem.

Ben-Tor, A., Y. Portugali and M. Avissàr (1979). The Second Season of Excavations at Tel Yoqne'am, 1978. Preliminary Report. *IEJ*, 29: 65–83, pls. 9–11.

Ben-Tor, A. and R. Rosenthal (1978a). The First Season of Excavations at Tel Yoqne'am, 1977. *IEJ*, 28: 57–82, pls. 16–18.

(1978b). Tel Yokneam (1977). In Chronique archéologique, *RB*, 85: 99–100, figs. 4–5, pls. VII–VIII.

Benvenisti, M. (1965). *Crusader Castles in Israel*. Jerusalem. [in Hebr.]

(1970). *The Crusaders in the Holy Land*. Jerusalem.

(1977). Montfort. In *EAEHL*, vol. III, pp. 886–8.

(1982). *Bovaria – babriyya*: A Frankish Residue on the Map of Palestine. In Kedar, Mayer and Smail 1982: 130–52.

Beretti, R. (1987). Al-Wu'eira, un esempio di rioccupazione, in ricognizione agli impianti fortificati di epoca crociata in Transgiordania. *Castellum*, 17–18.

Berggötz, O. (1991). *Der Bericht des Marsilio Zorzi: Codex Querini – Stampalia IV3 (1064)*. Kieler Werkstücke, Reihe C: Beiträge zur europäischen Geschichte des frühen und hohen Mittelalters, vol. II. Frankfurt am Main.

Bernie, V., M. Milwright and E.J. Simpson (1992). An Architectural Survey of Muslim Buildings in Tiberias. *Levant*, 24: 95–129.

Beyer, G. (1936). Das Gebiet der Kreuzfahrerherrschaft Caesarea in Palästina. *ZDPV*, 59: 1–91.

(1940). Neapolis und sein Gebiet in der Kreuzfahrerzeit. *ZDPV*, 63: 155–209.

(1942). Die Kreuzfahrergebiete von Jerusalem und St. Abraham. *ZDPV*, 65: 165–211.

(1945). Die Kreuzfahrergebiete Akko und Galilaea. *ZDPV*, 67 (1944–5): 183–260.

(1951). Die Kreuzfahrergebiete Sudwestpalastinas. *ZDPV*, 68 (1946–51): 148–281.

Beyer, G. and A. Alt (1953). Civitas Ficuum. *ZDPV*, 69: 75–82.

Bikai, P. and P. Bikai (1987). Tyre at the End of the Twentieth Century. *Berytus*, 35: 69–96.

Biller, T. (1989). Die Johanniterburg Belvoir am Jordan: zum frühen Burgenbau der Ritterorden im Heiligen Land. *Architectura: Zeitschrift fur Geschichte der Baukunst/Journal of the History of Architecture*: 105–36.

Biran, A. (1966). Athlit. *CNI*, 17: 18, pl. 2.

(1967). Archaeological Activities, 1966. *CNI*, 18.

(1968). Archaeological Activities 1967. *CNI*, 19: 29–48.

(1993). Yesud ha-Ma'ala. In *NEAEHL*, vol. IV, p. 1510.

Biran, A. and Y. Shoham (1987). Remains of a Synagogue and of Sugar Installations at Yesud Hama'alah. *Eretz-Israel*, 19: 199–207, 78*. [in Hebr. with Eng. summary]

Bliss, F.J. (1895). Narrative of an Expedition to Moab and Gilead in March, 1895. *PEFQS*: 203–35.

(1899). First Report on the Excavations at Tell-es-Sâfi. *PEFQS*: 317–33.

(1900). Third Report on the Excavations at Tell es-Sâfi. *PEFQS*: 16–29.

Bliss, F.J. and R.A.S. Macalister (1902). *Excavations in Palestine During the Years 1898–1900*. London.

Boase, T.S.R. (1967). *Castles and Churches of the Crusading Kingdom*. London.

(1971). *Kingdoms and Strongholds of the Crusaders*. London.

(1977). Contributions to Hazard (1977).

Boaz, A. (1990). Bet Shean, Crusader Fortress – Area Z. *ESI*, 9 (1989–90): 129, fig. 120.

Boniface of Ragusa (1577). *Liber de Perenni Cultu Terrae Sanctae*, ed. C. de Tarvisio. Venice (1875).

Boraas, R.S. and S.H. Horn (1969). *Heshbon 1968. The First Campaign at Tell Ḥesbân. A Preliminary Report*. Andrews University Monographs, vol. II. Berrien Springs, Michigan.

Bouillon, C. (1898). Aux rives du Jourdain. *Echos d'Orient*, 1 (1897–8): 290–300, 330–45, 368–80.

Bowen, B. (1981). *Ajlun Castle – Qalat al Rabad*. Jordan Dept of Antiquities, Amman.

Bralevski, J. (1946). On the Cemeteries of Acre in the XIIIth Century. *BJPES*, 12 (1945–6): 165–7.

Brooker, C.H. and E.A. Knauf (1988). Notes on Crusader Transjordan. *ZDPV*, 104: 184–8, pls. 14–15.

Broshi, M. (1972). Jérusalem: Quartier arménien. In Chronique archéologique, *RB*, 79: 578–81, pls. XLVIII–XLIX.

(1977). Along Jerusalem's Walls. *Biblical Archaeologist*, 40.1: 11–17.

(1987). Al-Malek al-Muazzam Isa – Evidence in a New Inscription. *Eretz-Israel*, 19: 299–302, 82*. [in Hebr. with Eng. summary]

Broshi, M. and S. Gibson (1994). Excavations along the Western and Southern Walls of the Old City of Jerusalem. In H. Geva (ed.), *Ancient Jerusalem Revealed*, pp. 147–55. Jerusalem.

Broshi, M. and Y. Tsafrir (1977). Excavations at the Zion Gate, Jerusalem. *IEJ*, 27: 28–37, pls. 2–3.

Brown, R.M. (1987). A 12th Century A.D. Sequence from Southern Transjordan: Crusader and Ayyubid Occupation at el-Wu'eira. *ADAJ*, 31: 267–88.

(1988). Summary Report of the 1986 Excavations. Late Islamic Shobak. *ADAJ*, 32: 225–45.

(1989a). Excavations in the 14th Century A.D. Mamluk Palace at Kerak. *ADAJ*, 33: 287–304.

(1989b). Kerak Castle. In D. Homès-Fredericq and J.B. Hennessy (eds.), *Archaeology of Jordan*, vol. II.i, pp. 341–7. Akkadica, Supplementum, vols. III, VII–VIII (2 vols.). Leuven (1986–9).

(1989c). Shobak Castle. In D. Homès-Fredericq and J.B. Hennessy (eds.), *Archaeology of Jordan*, vol. II.ii, pp. 559–66. Akkadica, Supplementum, vols. III, VII–VIII (2 vols.). Leuven (1986–9).

(1989d). Wueira (el). In D. Homès-Fredericq and J.B. Hennessy (eds.), *Archaeology of Jordan*, vol. II.ii, pp. 625–31. Akkadica, Supplementum, vols. III, VII–VIII (2 vols.). Leuven (1986–9).

Brünnow, R.E. and A. von Domaszewski (1904). *Die Provincia Arabia*, 3 vols. Strasbourg (1904–9).

van Bruyn, C. (1725). *Voyage au Levant*, 4 vols. Paris.

Buckingham, J.S. (1822). *Travels in Palestine*, 2 vols. London.

Bull, R.J. (1987) (ed.). 'The Joint Expedition to Caesarea Maritima. Preliminary Reports.' Drew University, Madison, New Jersey (on microfiche).

Bull, R.J. and E.F. Campbell (1968). The Sixth Campaign at Balâtah (Shechem). *BASOR*, 190: 2–41.

Bull, R.J., E.M. Krentz, O.J. Storvick and M. Spiro (1990). The Joint Expedition to Caesarea Maritima: Tenth Season, 1982. *BASOR*, Supplement 27: 69–94.

Bull, R.J. and L.E. Toombs (1972). Caesarea. In Notes and News, *IEJ*, 22: 178–80.

Bunimovitz, S. and Z. Ledermann (1993). Beth-Shemesh. In *NEAEHL*, vol. I, pp. 249–53.

Burckhardt, J.L. (1822). *Travels in Syria and the Holy Land*. London.

Burgoyne, M.H. (1976). *The Architecture of Islamic Jerusalem*. Jerusalem.

Burgoyne, M.H. and D.S. Richards (1987). *Mamlūk Jerusalem: An Architectural Study*. [London.]

Buselli, R. (1886). *L'Emmaus evangelico*, 4 parts. Milan.

Calano, C. (1980). San Giovanni d'Acri: contributi alla conoscienza di una città crociata. *Palladio*, 3: 7–40.

Campbell, E.F. (1991). *Shechem, II. Portrait of a Hill Country Vale. The Shechem Regional Survey*. ASOR Archaeological Reports, vol. II. Atlanta, Georgia.

Chaver, Y. (1986). Afeq Pass at the Sources of the Yarqon River. *Israel Land and Nature*, 11.3: 140–4.

Chéhab, M. (1948). Chronique. *BMB*, 8 (1946–8): 159–73.

(1950). Chronique. *BMB*, 9 (1949–50): 107–17.

(1955). Chronique. *BMB*, 12: 47–58.

(1975). *Tyr à l'époque des croisades*, I. *Histoire militaire et diplomatique*, 2 vols. = *BMB*, 27–8.

(1979). *Tyr à l'époque des croisades*, II. *Histoire sociale, économique et religieuse*, 2 vols. Paris.

Clermont-Ganneau, C. (1880). *Etudes d'archéologie orientale*. 2 vols. Paris (1880–95).

(1885). Rapports sur une mission en Palestine et en Phénicie entreprise en 1881, Cinquième rapport. *Archives des Missions scientifiques et littéraires*, 3rd series, 11: 157–251.

(1888). *Recueil d'archéologie orientale*, 8 vols. Paris (1888–1924).

(1896). *Archaeological Researches in Palestine During the Years 1873–1874*, 2 vols. London (1899, 1896).

Cohen, A. (1989). *Economic Life in Ottoman Jerusalem*. Cambridge Studies in Islamic Civilization. Cambridge.

Collinet, P. (1925). *Etudes historiques sur le droit de Justinien*, II. *Histoire de l'Ecole de Droit de Beyrouth*. Paris.

Conder, C.R. (1874). Lieut. Claude R. Conder's Reports [XVI–XXI]. *PEFQS*: 11–24, 35–64, 178–87.

(1875). The Survey of Western Palestine. Lieut. Claude R. Conder's Reports [XXII–XXXV]. *PEFQS*: 5–27, 63–94, 125–68, 188–95.

(1878). *Tent Work in Palestine*, 2 vols. London.

(1890). The Old Wall Outside Jerusalem. *PEFQS*: 39.

Conder, C.R. and H.H. Kitchener (1881). *The Survey of Western Palestine: Memoirs of the Topography, Orography, Hydrography and Archaeology*, 3 vols. London (1881–3).

Conteneau, G. (1920). Mission archéologique à Sidon (1914). *Syria*, 1: 16–55, 108–54, 198–229, 287–317, pls. V–VI, X–XV, XIX–XXI.

(1923). Deuxième mission archéologique à Sidon (1920). *Syria*, 4: 261–81.

Corbo, V. (1975). *Cafarnao*, I. *Gli edifici della città*. SBF, Coll. maj., vol. XIX. Jerusalem.

Coughenour, R.A. (1976). Preliminary Report on the Exploration and Excavation of Mugharat el Wardeh and Abu Thawab. *ADAJ*, 21: 71–8, pls. XXXI–XXXII.

(1989). Mugharat el Wardeh. In D. Homès-Fredericq and J.B. Hennessy (eds.), *Archaeology of Jordan*, vol. II.ii, pp. 386–90. Akkadica, Supplementum, vols. III, VII–VIII (2 vols.). Leuven (1986–9).

Creswell, K.A.C. (1959). *The Muslim Architecture of Egypt*, 2 vols. Oxford.

Crowfoot, J.W. (1945). Ophel Again. *PEQ*: 66–104, pls. VII–XVII.

Dahlberg, B.T. and K.G. O'Connell (1989). *Tell el-Hesi. The Site and the Expedition*. The Joint Archaeological Expedition to Tell al-Hesi, vol. IV. Winona Lake, Indiana.

Damati, E. (1985). Safed. *ESI*, 4: 98.

(1986). Safed: Citadel. *ESI*, 5: 93–4.

(1989). Safed Citadel. *ESI*, 7–8: 159–60.

(1990). Safed Citadel. *ESI*, 9 (1989–90): 13.

Dapper, O. (1677). *Naukeurige Beschrijving van gantsch Syrie, en Palestijn, of Heilige Lant*. Amsterdam.

Dar, S. (1984). Ḥ. Sumaq. *IEJ*, 34: 270–1.

(1986). *Landscape and Pattern: An Archaeological Survey of Samaria, 800 B.C.E.–636 C.E.*, 2 vols. BAR, International Series, vol. CCCVIII. Oxford.

(1988). Ḥorvat Summaqa. *IEJ*, 6 (1987–8): 98–9, figs. 39–40.

(1990). Ḥorvat Summaq–1988/1989. *ESI*, 9 (1989–90): 25–7.

(1993). Sumaqa, Ḥorvat. In *NEAEHL*, vol. IV, pp. 1412–15.

Dar, S. and D. Adnan-Bayewitz (1983a). Tiberias. In Notes and News, *IEJ*, 33: 114–15.

(1983b). Tiberias. *ESI*, 2: 103.

Dar, S. and Mintzker, J. (1987). *Qāqūn*, Turris Rubea and Montdidier: Three Crusader Sites in 'Ēmeq Ḥēfer. *ZDPV*, 103: 192–213.

Dauphin, C. (1979a). Dor, Byzantine Church. In Notes and News, *IEJ*, 29: 235–6, pl. 29.

(1979b). Shelomi (1978). In Chronique archéologique, *RB*, 86: 437, pl. XVII.

Davie, M.F. (1987). Maps and the Historical Topography of Beirut. *Berytus*, 35: 141–64.

Dean, B. (1927). *A Crusaders' Fortress in Palestine: A Report of Excavations Made by the Museum, 1926*. Part II of the Bulletin of the Metropolitan Museum of Art, New York. Reprinted as *The Crusaders' Fortress of Montfort*, with introduction by M. Benvenisti, Jerusalem (1982).

Deschamps, P. (1933). Deux positions stratégiques des croisés à l'est du Jourdain: Ahamant et el Habis. *Revue historique*, 172: 42–57.

(1934). Les châteaux des croisés en Terre Sainte, I. *Le Crac des Chevaliers*, text and album. Bibliothèque archéologique et historique, vol. XIX. Paris.

(1935). Une grotte-forteresse des croisés au delà du Jourdain: el Habis en Terre de Suète. *JA*, 227: 285–99.

(1937). Les deux Cracs des croisés. *JA*, 229: 494–500.

(1939a). *Les châteaux des croisés en Terre Sainte*, II. *La défense du royaume de Jérusalem: étude historique, géographique et monumentale*, text and album. Bibliothèque archéologique et historique, vol. XXXIV. Paris.

(1939b). Une grotte-forteresse des croisés dans le Liban: la Cave de Tyron. In *Mélanges syriens offerts à M. René Dussaud*, vol. II, pp. 873–82.

(1943). Étude sur un texte latin énumérant les possessions musulmanes dans le royaume de Jérusalem vers l'année 1239. *Syria*, 23 (1942–3): 86–104, pls. VII–VIII.

(1964). *Terre Sainte romane*. Zodiaque, La Nuit des Temps, vol. XXI. La Pierre-Qui-Vire.

(1973). *Les châteaux des croisés en Terre Sainte*, III. *La défense du comté de Tripoli et de la principauté d'Antioche*, text and album. Bibliothèque archéologique et historique, vol. XC. Paris.

Desimoni, C. (1884). Quatre titres de propriétés des génois à Acre et à Tyr. *AOL*, 2: 213–30.

DeVries, B. (1991). Archaeology in Jordan. *AJA*, 95: 253–80.

(forthcoming). *Hesban*, IX. *Ayyubid-Mamluk Strata*.

Dichter, B. (1973). *The Maps of Acre: An Historical Cartography*. Acre.

(1979a). *The Orders and Churches of Crusader Acre*. Acre.

(1979b). *Akko: A Bibliography*. Acre.

Dorrell, P.G. (1993). The Spring at Jericho from Early Photographs. *PEQ*, 125: 95–114.

Dothan, M. (1951). Archaeological News from Israel, 5. Arab and Crusader Periods. *Bulletin of the Dept of Antiquities of the State of Israel*, 3: 13, pl. VII. [in Hebr.]

(1955). The Excavations at 'Afula. *'Atiqot*, 1: 18–63 [in Hebr.]

(1964). Remains of Muslim Buildings at Ashdod. *Eretz-Israel*, 7: 98–101, 172*. [in Hebr. with Eng. summary]

(1973). Accho. In Notes and News, *IEJ*, 23: 257–8.

(1974). 'Akko. In Notes and News, *IEJ*, 24: 276–9, pl. 60d.

(1975a). Tel Akko. In Chronique archéologique, *RB*, 82: 84–6.

(1975b). Acre. In Chronique archéologique, *RB*, 82: 566–71, pl. XLVI.

(1975c). 'Afula. In *EAEHL*, vol. I, pp. 32–6.

(1976a). Akko: Interim Excavation Report. First Season, 1973/4. *BASOR*, 224: 1–48.

(1976b). 'Akko, 1976. In Notes and News, *IEJ*, 26: 207–8.

(1978). Akko (1976–1977). In Chronique archéologique, *RB*, 85: 92–4, pls. V–VI.

(1993a). Acco: Tel Acco; Excavations in the Modern City. In *NEAEHL*, vol. I, pp. 17–24.

(1993b). 'Afula. In *NEAEHL*, vol. I, pp. 37–9.

Dothan, M. and E. Linder (1974). *Akko. Land and Sea Excavations*. Haifa.

Dowling, T.E. (1896). Kerak in 1896. *PEFQS*: 327–32.

Drake, C.F.T. (1872). The Survey. *PEFQS*: 77–92.

(1873). Reports [XIII–XIV]. *PEFQS*: 99–111.

(1875). The Survey of Palestine. Mr. Tyrwhitt Drake's Report [XIX]. *PEFQS*: 27–34.

Druks, A. (1984). Akko, Fortifications. *ESI*, 3: 2–4.

Dudman, H. (1988). *Tiberias*. Jerusalem.

Dunand, M. (1939). Chronique. *BMB*, 3: 77–85.

(1940). Chronique. *BMB*, 4: 117–25.

(1941). Chronique. *BMB*, 5: 87–93.

(1967). Rapport préliminaire sur les fouilles de Sidon en 1964–1965. *BMB*, 20: 27–44.

Duncan, A. (1982). *Castles of Jordan*. [Amman.]

Duncan, J.G. (1928). Es-Salt. *PEFQS*: 28–36, pl. VII.

Dussaud, R. (1927). *Topographie historique de la Syrie antique et médiévale*. Bibliothèque archéologique et historique, vol. IV. Paris.

Dussaud, R., P. Deschamps and H. Seyrig (1931). *La Syrie antique et médiévale illustrée*. Bibliothèque archéologique et historique, vol. XVII. Paris.

Eakins, J.K. (1993). *Tell el-Hesi. The Muslim Cemetery in Fields V and VI/IX (Stratum II)*. The Joint Archaeological Expedition to Tell el-Hesi, vol. v. Winona Lake, Indiana.

Edbury, P.W. (1985) (ed.). *Crusade and Settlement: Papers Read at the First Conference of the Society for the Study of the Crusades and the Latin East and Presented to R.C. Smail*. Cardiff.

El'ad, A. (1982). The Coastal Cities of Palestine During the Early Middle Ages. *Jerusalem Cathedra*, 2: 146–67.

Elisséeff, N. (1960). Bayrūt. In *EI*, 2nd edition, vol. I, cols. 1137–8. Leiden.

Ellenblum, R. (1989). Who Built Qal'at al-Ṣubayba? *Dumbarton Oaks Papers*, 43: 103–12.

(1991). 'Frankish Rural Settlement in Crusader Palestine.' Unpublished Ph.D. thesis, Hebrew University of Jerusalem. [in Hebr. with Eng. summary]

(1992). Construction Methods in Frankish Rural Settlements. In Kedar 1992: 168–89.

(forthcoming). *Frankish Rural Settlement in Crusader Palestine*. Cambridge.

Ellenblum, R., R. Rubin and G. Solar (1996). Khirbat al-Lawza, a Frankish Farm House in the Judean Hills in Central Palestine. *Levant*, 28: 189–98.

Enlart, C. (1925). *Les monuments des croisés dans le royaume de Jérusalem: architecture religieuse et civile*, 2 vols. and 2 albums. Bibliothèque archéologique et historique, vols. VII–VIII. Paris (1925–8).

Escobar, J. (1976a). *Tecua*. Jerusalem.

(1976b). Estudio de los restos arqueologicos de Tecoa. *LA*, 26: 5–26, pls. 1–12.

Eydoux, H.-P. (1982). *Les châteaux du soleil: forteresses et guerres des croisés*. Paris.

Faber, Felix (1480–3). *The Book of the Wanderings of Brother Felix Fabri*, trans. A. Stewart. In *PPTS*, vols. VII–X (2 vols.), London (1887–97).

Fargo, V. (1993). Ḥesi, Tel. In *NEAEHL*, vol. II, pp. 630–4.

Favreau[-Lilie], M.-L. (1977). Die Kreuzfahrerherrschaft Scandalion (Iskanderūne). *ZDPV*, 93: 12–29.

(1980). Landesaubau und Burg während der Kreuzfahrerzeit Ṣafad in Obergaliläa. *ZDPV*, 96: 67–87.

(1982). The Teutonic Knights in Acre after the Fall of Montfort (1271): Some Reflections. In Kedar, Mayer and Smail 1982: 272–84.

Fedden, R. (1950). *Crusader Castles: A Brief Study in the Military Architecture of the Crusades*. London.

Fedden, R. and J. Thomson (1957). *Crusader Castles*. London.

Finkelstein, I. and Y. Magen (1993) (eds.). *Archaeological Survey of the Hill Country of Benjamin*. Jerusalem.

Fischer, M., B. Isaac and I. Roll (1996). *Roman Roads in Judaea, vol. II. The Jaffa–Jerusalem Roads*. BAR, International Series, vol. DCXXVIII. Oxford.

Flinder, A. (1977). The Island of Jezirat Fara'un. Its Ancient Harbour, Anchorage and Marine Defence Installations. *International Journal of Nautical Archaeology and Underwater Exploration*, 6.2: 127–39.

(1989). Is This Solomon's Seaport? *Biblical Archaeology Review*, 15.4: 30–43.

Flinder, A., E. Linder and E.T. Hall (1993). Survey of the Ancient Harbour of Akko, 1964–1966. In M. Heltzer, A. Segal and D. Kaufman (eds.), *Studies in the Archaeology and History of Ancient Israel in Honour of Moshe Dothan*, pp. 199–225. Haifa.

Foerster, G. (1975). Dor. In *EAEHL*, vol. I, pp. 334–7.

(1976). Herodium. In *EAEHL*, vol. II, pp. 502–10.

de Forbin, Comte L.N.P.A. (1819). *Voyage dans le Levant*. Paris.

Forest, C. and J.D. Forest (1982). Fouilles à la municipalité de Beyrouth (1977). *Syria*, 59: 1–26.

Forstreuter, K. (1967). *Der Deutschen Orden am Mittelmeer*. Quellen und Studien zur Geschichte des Deutschen Ordens, vol. II. Bonn.

Franciscan Fathers (1977). *Guide to Jordan*. Jerusalem.

Frank, F. (1934). Aus der 'Araba I: Reiserberichte. *ZDPV*, 57: 191–280.

Frankel, R. (1980). Three Crusader Boundary Stones from Kibbutz Shomrat. *IEJ*, 30: 199–201.

(1985). Western Galilee, oil presses. *ESI*, 4: 110–14.

(1986a). I cippi confinari genovesi dal Kibbutz Shomrat. In G. Airaldi and B.Z. Kedar (eds.), *I Comuni italiani del regno crociato di Gerusalemme*, pp. 691–5. Collana storica di fonti e studi, vol. XLVIII. Genoa.

(1986b). Ḥorvat Din'ala. *ESI*, 5: 21–3.

(1987a). The North-West Corner of Crusader Acre. *IEJ*, 37: 256–61, pls. 31–2.

(1987b). Oil Presses in Western Galilee and the Judaea – A Comparison. In Heltzer and Eitan 1987: 63–80.

(1988). Topographical Notes on the Territory of Acre in the Crusader Period. *IEJ*, 38: 249–72.

(1993). Montfort. In *NEAEHL*, vol. III, pp. 1070–3.

Frankel, R. and N. Gatzov (1986). The History and Plan of Montfort Castle. *Qadmoniot*, 19: 52–7. [in Hebr.]

Franken, H.J. and J. Kalsbeek (1975). *Potters of a Medieval Village in the Jordan Valley. Excavations at Tell deir 'Allā: A Medieval Tell, Tell Abu Gourdan, Jordan*. North Holland Ceramic Studies in Archaeology, vol. III. Amsterdam/ Oxford/New York.

Frenkel, J. (1987). Oil and Olives in the Land of Israel in the Early Muslim Period (634–1099). In Heltzer and Eitan 1987: 57–62.

Friedman, E. (1971). The Medieval Abbey of St. Margaret of Mount Carmel. *Ephemerides Carmeliticae*, 22: 295–348.

(1979). *The Latin Hermits of Mount Carmel: A Study in Carmelite Origins*. Institutum Historicum Teresianum, Studia, vol. I. Rome.

Fritsch, C.T. and I. Bendor (1961). The Link Marine Expedition to Israel. *Biblical Archaeologist*, 24: 50–9.

Frova, A., M. Avi-Yonah and A. Negev (1975). Caesarea. In *EAEHL*, vol. I, pp. 270–85

Fulco, W.J. (1975). Monnaies de Tell Keisan 1971–1974. *RB*, 82: 234–9, pls. XVIII–XIX.

Gal, Z. (1991). *Map of Gazit (46)*. 19–22. Archaeological Survey of Israel. Jerusalem. [in Hebr. with Eng. summary]

Garstang, J. (1921a). The Fund's Excavation of Askalon. *PEFQS*: 12–16.

(1921b). The Excavation of Askalon, 1920–1921. *PEFQS*: 73–5.

(1922a). The Excavations at Askalon. *PEFQS*: 112–19.

(1922b). Eighteen Months' Work of the Department of Antiquities for Palestine. July, 1920–December, 1921. *PEFQS*: 57–62.

(1922c). Geography of the Plain of Acre (S). *Bulletin of the British School of Archaeology in Jerusalem*, 2: 10–12.

(1924a). Ascalon. *PEFQS*: 24–35, fig. 5, pls. I–III.

(1924b). Tanturah (Dora). *Bulletin of the British School of Archaeology in Jerusalem*, 4: 35–45, pls. I–IV; 6: 64–73, pls. I–V.

Gaudefroy-Demombynes, M.G. (1923). *La Syrie à l'époque des mamelouks d'après les auteurs arabes*. Bibliothèque archéologique et historique, vol. III. Paris.

Gavin, C. (1985). Jordan's Environment in Early Photographs. In A. Hadidi (ed.), *Studies in the History and Archaeology of Jordan*, vol. II, pp. 279–85. London.

Geikie, C. (1887). *The Holy Land and the Bible*, 2 vols. London.

Geraty, L.T. (1975). Hesbân (Ḥeshbon). In Chronique archéologique, *RB*, 82: 576–86, pl. XLVIII.

(1993). Heshbon. In *NEAEHL*, vol. II, pp. 626–30.

Gertwagen, R. (1987). Tel Ḥanaton – 1987. *Hadashot Arkheologiot*: 22–3, figs. 17–19. [in Hebr.]

(1988). The Crusader Site of Hanaton: Report of the First Season. *CMS News* 15. University of Haifa, Center for Maritime Studies. Haifa.

(1989a). Land Excavation and Underwater Survey at the Southern End of the Old City of Akko – The so-called 'Pisan Harbour'. *CMS News* 16. University of Haifa, Center for Maritime Studies. Haifa.

(1989b). Underwater Salvage Excavation at the Eastern Flank of the Harbour at Akko. *CMS News* 16. University of Haifa, Center for Maritime Studies. Haifa.

(1989c). Tel Ḥannaton – 1987. *ESI*, 7–8 (1988–9): 71–2, figs. 59–61.

(1992a). The Fortress. In The Bet She'an Excavation Project (1989–1991), *ESI*, 11: 56–9, figs. 75–81.

(1992b). Archaeological Excavations of Medieval Beit-Shean – The Medieval Castle – Preliminary Report of 1980–1992 Seasons. *Hadashot Arkheologiot*, 98. [in Hebr.]

(1993). Tel Hanaton – Beginning of a New Touristic Archaeological Site. *Baekem*, September. Emek Israel Municipality.

Gertwagen, R., and G. Finkelstein (1992). Serail Bypass Road. In The Bet She'an Excavation Project (1989–1991), *ESI*, 11: 60.

Geva, H. (1983). Excavations in the Citadel of Jerusalem, 1979–1980. Preliminary Report. *IEJ*, 33: 55–71.

(1994). Excavations at the Citadel of Jerusalem, 1976–1980. In H. Geva (ed.), *Ancient Jerusalem Revealed*, pp. 156–67. Jerusalem.

Gibson, S. (1982). Jerusalem (North-East): Archaeological Survey. In Notes and News, *IEJ*, 32: 156–7.

Gichon, M. (1975). The Sites of the Limes in the Negev. *Eretz-Israel*, 12: 149–66. [in Hebr.]

(1987). The Bath-House at Emmaus. *Bulletin of the Anglo-Israel Archaeological Society*, 6 (1986–7): 54–7.

(1993a). *En Boqeq. Ausgrabungen in einer Oase am Toten Meer*, vol. I. Mainz am Rhein.

(1993b). Emmaus: The Southern Baths. In *NEAEHL*, vol. II, pp. 387–9.

Glidden, H.W. (1952). The Mamluke Origin of the Fortified Khan at al-'Aqabah, Jordan. In G.C. Miles (ed.), *Archaeologica Orientalia in Memoriam Ernst Herzfeld*, pp. 116–18. New York.

Glücksmann, G. and R. Kool (1995). Crusader Period Finds from the Temple Mount Excavations in Jerusalem. *'Atiqot*, 26: 87–104.

Glueck, N. (1935). *Explorations in Eastern Palestine*, vol. II. AASOR, vol. XV.

(1951). *Explorations in Eastern Palestine*, vol. III. AASOR, vols. XVIII–XIX.

(1970). *The Other Side of the Jordan*. Cambridge, Mass.

Goldfuss, H. (1984). Jaffa Gate. *ESI*, 3: 53–5.

Goldmann, Z. (1959). *Guide to the Crypt of St. John*. Acre.

(1962a). Newly Discovered Crusaders' Inscription in Acre (Preliminary Report). *CNI*, 13: 33–4, pl. IV.

(1962b). The Refectory of the Order of St. John in Acre. *CNI*, 12: 15–19, pls. I–IV.

(1966). The Hospice of the Knights of St. John in Akko. *Archaeology*, 19: 182–9.

(1967). The Hospice of the Knights of St. John in Akko. In *Archaeological Discoveries in the Holy Land*. Archaeological Institute of America.

(1974). Le Couvent des Hospitaliers à Saint Jean d'Acre. *Bible et Terre Sainte*, 160: 8–18.

(1987). *Akko in the Time of the Crusaders: The Convent of the Order of St. John*. Acre.

(1993). Acco: Excavations in the Modern City [II]. In *NEAEHL*, vol. I, pp. 24–7.

Gordon, R.L. (1987). Er-Rumman Survey 1985. *ADAJ*, 31: 289–98.

Gotein, S.D. (1982). Jerusalem in the Arab Period (638–1099). *Jerusalem Cathedra*, 2: 168–96.

Goujon, J. (1670). *Histoire et voyage de Terre Sainte*. Lyons.

Graboïs, A. (1970). La cité de Baniyas et le château de Subeibeh pendant les croisades. *Cahiers de civilisation médiévale*, 13: 43–62.

(1987). The City of Baniyas and the Castle of Subeibeh. In B.Z. Kedar (ed.), *The Crusaders in their Kingdom 1099–1291*, pp. 148–68. Jerusalem. [in Hebr.]

Grant, E. (1926). Rāmallāh. Signs of the Early Occupation of this and other Sites. *PEFQS*: 186–95.

Grant, E. and G.E. Wright (1938). *Ain Shems Excavations (Palestine). Part IV (Pottery)*. Biblical and Kindred Studies, vol. VII. Haverford, Pennsylvania.

(1939). *Ain Shems Excavations (Palestine). Part V (Text)*. Biblical and Kindred Studies, vol. VIII. Haverford, Pennsylvania.

Great Britain: Naval Intelligence Division (1943a). *Syria*. Geographical Handbook Series, B.R. 513. London.

(1943b). *Palestine and Transjordan*. Geographical Handbook Series, B.R. 514. London.

Grossmann, E. (1991). Apollonia, Underwater Survey. *ESI*, 10: 119, fig. 131.

Guérin, V. (1857). Description des ruines d'Ascalon. *Bulletin de la Société de Géographie de Paris*, 4th series, 13: 81–95.

(1868). *Description géographique, historique et archéologique de la Palestine*, vol. I. *Judée*, 3 vols. Paris (1868–9).

(1874). *Description géographique, historique et archéologique de la Palestine*, vol. II. *Samarie*, 2 vols. Paris (1874–5).

(1880). *Description géographique, historique et archéologique de la Palestine*, vol. III. *Galilée*, 3 vols. Paris.

Guide Bleu (1932). *Syrie – Palestine – Iraq – Transjordanie*. Paris.

(1975). *Liban*. Paris.

(1981). *Israël, Golan, Cisjordanie, Bande de Gaza, Côte orientale du Sinaï*. Paris.

Guthe, H. (1879). Die Ruinen Ascalons. *ZDPV*, 2: 164–9, pl. V.

Gütterling, W. (1921). Tecoa. *Palästina Jahrbuch*, 17.

de Haas, H., H.E. LaGro and M. Steiner (1989). First Season of Excavations at Tell Abū Ṣarbuṭ, 1988. A Preliminary Report. *ADAJ*, 33: 323–6.

(1992). Second and Third Seasons of Excavations at Tell Abu Sarbuṭ, Jordan Valley (Preliminary Report). *ADAJ*, 36: 333–43.

Hai, M. (1983). A Hike along the Snir River. *Israel Land and Nature*, 8.2 (1982–3): 72–6.

Hall, E.T., A. Flinder and E. Linder (1968). Acre. In Chronique archéologique, *RB*, 75: 421–2.

Hamilton, R.W. (1947). *The Church of the Nativity, Bethlehem: A Guide*. Jerusalem.

(1959). *Khirbat al Mafjar: An Arabian Mansion in the Jordan Valley*. Oxford.

Hammond, N. (1995). Crusaders Carve Crude Niche in History. *The Times* (6 Feb., and letters 10 Feb.).

Hammond, P.C. (1965). Hébron. In Chronique archéologique, *RB*, 72: 267–70, pls. XVIII–XIX.

(1970). *The Crusader Fort on El-Habis at Petra: Its Survey and Interpretation*. Middle East Center, University of Utah, Research Monograph, vol. II. Salt Lake City.

Hanauer, J.E. (1896). A Visit to Arsuf. *PEFQS*: 165.

(1903). Sculptured Figures from the Muristan and Other Notes. *PEFQS*: 77–86.

Harding, G.L. (1967). *The Antiquities of Jordan*, new edition. London/Amman.

Harper, R.P. (1986). In P. Freeman and D. Kennedy (eds.), *The Defence of the Roman and Byzantine East*, BAR International Series, vol. CCXCVIII, pp. 329–36. Oxford.

(1987). BSAJ Excavations 1985–1986. *Levant*, 19: 219–20.

(1988). Belmont (Suba). In Chronique archéologique, *RB*, 95: 277–9, fig. 26, pl. IXb.

(1989a). Belmont Castle (Suba) – 1987. *ESI*, 7–8 (1988–9): 13–14, fig. 11.

(1989b). Belmont Castle (Suba) – 1988. *Hadashot Arkheologiot*, 94: 48–9, fig. 49. [in Hebr.]

(1990). Belmont Castle (Suba) – 1988. *ESI*, 9 (1989–90): 57–8, fig. 49.

(1992). The Jerusalem School (B.S.A.J.) in Spring and Summer 1991. *PEQ*, 124: 78–9.

Harper, R.P. and D. Pringle (1986). Belmont (Suba) – 1986. *ESI*, 5: 12–13, fig. 6.

(1987). Scavi al castello di Belmont (Suba), Israele, 1986. *Notiziario di archeologia medievale*, 45: 6.

(1988). Belmont Castle: A Historical Notice and Preliminary Report of Excavations in 1986. *Levant*, 20: 101–18.

(1989). Belmont Castle 1987: Second Preliminary Report of Excavations. *Levant*, 21: 47–61.

Hartal, M., Z. Ma'oz and V. Tzaferis (1985). Banias. *ESI*, 4: 7–9.

Hartmann, R. (1960). 'Athlith. In *EI*, new edition, vol. I, col. 737. Leiden/London.

Hartmann, R. and B. Lewis (1960). 'Askalān. In *EI*, new edition, vol. I, cols. 710–11. Leiden/London.

Hazard, H.W. (1975). Caesarea and the Crusades. In C.T. Fritsch (ed.), *Studies in the History of Caesarea Maritima*, BASOR Supplemental Series, vol. XIX, pp. 79–114. Missoula, Montana.

(1977) (ed.). *The Art and Architecture of the Crusader States*. A

History of the Crusades, ed. K.M. Setton, vol. IV. Madison, Wisconsin.

Heltzer, M. and D. Eitan (1987) (eds.). *Olive Oil in Antiquity: Israel and Neighbouring Countries from Neolith to Early Arab Period*. Haifa.

Hennessy, B. (1968). Jérusalem (Porte de Damas). In Chronique archéologique, *RB*, 75: 250–53, pls. XXVIII–XXIX.

(1970). Preliminary Report on Excavations at the Damascus Gate, Jerusalem, 1964–6. *Levant*, 2: 22–7, pls. XIII–XXIV.

Heyck, E. (1900). *Die Kreuzzüge und das Heilige Land*. Monographien zur Weltgeschichte, vol. XII. Bielefeld/Leipzig.

van der Heyden, A. (1993). Crusader Castles in Israel. *Ariel*, 93: 15–28.

Heydenreich, L.H. (1965). Ein Jerusalem-Plan aus der Zeit der Kreuzfahrer. *Miscellanea Pro Arte: Festschrift für Hermann Schnitzler*, pp. 83–90. Düsseldorf.

Hirschfeld, Y. (1985). *Archaeological Survey of Israel. Map of Herodium (108/2), 17–11*. Jerusalem. [in Hebr. and Eng.]

(1992). *A Guide to Antiquity Sites in Tiberias*. Jerusalem.

Hoade, E. (1946). *Guide to the Holy Land*. Jerusalem.

(1966). *East of the Jordan*, 2nd edition. Jerusalem.

(1978). *Guide to the Holy Land*, 9th edition. Jerusalem.

Hohlfelder, R. and J.P. Oleson (1980). Sebastos, the Harbor Complex of Caesarea Maritima, Israel: The Preliminary Report of the 1978 Underwater Exploration. In M. Sears and D. Merriman (eds.), *Oceanography: The Past*, pp. 765–79. New York.

(1981). Underwater Excavations at Sebastos – The Harbor Complex of Caesarea Maritima (Israel): The 1980 Season. In G.P. Watts (ed.), *Underwater Archaeology: The Challenge Before Us: The Proceedings of the Twelfth Conference on Underwater Archaeology*, pp. 267–75. San Marino, California.

Hohlfelder, R., J.P. Oleson, A. Raban and R.L. Vann (1982). Caesarea, Ancient Harbor 1980–1982. *ESI*, 1: 16–19.

(1983). Sebastos, Herod's Harbor at Caesarea Maritima. *Biblical Archaeologist*, 46: 133–43.

Holland, D.L. (1973). The Joint Expedition to Caesarea-Maritima, 1972. *ASOR Newsletter*, 5 (1972–3): 1–4.

von Holst, N. (1981). *Der Deutsche Ritterorden und seine Bauten, von Jerusalem bis Sevilla, von Thorn bis Narwa*. Berlin.

Holum, K.G., and A. Raban (1993). Caesarea. In *NEAEHL*, vol. I, pp. 270–2, 282–6.

Holum, K.G. *et al.* (1988). *King Herod's Dream: Caesarea on the Sea*. New York/London.

Hornstein, A. (1898). A Visit to Kerak and Petra. *PEFQS*: 94–103.

Horsfield, G. and A. (1938). Sela: Petra, the Rock of Edom and Nabatene. *QDAP*, 7: 1–42, pls. I–LXXIV.

Horwitz, L.K., Tchernov and S. Dar (1990). Subsistence and Environment on Mount Carmel in the Roman–Byzantine and Medieval Periods: The Evidence from Kh. Sumaqa. *IEJ*, 40: 287–304.

Hubatsch, W. (1966). Montfort und die Bildung des Deutschordensstaates im Heiligen Lande. *Nachrichten der Akademie der Wissenschaften in Göttingen*, 1st series, Phil.-hist. Klasse, 51: 161–99.

Humbert, J.B. and E. Nodet (1979). Tell Keisan (1979). In Chronique archéologique, *RB*, 86: 444–9, pl. XIX.

Huygens, R.B.C. (1965). Un nouveau texte du traité 'De Constructione Castri Saphet'. *Studi medievali*, 3rd series, 6.1: 355–87.

(1968). Monuments de l'époque des croisades: réflections à propos de quelques livres récentes. *Bibliotheca Orientalis*, 25: 9–14.

(1981). *De Constructione Castri Saphet: construction et fonctions d'un château fort franc en Terre Sainte*. Koninklijke Nederlandse Akademie van Wetenschappen Afdeling Letterkunde, Verhandelingen Nieuwe Reeks, vol. CXI. Amsterdam/Oxford/New York.

Ibn al-Furāt (c.1375). *Ayyubids, Mamlukes and Crusaders*, ed. and trans. U. and M.C. Lyons, 2 vols. Cambridge.

Ilan, Z. (1982). Horvat 'Erav. *ESI* 1: 26–7, fig.

(1988). Ḥorvat 'Erav. *ESI*, 6 (1987–8): 53–4, fig. 18.

(1989). Ḥorvat Arbel. In Notes and News, *IEJ*, 39: 100–2.

(1993). 'Erav, Ḥorvat. In *NEAEHL*, vol. II, p. 422.

Ilan, Z. and E. Damati (1984). Khirbet Marus – 1984. *ESI*, 3: 73–6.

(1985). Marous – An Ancient Jewish Fortified Village in Upper Galilee. *Israel Land and Nature*, 10.2 (1984–5): 60–9.

(1986). Meroth (Kh. Marus) – 1986. *ESI*, 5: 64–8, figs. 31–3, photos. 5–6.

(1987a). Kh. Marus (Merot), 1985–1986. In Notes and News, *IEJ*, 37: 54–7.

(1987b). The Synagogue and Beth-Midrash at Ancient Meroth. *Qadmoniot*, 20.3–4: 87–96 [in Hebr.].

Irby, C.L. and J. Mangles (1823). *Travels in Egypt and Nubia, Syria and Asia Minor; During the Years 1817 & 1818*. London.

(1861). *Travels in Egypt and Nubia, Syria, and the Holy Land; Including a Journey Round the Dead Sea, and through the Country East of the Jordan*, new edition. London.

Isambert, E. (1861). *Itinéraire descriptif, historique et archéologique de l'Orient*. Paris.

Israel (1964). Schedule of Monuments and Historical Sites. *Reshumot Yalqut ha-Pirsumim* [Official Gazette Announcements], 1091 (18 May): 1349–561, i–xliii. [in Hebr.]

Israel: Department of Antiquities (1955). *Short Guide to the Ruins of Caesarea*. Jerusalem.

Israel: Nature Reserves Authority (1993). *Ein Afek*. Jerusalem.

Jacoby, D. (1977). L'expansion occidentale dans le Levant: les vénétiens à Acre dans la seconde moitié du treizième siècle. *Journal of Medieval History*, 3: 225–64.

(1979). Crusader Acre in the Thirteenth Century: Urban Layout and Topography. *Studi medievali*, 3rd series, 20.1: 1–45, figs. 1–4.

(1982). Montmusard, Suburb of Crusader Acre: The First Stage of its Development. In Kedar, Mayer and Smail 1982: 205–17.

(1989a). Les Communes italiennes et les ordres militaires à Acre: aspects juridiques, territoriaux et militaires (1104–1187, 1191–1291). In M. Balard (ed.), *Etat et colonisation au Moyen Age et à la Renaissance: Actes du Colloque de Reims 1987*, pp. 193–214. Lyons.

(1989b). L'évolution urbaine et la fonction méditerra-néenne d'Acre à l'époque des croisades. In E. Poleggi (ed.), *Città portuali del Mediterraneo, Storia e Archeologia: Atti del Convegno internazionale di Genova 1985*, pp. 95–109. Genoa.

(1993). Three Notes on Crusader Acre. *ZDPV*, 109: 83–96.

Jacoby, Z. (1982a). The Workshop of the Temple Area in Jerusalem in the Twelfth Century: Its Origin, Evolution and Impact. *Zeitschrift für Kunstgeschichte*, 45: 325–94.

(1982b). The Impact of Northern French Gothic on Crusader Sculpture in the Holy Land. In *Il Medio Oriente e l'Occidente nell'arte del XIII secolo: Atti del XXIV Convegno internazionale di Storia dell'Arte*, pp. 123–7, figs. 96–113. Bologna.

James of Verona (Giacomo da Verona)(1335). Le pèlerinage du moine augustin Jacques de Vérone (1335), ed R. Röhricht. *ROL*, 3: 155–302.

Jidejian, N. (1969). *Tyre Through the Ages*. Beirut.

(1971). *Sidon Through the Ages*. Beirut.

(1973). *Beirut Through the Ages*. Beirut.

Johns, C.N. (1931). Medieval 'Ajlun, I. The Castle. (Qal'at ar-Rabad). *QDAP*, 1: 21–33, pls. XX–XXVI.

(1932). Excavations at Pilgrims' Castle ('Atlīt). The Faubourg and its Defences. *QDAP*, 1: 111–29, pls. XL–LIII.

(1934a). Medieval Slip-Ware from Pilgrims' Castle, 'Atlīt (1930–1). *QDAP*, 3: 136–44, pls. XLIX–LVII.

(1934b). Excavations at Pilgrims' Castle, 'Atlīt (1932); the Ancient Tell and the Outer Defences of the Castle. *QDAP*, 3: 145–64, pls. XLVIII–LXV.

(1935). Excavations at Pilgrims' Castle, 'Atlīt (1931–2). An Unfinished Church in the Suburb. *QDAP*, 4: 122–37, pls. LXXI–LXXV.

(1936a). Excavations at Pilgrims' Castle, 'Atlīt (1932–3); Stables at the South-West of the Suburb. *QDAP*, 5: 31–60, pls. XVIII–XXVIII.

(1936b). Excavations at the Citadel, Jerusalem. *QDAP*, 5; 127–31, pls. LXVIII–LXXIII.

(1937). *Palestine of the Crusaders: A Map of the Country on Scale 1:350,000 with Historical Introduction & Gazetteer*. Survey of Palestine. Jaffa.

(1939). Contributions to Grant and Wright 1939: 86–8, 147–9.

(1940). Excavations at the Citadel, Jerusalem 1934–9. *PEQ*, 36–56, pls. III–VIII.

(1944). *Guide to the Citadel of Jerusalem*. Jerusalem.

(1947). *Guide to 'Atlīt: The Crusader Castle, Town & Surroundings*. Jerusalem.

(1950). The Citadel, Jerusalem. A Summary of Work since 1934. *QDAP*, 14: 121–90, pls. XLVII–LXIV.

(1975). 'Atlit. In *EAEHL*, vol. I, pp. 130–40.

Johns, J. (1993). Snakes, Lions of the Desert and the Elephant of Christ. *Oxford Today*, 5.2: 9–11.

Johns, J., A. McQuitty, R. Falkner *et al.* (1989). The Fāris Project: Preliminary Report upon the 1986 and 1988 Seasons. *Levant*, 21: 63–95.

Johnson, D. (1995). Crusader Castles in the Kingdom of Jerusalem. *Newsletter of the Castle Studies Group*, 8 (1994–5): 4–13.

Jowett, W. (1825). *Christian Researches in Syria and the Holy Land*. London.

Kalayan, H. (1968). *A New Outlook into the History of Architecture Through the Tools Used as Schools of Masonry*. Reprinted from *Al-Mouhandess*, 11 (April). Beirut.

(1973). The Sea Castle of Sidon. *BMB*, 26: 81–9.

Kammerer, A. (1929). *Pétra et la Nabatène*, 2 vols. Paris (1929–30).

Kaplan, H. and J. Kaplan (1976). Jaffa. In *EAEHL*, vol. II, pp. 532–41.

Kaplan, J. (1960). In Notes and News, *IEJ*, 10: 121–2.

(1966). Tel Aviv – Yafo. In Notes and News, *IEJ*, 16: 282–3.

(1967). Jaffa. In Chronique archéologique, *RB*, 74: 87–8, pl. XIVb.

(1972). The Archaeology and History of Tel Aviv – Jaffa. *Biblical Archaeologist*, 35.3: 66–95.

(1974). Tel Aviv – Yafo. In Notes and News, *IEJ*, 24: 137–8.

(1975a). Jaffa, Tel Aviv. In Chronique archéologique, *RB*, 82: 257–63, pl. XXIV.

(1975b). Ashdod-Yam. In *EAEHL*, vol. I, pp. 119–20.

(1993). Ashdod-Yam. In *NEAEHL*, vol. I, pp. 102–3.

Kark, R. (1989). Cartographic Sources for the Study of Jaffa from the Napoleonic Siege until the British Conquest. *Israel – People and Land: Eretz Israel Museum Yearbook*, new series, 5–6 (1987–9): 173–98, 20*. [in Hebr. with Eng. summary]

Kedar, B.Z. (1982). Ein Hilferuf aus Jerusalem von September 1187. *Deutsches Archiv für Erforschung des Mittelalters*, 38: 112–22 (reprinted in Kedar 1993: ch. x).

(1989). The Frankish Period. In A.D. Crown (ed.), *The Samaritans*, pp. 82–94. Tübingen (reprinted in Kedar 1993: ch. XIX).

(1992) (ed.). *The Horns of Ḥaṭṭīn*. Proceedings of the Second Conference of the Society for the Study of the Crusades and the Latin East, Jerusalem and Haifa 2–6 July 1987. Jerusalem/London.

(1993). *The Franks in the Levant, 11th to 14th Centuries*. Variorum Collected Studies Series, vol. CCCCXXIII. London.

(forthcoming). The Outer Walls of Frankish Acre. *'Atiqot*, 28 (1997).

Kedar, B.Z. and A. Kaufman (1975). Radiocarbon Measurements of Medieval Mortars: A Preliminary Report. *IEJ*, 25: 36–8.

Kedar, B.Z., H.E. Mayer and R.C. Smail (1982) (eds.). *Outremer: Studies in the History of the Crusading Kingdom of Jerusalem, presented to Joshua Prawer*. Jerusalem.

Kedar, B.Z. and W.G. Mook (1978). Radiocarbon Dating of Mortar from the City-Wall of Ascalon. *IEJ*, 28: 173–6, pl. 26d.

Kedar, B.Z. and R.D. Pringle (1985). La Fève: A Crusader Castle in the Jezreel Valley. *IEJ*, 35: 164–79, pls. 20–1.

Kedar, B.Z. and E. Stern (1995). A Vaulted East–West Street in Acre's Genoese Quarter. *'Atiqot*, 26: 105–11.

Keel, O. and M. Küchler (1982). *Orte und Landschaften der Bibel: Ein Handbuch und Studienreiseführer zum Heiligen Land*, vol. II. *Die Süden*. Zurich.

Kempinski, A. (1978). Shiloh. In *EAEHL*, vol. IV, pp. 1098–100.

Kennedy, A.B.W. (1925). *Petra: Its History and Monuments*. London.

Kennedy, H. (1994). *Crusader Castles*. Cambridge.

Kenyon, K.M. (1962). Excavations in Jerusalem, 1961. *PEQ*: 72–89, pls. XVII–XXV.

(1963). Excavations in Jerusalem, 1962. *PEQ*: 7–21, pls. I–X.

(1967). *Jerusalem: Excavating 3000 Years of History*. [London.]

Kesten, A. (1962). *Acre. The Old City. Survey and Planning*. Israel: Prime Minister's Office, Dept for Landscaping and the Preservation of Historic Sites. Jerusalem.

(1993). *The Old City of Acre: Re-examination Report 1993*. Acre.

Khalidi, W. (1992) (ed.). *All that Remains: The Palestinian Villages Occupied and Depopulated by Israel in 1948*. Washington, D.C.

Khouri, R.G. (1986). *Petra: A Guide to the Capital of the Nabataeans*. London/New York.

(1988a). *Petra: A Brief Guide to the Antiquities*. Amman.

(1988b). *The Antiquities of the Jordan Rift Valley*. Amman.

Khouri, R.G. and D. Whitcomb (1988). *Aqaba. Port of Palestine on the China Sea*. Al Kutba Guides. Amman.

King, D.J.C. (1946). Unpublished descriptions and plans of castles in Syria, Lebanon, Palestine and Transjordan. Typed copy given to C.N. Johns and now deposited with the PEF, London.

King, G.R.D. *et al.* (1987). Survey of Byzantine and Islamic Sites in Jordan. Third Season. Preliminary Report (1982). The Southern Ghor. *ADAJ*, 31: 439–59.

Kitchener, H.H. (1877). Lieutenant Kitchener's Reports [II–VI]. *PEFQS*: 116–25, 165–78.

(1878). List of Photographs Taken in Galilee with Descriptions. *PEFQS*: 134–41.

(1917). Our Ride from Gaza to Jerusalem, with a Description of the Greek Holy Fire. *PEFQS*: 66–72.

Kjaer, H. (1927). The Danish Excavation of Shiloh. Preliminary Report. *PEFQS*: 202–13.

(1930). The Excavation of Shilo: The Place of Eli and Samuel. Preliminary Report of the Excavations of 1929. *JPOS*, 10: 87–174.

(1931). A Summary Report of the Second Danish Expedition, 1929. *PEFQS*: 71–88.

Kloner, A. (1974). History of Ashdod Yam. *Nature and Land*, 16 (1973–4): 21–4. [in Hebr.]

(1983a). Bet Guvrin: Medieval Church and Fortifications. *Hadashot Arkheologiot*, 83: 52–3. [in Hebr.]

(1983b). Two Crusader Sites in the South Judean Foothills. *Israel – Land and Nature*, 8.2 (1982–83): 58–60.

(1985). The Amphitheatre of Beth-Guvrin/Eleutheropolis. *Qadmoniot*, 18: 38–43. [in Hebr.]

(1987). Crusader Bet Govrin – An Archaeological Survey. In B.Z. Kedar (ed.), *The Crusaders in their Kingdom, 1099–1291*, pp. 132–47. Jerusalem. [in Hebr.]

(1993). Beth Guvrin. In *NEAEHL*, vol. I, pp. 195–201.

Kloner, A. and D. Chen (1983). Bet Govrin: Crusader Church and Fortifications. *ESI*, 2: 12–13.

Kochavi, M. (1972) (ed.). *Judaea, Samaria and the Golan: Archaeological Survey 1967–1968*. The Archaeological Survey of Israel, vol. I. Jerusalem. [in Hebr.]

(1993). Zeror, Tel. In *NEAEHL*, vol. IV, pp. 1524–6.

Kochavi, M. and I. Beit-Arieh (1994). *Map of Rosh ha-ʿAyin (78)*. Archaeological Survey of Israel. Jerusalem. [in Hebr. and Eng.]

Kootwyk, J. (I. Cotovicus) (1619). *Itinerarium Hierosolymitanum et Syriacum*. Antwerp.

Kopp, C. (1929). *Elias und Christentum auf dem Karmel*. Collectanea Hierosolymitana, vol. CXI. Paderborn.

(1949). Christian Sites Around the Sea of Galilee, I. Capernaum. *Dominican Studies*, 2.3: 213–35.

de Laborde, L. (1830). *Voyage de l'Arabie Pétrée*. Paris.

Lagrange, M.J. (1894). Chronique. *RB*, 3: 136–41.

(1897). Notre exploration de Pétra. *RB*, 6: 208–30.

Langé, S. (1965). *Architettura delle crociate in Palestina*. Como.

Langendorf, J.-J. and G. Zimmermann (1964). Trois monuments inconnus des croisés. *Genava*, new series, 12: 123–65.

le Lasseur, D. (1922). Mission archéologique à Tyr (avril–mai 1921). *Syria*, 3: 1–26, 116–33, pls. I–III, XXIII–XXVI.

Lauffray, J. (1945). Forums et monuments de Béryte. *BMB*, 7 (1944–5): 13–80.

Lawlor, J.I. (1979). Hesban (Heshbon) 1978. In Chronique archéologique, *RB*, 86: 115–17, pl. v.a–c.

Lawrence, T.E. (1936). *Crusader Castles*, 2 vols. London.

(1939). *Oriental Assembly*, ed. A.W. Lawrence. London.

(1988). *Crusader Castles*, new edition with introduction and notes by D. Pringle. Oxford.

Lenzen, C.J., J. Kareem and S. Thorpe (1987). The Jisr Sheikh Hussein Project, 1986. *ADAJ*, 31: 313–19.

Le Strange, G. (1890). *Palestine Under the Moslems*. London.

Levine, L. (1975). *Roman Caesarea: An Archaeological–Topographical Study*. Qedem, vol. II. Jerusalem.

Levy, Y. (1988). Netanya, Umm Khaled. *ESI*, 6 (1987–8): 87–8.

Linder, E. (1971). Underwater Archaeology. – A New Dimension in the Study of Israel in Antiquity. *Qadmoniot*, 4: 44–55. [in Hebr.]

Linder, E. and O. Leenhardt (1964). Recherches d'archéologie sous-marine sur la côte méditerranéenne d'Israël. *Revue archéologique*, 1: 47–51.

Linder, E., and A. Raban (1965). Underwater Survey in the Harbour of Acre (1964). In *Western Galilee and the Coast of Galilee*, pp. 180–94. Jerusalem. [in Hebr.]

Lindner, M. (1983). *Petra und das Königreich der Nabatäer*. Munich.

(1985). *Petra: Der Führer durch die antike Stadt/The Guide Through the Antique City*. Fürth.

Link, E.A. (1956). *Survey Trip to Israel: The Port of Caesarea, the Port of Acre, the Lake of Tiberias*. New York.

Loffreda, S. (1968). The First Season of Excavations at Tabgha (near Capharnaum)(March 25th–June 20th) – Preliminary Report. *LA*, 18: 238–43.

(1970). *Scavi di et-Tabgha. Relazione finale della campagna di scavi 25 marzo – 20 giugno 1969*. SBF, Coll. min., vol. VII. Jerusalem.

(1972). *A Visit to Capharnaum.* The Holy Places of Palestine. Jerusalem.

(1975). *I Santuari di Tabgha.* Luoghi Santi della Palestina. Jerusalem.

(1980). *A Visit to Capharnaum.* The Holy Places of Palestine, 7th edition. Jerusalem.

(1982). Documentazione preliminare degli oggetti della XIV campagna di scavi a Cafarnao. *LA,* 32: 409–26, pls. 83–96.

(1983). Nuovi contributi di Cafarnao per la ceramologia palestinese. *LA,* 33: 347–72, pls. 29–48.

Loffreda, S. and V. Tzaferis (1993). Capernaum. In *NEAEHL,* vol. I, pp. 291–6.

Luttrell, A. (1994). The Hospitallers' Medical Tradition: 1291–1530. In Barber 1994b: 64–81.

de Luynes, M. le duc (H.T.P.J. d'Albert) (1871). *Voyage d'exploration à la Mer Morte, à Petra, et sur la rive gauche du Jourdain,* 2 vols., ed. C.J.M. de Vogüé. Paris (1871–6).

Mabry, J. and G. Palumbo (1988a). Survey in the Wadi el-Yabis (Irbid District, Jordan), 1987. *Syria,* 65: 425–7.

(1988b). The 1987 Wadi el-Yabis Survey. *ADAJ,* 32: 275–305.

Macalister, R.A.S. (1930). *A Century of Excavation in Palestine,* 2nd edition. London.

Macalister, R.A.S. and E.W.G. Masterman (1907). Diary of a Visit to Safed. *PEFQS:* 91–130.

McCown, C.C. (1931). Archaeology in Palestine in 1930. *BASOR,* 41: 2–18.

MacDonald, B.M. (1992). *The Southern Ghors and Northeast 'Arabah Archaeological Survey.* Sheffield Archaeological Monographs, vol. V. Sheffield.

MacDonald, B.M. *et al.* (1987). Southern Ghors and Northeast 'Arabah Archaeological Survey 1986, Jordan, A Preliminary Report. *ADAJ,* 31: 391–413.

(1988). Southern Ghors and Northeast 'Araba Archaeological Survey 1985 and 1986, Jordan: A Preliminary Report. *BASOR,* 272: 23–45.

Mackenzie, D. (1913). The Philistine City of Askelon. *PEFQS:* 8–23.

MacLeish, K. (1961). Sea Search into the History of Caesarea. *Life,* 5.18: 72–82.

McQuitty, A. (1993a). Khirbat Faris 1993. *Newsletter of the British Association for Near Eastern Archaeology,* 6: 45–6.

(1993b). Khirbat Faris. In B. DeVries and P. Bikai, Archaeology in Jordan, *AJA,* 97: 457–520 (pp. 506–7, fig. 59).

(1994a). In British Institute at Amman for Archaeology and History: Research Grants: 1993–4. *Levant,* 26: 237.

(1994b). Khirbat Faris. *PEQ,* 126: 88.

McQuitty, A. and R. Falkner (1993). The Faris Project: Preliminary Report on the 1989, 1990 and 1991 Seasons. *Levant,* 25: 37–61.

Mader, A.E. (1918). *Altchristliche Basiliken und Lokaltraditionen in Südjudäa. Archäologische und topographische Untersuchungen.* Studien zur Geschichte und Kultur des Altertums, vol. VIII.v–vi. Paderborn.

Maeir, A.M. (1980). Mount Zion Gleanings. *IEJ,* 40: 68–70, pl. 8.

Magen, M. (1984). Excavations at the Damascus Gate, 1979–1984. *Qadmoniot,* 17: 117–20. [in Hebr.]

(1988). Recovering Roman Jerusalem – The Entry Beneath Damascus Gate. *Biblical Archaeology Review,* 15.3: 48–56.

(1994). Excavations at the Damascus Gate, 1979–1984. In H. Geva (ed.), *Ancient Jerusalem Revealed,* pp. 281–6. Jerusalem.

Magness, J. (1991). The Walls of Jerusalem in the Early Islamic Period. *Biblical Archaeologist,* 54: 208–17.

Maier, A. (1993). Jerusalem, Mamilla (2). *ESI,* 12: 61–2, figs. 69–72.

Maisler [Mazar], B. (1939). Tell Kurdâne (Aphek?) in the Plain of Acre. *BJPES,* 6: 151–8. [in Hebr.]

Makhouly, N. (1941). *Guide to Acre.* Jerusalem.

Makhouly, N. and M. Avi-Yonah (1934). The Byzantine Church at Suhmātā. *QDAP,* 3: 92–105.

Makhouly, N. and C.N. Johns (1946). *Guide to Acre,* 2nd edition. Jerusalem.

Mallon, A. (1924). Voyage d'exploration au sud-est de la Mer Morte. *Biblica,* 5: 413–55.

Mann, S. (1979). Ancient Jericho's Sweet Tooth. *Jerusalem Post Magazine* (7 Sept.): 12–13.

Ma'oz, Z.U. (1993). Banias. In *NEAEHL,* vol. I, pp. 136–43.

al-Maqrīzī (*c.*1400a). *A History of the Ayyubid Sultans of Egypt,* trans. R.J.C. Broadhurst. Boston (1980).

(*c.*1400b). *Histoire des sultans mamlouks de l'Egypte,* trans. M. Quatremère, 2 vols. (4 parts). Paris (1837–45).

Margalit, S. (1993). Jerusalem, the Butchers' Bazaar. *ESI,* 12: 114, fig. 129.

Margovsky, Y. (1971). Jérusalem: Bordj Kabrit et environs. In Chronique archéologique, *RB,* 78: 597–8, pl. XXXII.

Marino, L. (1993). Petra, Wu'eira. In B. DeVries and P. Bikai, Archaeology in Jordan, *AJA,* 97: 457–520 (pp. 511–12, fig. 42).

Marino, L. *et al.* (1990a). The Crusader Settlement in Petra. *Fortress,* 7: 3–13.

(1990b). La Fortezza crociata di Wu'eira (Giordania). Indagini sulle strutture e sui materiali. *Castellum.*

Mariti, G. (1769). *Viaggi per l'isola di Cipro e per la Sorìa e Palestina fatti . . . dall'anno 1760 al 1768,* 9 vols. Florence (1769–76).

Marmardji, A. (1951). *Textes géographiques arabes sur la Palestine.* Études bibliques. Paris.

Marshall, C. (1992). *Warfare in the Latin East, 1192–1291.* Cambridge Studies in Medieval Life and Thought, 4th series, vol. XVII. Cambridge.

Masterman, E.W.G. (1914). Safed. *PEFQS:* 169–79.

(1919). A Visit to the Ruined Castles of the Teutonic Knights. *PEFQS:* 71–5.

(1928). A Crusaders' Fortress in Palestine. *PEFQS:* 91–7.

Maundrell, H. (1697a). A Journey From Aleppo to Jerusalem at Easter, A.D. 1697. In Wright 1848: 383–512.

(1697b). *A Journey From Aleppo to Jerusalem in 1697,* with introduction by D. Howell. Beirut (1963).

Mayer, H.E. (1990). *Die Kreuzfahrerherrschaft Montréal (Šōbak): Jordanien im 12 Jahrhundert.* Abhandlungen des Deutschen Palästinavereins, vol. XIV. Wiesbaden.

Mayer, L.A. (1934). Saturna Epigraphica Arabica, III, Isdūd. *QDAP,* 3: 24–5, pl. XIII.

Mayer, L.A. and J. Pinkerfeld (1950). *Some Principal Muslim Religious Buildings in Israel*. Israel: Ministry of Religious Affairs. Jerusalem.

Mayer, L.A. and A. Reifenberg (1940). The Synagogue of Eshtemoʿa: Preliminary Report. *JPOS*, 19 (1939–40): 314–26, pls. XXIII–XXX.

Mazar, A. (1986a). The Excavations at Tell Qasile During 1983–1984. *Israel – People and Land: Haaretz Museum Yearbook*, new series, 2–3 (1985–6): 9–20, 7*. [in Hebr. with Eng. summary]

(1986b). Excavations at Tell Qasile, 1982–1984: Preliminary Report. *IEJ*, 36: 1–15, pl. 2b.

(1989). Tel Qasila – 1986/1987. *ESI*, 7–8 (1988–9): 147–8, fig. 123.

(1993). Qasile, Tell. In *NEAEHL*, vol. IV, pp. 1204–12.

Mazar, B. (1975). *The Mountain of the Lord*. New York.

Mazor, G. (1984a). [Har Hazofim]. *Hadashot Arkheologiot*, 84: 45.

(1984b). [Har Hazofim]. *ESI*, 3: 57.

Meinardus, O. (1969). Notes on the Laurae and Monasteries of the Wilderness of Judaea (III). *LA*, 19: 305–27.

Meistermann, B. (1909). *Guide du Nil au Jourdain par le Sinaï et Pétra*. Paris.

(1936). *Guide de Terre Sainte*, 3rd edition. Paris.

du Mesnil du Buisson, Le comte (1921). Les anciennes défenses de Beyrouth. *Syria*, 3: 235–57, 317–27, pls. XXXV–XL, XLVI–LIII.

Meyer, J. (1964). Es-Samariya, ein Kreuzfahrersitz in Westgaliläa. *Jahrbuch des Romisch-Germanischen Zentralmuseums Mainz*, 11: 198–202.

(1978). The Early Arab and Crusader Periods. In D. Lazar (ed.), *Archaeology of Nahariya*. Nahariya. [in Hebr.]

Meyers, E.M. (1978). Shemaʿ, Khirbet. In *EAEHL*, vol. IV, pp. 1094–7.

Meyers, E.M. and D. Barag (1977). Meiron. In *EAEHL*, vol. III, pp. 856–62.

Meyers, E.M. and R.S. Hanson (1976). Meiron. *RB*, 83: 93–6. pl. XVIII–XIX.

Meyers, E.M., A.T. Kraabel and J.F. Strange (1976). *Ancient Synagogue Excavations at Khirbet Shemaʿ, Upper Galilee, Israel 1970–1972*. AASOR, vol. XLII. Durham, N.Carolina.

Meyers, E.M., E. Netzer and C.L. Meyers (1986). [Sepphoris]. *Biblical Archaeologist*, 49.1: 4–19.

(1988). Ṣippori (Sepphoris) – 1986. *ESI*, 6 (1987–8): 95–8.

(1992). *Sepphoris*. Winona Lake, Indiana.

Miller, J.M. (1991) (ed.). *Archaeological Survey of the Kerak Plateau, Conducted During 1978–1982*. ASOR Archaeological Reports, I. Atlanta, Georgia.

Minnis, D. and Y. Bader (1988). A Comparative Analysis of Belvoir (Kawkab al-Hawa) and Qalʿat al-Rabad (ʿAjlun Castle). *ADAJ*, 32: 255–64.

Mittmann, S. (1970). *Beiträge zur Siedlungs- und Territorialgeschichte des Nordlich Ostjordanlandes*. Abhandlungen des Deutschen Palästinavereins. Wiesbaden.

(1971). [Kh. Karmil]. *ADAJ*, 16: 87–.

Mortet, V. and P. Deschamps (1911). *Recueil de textes relatifs à l'histoire de l'architecture et à la condition des architectes en France au moyen-âge*, 2 vols. Paris (1911–29).

von Mülinen, E. (1907, 1908a). Beiträge zur Kenntnis des Karmels. *ZDPV*, 30 (1907): 117–207; 31 (1908): 1–258.

(1908b). *Beiträge zur Kenntnis des Karmels*. Leipzig (repr. Lichtenstein 1970).

Müller-Wiener, W.M. (1966). *Castles of the Crusaders*. London.

Musil, A. (1907). *Arabia Petraea*, 3 vols. Vienna (1907–8).

Nau, M.F. (1899). Croisé lorrain Godefroy de Asha. *JA*: 421–31.

Neʿeman, Y. (1990). *Archaeological Survey of Israel: Map of Maʿamit (54), 15–20*. Jerusalem. [in Hebr. with Eng. summary]

Negev, A. (1960a). Caesarea. In Notes and News, *IEJ*, 10: 127, 264–5.

(1960b). Caesarea Maritima. *CNI*, 11.4: 17–22.

(1961a). Caesarea. In Notes and News, *IEJ*, 11: 81–3.

(1961b). Césarée Maritime. *Bible et Terre Sainte*, 41: 13–15.

(1962). Césarée Maritime. In Chronique archéologique, *RB*, 69: 412–15, pls. XLVI–XLVII.

(1963). Where Vespasian was Proclaimed Emperor: Caesarea Maritima on the Coast of Israel – A Summary of Recent Excavations. Part I: The Crusader and Arab Cities. *Illustrated London News*, 6482 (Oct.): 684–6.

(1984). Khirbet Susiya. *ESI*, 3: 101–2.

(1985). Excavations at Carmel (Kh. Susiya) in 1984: Preliminary Report. *IEJ*, 35: 231–2, pls. 27–32.

Negev, A., A. Frova and M. Avi-Yonah (1993). Caesarea. Excavations in the 1950s and 1960s. In *NEAEHL*, vol. I, pp. 272–80.

Negev, A. and Z. Yeivin (1993). Susiya, Khirbet. In *NEAEHL*, vol. IV, pp. 1412–21.

Netzer, E. (1981). *Greater Herodium*. Qedem, vol. XIII. Jerusalem.

Netzer, E. and Z. Weiss (1993). Zippori – 1990/1991. *ESI*, 12: 13–15, figs. 19–20.

(1994). *Zippori*. Jerusalem.

Nicolle, D. (1988). ʿAin al Ḥabīs. The Cave de Sueth. *Archéologie médiévale*, 18: 113–40.

(1989). ʿAin Habis. In D. Homès-Fredericq and J.B. Hennessy, *Archaeology of Jordan, vol. II.i*, pp.141–9. Akkadica, Supplementum, vols. III, VII–VIII (2 vols.). Leuven (1986–9).

Northedge, A. (1983). The Fortifications of Qalʿat Amman (ʿAmman Citadel): Preliminary Report. *ADAJ*, 27: 437–59.

Northedge, A. *et al.* (1993). *Studies on Roman and Islamic Amman: The Excavations of Mrs C.-M. Bennett and Other Investigations, vol. I. History, Site and Architecture*. British Academy Monographs in Archaeology, vol. III. London.

Ohata, K. (1966). *Tel Zeror, vol. I. Preliminary Report of the Excavation. First Season 1964*. Tokyo.

(1967). *Tel Zeror, vol. II. Preliminary Report of the Excavation. Second Season 1965*. Tokyo.

(1970). *Tel Zeror, vol. III. Report of the Excavation. Third Season 1966*. Tokyo.

Onn, A. (1991). Tiberias. *ESI*, 10: 166–7.

Orfali, G. (1922). La dernière période de l'histoire de Capharnaüm. *JPOS*, 2: 87–93.

Ory, S. (1975). *Archives Max Van Berchem conservées à la Bibliothèque Publique et Universitaire de Genève: Catalogue de la photothèque*. Beirut.

Ovadiah, A. (1970). *Corpus of the Byzantine Churches in the Holy Land*. Theophaneia, vol. XXII. Bonn.

Ovadiah, A. and C. Gomez de Silva (1981, 1982, 1984). Supplementum to the Corpus of the Byzantine Churches in the Holy Land. *Levant*, 13 (1981): 200–61; 14 (1982), 122–70; 16 (1984): 129–65.

Palestine, Government of (1929). Provisional Schedule of Historical Sites and Monuments, ed. E.T. Richmond. *Official Palestine Gazette Extraordinary* (15 June).

(1933). Schedule of Historical Monuments and Historical Sites [Additions], ed. R.W. Hamilton. *Official Palestine Gazette Extraordinary*, 387 (7 Sept.).

(1944). Schedule of Historical Monuments and Sites, Suppl. no. 2, ed. R.W. Hamilton. *Palestine Gazette Extraordinary*, 1375 (25 Nov.).

(1948). *Department of Antiquities. Geographical List of the Record Files, 1918–1948*. Israel Department of Antiquities. Jerusalem (1976).

Palestine Exploration Fund (1881). *The Survey of Western Palestine: Special Papers*. London.

Pearlman, M. and A. Negev (1963). *Caesarea*. Jerusalem.

Pearlman, M. and Y. Yannai (1964). *Historical Sites in Israel*. London.

Peled, A. and Y. Friedman (1987). Did the Crusaders Build Roads? *Qadmoniot*, 20: 119–23. [in Hebr.]

Perkins, A. (1951). Archaeological News. The Near East. *American Journal of Archaeology*, 55: 81–102.

Petrozzi, M.T. (1971). *Ain Karim*. Luoghi Santi della Palestina. Jerusalem.

(1973). *Samaria*. Luoghi Santi della Palestina. Jerusalem.

(1976). *Il Monte Tabor e dintorni*. Luoghi Santi della Palestina. Jerusalem.

Phythian-Adams, W.J. (1921). History of Askalon. *PEFQS*: 76–90.

(1922). The Site of Ibleam. *PEFQS*: 142–7.

(1923). Report on the Stratification of Askalon. *PEFQS*: 60–84.

Pictorial Archive (n.d.). *Near Eastern History: The Crusades* (35 mm colour slide set). Jerusalem.

Pierotti, E. (1869). *Macpela ou tombeau des Patriarches à Hébron*. Lausanne.

Pipano, S. (1988). Ashdod-Yam: An Early Muslim Fortress on the Mediterranean Coast. *Israel Land and Nature*, 13.4: 163–7.

Pococke, R. (1743), *A Description of the East and Some Other Countries*, 2 vols. London (1743–5).

Poidebard, A. (1939). *Un grand port disparu. Tyr. Recherches aériennes et sous-marines 1934–1936*. Bibliothèque archéologique et historique, vol. XXIX. Paris.

Poidebard, A. and J. Lauffray (1951). *Sidon. Aménagements antiques du port de Saïda: étude aérienne, au sol et sous-marine 1946–1950*. Beirut.

Porath, Y. (1983). Fasa'el Area. *ESI*, 2: 31–2.

(1986a). Nethanya ('Umm Khalid). *Hadashot Arkheologiot*, 88: 14–15. [in Hebr.]

(1986b). Netanya, Umm Khaled. *ESI*, 5: 85–6, fig. 44.

(1987). Umm Khalid, Netanya, 1985–1986. In Notes and News, *IEJ*, 37: 57–9.

(1989a). Tel 'Afar. *ESI*, 7–8 (1988–9): 1–3, figs. 1–2.

(1989b). Arsuf Castle. *ESI*, 7–8 (1988–9): 198.

Porath, Y., Y. Neeman and R. Badihi (1990). Caesarea. *ESI*, 9 (1989–90): 132–4.

Porter, J.L. (1867). *The Giant Cities of Bashan; and Syria's Holy Places*. London.

Prag, K. (1989). *Jerusalem*. Blue Guide. London/New York.

Prausnitz, M.W. (1972). Romena (Haifa). In Notes and News, *IEJ*, 22: 246–7.

(1974). Romena (Haifa). In Notes and News, *IEJ*, 24: 142–3.

(1975). Rosh Maya (Kh. Rushmiya) – Haifa. In Chronique archéologique, *RB*, 82: 591–4.

Prawer, J. (1952). The Settlement of the Latins in Jerusalem. *Speculum*, 27: 490–503.

(1953). Historical Maps of Acre. *Eretz-Israel*, 2: 175–84, pls. XX–XXIII. [in Hebr.]

(1956). Ascalon and the Ascalon Strip in Crusader Politics. *Eretz-Israel*, 4: 231–48. [in Hebr.]

(1958). The City and Duchy of Ascalon in the Crusader Period. *Eretz-Israel*, 5: 224–37, pl. 26. [in Hebr.]

(1967). History of the Crusader Castle of Kaukab al-Hawa. *Yediot*, 31: 236–49. [in Hebr.]

(1972). *The Latin Kingdom of Jerusalem: European Colonialism in the Middle Ages*. London.

(1973). I Veneziani e le colonie nel regno latino di Gerusalemme. In *Venezia e il Levante fino al sec. XV*, pp. 625–56. Civiltà veneziana, Studi, vol. XXVII.i–ii. Venice.

(1975). *Histoire du Royaume latin de Jérusalem*, 2nd edition, 2 vols. Paris.

(1976). Jerusalem in Crusader Days. In Yadin 1976: 102–8.

(1977). Crusader Cities. In H.M. Miskimin, D. Herlihy and A.L. Udovitch (eds.) *The Medieval City*, pp. 179–201. New Haven/London.

(1980). *Crusader Institutions*. Oxford.

(1981). The Archaeological Research of the Crusader Period. In *Thirty Years of Archaeology in Israel 1948–1978*, pp. 117–28. Jerusalem. [in Hebr.]

(1984). A Contribution to the Medieval Topography of Jerusalem – The Crusader Conquest of 1099. *Eretz-Israel*, 17: 312–24, 13*–14*. [in Hebr. with Eng. summary]

(1985). The Jerusalem the Crusaders Captured: A Contribution to the Medieval Topography of the City. In Edbury 1985: 1–16.

Prawer, J. and M. Benvenisti (1970). Palestine under the Crusaders. *Atlas of Israel*, sheet IX/10. Jerusalem/Amsterdam.

Pringle, R.D. (1981a). Some Approaches to the Study of Crusader Masonry Marks in Palestine. *Levant*, 13: 173–99.

(1981b). The Medieval Pottery of Palestine and Transjordan (A.D. 636–1500): An Introduction, Gazetteer and Bibliography. *Medieval Ceramics*, 5: 45–60.

(1982). Les édifices ecclésiastiques du royaume latin de Jérusalem: une liste provisoire. *RB*, 89: 92–8.

(1983a). Two Medieval Villages North of Jerusalem: Archaeological Investigations in al-Jib and ar-Ram. *Levant*, 15: 141–77, pls. XVI–XXIIa.

(1983b). Review of Kedar, Mayer and Smail 1982. In *Jerusalem Post Magazine* (28 Jan.): 12.

(1983c). Burj el-Ahmar. *Hadashot Arkheologiot*, 83: 22–4. [in Hebr.]

(1983d). Burj el-Ahmar – 1983. *ESI*, 2: 17–18.

(1984a). King Richard I and the Walls of Ascalon. *PEQ*, 116: 133–47.

(1984b). Excavations at al-Burj al-Ahmar, July–August 1983: An Interim Report. *Notiziario di archeologia medievale*, 37: 7; 38: 21–2.

(1984c). Excavations at al-Burj al-Ahmar, July–August 1983: An Interim Report. *Bulletin of the Society for the Study of the Crusades and the Latin East*, 4: 16–19.

(1984d). Al-Burj al-Ahmar Excavations. *PEQ*, 116: 77.

(1984e). El-Burj al-Ahmar (H. Burgeta), 1983. In Notes and News, *IEJ*, 34: 52–5, fig. 1, pl. 7b.

(1984f). El-Burj el-Ahmar 1983. In Chronique archéologique, *RB*, 91: 267–71, fig. 11, pl. IX.

(1984g). Review of Huygens 1981. In *Speculum*, 59: 165–7.

(1985a). Magna Mahumeria (al-Bīra): The Archaeology of a Frankish New Town in Palestine. In Edbury 1985: 147–68.

(1985b). Medieval Pottery from Caesarea: The Crusader Period. *Levant*, 17: 171–202, pl. XVII.

(1985c). Reconstructing the Castle of Safad. *PEQ*, 117: 139–49.

(1986a). *The Red Tower (al-Burj al-Ahmar): Settlement in the Plain of Sharon at the Time of the Crusaders and Mamluks, A.D. 1099–1516*. British School of Archaeology in Jerusalem, Monograph Series, vol. I. London.

(1986b). A Thirteenth-Century Hall at Montfort Castle in Western Galilee. *Antiquaries Journal*, 66: 52–81, pls. VI–XIII.

(1987). Crusader Settlement and the Landscape: Some Reflections on Method in the Light of Recent Archaeological Work. In B.Z. Kedar (ed.), *The Crusaders in their Kingdom, 1099–1291*, pp. 55–62. Jerusalem. [in Hebr.]

(1988). Introduction and Notes. In Lawrence 1988.

(1989). Crusader Castles: The First Generation. *Fortress*, 1: 14–25.

(1991a). Survey of Castles in the Crusader Kingdom of Jerusalem, 1989: Preliminary Report. *Levant*, 23: 87–91.

(1991b). Crusader Jerusalem. *BAIAS*, 10 (1990–1): 105–13.

(1992). Aqua Bella: The Interpretation of a Crusader Courtyard Building. In Kedar 1992: 147–67.

(1993). *The Churches of the Crusader Kingdom of Jerusalem: A Corpus*, 3 vols. (in progress). Cambridge.

(1994a). Burj Bardawil and Frankish Settlement North of Ramallah in the Twelfth Century. In K. Athamina and R. Heacock (eds.), *The Frankish Wars and their Influence on Palestine*, pp. 30–59. Bir Zeit.

(1994b). Towers in Crusader Palestine. *Château-Gaillard:*

études de castellologie médiévale, vol. XVI. *Actes du colloque internationale tenu à Luxembourg, 1992*, pp. 335–50. Caen.

(1994c). Templar Castles on the Road to the Jordan. In Barber 1994b: 148–66.

(1995a). Town Defences in the Crusader Kingdom of Jerusalem. In I. Corfis and M. Wolfe (eds.), *The Medieval City Under Siege*, pp. 69–121. Woodbridge.

(1995b). Architecture in the Latin East. In J.S.C. Riley-Smith (ed.), *The Oxford Illustrated History of the Crusades*, pp. 160–83. Oxford/New York.

(forthcoming: a). Belvoir Castle. In J.S. Turner (ed.), *The Dictionary of Art*. London.

(forthcoming: b). The Castle and Lordship of Mirabel.

Pringle, R.D. and P.E. Leach (1983). A Byzantine Building at Burham, near Ramallah. *LA*, 33: 319–26, pls. 9–12.

Pringle, R.D., A. Petersen, M. Dow and C. Singer (1994). Qal'at Jiddin: A Castle of the Crusader and Ottoman Periods in Galilee. *Levant*, 26: 135–66.

Prutz, H. (1881). Die Besitzungen des Johanniterordens in Palästina und Syrien. *ZDPV*, 4: 157–93.

Quaresmi, F. (1626a). *Historica, Theologica et Moralis Terrae Sanctae Elucidatio*, ed. C. de Tarvisio. 2 vols. Venice (1880–1).

(1626b). *Elucidatio Terrae Sanctae*, partial ed. and Ital. trans. S. de Sandoli. SBF, Coll. maj., vol. XXXII. Jerusalem (1989).

Quatremère, M. (1837). *Histoire des sultans mamlouks de l'Egypte, écrite en arabe par Taki-eddin-Ahmed-Makrizi, traduite en français et accompagnée de notes*, 2 vols. (in 4 parts). Paris (1837–42).

Raban, A. (1978). Dor – 1977. In Chronique archéologique, *RB*, 85: 410–11, fig. 4.

(1984). Caesarea Harbor – 1984. *ESI*, 3: 13–15.

(1986). Caesarea Harbor – 1986. *ESI*, 5: 19–20.

(1989). *The Harbours of Caesarea Maritima: Results of the Caesarea Ancient Harbour Excavation Project, 1980–1985*, ed. J.P. Oleson, vol. I. *The Site and the Excavations*, 2 vols. Center for Maritime Studies, University of Haifa, Publications, vol. III/BAR International Series, vol. CCCCXCI. Oxford.

(1993a). Acco: Maritime Acco. In *NEAEHL*, vol. I, pp. 29–31.

(1993b). Caesarea: Maritime Caesarea. In *NEAEHL*, vol. I, pp. 286–91.

Raban, A., R.L. Hohlfelder, J.P. Oleson and R.L. Vann (1983). Caesarea, Ancient Harbour – 1983. *ESI*, 2: 18–21.

Raban, A. and K.G. Holum (1991). Caesarea – 1990. *ESI*, 10: 109–12.

Raban, A., K.G. Holum and J.A. Blakely (1993). *The Combined Caesarea Expeditions: Field Report of the 1992 Season*, 2 vols. University of Haifa, Recanati Center for Maritime Studies, Publication, vol. IV. Haifa.

Raban, A. and A. Linder (1978). Caesarea: The Herodian Harbor. *International Journal of Nautical Archaeology*, 7: 238–43.

(1993). 'Atlit: Maritime 'Atlit. In *NEAEHL*, vol. I, pp. 117–20.

Raban, A. and R. Stieglitz (1988). Caesarea, Ancient Harbour, 1987. In Notes and News, *IEJ*, 38: 273–8.

Raban, A., R. Stieglitz and A. Engert (1989). Caesarea and its Harbor – 1987/1988. *ESI*, 7–8 (1988–9): 33–42, figs. 32–41.

Raban, A. *et al.* (1990). Caesarea and its Harbour: A Preliminary Report on the 1988 Season. *IEJ*, 40: 241–56, pls. 25–7.

Rahmani, L.Y. (1971). On Some Medieval Antiquities from the Holy Land. *IEJ*, 21: 55–9, pls. 7–8.

(1980a). Miscellanea – Roman to Medieval. '*Atiqot*, English series, 14: 103–13, pls. XXII–XXV.

(1980b). Two Hoards of 'Moneta Regis' Coins Found in Northern Israel. *Israel Numismatic Society*, 4: 72–6, pls. 17–20.

Rangé, P. (1923). Wanderfahrten in Galilaea, XII: Zur Deutschritterburg Montfort. *Jahrbuch des Bundes der Asienkämpfer*, 3: 122–4.

(1935a). Montfort. *ZDPV*, 58: 84–9.

(1935b). Montfort, die Deutschritterburg in Palästina. *Orientrundschau hg. v. Bund der Asienkämpfer*, 17: 89–90.

Razi, Z. and E. Braun (1992). The Lost Crusader Castle of Tiberias. In Kedar 1992: 95–129.

Reich, R. (1983). Archaeological Sites in the Area of Nathanya. In A. Shmu'eli and M. Brawer (eds.), *Sepher Nethania*, pp. 101–14. Tel Aviv/Nathanya. [in Hebr.]

Reich, R., E. Shukron and Y. Billig (1993). Jerusalem, Mamilla (1). *ESI*, 12: 59–61, fig. 69.

Reifenberg, A. (1951). Caesarea: A Study in the Decline of a Town. *IEJ*, 1 (1950–1): 20–32, pls. VIII–XVI.

Renan, E.M. (1864). *Mission en Phénicie*, 2 vols. Paris.

Rey, E.G. (1866). Rapport sur une mission scientifique accomplie en 1864–1865 dans le nord de la Syrie. *Archives des missions scientifiques et littéraires*, 2nd series, 3: 329–73.

(1871). *Etude sur les monuments de l'architecture militaire des croisés en Syrie*. Collection des documents inédites sur l'histoire de France, series 1, Histoire politique. Paris.

(1878). Étude sur la topographie de la ville d'Acre au XIIIe siècle. *Mémoires de la Société nationale des Antiquaires de France*, 39: 115–45.

(1883). *Les colonies franques de Syrie aux XII^ME ET XIII^me siècles*. Paris.

(1884). Les périples des côtes de Syrie et de la Petite Arménie. *AOL*, 2.1: 329–53.

(1888). Supplément à l'étude sur la topographie de la ville d'Acre. *Mémoires de la Société nationale des Antiquaires de France*, 49: 1–18.

Richard, J. (1953). Colonies marchandes privilegiées et marché seigneurial: la fonde d'Acre et ses droitures. *Le Moyen-Age*, 60: 325–39.

(1954). Les listes des seigneuries dans le livre de Jean d'Ibelin sur l'Assebèbe et Mimars. *Revue historique de droit français et étranger*, 4th series, 32: 565–77.

(1965). Sur un passage du 'Pèlerinage de Charlemagne': le marché de Jérusalem. *Revue belge de philosophie et d'histoire*, 43: 552–5. Reprinted in Richard 1976.

(1966). La confrérie des mosserins d'Acre et les marchands de Mossoul au XIIIe siècle. *L'Orient syrien*, 11: 451–60.

(1976). *Orient et occident au moyen âge: contacts et relations (XIIe–XVe s.)*. Variorum Collected Studies. London.

(1991). *Notice sur la vie et travaux de Paul Deschamps*. Paris.

Riley-Smith, J.S.C. (1967). *The Knights of St. John in Jerusalem and Cyprus, c.1050–1310*. A History of the Order of the Hospital of St John of Jerusalem, vol. 1. London.

(1971). Historical Introduction and Notes. In Ibn al-Furāt c.1375.

(1973). *The Feudal Nobility and the Kingdom of Jerusalem, 1174–1277*. London.

(1990) (ed.). *The Atlas of the Crusades*. London.

Ringel, J. (1975). *Césarée de Palestine: étude historique et archéologique*. Paris.

Roberts, D. (1842a). *The Holy Land: Syria, Idumea, Arabia, Egypt & Nubia, from Drawings Made on the Spot by David Roberts, R.A., with Historical Descriptions by the Revd. G. Croly, L.L.D., Lithographed by L. Hague*, 3 vols. London.

(1842b). *The Holy Land*. Reprint of 1842 edition, with additional material, ed. N. Ran, 5 parts. Jerusalem (1982).

Robinson, E. (1841). *Biblical Researches in Palestine, Mount Sinai and Arabia Petraea: A Journal of Travels in the Year 1838*, 3 vols. London.

(1856). *Later Biblical Researches in Palestine and the Adjacent Regions: A Journal of Travels in the Year 1852*. London.

Röhricht, R. (1887). Studien zur mittelalterlichen Geographie und Topographie Syriens. *ZDPV*, 10: 195–344.

(1898). *Geschichte des Königsreichs Jerusalem (1100–1291)*. Innsbruck.

Roger, E. (1664). *La Terre Sainte, ou description topographique très-particulière des Saintes Lieux et de la Terre de Promission*. Paris.

Roll, I. (1991). Apollonia – 1990. *ESI*, 10: 118.

Roll, I. and E. Ayalon (1977). *Apollonia – Arsuf 1977*. Israel Dept of Antiquities and Museums/Tel Aviv University.

(1982). Apollonia/Arsur – A Coastal Town in the Southern Sharon Plain. *Qadmoniot*, 15: 16–22. [in Hebr.]

(1985). The Market Street (suq) of Apollonia-Arsuf during the Early Arab Period. *Israel – People and Land: Haaretz Museum Yearbook*, new series, 2–3 [20–1]: 107–18, 11\*–12\*. [in Hebr. with Eng. summary]

(1987). The Market Street at Apollonia-Arsuf. *BASOR*, 267: 61–76.

(1989). *Apollonia and Southern Sharon – Model of a Coastal City and its Hinterland*. Kibbutz Hamenhad/Tel Aviv University/Israel Exploration Society. [in Hebr.]

(1993). Apollonia – Arsuf. In *NEAEHL*, vol. I, pp. 72–5.

Roman, Y. (1993). Bridge over Gentle Water. *Eretz Magazine* (Winter): 35–50.

Ronen, A. and Y. Olami (1978). *Archaeological Survey of Israel, I: 'Atlit Map [14–23]*. Jerusalem. [in Hebr. with Eng. summary]

(1983). *Archaeological Survey of Israel: Map of Haifa-East (23)*, 15–24. Jerusalem. [in Hebr. with Eng. summary]

Rothenberg, B. (1961). *God's Wilderness: Discoveries in Sinai*. London.

Rothschild, J.J. (1938). The Fortified Zone of the Plain of Esdraelon. *PEQ*: 41–54, pl. III.

(1949). Kurdaneh. *PEQ*: 58–66, pls. VI–VIII.

Rubin, R. and M. Jägendorf (1992). *The Tower of David: Museum of the History of Jerusalem.* Jerusalem.

Runciman, S. (1951). *A History of the Crusades,* 3 vols. Cambridge (1951–4).

Rustum, A.J. (1926). Akka (Acre) and its Defences. *PEFQS:* 143–57.

Saarisalo, A. and H. Palva (1966). *A Byzantine Church at Kafer Kama.* Studia Orientalia, vol. xxx. Helsinki.

Saidah, R. (1967). Chronique. *BMB,* 20: 155–80.

(1969). Archaeology in the Lebanon 1968–1969. *Berytus,* 18: 119–42.

Saller, S.J. (1946). *Discoveries at St. John's, 'Ein Karim, (1941–1942).* SBF, Coll. maj., vol. iii. Jerusalem.

(1957). *Excavations at Bethany (1949–1953).* SBF, Coll. maj., vol. xii. Jerusalem.

de Sandoli, S. (1966). *Le Sanctuaire de Emmaüs.* Jerusalem.

(1968). *Il Santuario di Emmaus e luoghi biblici circonvicini,* 2nd edition. Jerusalem.

(1974). *Corpus Inscriptionum Crucesignatorum Terrae Sanctae (1099–1291).* SBF, Coll. maj., vol. xxi. Jerusalem.

Sauer, J.A. (1973). *Heshbon Pottery. A Preliminary Report on the Pottery from the 1971 Excavations at Tell Ḥesbân.* Andrews University Monographs, vol. vii. Berrien Springs, Michigan.

(1975). Review of Tushingham 1972. In *ADAJ,* 20: 103–9.

(1976). Pottery Techniques at Tell Deir 'Allā. *BASOR,* 224: 91–4.

de Saulcy, F. (1853). *Voyage autour de la Mer Morte et dans les terres bibliques exécutée de décembre 1850 à avril 1851,* 2 vols and atlas. Paris.

(1854). *Narrative of a Journey Round the Dead Sea and in the Bible Lands in 1850 and 1851,* 2nd edition, ed. E. de Warren, 2 vols. London.

(1865). *Voyage en Terre Sainte,* 2 vols. Paris.

Savignac, R. (1903). Ou'aïrah. *RB,* 12: 114–20.

(1913). Chronique: une visite à l'île de Graye. *RB,* new series, 10: 588–96, pls. i–ii.

(1936). Sur les pistes de Transjordanie méridionale. *RB,* 45: 235–62, pls. vii–xiii.

Schick, C. (1867). Studien über Strassen und Eisenbahn Anlagen zwischen Jaffa und Jerusalem. *Mitteilungen aus Justus Perthes geographischer Anstalt von A. Petermann,* 13: 124–32. Gotha.

(1873). [Muristan]. *PEFQS:* 72.

(1878a). Die antiken Reste an der Nordwestmauer von Jerusalem. *ZDPV,* 1: 15–23, pls. ii–iv.

(1878b). Der Davids Turm in Jerusalem. *ZDPV,* 1: 226–37.

(1879). New Discoveries in the North of Jerusalem. *PEFQS:* 198–200.

(1889). Recent Discoveries in Jerusalem ii: The Muristan. *PEFQS:* 113–14.

(1890). Discoveries North of Damascus Gate. *PEFQS:* 9–11, plan.

(1891). Reports from Jerusalem: Letters from Herr Schick. *PEFQS:* 198–204.

(1893). Letters from Herr Baurath von Schick. *PEFQS:* 20–5, 119–37, 191–203, 282–99.

(1894). Notes from Herr Baurath von Schick. *PEFQS:* 146–7.

(1897). Khan ez Zeit. *PEFQS:* 29–33.

(1898). Birket es Sultan, Jerusalem. *PEFQS:* 224–9.

(1899). Reports. *PEFQS:* 36–42, 213–17.

(1901a). Kubeibeh (Emmaus). *PEFQS:* 165–7.

(1901b). Neubau der Kirche in el-Kubebe. *Mittheilungen und Nachrichten des Deutschen Palästina-Vereins,* 7: 9–13.

(1902). The Muristan, or the Site of the Hospital of St. John at Jerusalem. *PEFQS:* 42–56.

Schiller, E. (1979). *The First Photographs of the Holy Land.* Jerusalem.

(1980). *The First Photographs of Jerusalem & the Holy Land.* Jerusalem.

(1981). *The Holy Land in Old Maps and Prints.* Jerusalem.

Schneider, A.M. (1934). [Burj Baitin]. *ZDPV,* 57: 186–90.

(1938). Südjudäischen Kirchen. *ZDPV,* 61: 96–108.

Schumacher, G. (1888). *The Jaulan.* London.

(1895). Reports fom Galilee. *PEFQS:* 110–14.

(1910). The Great Water Passage of Khirbat Bel'ameh. *PEFQS:* 107–12, pl. iii.

(1917). Unsere Arbeiten im Ostjordanlande. *ZDPV,* 40.

(1926). *Der 'Adschlun.* Leipzig.

Seger, J.D. (1987). Tel Halif, 1986. In Notes and News, *IEJ,* 37: 192–5.

Séjourné, M. (1895). Chronique de Jérusalem. *RB,* 4: 253–69, 611–22.

Seligman, J. (1994). Excavations in the Crusader Fortress at Beth-Shean. *Qadmoniot,* 27: 138–41. [in Hebr.]

(1995). Bet She'an, Citadel. *Hadashot Arkheologiot,* 103: 38–41, figs. 37–42. [in Hebr.]

Shapiro, S. (1978). Crusader Jaffa. *Jerusalem Post* (24 Feb.): 7.

Sharon, M. (1977). The Ayyubid Walls of Jerusalem: A New Inscription from the Time of Al-Mu'aẓẓam 'Īsā. In M. Rosen-Ayalon (ed.), *Studies in Memory of Gaston Wiet,* pp. 179–93. Jerusalem.

(1978). Ḳayṣariyya. In *EI,* 2nd edition, vol. iv, cols. 841–2.

(1994). *Egyptian Caliph and English Baron: The Story of an Arabic Inscription from Ashkelon.* Jerusalem.

(1995). A New Fāṭimid Inscription from Ascalon and its Historical Setting. *'Atiqot,* 26: 61–86.

Shenhav, A. (1986). Ḥorvat Ḥanot (Kh. el-Khan). *ESI,* 5: 46–7.

Simpson, E.J., V. Bernie and M. Milwright (1991). Tiberias, Survey of Islamic Buildings. *ESI,* 10: 4.

Singer, C. (1991). Survey of Yehi'am Fortress (Judin Castle) in Western Galilee, July–August 1991. Unpublished report for British School of Archaeology in Jerusalem.

Sion, O. (1993). Wadi el-Qilt Map, Survey. *ESI,* 12: 50–1, fig. 58.

Sivan, R. and G. Solar (1984). Discoveries in the Jerusalem Citadel, 1980–1984. *Qadmoniot,* 17: 111–17. [in Hebr.]

(1994). Excavations in the Jerusalem Citadel, 1980–1988. In H. Geva (ed.), *Ancient Jerusalem Revealed,* pp. 168–76. Jerusalem.

Smail, R.C. (1956). *Crusading Warfare (1097–1193).* Cambridge Studies in Medieval Life and Thought, n.s., vol. iii. Cambridge.

(1973). *The Crusaders in Syria and the Holy Land*. Ancient Peoples and Places Series, vol. LXXXII. London.

Solar, G. and R. Sivan (1984). Jerusalem: Citadel Moat. *ESI*, 3: 47–8.

Spijkerman, A. (1975). *Cafarnao*, vol. III. *Catalogo delle monete della città*. SBF, Coll. maj., vol. XIX.iii. Jerusalem.

SSCLE [Society for the Study of the Crusades and the Latin East] (1987). *A Display of Crusader Sculpture at the Archaeological Museum (Rockefeller), on the Occasion of the Second SSCLE Conference, Jerusalem and Haifa, July 2–6, 1987*. Texts by T. Ornan, J. Prawer and Z. Jacoby. Jerusalem.

Stager, L.E. (1991). Eroticism & Infanticide at Ashkelon. *Biblical Archaeology Review*, 17.4: 34–53, 72.

(1993). Ashkelon. In *NEAEHL*, vol. I, pp. 103–12.

Stager, L.E. and D. Esse (1986). Ashkelon – 1985/1986. *ESI*, 5: 2–6, figs. 3–4.

(1987). Ashkelon, 1985–1986. In Notes and News, *IEJ*, 37: 68–72.

Stern, E. (1978). *Excavations at Tel Mevorakh (1973–1976), Part One. From the Iron Age to the Roman Period*. Qedem, vol. IX. Jerusalem.

(1985). Tel Dor – 1984. *ESI*, 4: 21–4.

(1993). Zafit, Tel. In *NEAEHL*, vol. IV, pp. 1522–4.

(1994). *Dor: Ruler of the Seas: Twelve Years of Excavations at the Israelite–Phoenician Harbor Town on the Carmel Coast*. Jerusalem.

Stern, E., K. Ravneh, S.A. Kingsley and A. Raban (1993). Dor. In *NEAEHL*, vol. I, pp. 357–72.

Sternberg, G. (1915). Studien aus dem Deutschen Evang. Institut für Altertumwissenschaft im Jerusalem, 27: Bethel. *ZDPV*, 38: 1–40, pl. I.

Stieglitz, R.R. and A. Raban (1987). Caesarea Ancient Harbours Excavation Project, 1986. In Notes and News, *IEJ*, 37: 187–90, pls. 22–3.

Sukenik, E.L. (1948). *Archaeological Investigations at 'Affūla Conducted on Behalf of the Hebrew University, Jerusalem*. Jerusalem.

Sukenik [Yadin], Y. (1946). An Ayyubid Inscription from Beith-Hanun. *BJPES*, 12 (1945–6): 84–91, pl. I. [in Hebr. with Eng. summary]

Suleiman, E. and A. Betts (1981). Rescue Excavations at Tell Sahl es-Saraket 1978/1979. *ADAJ*, 25: 227–34.

Suriano, F. (1485). *Treatise on the Holy Land*, trans. T. Bellorini and E. Hoade. SBF, Coll. maj., vol. VIII. Jerusalem (1949).

Thomson, W.M. (1858). *The Land and the Book*, 2 vols. New York.

(1876). *The Land and the Book*. London.

Tibble, S. (1989). *Monarchy and Lordships in the Latin Kingdom of Jerusalem 1099–1291*. Oxford.

Tobler, T. (1853). *Topographie von Jerusalem und seiner Umgebung*, 2 vols. Berlin (1853–4).

Tombs, L.E. (1985). *Tell el Ḥesi. Modern, Military and Muslim Cemetery in Field I, Strata I–II*. The Joint Archaeological Expedition to Tell el-Hesi, vol. II. Waterloo, Ontario.

Tristram, H.B. (1874). *The Land of Moab: Travels and Descriptions on the East Side of the Dead Sea and the Jordan*. London.

Tsafrir, Y. (1990). The 'Massive Wall' East of the Golden Gate, Jerusalem. *IEJ*, 40: 280–86.

Tushingham, A.D. (1972). *The Excavation at Dibon (Dhībân) in Moab. The Third Campaign*. AASOR, vol. XL. Cambridge, Mass.

(1985). *Excavations in Jerusalem 1961–1967*, vol. I. Toronto.

(1993). Dibon. In *NEAEHL*, vol. I, pp. 350–52.

Tzaferis, V. (1982). Kefar Nahum. *ESI*, 1: 61–2.

(1983). New Archaeological Evidence on Ancient Capernaum. *Biblical Archaeologist*, 46.4: 198–204.

(1989). *Excavations at Capernaum*, vol. I. *1978–1982*. Winona Lake, Indiana.

Tzaferis, V. and R. Avner (1990a). Banias – 1989. *ESI*, 9 (1989–90): 3–4.

(1990b). The Excavations at Banias. *Qadmoniot*, 23: 110–14. [in Hebr.]

(1991). Banias – 1990. *ESI*, 10: 1–2.

Tzaferis, V. and S. Israeli (1993). Banias – 1991. *ESI*, 12: 1–3, figs. 1–4.

Tzaferis, V. and T. Muttat (1988). Banias – 1986. *ESI*, 6 (1987–8): 2–3.

Tzaferis, V., M. Peleg and Z. Ma'oz (1989). Banias Excavation Project – 1988. *ESI*, 7–8 (1988–9): 10–11.

Ussishkin, D. and J. Woodhead (1992). Excavations at Tel Jezreel 1990–1991: Preliminary Report. In *Excavations at Tel Jezreel 1990–1991*, pp. 3–56. Tel Aviv University, Institute of Archaeology Reprint Series, vol. VIII. Tel Aviv.

(1994). Excavations at Tel Jezreel 1992–1993: Second Preliminary Report. *Levant*, 26: 1–48.

Van Berchem, M. (1902). Notes sur les Croisades. *JA*, 9th series, 29: 385–456. Reprinted in Van Berchem 1978: II, 903–74.

(1903). Inscription arabe de Banias. *RB*, 12: 421–4. Reprinted in Van Berchem 1978: I, 297–300.

(1978). *Opera Minora*, 2 vols. Geneva.

Van Berchem, M. and E. Fatio (1913). *Voyage en Syrie*. Mémoires publiés par les membres de l'Institut français d'archéologie orientale du Caire, vols. XXXVII–XXXVIII. Cairo (1913–15).

Van de Velde, C.W.M. (1861). *Reise durch Syrien und Palästina in den Jahren 1851 und 1852*. Gotha.

Van der Kooij, G. (1993). Deir 'Alla, Tell. In *NEAEHL*, vol. I, pp. 338–42.

Van der Kooij, G. and M.M. Ibrahim (1990) (eds.). *Picking up the Threads ... A Continuing Review of Excavations at Dair Alla, Jordan*. Leiden.

Van Egmond, J.G. and J. Heyman (1757). *Reizen door een gedeelte van Europa, Klein Asien, verscheide Eilanden van de Archipel, Syrien, Palestina of het H. Land, Aegypten, den Berg Sinai*, 2 vols. Leiden (1757–8).

Van Kasteren, J.P. (1897). Notes de géographie biblique. Dalmanutha, Magadan, Mageth. – Doch. *RB*, 6: 93–104.

Vannini, G. (1990). Insediamenti di età crociata in Transgiordania. *LA*, 40: 476–8.

de Vaux, R. (1938). Chronique. Exploration de la région de Salt. *RB*, 47: 398–425. pls. XVII–XXIII.

(1946). Notes archéologiques et topographiques. *RB*, 53: 160–74.

de Vaux, R. *et al.* (1993). Fara'ah, Tell el- (North). In *NEAEHL*, vol. II, pp. 433–40.

Vincent, H. (1898). Chronique. Notes de voyage. *RB*, 7: 424–51.

(1899). Chronique. Les fouilles anglaises. *RB*, 8: 605–8.

(1903). Les ruines d''Amwas. *RB*, 12: 571–99.

(1908). Chronique. A travers Jérusalem, notes archéologiques. *RB*, n.s., 5: 267–79.

(1913). Chronique. Jérusalem. Fouilles aux abords de la Tour Pséphina. *RB*, n.s., 10: 89–96.

(1924). Jérusalem. Glanures archéologiques. *RB*, 33: 431–7.

(1927). La Troisième Enceinte de Jérusalem. *RB*, 36: 516–48, pls. XIII–XIX.

(1931). Les Monuments de Qoubeibeh. *RB*, 40: 57–91, pls. I–V.

Vincent, H. and F.M. Abel (1914). *Jérusalem: recherches de topographie, d'archéologie et d'histoire*, vol. II. *Jérusalem nouvelle*, 4 fascs. and album. Paris (1914–26).

(1932). *Emmaüs, sa basilique et son histoire.* Paris.

Vincent, L.H., E.J.H. Mackay and F.M. Abel (1923). *Hébron: le Ḥaram el-Khalîl: Sépulture des Patriarches*, 2 vols. Paris.

Volterra, H.V. (1989). Acri – salvaguardia e rivalutazione dei quartieri fondati dalle repubbliche marinare. In E. Poleggi (ed.), *Città portuali del Mediterraneo, storia e archeologia. Atti del Convegno internazionale di Genova 1985*, pp. 111–14. Genoa.

Warren, C. (1869). Notes on a Visit to Saida in July 1869. *PEFQS* (1869–70): 136–41.

(1870). Inscriptions and Masons' Marks. *PEFQS*: 324–9.

Warren, C. and C.R. Conder (1884). *The Survey of Western Palestine: Jerusalem.* London.

Waterman, L. (1937). *Preliminary Report of the University of Michigan Excavations at Sephoris, Palestine, in 1931.* Michigan.

Weinberg, G.D. (1968). Es-Samiriya. In Notes and News, *IEJ*, 18: 198–9.

(1987). A Glass Factory of Crusader Times in Northern Israel (Preliminary Report). *Annales du 10ᵉ Congrès de l'Association internationale pour l'Histoire du Verre, Madrid–Ségovie, 23–28 septembre 1985*, pp. 305–17. Amsterdam.

Weippert, M. (1964). Archäologische Jahresbericht. *ZDPV*, 80: 150–93.

Weiss, Z. (1993). Sepphoris. In *NEAEHL*, vol. IV, pp. 1324–8.

Whitcomb, D. (1987a). A Brief Report on the 1986 and 1987 Seasons at Aqaba. *LA*, 37: 411–12.

(1987b). Excavations in 'Aqaba. First Preliminary report. *ADAJ*, 31: 247–66.

(1988). Medieval Aqaba: A Brief Report on the 1986 and 1987 Seasons. *Syria*, 65: 423–5, fig. 5.

(1989). 'Aqaba (Ayla). In D. Homès-Fredericq and J.B. Hennessy, *Archaeology of Jordan*, vol. II.ii, pp. 178–83. Akkadica, Supplementum, vols. III, VII–VIII (2 vols.). Leuven (1986–9).

(1992). The Islamic Period as Seen from Selected Sites. In MacDonald 1992: 113–18.

Wightman, G. (1989). *The Damascus Gate, Jerusalem: Excavations by C.-M. Bennett and J.B. Hennessy at the Damascus Gate, Jerusalem, 1964–66.* BAR International Series, vol. DXIX. Oxford.

(1994). *The Walls of Jerusalem from the Canaanites to the Mamluks.* Mediterranean Archaeology, Supplement, vol. IV. Sydney.

Wilson, C.W. (1865). *Ordnance Survey of Jerusalem.* London. Facsimile edition, Jerusalem (1970).

(1880a). *Picturesque Palestine, Sinai and Egypt*, 4 vols. London (no date).

(1880b). *Picturesque Palestine, Sinai and Egypt*, 4 vols. Jerusalem (1976).

Wilson, C.W. and C. Warren (1871). *The Recovery of Jerusalem.* New York.

Winnett, F.V. and W.L. Reed (1964). *The Excavations at Dibon (Dhîbân) in Moab.* AASOR, vols. XXXVI–XXXVII (for 1957–8). New Haven.

Winter, P.H. (1944). *Acre Report*, 4 vols. Govt of Palestine, Public Works Department. Jerusalem.

Wolff, S.R. (1991). Archaeology in Israel. *AJA*, 95: 498–538.

(1994). Archaeology in Israel. *AJA*, 98: 481–519.

Wood, J. (1993). The Fortifications of Amman Citadel. *Fortress*, 16: 3–15.

Woolley, C.L. and T.E. Lawrence (1936). *The Wilderness of Zin*, new edition. London.

Wright, G.E. (1975). Beth-Shemesh. In *EAEHL*, vol. I, pp. 248–53.

Wright, T. (1848). *Early Travels in Palestine.* London.

Yadin, Y. (1976) (ed.). *Jerusalem Revealed: Archaeology in the Holy City 1968–1974.* Jerusalem.

Yeivin, Z. (1967). Exploration archéologique en Israël. In Chronique archéologique, *RB*, 74: 94–6.

(1973). Archaeological Activities in Samaria. In *Eretz Shomron: The Thirtieth Archaeological Convention, September 1972*, pp. xix–xx, 147–162. Jerusalem. [in Hebr. with Eng. summary]

(1981). The Synagogue of Eshtemoa. In L.I. Levine (ed.), *Ancient Synagogues Revealed*, pp. 120–2. Jerusalem.

(1982). Korazin. *ESI*, 1: 64–7.

(1993). Eshtemoa. In *NEAEHL*, vol. II, pp. 423–6.

Yeivin, Z. *et al.* (1988). The Bet Shean Project. *ESI*, 6 (1987–8): 7–45.

Yogev, O. and A. Rochman. (1985) Tel Sumeiriya. *ESI*, 4: 103–4.

Yule, B. and P. Rowsome (1994). *Caesarea Maritima. Area I 14 Excavations – The 1993 Season. Interim Report on the Excavation of a Sondage Through Sediments Filling the Inner Harbour, and an Overlying Arab and Crusader Sequence.* [London.]

Zayadine, F. (1985). Caravan Routes Between Egypt and Nabataea and the Voyage of Sultan Baybars to Petra in 1276. In A. Hadidi (ed.), *Studies in the History and Archaeology of Jordan*, vol. II, pp. 159–174. Amman/London.

Zschokke, H. (1865). *Das neuestestamentliche Emmaus.* Schaffhausen.

# MAPS

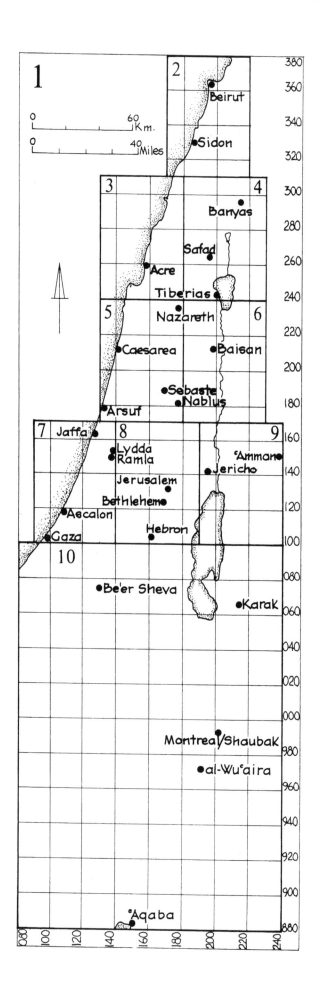

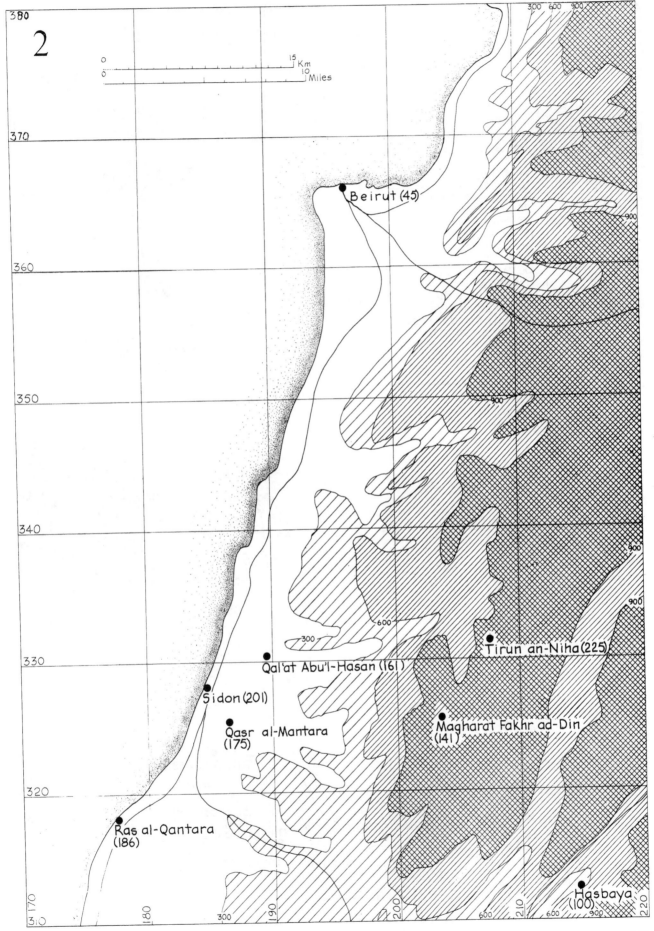

380

2

0                  15 Km
0                 10 Miles

300 600 900

370

● Beirut (45)

900

360

350

900

340

900

600

300

900

330

Qal'at Abu'l-Hasan (161)

● Tirun an-Niha (225)

● Sidon (201)

● Qasr al-Mantara
(175)

● Magharat Fakhr ad-Din
(141)

320

● Ras al-Qantara
(186)

310

170        180      300      190      200      210     600    600   900   220

● Hasbaya
(100)

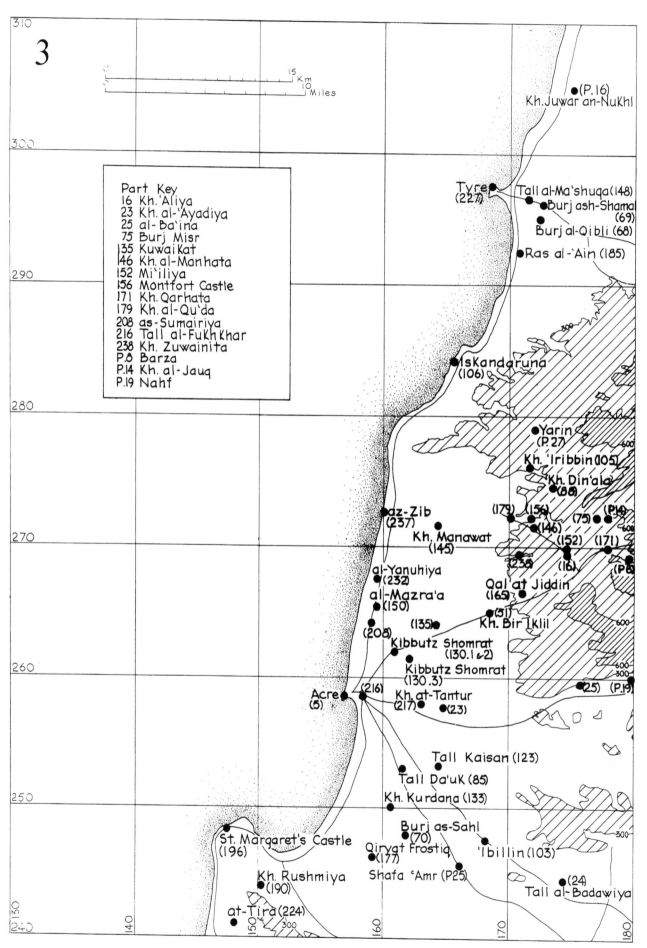

3

15 Km
10 Miles

Part Key
16 Kh.ʿAliya
23 Kh. al-ʿAyadiya
25 al-Baʿina
75 Burj Misr
135 Kuwaikat
146 Kh. al-Manhata
152 Miʿiliya
156 Montfort Castle
171 Kh. Qarhata
179 Kh. al-Quʿda
208 as-Sumairiya
216 Tall al-Fukhkhar
238 Kh. Zuwainita
P.8 Barza
P.14 Kh. al-Jauq
P.19 Nahf

Kh. Juwar an-Nukhl ● (P.16)

Tyre ● Tall al-Maʿshuqa (148)
(227)
● Burj ash-Shamal
● (69)
Burj al-Qibli (68)

● Ras al-ʿAin (185)

● Iskandaruna
(106)

● Yarin
(P.27)
Kh. ʿIribbin (105)
● Kh. Dinʿala
● (88)

az-Zib ● (179) (156) (75) (P14)
(237) ● ● ●
● Kh. Manawat (146)
(145) (152) (171)
al-Yanuhiya ● (238) (16) (P.8)
(232)
al-Mazraʿa Qalʿat Jiddin
(150) (165)
(135) ● (51)
(208) ● Kh. Bir Iklil
Kibbutz Shomrat
(130.1&2)
Kibbutz Shomrat
(130.3)
(25) (P.19)
Acre ● (216)
(5) Kh. at-Tantur
(217) (23)

Tall Kaisan (123)

Tall Daʿuk (85)

● Kh. Kurdana (133)

Burj as-Sahl
St. Margaret's Castle (70)
(196) Qiryat Frostig ʿIbillin (103)
(177)
Kh. Rushmiya Shafa ʿAmr (P25) (24)
(190) Tall al-Badawiya

at-Tira (224)

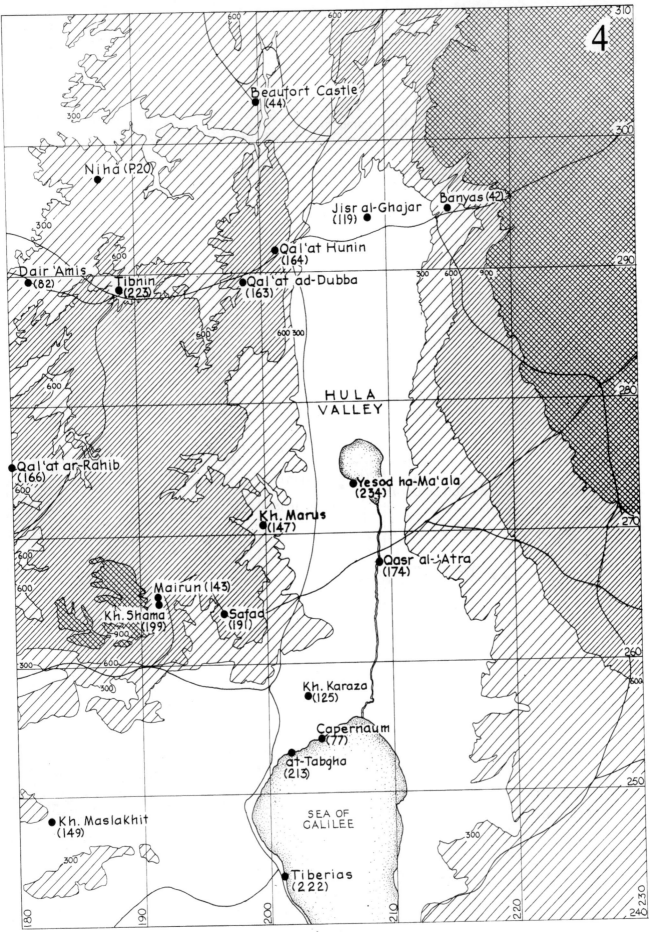

4

Beaufort Castle
(44)

Niha (P20)

Jisr al-Ghajar
(119)

Banyas (42)

Qal'at Hunin
(164)

Dair 'Amis
(82)

Tibnin
(223)

Qal'at ad-Dubba
(163)

HULA
VALLEY

Qal'at ar-Rahib
(166)

Yesod ha-Ma'ala
(234)

Kh. Marus
(147)

Qasr al-'Atra
(174)

Mairun (143)

Kh. Shama
(199)

Safad
(191)

Kh. Karaza
(125)

Capernaum
(77)

at-Tabgha
(213)

Kh. Maslakhit
(149)

SEA OF
GALILEE

Tiberias
(222)

145

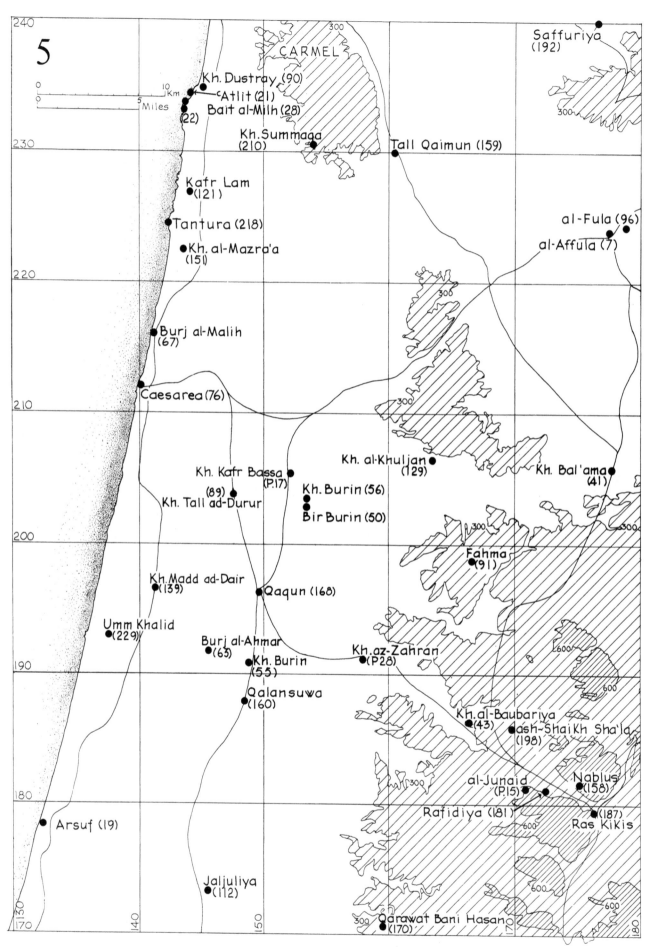

5

Saffuriya
(192)

CARMEL

Kh. Dustray (90)
Atlit (21)
Bait al-Milh (28)
(22)

Kh. Summaqa
(210)

Tall Qaimun (159)

Kafr Lam
(121)

al-Fula (96)
al-Affula (7)

Tantura (218)

Kh. al-Mazra'a
(151)

Burj al-Malih
(67)

Caesarea (76)

Kh. Kafr Bassa
(89)        (P.17)

Kh. al-Khuljan
(129)

Kh. Bal'ama
(41)

Kh. Burin (56)

Kh. Tall ad-Durur

Bir Burin (50)

Fahma
(91)

Kh. Madd ad-Dair
(139)

Qaqun (168)

Umm Khalid
(229)

Burj al-Ahmar
(63)

Kh. az-Zahran
(P28)

Kh. Burin
(55)

Kh. al-Baubariya
(43)

ash-Shaikh Sha'la
(198)

Qalansuwa
(160)

al-Junaid
(P.15)

Nablus
(158)

Rafidiya (181)

Ras Kikis
(187)

Arsuf (19)

Jaljuliya
(112)

Qarawat Bani Hasan
(170)

146

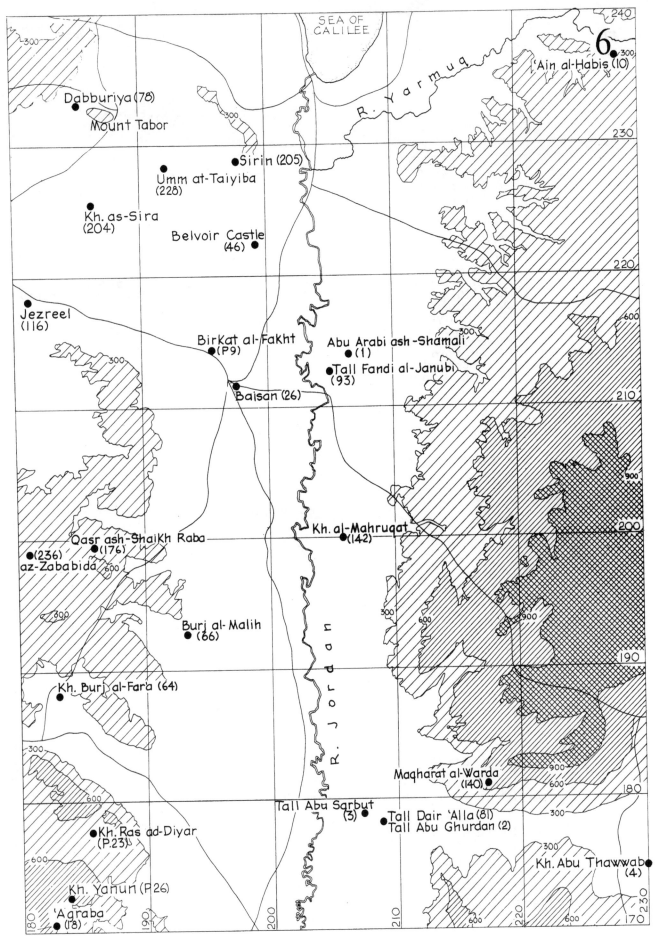

SEA OF
GALILEE

R. Yarmuq

6.

'Ain al-Habis (10)

Dabburiya (78)

Mount Tabor

Sirin (205)

Umm at-Taiyiba
(228)

Kh. as-Sira
(204)

Belvoir Castle
(46)

Jezreel
(116)

Birkat al-Fakht
(P9)

Abu Arabi ash-Shamali
(1)

Tall Fandi al-Janubi
(93)

Baisan (26)

Kh. al-Mahruqat
(142)

Qasr ash-Shaikh Raba
(176)

(236)
az-Zababida

Burj al-Malih
(66)

R. Jordan

Kh. Burj al-Fara (64)

Maqharat al-Warda
(140)

Tall Abu Sarbut
(3)

Tall Dair 'Alla (81)
Tall Abu Ghurdan (2)

Kh. Ras ad-Diyar
(P.23)

Kh. Abu Thawwab
(4)

Kh. Yanun (P.26)

'Aqraba
(18)

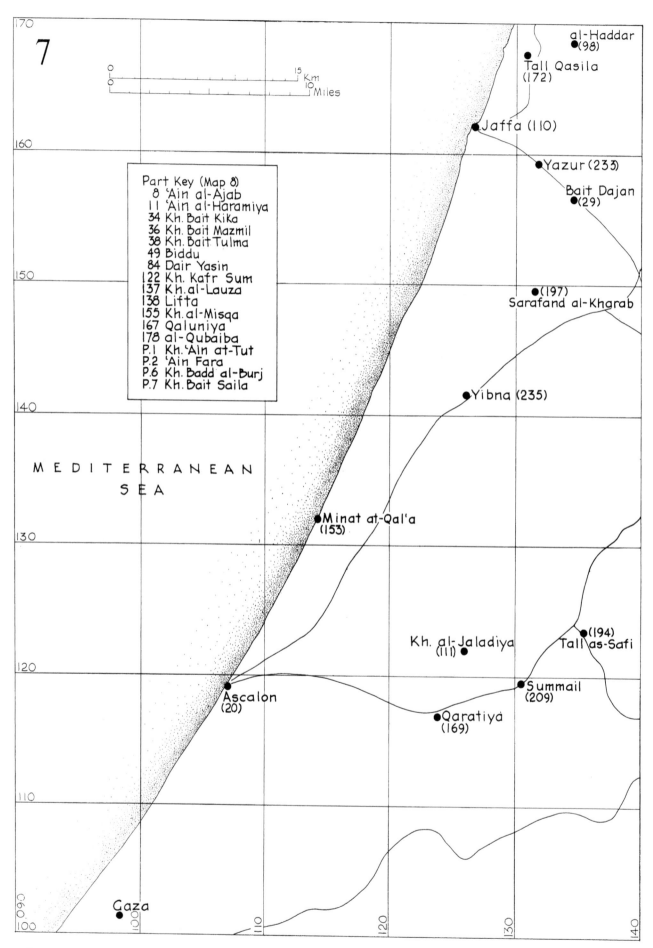

7

0
0 |‑‑‑‑‑‑‑‑‑‑‑‑‑‑‑‑‑‑‑‑‑| 15 Km
0 |‑‑‑‑‑‑‑‑‑‑‑‑‑‑‑‑‑| 10 Miles

al‑Haddar
●(98)

●Tall Qasila
(172)

●Jaffa (110)

●Yazur (233)

Bait Dajan
●(29)

Part Key (Map 8)
  8 'Ain al‑Ajab
 11 'Ain al‑Haramiya
 34 Kh. Bait Kika
 36 Kh. Bait Mazmil
 38 Kh. Bait Tulma
 49 Biddu
 84 Dair Yasin
122 Kh. Kafr Sum
137 Kh. al‑Lauza
138 Lifta
155 Kh. al‑Misqa
167 Qaluniya
178 al‑Qubaiba
P.1 Kh. 'Ain at‑Tut
P.2 'Ain Fara
P.6 Kh. Badd al‑Burj
P.7 Kh. Bait Saila

●(197)
Sarafand al‑Kharab

●Yibna (235)

M E D I T E R R A N E A N
S E A

●Minat at‑Qal'a
(153)

●(194)
Tall as‑Safi

Kh. al‑Jaladiya
(111) ●

●Summail
(209)

●Ascalon
(20)

●Qaratiya
(169)

●Gaza

148

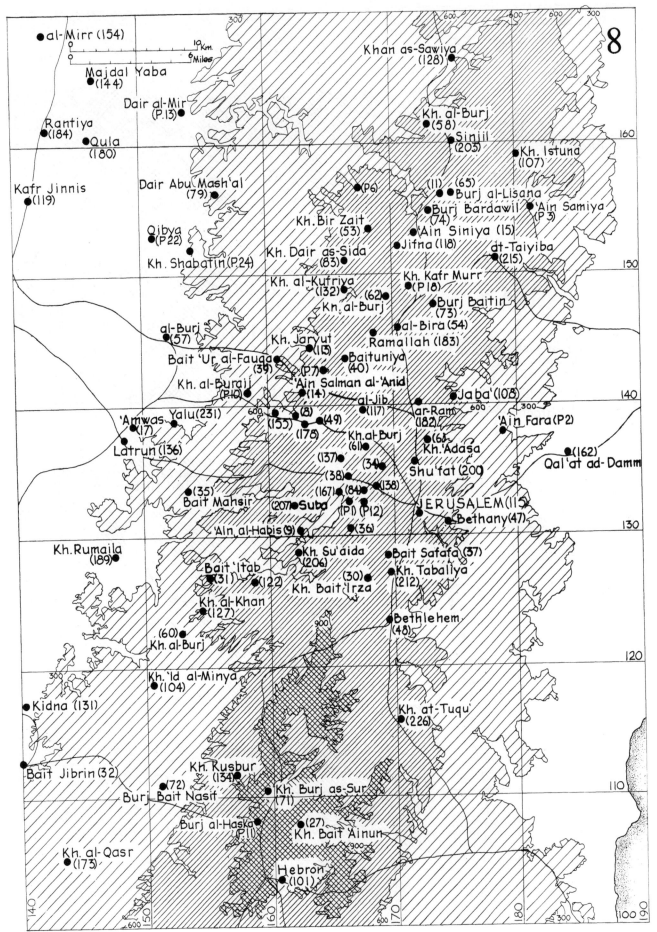

al-Mirr (154)

Majdal Yaba (144)

Dair al-Mir (P.13)

Rantiya (184)

Qula (180)

Kafr Jinnis (119)

Dair Abu Mash'al (79)

Qibya (P22)

Kh. Shabatin (P.24)

Khan as-Sawiya (128)

Kh. al-Burj (58)

Sinjil (203)

Kh. Istuna (107)

(11) (65)

Burj al-Lisana

Burj Bardawil (74)

'Ain Samiya (P3)

(P6)

Kh. Bir Zait (53)

'Ain Siniya (15)

Jifna (118)

dt-Taiyiba (215)

Kh. Dair as-Sida (83)

Kh. al-Kufriya (132)

Kh. Kafr Murr (P18)

(62)

Kn. al-Burj

Burj Baitin (73)

al-Bira (54)

al-Burj (57)

Kh. Jaryut (13)

Ramallah (183)

Bait 'Ur al-Fauqa (39)

Baituniya (40)

(P7)

Kh. al-Buraij (P10)

'Ain Salman al-'Anid (14)

al-Jib (117)

Jaba' (108)

ar-Ram (182)

(8)

'Amwas (17)

Yalu (231)

'Ain Fara (P2)

(155)

(49)

600

Latrun (136)

(176)

Kh. al-Burj (61)

(64)

Kh. 'Adasa

(162)

Qal'at ad-Damm

(137)

Shu'fat (200)

(34)

(38)

(138)

(35)

Bait Mahsir

(167)

(84)

JERUSALEM (115)

(207) Suba

(P1) (P12)

Bethany (47)

'Ain al-Habis (9)

(36)

Kh. Rumaila (189)

Kh. Su'aida (206)

Bait Safafa (37)

Bait 'Itab (131)

(122)

(30)

Kh. Tabaliya (212)

Kh. Bait 'Irza

Kh. al-Khan (127)

(60)

Kh. al-Burj

Bethlehem (48)

Kh. 'Id al-Minya (104)

Kidna (131)

Kh. at-Tuqu' (226)

Bait Jibrin (32)

Kh. Rusbur (134)

(72)

Burj Bait Nasif

Kh. Burj as-Sur (71)

Burj al-Haska (P11)

(27)

Kh. Bait 'Ainun

Kh. al-Qasr (173)

Hebron (101)

8

160

150

140

130

120

110

100

140

150

160

170

180

190

149

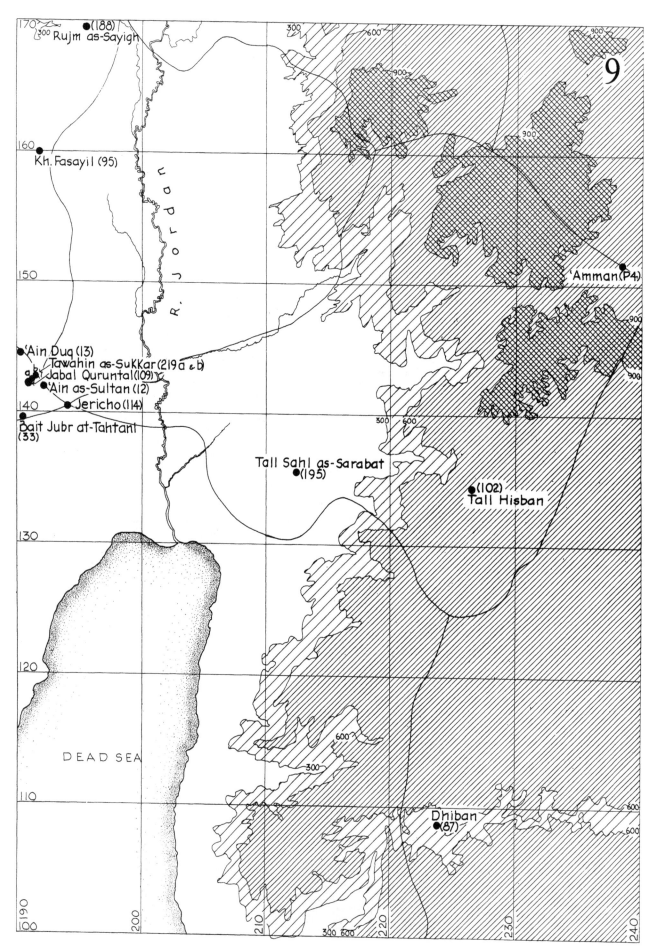

9

‘(188)
Rujm as-Sayigh

Kh.Fasayil (95)

R. Jordan

‘Amman(P4)

‘Ain Duq (13)
Tawahin as-Sukkar(219a &b)
Jabal Quruntal(109)
‘Ain as-Sultan (12)
Jericho (114)
Bait Jubr at-Tahtani
(33)

Tall Sahl as-Sarabat
(195)

(102)
Tall Hisban

DEAD SEA

Dhiban
(87)

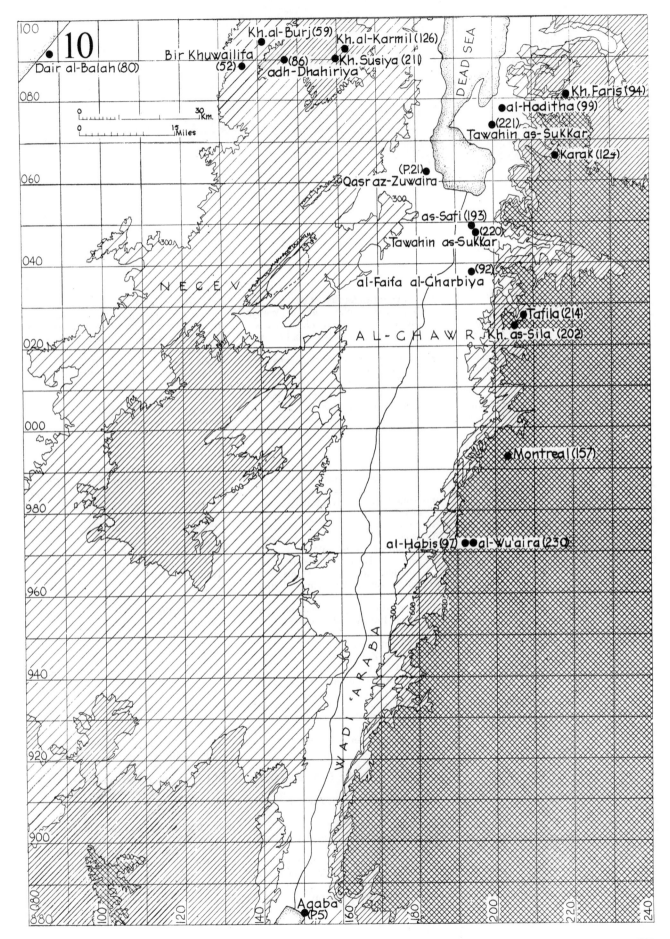

10

Dair al-Balah (80)

Kh.al-Burj (59)

Bir Khuwailifa (52)

Kh.al-Karmil (126)

(86)

adh-Dhahiriya

Kh. Susiya (210)

DEAD SEA

Kh. Faris (94)

al-Haditha (99)

(221)

Tawahin as-Sukkar

Karak (124)

(P.21)

Qasr az-Zuwaira

300

as-Safi (193)

(220)

Tawahin as-Sukkar

(92)

al-Faifa al-Gharbiya

N E G E V

300

Tafila (214)

Kh. as-Sila (202)

A L - G H A W R

600

Montreal (157)

al-Habis (97)

al-Wu aira (230)

600

W A D I   ' A R A B A

600

Aqaba (P.5)

0      30 Km.

0      15 Miles

151

# INDEX OF PLACE-NAMES

Note: The system used here for transliterating Arabic names appearing in written sources differs slightly from the simplified method of transcription used for modern place-names; the former are therefore distinguished in the index by *italics*.

Abelina *see* 'Ibillin (**no. 103**)
Abrahe Ortus *see* 'Ain Duq (**no. 13**), *and* Tawahin as-Sukkar (**no. 219**)
Abu Arabi ash-Shamali (**no. 1**), 13, 15, map 6
Abu Ghosh (castellum Emmaus), 13, 14
Abu Ghurdan, Tall (near Tall Dair 'Alla) (**no. 2**), 12, 15, map 6
Abu Sarbut, Tall (**no. 3**), 13, 15, map 6
Abu Sinan (Busenen), 119
Abu Thawwab, Kh. (**no. 4**), 14, 15, map 6
Acre (**no. 5**), 3, 6, 13, 14, 15–17, figs. 1, 3, 5, pls. I–IV, tables 1–2, map 3
  Burj al-Khazna, fig. 3.1
  Burj as-Sultan, 15, fig. 3.9, pl. II, table 3, estate in territory of, 11
  Hospital, 17, fig. 3.4
  Khan al-Faranj, fig. 3.8
  Khan al-'Umdan, fig. 3.12
  Khan ash-Shuna, fig. 3.11, pl. IV
  Montmusard, 15
  siege works near, 10
  Tower of the Flies, 17, fig. 3.14
'Adasa, Kh. (Adasa, Hadessa) (**no. 6**), 11, 17–18, map 8
'Addasa, Kh., 18
'Adullam, H. *see* 'Id al-Minya, Kh. (**no. 104**)
Adumin *see* Qal'at ad-Damm (**no. 162**)
Afeq, Tel *see* Kurdana, Kh. (**no. 133**)
Al-'Affula ('Afula) (**no. 7**), 18, pl. V, table 3, map 5
'Afra *see* at-Taiyiba (**no. 215**)
'Afrabala *see* Umm at-Taiyiba (**no. 228**)
Afula *see* al-'Affula (**no. 7**)
Ahamant *see* 'Amman (**no. P4**)
Aila *see* Aqaba (**no. P5**)
'Ain al-Ajab (**no. 8**), 13, 18, map 8
'Ain al-Habis (Desert of St John) (**no. 9**), 18, table 3, map 8
'Ain al-Habis (Cava de Suet, praesidium ... in regione Suita/Suhite, *Habis Jaldak*) (**no. 10**), 10, 18, map 6

'Ain al-Haramiya (Spring of the Brigands/Templars; *Birkat al-Dāwiyya*) (**no. 11**), 13, 14, 18–19, pl. VI, map 8
'Ain as-Sinjib/Sinjil *see* Bal'ama, Kh. (**no. 41**)
'Ain as-Sultan (Elisha's Spring, Fons Helysei) (**no. 12**), 13, 19, map 9
'Ain at-Tina *see* Burj as-Sahl (**no. 70**)
'Ain at-Tut, Kh. (**no. P1**), 111, 112, map 8
'Ain Arik (Beth 'Ariq) (**no. R1**), 116
'Ain Duq (Abrahe Ortus, Campi Abraham, Jardinz Abraham) (**no. 13**), 13, 19, pl. VII, map 9
'Ain Fara (Farafronte) (**no. P2**), 112, map 8
'Ain Karim, St John in the Woods, 13
'Ain Salman al-'Anid (Kh. Salman) (**no. 14**), 13, 19, fig. 4, table 4, map 8
'Ain Samiya (Kh. Samiya) (**no. P3**), 112, map 8
'Ain Sarin, 1
'Ain Shams (Aineseins?, Ainesens?) *see* Rumaila, Kh. (**no. 189**)
'Ain Siniya (Valdecurs, Aineseins?, Ainesens?) (**no. 15**), 12, 20, map 8
'Ain Tulma, Kh. *see* Bait Tulma, Kh. (**no. 38**)
'Aineseins (Ainesens) *see* 'Ain Siniya (**no. 15**) *and* Rumaila, Kh. (**no. 189**)
'Ajjul, 1
'Ajlun (Qal'at ar-Rabad), 2
Akhziv *see* az-Zib (**no. 237**)
'Akka ('Akko) *see* Acre (**no. 5**)
'Akko, Tel *see* Tall al-Fukhkhar (**no. 216**)
'Aliya, Kh. (**no. 16**), 20, table 3, map 3
'Amir, Kh. al- *see* Dair al-Mir (**no. P13**)
'Amman (Ahamant, Haman) (**no. P4**), 112–13, map 9
'Amwas (Emaus, Emmaus) (**no. 17**), 12, 20, map 8
Antioch, 6
Aqab (Aila, 'Ayla, Elat, Elim) (**no. P5**), 113, map 10
'Aqraba (**no. 18**), 11, 12, 20, map 6
  al-Hisn, 20
Aqua Bella *see* 'Iqbala, Kh.
'Aqudim, H. *see* Qu'da, Kh. al- (**no. 179**)
Aram *see* ar-Ram (**no. 182**)
Arbel (H. Arbel) *see* Irbid, Kh. (**no. R7**)
Ard Al-Qasr *see* Qasr ash-Shaikh Raba (**no. 176**)
Arshaf, Tel *see* Arsuf (**no. 19**)

Arsuf (Arsur, Tel Arshaf) (**no. 19**), 5, 6, 10, 11, 20–1, figs. 1, 5, tables 1–2, map 5
Ascalon (Ashqelon, 'Asqalan) (**no. 20**), 3, 5, 6, 21, 52, figs. 1, 6, pl. VIII, tables 1–2, map 7
Ashdod, Tel *see* Isdud (**no. R8**)
Ashdod Yam, H. *see* Minat al-Qal'a (**no. 153**)
Ashqelon *see* Ascalon
Asnerie *see* Jerusalem (**no. 115**)
'Asqalan *see* Ascalon
Assabebe *see* Hasbaya (**no. 100**)
*al-Aswīt* *see* Habis, al- (**no. 97**)
'Athlith *see* 'Atlit (**no. 21**)
'Atlit ('Athlit, Castrum Peregrinorum/Filii dei, Chastiau Pelerin, Pilgrims' Castle) (**no. 21**), 3, 5, 6, 10, 11, 13, 14, 22–3, 24, 26, figs. 1, 7–9, pl. IX, tables 1–3, map 5
  tower, 1.3 km SSW of (**no. 22**), 14, 24, fig. 8, table 3
'Ayadiya, Kh. al- (*al-Ghayadah*, la Hadia, H. Uza) (**no. 23**), 11, 24, map 3
'Ayadīya, Tall al- *see* Tantur, Kh. al- (**no. 217**)
al-'Azariya *see* Bethany (**no. 47**)
*Ayla* *see* Aqaba (**no. P5**)
*Azdūd* *see* Isdud (**no. R8**)
'Azor *see* Yazur (**no. 233**)
Azot *see* Isdud (**no. R8**)

al-Babariyya *see* Sarafand al-Kharab (**no. 197**)
al-Babriya *see* Fahma (**no. 91**)
Babriya, Kh. al- *see* Baubariya, Kh. al- (**no. 43**)
le Bace *see* al-Bassa (**no. R2**)
Badawiya, Tall al- (Kh. Ibdawiya, Tel Hannaton) (**no. 24**), 7, 24, fig. 10, pl. X, table 3, map 3
al-Badd *see* Bait Mahsir (**no. 35**)
Badd al-Balad *see* Baituniya (**no. 40**)
Badd al-Burj, Kh. (Burj Bardawil) (**no. P6**), 113, map 8
Badd Bunduq *see* Qarawat Bani Hassan (**no. 170**)
al-Ba'ina (casale S. Georgii, Saint Jorge Labane/de la Baene, Sangeor) (**no. 25**), 10, 24–5, tables 3, 4, map 3
al-Baiqa *see* Latrun (**no. 136**)
Bairut *see* Beirut (**no. 45**)

Baisan (Beisan, Bessan, Bethsan, Bet
  She'an) (**no. 26**), 7, 10, 11, 13, 25, figs.
  1, 11, pl. XI, tables 1, 3, map 6
Bait 'Ainun, Kh. (**no. 27**), 11, 26, table 4,
  map 8
Bait al-Milh (Salt Island) (**no. 28**), 14, 26,
  fig. 8, table 3, map 5
Bait Dajan (Bedeian, Casellum
  Maen/Medium) (**no. 29**), 10, 26,
  map 7; *see also* Ras ad-Diyar, Kh.
  (**no. P23**)
Bait Hanina, 112
Bait Hanun, 1
Bait 'Irza, Kh. (**no. 30**), 12, 26, map 8
Bait 'Itab (Beitatap, Bethaatap, Bethahatap)
  (**no. 31**), 10, 11, 24, 26–7, fig. 12, pls.
  XII–XIII, table 4, map 8
Bait Jibrin (Beit Gibelin, Bersabea, Bet
  Guvrin, Bethgibelin, Gybelin, Ybelin
  Hospitalariorum) (**no. 32**), 10, 11, 12,
  27, fig. 1, table 1, map 8
Bait Jubr at-Tahtani (**no. 33**), 6, 27, fig. 13,
  pl. XIV, table 3, map 9
Bait Kika, Kh. (Belrit Kykay, Kh. Maqiqa,
  Ramot) (**no. 34**), 7, 27–8, pl. XV, table
  3, map 8
Bait Lahm *see* Bethlehem (**no. 48**)
Bait Mahsir (Bet Me'ir; including al-Badd)
  (**no. 35**), 14, 28, map 8
Bait Mazmil, Kh. (**no. 36**), 12, 28, map 8
Bait Mizza, Kh. (H. Ha-Moza, Mevasseret
  Yerushalayim) (**no. 239**), 111
Bait Nasib, Kh. *see* Burj Bait Nasif (**no. 72**)
Bait Nasib ash-Sharqiya, Kh. (near Burj
  Bait Nasif, **no. 72**), 42, table 3
Bait Nuba, 113
Bait Safafa (Bethafava, Bethsaphace) (**no.
  37**), 7, 11, 28–9, pl. XVI, table 3, map 8
  Bubalia, 29
  al-Burj, 28–9
Bait Saila (Bait Sila) (**no. P7**), 113, map 8
Bait Sur *see* Burj as-Sur, Kh. (**no. 71**)
Bait Suriq, fig. 1, table 1
Bait Tulma, Kh. (Kh. 'Ain Tulma, H. Bet
  Telem, H. 'En Telem, Tolma) (**no. 38**),
  12, 13, 29, map 8
Bait 'Ur al-Fauqa (Bethoron Superior,
  Vetus Bethor; including al-Burj) (**no.
  39**), 29, table 3, map 8
Bait Yunan an-Nabi *see* Tabaliya, Kh. (**no.
  212**)
Baituniya (Beitiumen, Urniet; including
  Badd al-Balad) (**no. 40**), 14, 29, map 8
Bal'ama, Kh. (Castellum Beleismum,
  Chastiau St Job) (**no. 41**), 7, 13, 29–30,
  pls. XVII–XVIII, table 3, map 5
  'Ain as-Sinjib/Sinjil, 29
Balqa' province 50
Banyas (Belinas, Paneas) (**no. 42**), 5, 30, fig.
  1, tables 1–2, map 4
al-Bardawil *see* Qasr Bardawil (**no. R14**)
Baruth *see* Beirut (**no. 45**)
Barza, Kh. (H. Barzayit, Berzei, Berzey)
  (**no. P8**), 113, map 3
al-Bassa (le Bace, *al-Basah*, Lebassa,
  Shelomi) (**no. R2**), 116
al-Baubariya *see* Burj Bardawil (**no. 74**)
al-Baubariya *see* Jifna (**no. 118**)
al-Baubariya *see* Latrun (**no. 136**)
al-Baubariya *see* Rantiya (**no. 184**)

al-Baubariya *see* ash-Shaikh Sha'ala (**no.
  198**)
al-Baubariya *see* az-Zababida (**no. 236**)
Baubiyra, Kh. al- (Kh. al-Babriya) (**no. 43**),
  11, 30, map 5
Baubriya, Kh. *see* Manawat, Kh. (**no. 145**)
Beaufort Castle (Belfort, Qal'at ash-Shaqif
  Arnun) (**no. 44**), 5, 7, 10, 11, 31, figs. 1,
  14, pl. XIX, tables 1, 3, map 4
Beauverium *see* Qastal (**no. R15**)
Bedeian *see* Bait Dajan (**no. 29**)
Be'er Borin *see* Bir Burin (**no. 50**)
Beirut (Bairut, Baruth, Beritum, Berytum,
  Beyrouth) (**no. 45**), 5, 6, 32, figs. 1, 15,
  tables 1–2, map 2
Beisan *see* Baisan (**no. 26**)
Beit Gibelin *see* Bait Jibrin (**no. 32**)
Beitatap *see* Bait 'Itab (**no. 31**)
Beithsur *see* Burj as-Sur, Kh. (**no. 71**)
Beitiumen *see* Baituniya (**no. 40**)
Belfort *see* Beaufort Castle (**no. 44**)
Belfort *see* Dair Abu Mash'al (**no. 79**)
Belhasem *see* Qal'at Abu'l-Hasan (**no. 161**)
Belinas *see* Banyas (**no. 42**)
Bellifortis (Belfort) *see* Dair Abu Mash'al
  (**no. 79**)
Belmont *see* Suba (**no. 207**)
Belrit Kykay *see* Bait Kika, Kh. (**no. 34**)
Belveer *see* Qastal (**no. R15**)
Belvoir Castle (Coquet, Kaukab al-Hawa,
  Kokhav ha-Yarden) (**no. 46**), 6, 10, 11,
  14, 32–3, 95, fig. 16, pls. XX–XXI, map 6
Beritum *see* Beirut (**no. 45**)
Bersabea *see* Bait Jibrin (**no. 32**)
Berytum *see* Beirut (**no. 45**)
Berzei (Berzey) *see* Barza, Kh. (**no. P8**)
Bessan *see* Baisan (**no. 26**)
Bet Bad, H. *see* Umm ar-Ras
  ash-Shamaliya, Kh. (**no. R20**)
Bet Guvrin *see* Bait Jibrin (**no. 32**)
Bet Me'ir *see* Bait Mahsir (**no. 35**)
Bet She'an *see* Baisan (**no. 26**)
Bet Shemesh, Tel *see* Rumaila, Kh. (**no.
  189**)
Bet Telem, H. *see* Bait Tulma, Kh. (**no. 38**)
Bet Zeneita, H. *see* Zuwainita, Kh. (**no.
  238**)
Beth 'Ariq *see* 'Ain Arik (**no. R1**)
Bethaatap (Bethahatap) *see* Bait 'Itab (**no.
  31**)
Bethafava *see* Bait Safafa (**no. 37**)
Bethania *see* Bethany (**no. 47**)
Bethany (al-'Azariya, Bethania, S. Lazarus)
  (**no. 47**), 6, 11, 13, 14, 33, table 3, map
  8
Bethel *see* Burj Baitin (**no. 73**)
Bethenase *see* Burj Bait Nasif (**no. 72**)
Bethgibelin *see* Bait Jibrin (**no. 32**)
Bethlehem (Bait Lahm, Bethleem) (**no. 48**),
  5, 14, 33, fig. 1, tables 1, 3, map 8
Bethoron Superior *see* Bait 'Ur al-Fauqa
  (**no. 39**)
Bethsame Iudae (Bethsames) *see* Rumaila,
  Kh. (**no. 189**)
Bethsan *see* Baisan (**no. 26**)
Bethsaphace *see* Bait Safafa (**no. 37**)
Bethsura *see* Burj as-Sur, Kh. (**no. 71**)
Beyrouth *see* Beirut (**no. 45**)
Biddu (**no. 49**), 12, 33–4, map 8
  Shaikh Abu Talal, 33

Bir Burin (Be'er Borin) (**no. 50**), 13, 34,
  map 5
Bir Iklil, Kh. (Clie, Clil, *Iklil*, Kh. Iklil,
  Kalil, H. Kalil) (**no. 51**), 14, 34, map 3
Bir Khuwailifa (Reonde Cisterne, Rotunda
  Cisterne) (**no. 52**), 13, 34, map 1
Bir Nabala (**no. 240**), 111
Bir Summail *see* Summail (**no. 209**)
Bir Zait, Kh. (**no. 53**), 11, 34, fig. 17, pl.
  XXII, map 8
al-Bira (Birra, Castrum
  Maome/Mahomaria, Magna
  Mahomaria, Mahomeria major,
  Mahumeria) (**no. 54**), 2, 3, 6, 7, 11, 13,
  14, 35, figs. 1, 18, pl. XXIII, tables 1,
  3–4, map 8
*Birkat al-Dawiyya* *see* 'Ain al-Haramiya
  (**no. 11**)
Birkat al-Fakht (**no. P9**), 113, map 6
Birkat as-Sultan *see* Jerusalem (**no. 115**)
Birra *see* al-Bira (**no. 54**)
Biyar, Kh. al- *see* Farraj, Kh. (**no. 242**)
Blanca Guarda (Blanchegarde) *see* Safi, Tall
  as- (**no. 194**)
Borin, H. *see* Burin, Kh. (**no. 56**)
Bubalia, *see* Bait Safafa (**no. 37**)
Buraij, Kh. al- (al-Burj) (**no. P10**), 113, map 8
Bures *see* Dabburiya (**no. 78**)
Burgat Mishor, H. *see* Burj as-Sahl (**no. 70**)
Burgata, H. *see* Burj al-Ahmar (**no. 63**)
Buria *see* Burin, Kh. (**no. 55**)
Buria (Burie) *see* Dabburiya (**no. 78**)
Burin, Kh. (Buria, Burin, *Burin*, Casal neuf)
  (**no. 55**), 12, 35, map 5
Burin, Kh. (H. Borin) (**no. 56**), 12, 35, map
  5
al-Burj *see* Bait Safafa (**no. 37**)
al-Burj *see* Bait 'Ur al-Fauqa (**no. 39**)
al-Burj *see* Buraij, Kh. al- (**no. P10**)
al-Burj *see* Dair al-Mahruq (**no. P12**)
al-Burj *see* Jaba' (**no. 108**)
al-Burj *see* Jifna (**no. 118**)
al-Burj *see* Ramallah (**no. 183**)
al-Burj *see* Tantura (**no. 218**)
al-Burj (Qal'at Tantura, al-Habis, Gith, Git,
  Tarenta, Tharenta, H. Tittora) (**no. 57**),
  7, 10, 25, 35, fig. 19, table 3, map 8
Burj, Kh. al- (**no. 58**), 7, 37, pl. XXIV, table
  3, map 8
Burj, Kh. al- (Burj al-Bayyara, Castle of
  Figs, Castrum Ficuum, Fiyr, le Fier,
  Qal'at al-Burj) (**no. 59**), 7, 37, table 3,
  map 1
Burj, Kh. al- (Burj Sansan) (**no. 60**), 37,
  table 4, map 8
Burj, Kh. al- (Burj al-Jauz, Kh. al-Kurum,
  Ramot) (**no. 61**), 6, 13, 14, 37–8, fig. 20,
  pl. XXV, tables 1, 4, map 8
Burj, Kh. al- (near Kh. Salamiya, Salome)
  (**no. 62**), 38, pl. XXVI, table 3, map 8
Burj, Kh. al- *see* Burj al-Lisana (**no. 65**)
Burj, Kh. al- *see* Burj al-Malih (**no. 66**)
Burj, Kh. al- *see* Burj Bait Nasif (**no. 72**)
Burj al-Ahmar (H. Burgata, Kh. al-Burj
  al-'Atut, Red Tower, Tourre-Rouge,
  Turriclee, Turris Latinae, Turris
  Rubea) (**no. 63**), xvii, 7, 14, 38–9, fig.
  21, pl. XXVII, table 3, map 5
Burj al-'Atut, Kh. al- *see* Burj al-Ahmar
  (**no. 63**)

Burj at-Tut (**no. 241**), 111
Burj al-Bayyara *see* Burj, Kh. al- (**no. 59**)
Burj al-Far'a, Kh. (**no. 64**), 7, 11, 39, pl.
   xxviii, table 3, map 4
Burj al-Haska (Burj Haska) (**no. P11**), 113,
   map 8
Burj al-Jauz, al- *see* Burj, Kh. al- (**no. 61**)
Burj al-Lisana (Kh. al-Burj) (**no. 65**), 7, 11,
   39–40, table 3, map 8
Burj al-Malih (Kh. al-Burj) (**no. 66**), 10, 11,
   40, fig. 22, map 6
Burj al-Malih (*al-Malaha, al-Mallūha*, Tall
   al-Malat, Tel Tanninim, *Turris
   Salinarum*) (**no. 67**), 14, 41, table 3,
   map 5
Burj al-Qibli (**no. 68**), 41, table 3, map 3
Burj ar-Riha *see* Jericho (**no. 114**)
Burj al-Yaqur *see* Qarawat Bani Hassan
   (**no. 170**)
Burj ash-Shamal (le Tor de l'Opital?) (**no.
   69**), 41, table 3, map 3
Burj as-Sahl (H. Burgat Mishor) (**no. 70**),
   11, 41, fig. 23, map 3
'Ain at-Tina, 13, 41
Burj as-Sultan *see* Acre (**no. 5**)
Burj as-Sur, Kh. (Bait Sur, Beithsur,
   Bethsura) (**no. 71**), 41, pl. xxix, table 3,
   map 8
Burj Bait Nasif (Kh. Bait Nasib, Bethenase,
   Kh. al-Burj, H. Neziv) (**no. 72**), 7, 42,
   map 8
Burj Baitin (Bethel) (**no. 73**), 7, 42, pl. xxx,
   table 3, map 8
Burj Bardawil (**no. 74**), 12, 13, 42–3, fig. 24,
   map 8
al-Baubariya, 43, pl. xxxi
Burj Bardawil *see* Badd al-Burj, Kh. (**no. P6**)
*Burj Dahūq see* Da'uk, Tall (**no. 85**)
Burj Kufriya, Kh. *see* Kufriya, Kh. (**no. 132**)
Burj Misr (H. Mezad Abbirim) (**no. 75**), 43,
   table 3, map 3
Burj Sansan *see* Burj, Kh. al- (**no. 60**)
Busenen *see* Abu Sinan

Cabecie *see* al-Ghabasiya
Caco (Cacho) *see* Qaqun (**no. 168**)
Caesarea (Cesaire, Qaisariya, H. Qesari)
   (**no. 76**), 5, 6, 7, 13, 43–5, figs. 1, 25,
   pls. xxxii–xxxvi, tables 1–3, map 5
Cafarlet *see* Kafr Lam (**no. 121**)
Cafram *see* Shafa 'Amr (**no. P25**)
Cafresi (Cafriasif) *see* Kafr Yasif
Caimun *see* Qiamun, Tall (**no. 159**)
Calanson (Calansue, Calanzon) *see*
   Qalansuwa (**no. 160**)
Campi Abraham *see* 'Ain Duq (**no. 13**) *and*
   Tawahin as-Sukkar (**no. 219**)
Capernaum (Capharnaum, Kefar Nahum,
   Talhum) (**no. 77**), 12, 46, map 4
Capharkeme *see* Kafr Kama (**no. R10**)
Capharleth *see* Kafr Lam (**no. 121**)
Capharnaum *see* Capernaum (**no. 77**)
Caphason *see* Kafr Sum (**no. 122**)
Caphastrum *see* Istuna, Kh. (**no. 107**)
Cariatarba *see* Hebron (**no. 101**)
Carmelus *see* Karmil, Kh. al- (**no. 126**)
Casal de Châtillon *see* Mazra'a, Kh. al- (**no.
   151**)
Casal neuf *see* Burin, Kh. (**no. 55**)
Casale Balneorum *see* Yazur (**no. 233**)

Casale Huberti de Paci/Lamberti *see*
   az-Zib (**no. 237**)
Casale Latinae *see* Madd ad-Dair (**no. 139**)
Casale quod fuit Eustachii *see* Madd
   ad-Dair (**no. 139**)
Casale Rogerii de Chasteillon *see* Mazra'a,
   Kh. al- (**no. 151**)
Casale S. Egidii *see* Sinjil (**no. 203**)
Casale S. Georgii *see* al-Ba'ina (**no. 25**)
Casel des Plains *see* Yazur (**no. 233**)
Casel Destreiz *see* Dustray, Kh. (**no. 90**)
Casel Imbert *see* az-Zib (**no. 237**)
Casellum Balneorum/de Planis/de
   Templo *see* Yazur (**no. 233**)
Casellum Maen/Medium *see* Bait Dajan
   (**no. 229**)
Casellum S. Abacuc *see* Kafr Jinnis (**no. 120**)
Castellare Rogerii Longobardi *see* Umm
   Khalid (**no. 229**)
Castellum, S. Margaretha *see* St Margaret's
   Castle (**no. 196**)
Castellum Abrahami *see* Jabal Quruntul
   (**no. 109**)
Castellum Arnaldi/Arnulfi *see* Yalu (**no.
   231**)
Castellum Beleismum *see* Bal'ama, Kh. (**no.
   41**)
Castellum Beroart *see* Minat al-Qal'a (**no.
   153**)
Castellum Novum *see* Qal'at Hunin (**no.
   164**)
Castellum Novum (Castellum Novum
   Regis) *see* Mi'iliya (**no. 152**)
Castellum Vallis Moysis *see* al-Wu'aira (**no.
   230**)
Castellum Ziph *see* az-Zib (**no. 237**)
Castiaus/castiel S. Elyes *see* at-Taiyiba (**no.
   215**)
Castle of Figs *see* Burj, Kh. al- (**no. 59**)
Castle of St Elias *see* at-Taiyiba (**no. 215**)
Castrum Dumi *see* Qal'at ad-Damm (**no.
   162**)
Castrum Fabbarum/Fabe *see* al-Fula (**no.
   96**)
Castrum Ficuum *see* burj, Kh. al- (**no. 59**)
Castrum Filii Dei *see* 'Atlit (**no. 21**)
Castrum Maome/Mahomaria *see* Bira, al-
   (**no. 54**)
Castrum Peregrinorum *see* 'Atlit (**no. 21**)
Castrum Regis *see* Mi'iliya (**no. 152**)
Castrum Saboach *see* Montreal (**no. 157**)
Castrum S. Helyae *see* at-Taiyiba (**no. 215**)
Castrum Zafetanum *see* Shafa 'Amr (**no.
   P25**)
Caun Mons *see* Qaimont, Tall (**no. 159**)
Cava de Suet *see* 'Ain al-Habis (**no. 10**)
Cava Templi, castrum *see* St Margaret's
   Castle (**no. 196**)
Cave de Tyron *see* Tirun an-Niha (**no. 225**)
Caymont *see* Qaimun, Tall (**no. 159**)
Celle *see* as-Sila' (**no. 202**)
Cesaire *see* Caesarea (**no. 76**)
Chastel Arnoul/Arnold/Hernaut *see* Yalu
   (**no. 231**)
Chastel Neuf *see* Qal'at Hunin (**no. 164**)
le Chastelez *see* Qasr al-'Atra (**no. 174**)
Chastiau de Roi/dou Rei *see* Mi'iliya (**no.
   152**)
Chastiau Pelerin *see* 'Atlit (**no. 21**)
Chastiau S. Job *see* Bal'ama, Kh. (**no. 41**)

Chorazin *see* Karaza, Kh. (**no. 125**)
Cisterna Rubea *see* Qal'at ad-Damm (**no.
   162**)
Civitas Petracensis *see* Karak (**no. 124**)
Clepsta *see* Lifta (**no. 138**)
Clie (Clil) *see* Bir Iklil, Kh. (**no. 51**)
Coketum *see* Kuwaikat (**no. 135**)
Cola *see* Qula (**no. 180**)
Colonia *see* Qaluniya (**no. 167**)
Coquet *see* Belvoir Castle (**no. 46**)
Coquetum *see* Kuwaikat (**no. 135**)
Crac (le Crac de Montreal, Cracum Montis
   regalis) *see* Karak (**no. 124**)
Crac des Chevaliers, 6

Dabburiya (Buria, Burie, Dabereth) (**no.
   78**), 46, fig. 1, tables 1, 3, map 6
Dair, Kh. al- (Deira), 119
Dair Abu Mash'al (Belfort, Bellifortis) (**no.
   79**), 10, 11, 46, map 8
Dair al-Balah (Darom, Darum, *al-Dārūm*)
   (**no. 80**), 10, 46, fig. 1, table 1, map 10
Dair 'Alla, Tall (**no. 81**), 1, 13, 46, map 6;
   *see also* Abu Ghurdan, Tall
Dair al-Mahruq (al-Burj) (**no. P12**), 113,
   map 8
Dair al-Mir (Kh. al-'Amir) (**no. P13**), 114,
   map 8
Dair 'Amis (Dairrhamos, Derreme) (**no.
   82**), 13, 46, map 4
Dair as-Sida, Kh. (Dair Sa'ida) (**no. 83**), 12,
   46, map 8
Dair Surur (**no. R3**), 116
Dair Yasin (**no. 84**), 11, 47, 113, map 8
Dairrhamos *see* Dair 'Amis (**no. 82**)
Damietta (Torunum in sabulo), 6
Danehila (Danehyle) *see* Din'ala, Kh. (**no.
   88**)
Darom (Darum, *al-Dārūm*) *see* Dair
   al-Balah (**no. 80**)
Da'uk, Tall (Kh. Da'uk, Khan Da'uk, *Burj
   Dahūq, Da'ūq*, Doc, Dochum, Doke),
   (**no. 85**), 12, 13, 47, table 3, map 3
*Da'ūq see* Da'uk, Tall (**no. 85**)
David's Tower *see* Jerusalem (**no. 115**)
Deira *see* Dair, Kh. al-
Deirelcobebe *see* al-Qubaiba
Derina *see* Ras al-'Ain (**no. 185**)
Derreme *see* Dair 'Amis (**no. 82**)
Dersophath *see* Shu'fat (**no. 200**)
Desert of St John *see* al-Habis (**no. 9**)
Destrictum (Casel Destreiz, le Destroit) *see*
   Dustray, Kh. (**no. 90**)
adh-Dhahiriya (including al-Hisn) (**no. 86**),
   47, table 3, map 10
Dhiban (*Dhibān, Dhibyān*, Dibon) (**no. 87**),
   12, 47, map 9
Din'ala, Kh. (Danehyle, Danehile, H.
   Din'ala, Kh. Nu'aila) (**no. 88**), 12, 14,
   47, 119, map 3
Doc (Dochum, Doke) *see* Da'uk, Tall (**no.
   85**)
Doc (Docus) *see* Jabal Quruntul (**no. 109**)
Dor *see* Tantura (**no. 218**)
Durur, Kh. Tall ad- (Tel Zeror) (**no. 89**), 1,
   12, 14, 47, map 5
Dustray, Kh. (Casel Destreiz, le Destroit,
   Destrictum, Petra Incisa, H. Qarta)
   (**no. 90**), 6, 7, 11, 14, 47, figs. 8, 26,
   table 3, map 5

Ebron *see* Hebron (**no. 101**)
Effraon *see* Taiyiba, at- (**no. 215**)
'Elat *see* Aqaba (**no. P5**)
Elful (Elfule) *see* al-Fula (**no. 96**)
Elgedeide *see* Judaida, Kh.
Elim *see* Aqaba (**no. P5**)
Elisha's Spring *see* 'Ain as-Sultan (**no. 12**)
Emaus (Emmaus) *see* 'Amwas (**no. 17**)
'En Boqeq *see* Umm Baghag (**no. R21**)
'En Sheva' *see* at-Tabgha (**no. 213**)
'En Telem, H. *see* Bait Tulma, Kh. (**no. 38**)
'Erav, H. *see* 'Iribbin, Kh. (**no. 105**)
Eshtemoa *see* as-Samu' (**no. R18**)
Evlayim *see* 'Ibillin (**no. 103**)

Fahma (Fame) (**no. 91**), 48, table 4, map 5
  al-Babriya, 48
al-Faifa al-Gharbiya (Qasr al-Faifa) (**no. 92**), 13, 48, map 1
Fame *see* Fahma (**no. 91**)
Fandi al-Janubi, Tall (**no. 93**), 13, 48, map 6
Far'a, Kh. Tall al- (**no. R4**), 1, 116
Farafronte *see* 'Ain Fara (**no. P2**)
Faris, Kh. (Kh. Tadun) (**no. 94**), 12, 48, map 10
Farraj, Kh. (Kh. al-Biyar) (**no. 242**), 112
Fasayil, Kh. (Fasael, Kh. Fasa'il, Tall Fasa'il, Phesech) (**no. 95**), 13, 48, map 9
Fasil Danyal, Kh. (H. Pazelet), 119
la Feve *see* al-Fula (**no. 96**)
le Fier (Fiyr) *see* Burj, Kh. al- (**no. 59**)
Fons Helysei *see* 'Ain as-Sultan (**no. 12**)
Forbelet *see* Umm at-Taiyiba (**no. 228**)
Franche Garde *see* Qasr al-Mantara (**no. 174**)
Francheville *see* Rushmiya, Kh. (**no. 190**)
Frans Castiaus *see* Montfort Castle (**no. 156**)
Fukhkhar *see* Tall al-Fukhkhar (**no. 216**)
al-Fula (Elful, Elfule, castrum Fabe/Fabbarum, la Feve, Kibbutz Merhavya) (**no. 96**), 10, 11, 18, 49, map 5

Gabaa *see* Jaba' (**no. 108**)
Gabaon *see* al-Jib (**no. 117**)
Galatia (Galatidis, la Galatie) *see* Qaratiya (**no. 169**)
Gaza, 2, fig. 1, table 1
Gebea *see* Jaba' (**no. 108**)
Geladia (Geliadia) *see* Jaladiya, Kh. (**no. 111**)
Gezrael *see* Jezreel (**no. 116**)
al-Ghabasiya (Cabecie, le Ghabezie), 119
*al-Ghayadah see* 'Ayadiya, Kh. al- (**no. 23**)
Ghawr, 2
Gibelim *see* Yibna (**no. 235**)
Gibeon *see* al-Jib (**no. 117**)
Git (Gith) *see* al-Burj (**no. 57**)
Gov, H. *see* Jauq, Kh. al- (**no. P14**)
Gybelin *see* Bait Jibrin (**no. 32**)

al-Habis (al-*Aswīt*, Petra) (**no. 97**), 7, 49, fig. 27, pls. xxxvii–xxxviii, table 3, map 10
al-Habis *see* al-Burj (**no. 57**)
*Habis Jaldak see* 'Ain al-Habis (**no. 10**)
Habonim *see* Kafr Lam (**no. 121**)

Habs ad-Damm *see* Nablus (**no. 158**)
al-Haddar (Molendina Trium Pontium, Tres Pontes) (**no. 98**), 13, 14, 49, map 7
Hadessa *see* Adasa, Kh. (**no. 6**)
Hadia *see* 'Ayadiya, Kh. al- (**no. 23**)
al-Haditha (**no. 99**), 13, 49, map 10
Hafita *see* Madd ad-Dair (**no. 139**)
Haifa, fig. 1, table 1; *see also* St Margaret's Castle (**no. 196**)
Haifa-Romena *see* Rushmiya, Kh. (**no. 190**)
Haman *see* 'Amman (**no. P4**)
Hannaton, Tel *see* Badawiya, Tall al- (**no. 24**)
Hanot, H. *see* Khan, Kh. al- (**no. 127**)
Har Hazofim (Jerusalem) (**no. 243**), 111
Haram ash-Sharif *see* Jerusalem (**no. 115**)
Hasbaya (Assabebe, Hasbeya) (**no. 100**), 50, fig. 1, tables 1, 3, map 2
Hasi, Tall al- (*al-Hasī*, Tel Hesi) (**no. R5**), 1, 116
Hebron (Cariatarba, Ebron, al-Khalil, S. Abraham) (**no. 101**), 10, 12, 50, 114, fig. 1, table 1, map 8
Herodium (Herodion, Kh. Jabal Firdaus) (**no. R6**), 116
Heshbon *see* Hisban, Tall (**no. 102**)
Hesi, Tel *see* Hasi, Tall al- (**no. R5**)
Hiericho *see* Jericho (**no. 114**)
Hierusalem *see* Jerusalem (**no. 115**)
Hinnom Valley *see* Jerusalem (**no. 115**)
Hisban, Tall (Heshbon, Hisbān) (**no. 102**), 12, 13, 50–1, pl. xxxix, map 9
al-Hisn *see* 'Aqraba (**no. 18**)
al-Hisn *see* adh-Dhahiriya (**no. 86**)
Hisn, Tall al- (Baisan), 25
Hunin *see* Qal'at Hunin (**no. 164**)

Ibdawiya, Kh. *see* Badawiya, Tall al- (**no. 24**)
Ibelin *see* Yibna (**no. 235**)
'Ibillin (Abelina, Evlayim, Ibillin) (**no. 103**), 7, 51, table 3, map 3
'Id al-Minya, Kh. (H. 'Adullam, Kh,. 'Id al-Miya) (**no. 104**), 12, 51, map 8
Iericho *see* Jericho (**no. 114**)
Ierosolima (Ierusalem) *see* Jerusalem (**no. 115**)
Iezrael *see* Jezreel (**no. 116**)
*Iklil* (Kh. Iklil) *see* Bir Iklil, Kh. (**no. 51**)
'Iqbala, Kh. (Aqua Bella), 12, 14
Irbid, Kh. (Arbel, H. Arbel) (**no. R7**), 116
'Iribbin, Kh. (H. 'Erav) (**no. 105**), 12, 51, map 3
Isdud (Tel Ashdod, Azot, *Azdūd, Yazdūd*) (**no. R8**), 116–17
Iskandaruna (Iskandariya, Scandalion, Scandalium) (**no. 106**), 10, 11, 51, fig. 1, tables 1–2, map 3
Isle de Graye *see* Jazirat Fara'un (**no. R9**)
Istuna, Kh. (Caphastrum, Kh. Kafr Istuna) (**no. 107**), 7, 51, table 3, map 8
Iudin (Iudyn) *see* Qal'at Jiddin (**no. 165**)
Iyye Kidon *see* Kidna (**no. 131**)

Jaba' (Gabaa, Gebea; including al-Burj) (**no. 108**), 51–2, fig. 2g, table 3, map 8
Jabal ad-Duq *see* Jabal Quruntul (**no. 109**)
Jabal at-Tantur *see* Tantur, Kh. al- (**no. 217**)
Jabal Firdaus, Kh. *see* Herodium (**no. R6**)

Jabal Quruntul (Doc, Docus, castellum Abrahami, Jabal ad-Duq, Tahunat al-Hawa) (**no. 109**), 10, 52, map 9; *see also* Tawahin as-Sukkar (**nos. 219a/b**)
Jafenia *see* Jifna (**no. 118**)
Jaffa (Joppa, Joppe, Yafa, Yafo) (**no. 110**), 6, 11, 13, 14, 52, fig. 1, tables 1–2, map 7
Jaladiya, Kh. (Geliadia, Geladia) (**no. 111**), 52, table 3, map 7
Jaljuliya (Jorgilia, Jorgilra) (**no. 112**), 13, 52, map 5
Jami' al-Bahr *see* Tiberias (**no. 222**)
Jami' al-Masakin *see* Nablus (**no. 158**)
Jami' al-'Umari, 85
Japhe *see* Jaffa (**no. 110**)
Jarash, 2
Jardinz Abraham *see* 'Ain Duq (**no. 13**), *and* Tawahin as-Sukkar (**no. 219**)
Jaryut, Kh. (**no. 113**), 12, 13, 52, map 8
al-Jaulan (Golan), 2
Jauq, Kh. al- (H. Gov) (**no. P14**), 114, map 3
Jazirat Fara'un (al-Quraiya, Isle de Graye, Pharaoh's Island) (**no. R9**), 2, 13, 117
Jericho (Hiericho, Iericho, Jherico, ar-Riha) (**no. 114**), 10, 13, 52, fig. 1, tables 1, 3, map 9
  Burj ar-Riha, 52
Jerusalem (Hierusalem, Ierusalem, Ierosolima, al-Quds ash-Sharif, Yerushalayim) (**no. 115**), xvii, 2, 3, 5, 6, 13, 53–6, 90, figs. 1, 28, pls. xlii–xlv, table 1, map 8
  Asnerie, 56
  Birkat as-Sultan (Pool of Germanus), 56
  Citadel (David's Tower), 10, 11, 54–5, figs. 28–9, pl. xli, table 3
  David Street, 55
  Haram ash-Sharif (Temple Mount), 56
  Hinnom Valley, 56
  Mount Sion, 54
  Muristan, 55, pl. xlii
  Ophel, 56
  St Stephen's Gate, 5, 54, 56
  Siloam, 56
  Tancred's Tower, 54, pl. xl, table 3
  *see also* Har Hazofim
Jezreel (Gesreal, Iezrael, Parvum Gerinum, Tel Yizra'el, Zarain, Zir'in) (**no. 116**), 10, 56, map 6
Jherico *see* Jericho (**no. 114**)
al-Jib (Gabaon, Gibeon) (**no. 117**), 56–7, fig. 30, map 8
Jiddin, Kh. *see* Qal'at Jiddin (**no. 165**)
Jifna (Jafenia?; including al-Baubariya, al-Burj, al-Qurnaifa) (**no. 118**), 11, 14, 57, pls. xlvi–xlvii, table 4, map 8
Jisr al-Ghajar (**no. 119**), 14, 57, map 4
Joppa (Joppe) *see* Jaffa (**no. 110**)
Jordan Valley, 2, 13
Jorgilia (Jorgilra) *see* Jaljuliya (**no. 112**)
Judaida, Kh. (Elgedeide), 119
al-Junaid (**no. P15**), 114, map 5
Juwar an-Nukhl, Kh. (**no. P16**), 114, map 3

Kafartelum *see* Kafr Lam (**no. 121**)
Kafr ad-Dik, 13
Kafr Bassa, Kh. (**no. P17**), 14, 114, map 5
Kafr Istuna, Kh. *see* Istuna, Kh. (**no. 107**)

Kafr Jinnis (casellum S. Abacuc, al-Kanisa, saint Abaccu de Cantie, s. Abacuch de Quantie, s. Abacuc de Cansie) (**no. 120**), 58, table 3, map 8

Kafr Kama (Capharkeme, Kapharchemme) (**no. R10**), 117

Kafr Lam (Cafarlet, Capharleth, Habonim, Kafarletum, Kafr Lab) (**no. 121**), 10, 58, fig. 31, map 5

Kafr Murr, Kh. (Kh. Murara) (**no. P18**), 114

Kafr Sum, Kh. (Caphason) (**no. 122**), 11, 58–9, table 3, map 8

ash-Shaikh Musafar, Maqam, 59

Kafr Yasif (Cafresi, Cafriasif), 119

Kaisan, Tall (Napoleon's Hill, Tel Qison, Tolonum Rohardi de Chabor, Turon Dame Joiette) (**no. 123**), 10, 59, map 3

Kalensue *see* Qalansuwa (**no. 160**)

Kalil (H. Kalil) *see* Bir Iklil, Kh. (**no. 51**)

al-Kanisa *see* Kafr Jinnis (**no. 120**)

Kapharchemme *see* Kafr Kama (**no. R10**)

Karak (Crac, le Crac de Montreal, Cracum Montis regalis, Petra Deserti, Civitas Petracensis, *Karak al-Shawbak*) (**no. 124**), 2, 6, 10, 11, 14, 59–60, 114, figs. 1, 32, pls. XLVIII–LI, table 1, map 10

Karaza, Kh. (Chorazin, Korazin) (**no. 125**), 12, 60, map 4

Karmil, Kh. al- (Carmelus) (**no. 126**), 13, 61, fig. 2a, pls. LII–LIII, table 3, map 10

Kaukab al-Hawa *see* Belvoir Castle (**no. 46**)

*Kawkab see* Kuwaikat (**no. 135**)

Kefar Lakhish, H. *see* al-Qubaiba

Kefar Meron *see* Mairun (**no. 143**)

Kefar Nahum *see* Capernaum (**no. 77**)

al-Khalil *see* Hebron (**no. 101**)

Khan, Kh. al- (H. Hanot) (**no. 127**), 12, 61, map 8

Khan as-Sawiya (**no. 128**), 12, 61, pl. LIV, map 8

Khan at-Tujar *see* Nablus (**no. 158**)

Khan Da'uk *see* Da'uk, Tall (**no. 85**)

Khan Misqa *see* Misqa, Kh. al- (**no. 155**)

al-Khirba *see* Qasila, Tall (**no. 172**)

Khuljan, Kh. al- (Kh. al-Muntar, Kh. Umm Dar) (**no. 129**), 62, table 3, map 5

Kibbutz Bet ha-Emeq *see* Kuwaikat (**no. 135**)

Kibbutz Ma'barot *see* Madd ad-Dair (**no. 139**)

Kibbutz Merhavya *see* al-Fula (**no. 96**)

Kibbutz Shomrat (**no. 130**), 62, map 3

Kidna (Iyye Kidon) (**no. 131**), 62, table 4, map 8

Kokhav ha-Yarden *see* Belvoir Castle (**no. 46**)

Korazim *see* Karaza, Kh. (**no. 125**)

Kufriya, Kh. al- (Kh. Burj Kufriya, Tower of the Unbelievers) (**no. 132**), 12, 13, 62, map 8

Kurdana, Kh. (Tel Afeq, Tall Kurdana, Recordana, Recordane) (**no. 133**), 6, 7, 10, 11, 13, 62–4, fig. 33, pls. LV–LVIII, table 3, map 3

Kurum, Kh. al- *see* Burj, Kh. al- (**no. 61**)

Kusbur, Kh. (**no. 134**), 12, 64, map 8

Kuwaikat (Coketum, Coquetum, *Kawkab*, Kibbutz Bet ha-Emeq) (**no. 135**), 12, 62, 64, pl. LIX, map 3

Lacus Meleha *see* Yesod ha-Ma'ala (**no. 234**)

Lanahiam (Lanahie, Lanoye) *see* al-Yanuhiya (**no. 232**)

Land Castle *see* Sidon (**no. 201**)

Latrun (*al-Natrūn*, Toron des Chevaliers/de los Caballeros, Toronum Militum) (**no. 136**), 7, 10, 11, 64–5, fig. 34, pls. LX–LXI, table 3, map 8

al-Baubariya (al-Baiqa), 64

Lauza, Kh. al- (Kh. al-Lauz) (**no. 137**), 11, 13, 14, 65–6, pl. LXII, table 4, map 8

Lavi *see* Lubiya

Lebassa *see* al-Bassa (**no. R2**)

Lifta (Cleptsa, Me Neftoah) (**no. 138**), 12, 13, 14, 66, pl. LXIII, map 8

Losserin *see* Sirin (**no. 205**)

Lower Zohar *see* Qasr az-Zuwaira (**no. P21**)

Lubban Sharqiya (Lubanum), 119

Lubiya (Lubia, Lavi), 119

Lydda, 5, fig. 1, table 1

Ma'ale Adumin *see* Qal'at ad-Damm (**no. 162**)

Ma'alot *see* Mi'iliya (**no. 152**)

Madd ad-Dair, Kh. (Casale Latinae, casale quod fuit Eustachii, Hafita, Kibbutz Ma'barot, Mondisder, Mons Dederi, Montdidier) (**no. 139**), 67, table 3, map 5

Magharat al-Warda (**no. 140**), 14, 67, map 6

Magharat Fakhr ad-Din (**no. 141**), 10, 67, map 2

Magna Mahomaria *see* al-Bira (**no. 54**)

Mahomeria major *see* al-Bira (**no. 54**)

Mahomeriola *see* al-Qubaiba (**no. 178**)

Mahoz, H. *see* Makhuz, Kh.

Mahruqat, Kh. al- (**no. 142**), 13, 67, map 6

Mahumeria *see* al-Bira (**no. 54**)

Mahus *see* Makhuz, Kh.

*Māhūz Azdūd see* Minat al-Qal'a (**no. 153**)

Mairun (*Mayrūn*, Kefar Meron, Meiron, Meron) (**no. 143**), 12, 14, 67, map 4

Majdal Sadiq *see* Majdal Yaba (**no. 144**)

Majdal Yaba (Majdal Sadiq, H. Migdal Afeq, Mirabel, Mirabellum) (**no. 144**), 7, 67, figs. 1, 2b, 35, pls. LXIV–LXV, tables 1, 3, map 8

Makhuz, Kh. (Mahus, H. Mahoz), 119

*al-Malaha see* Burj al-Malih (**no. 67**)

Malat, Tall al- *see* Burj al-Malih (**no. 67**)

Maldoim *see* Qal'at ad-Damm (**no. 162**)

Malkat'ha, Kh. (H. Malka) (**no. R11**), 117

Mallah *see* Yesod ha-Ma'ala (**no. 234**)

*al-Mallūha see* Burj al-Malih (**no. 67**)

Manawat, Kh. (Kh. Baubriya, H. Manot, Manueth) (**no. 145**), 7, 11, 13, 14, 69–70, pls. LXVI–LXVII, table 3, map 3

Manhata, Kh. al- (Tarphile, Tertille, Kh. Tharfila, Tharthilla, Trefile) (**no. 146**), 12, 14, 70, pl. LXVIII, table 3, map 3

Manot, H. (Manueth) *see* Manawat, Kh. (**no. 145**)

Ma'oz Ziyyon *see* Qastal (**no. R15**)

Maqiqa, Kh. *see* Bait Kika, Kh. (**no. 34**)

Marish *see* Marus, Kh. (**no. 147**)

Maron *see* Qal'at Marun (**no. R13**)

Marqab (Margat), 6

Marus, Kh. (Marish, Merot) (**no. 147**), 12, 14, 70, map 4

Ma'shuqa, Tall al- (la Massoque, Nabi Ma'shuq) (**no. 148**), 10, 70, map 3

Maslakhit, Kh. (Miscalim, H. Mislah) (**no. 149**), 70, table 3, map 4

Massoque, la *see* Ma'shuqa, Tall al- (**no. 148**)

*Mayrūn see* Mairun (**no. 143**)

al-Mazra'a (*al-Mazra'ah*) (**no. 150**), 12, 70, map 3

Mazra'a, Kh. al- (casale Rogerii de Chasteillon, Casal de Châtillon, le Meseraa, H. Tafat) (**no. 151**), 70–1, table 3, map 5

Me Neftoah *see* Lifta (**no. 138**)

Meiron *see* Mairun (**no. 143**)

Mensa Domini/Ihesus Christi *see* at-Tabgha (**no. 213**)

Merle *see* Tantura (**no. 218**)

Meron *see* Mairun (**no. 143**)

Merot *see* Marus, Kh. (**no. 147**)

Meschium *see* Misqa, Kh. al- (**no. 155**)

le Meseraa *see* Mazra'a, Kh. al- (**no. 151**)

Meserefe *see* Mushairifa, Kh. al-

Mevasseret Ziyyon (Mevasseret Yerushalayim) *see* Qaluniya (**no. 167**); *see also* Bait Mizza, Kh. (**no. 239**)

Mezad Abbirim, H. *see* Burj Misr (**no. 75**)

Mezad 'Ateret *see* Qasr al-'Atra (**no. 174**)

Mezad Qarha *see* Qarhata, Kh. (**no. 171**)

Mezad Rahav *see* Qal'at Tahib (**no. 166**)

Mezad Zohar *see* Qasr az-Zuwaira (**no. P21**)

Mezudat Gadin *see* Qal'at Jiddin (**no. 165**)

Mezudat Hunin, H. *see* Qal'at Hunin (**no. 164**)

Mhalia *see* Mi'iliya (**no. 152**)

Migdal Afeq, H. *see* Majdal Yaba (**no. 144**)

Mi'iliya (Castellum Novum, Castellum Novum Regis, Chastiau de Roi/dou Rei, Ma'alot, Mhalia) (**no. 152**), 6, 10, 11, 47, 71–2, 83, figs. 1, 36, pls. LXIX–LXX, table 1, map 3

Minat al-Qal'a (H. Ashdod Yam, Castellum Beroart, *Māhūz Azdūd*) (**no. 153**), 10, 72, pl. LXXI, map 7

Mirabel (Mirabellum) *see* Majdal Yaba (**no. 144**)

al-Mirr (Molendina desubter Mirabellum) (**no. 154**), 13, 72, map 8

Miscalim (Mislah, H.) *see* Maslakhit, Kh. (**no. 149**)

Misqa, Kh. al- (Meschium, Khan Misqa) (**no. 155**), 12, 13, 72–3, fig. 37, map 8

Misrefot Yam *see* Mushairifa, Kh. al-

Mizpe Zohar (Upper Zohar) *see* Rujm az-Zuwaira (**no. R16**)

Molendina desubter Mirabellum *see* al-Mirr (**no. 154**)

Molendina Trium Pontium *see* al-Haddar (**no. 98**)

Mondisder *see* Madd ad-Dair (**no. 139**)

Monreal *see* Montreal (**no. 157**)

Mons Cain *see* Qaimun, Tall (**no. 159**)

Mons Dederi *see* Madd ad-Dair (**no. 139**)

Mons Garazim *see* Ras Kikis (**no. 187**)

Mons Regalis (Mont Real) *see* Montreal (**no. 157**)

Montdidier *see* Madd ad-Dair (**no. 139**)

Montfort Castle (Frans Castiaus, Qal'at al-Qarn, Qal'at al-Qurain, Starkenberg) (**no. 156**), 7, 10, 11, 13, 14, 73–5, figs. 38–9, pls. LXXII–LXXV, tables 3, 4, map 3

Montreal (Castrum Saboach, Monreal, Mons Regalis, Mont Real, Scobach, Shaubak, *al-Shawbak*) (**no. 157**), 6, 10, 11, 13, 75–6, fig. 1, pls. LXXVI–LXXVII, table 1, map 1

Mount Carmel, 10; *see also* St Margaret's Castle (**no. 196**)

Mount Garizim (Mons Garizim) *see* Ras Kikis (**no. 187**)

Mount Sion *see* Jerusalem (**no. 115**)

Mount Tabor, 2, 13, 14

Moza *see* Qaluniya (**no. 167**)

Moza, H. ha- *see* Bait Mizza, Kh. (**no. 239**)

Mubarak, Tall, 1

Mugharat al-Warda (**no. **)

Mukhalid *see* Umm Khalid (**no. 229**)

Muntar, Kh. al- *see* Khuljan, Kh. al- (**no. 129**)

Murara, Kh. *see* Kafr Murr, Kh. (**no. P18**)

*Musallīyīn, Tall al-* see Tall al-Fukhkhar (**no. 216**)

Mushairifa, Kh. al- (Meserefe, Misrefot Yam, Tel Rosh ha-Niqra, at-Taba'iq), 119

Nabi Bulus, Kh. an- (**no. R12**), 117

Nabi Ma'shuq *see* Ma'shuqa, Tall al- (**no. 148**)

Nabi Samwil, 112

Nablus (Neapolis, Naples; including Habs ad-Damm, Jami' al-Masakin, Khan at-Tujar) (**no. 158**), 1, 6, 76, fig. 1, tables, 1, 3, map 5

Nahf (Nef) (**no. P19**), 114, map 3

Nahr al-'Auja (River Yarqon), 49

Nahr al-Awali, 78

Naples *see* Nablus (**no. 158**)

Napoleon's Hill *see* Kaisan, Tall (**no. 123**)

Nathanya *see* Umm Khalid (**no. 229**)

*al-Natrūn* see Latrun (**no. 136**)

Nazareth, 5, fig. 1, table 1

Neapolis *see* Nablus (**no. 158**)

Nef *see* Nahf (**no. P19**)

Neziv, H. *see* Burj Bait Nasif (**no. 72**)

Niha (Nyha) (**no. P20**), 114, map 4

Nofekh *see* Rantiya (**no. 184**)

Noie *see* Yanuhiya, al- (**no. 232**)

Nova Villa *see* ar-Ram (**no. 182**)

Nu'aila, Kh. *see* Din'ala, Kh. (**no. 88**)

Nyha *see* Niha (**no. P19**)

Palmarea (near Tiberias), fig. 1, table 1

Palmaria (Palmer) *see* Tawahin as-Sukkar (**no. 220**)

Paneas *see* Banyas (**no. 42**)

Parva Mahomaria *see* al-Qubaiba (**no. 178**)

Parvum Gerinum *see* Jesreel (**no. 116**)

Pazelet, H. *see* Fasil Danyal, Kh.

Petra *see* al-Habis (**no. 97**)

Petra Deserti *see* Karak (**no. 124**)

Petra Incisa *see* Dustray, Kh. (**no. 90**)

Pharaoh's Island *see* Jazirat Fara'un (**no. R9**)

Phesech *see* Fasayil, Kh. (**no. 95**)

Pilgrim's Castle *see* 'Atlit (**no. 21**)

Pool of Germanus *see* Jerusalem (**no. 115**)

praesidium … in regione Suita/Suhite *see* 'Ain al-Habis (**no. 10**)

Qaimun, Tall (Caimun, Caun Mons, Caymont, Mons Cain, *al-Qaymūn*, Tel Yoqne'am) (**no. 159**), 5, 76–7, fig. 1, tables 1, 3, map 5

Qaisariya *see* Caesarea (**no. 76**)

al-Qal'a *see* Bait Dajan (**no. 29**)

Qalansuwa (Calanson, Calansue, Calanzon, Kalensue) (**no. 160**), 7, 11, 13, 77–8, figs. 1, 40, pl. LXXVIII, tables 1, 3–4, map 5

Qal'at Abu'l-Hasan (Belhasem) (**no. 161**), 10, 78, fig. 41, map 2

Qal'at al-Bahr *see* Sidon (**no. 201**)

Qal'at al-Burj *see* Burj, Kh. al- (**no. 59**)

Qal'at ad-Damm (Adumim, Castrum Dumi, Cisterna Rubea, Ma'ale Adumim, Maldoim, Rouge Cisterne, Turris Rubea) (**no. 162**), 7, 14, 78–9, figs. 2d, 42, pl. LXXIX, table 3, map 8

Qal'at ad-Dubba (Qal'at Dubal) (**no. 163**), 10, 79, table 3, map 4

Qal'at al-Fanish *see* Qaratiya (**no. 169**)

Qal'at al-Mu'azzam *see* Sidon (**no. 201**)

Qal'at al-Qarn/Quain *see* Montfort Castle (**no. 156**)

Qal'at an-Niha *see* Tirun an-Niha (**no. 225**)

Qal'at ar-Rabad *see* 'Ajlun

Qal'at ash-Shaqif Arnun *see* Beaufort Castle (**no. 44**)

Qal'at Dubal *see* Qal'at ad-Dubba (**no. 163**)

Qal'at Hunin (Castellum Novum, Chastel Neuf, H. Mezudat Hunin) (**no. 164**), 10, 79, figs. 1, 43, pl. LXXX, table 1, map 4

Qal'at Jiddin (Kh. Jiddin, Iudyn, Iudin, Mezudat Gadin, Yehi'am) (**no. 165**), 10, 11, 12, 13, 80–2, fig. 44, pls. LXXXI–LXXXIV, table 3, map 3

Qal'at Marun (Maron), (**no. R13**), 117

Qal'at Rahib (Qila' ar-Rahib, Raheb, Mezad Rahav) (**no. 166**), 12, 14, 82–3, table 3, map 4

Qal'at Subaiba (Qal'at Nimrud), 2

Qal'at Tantura *see* al-Burj (**no. 57**)

Qaluniya (Colonia, Mevasseret Ziyyon/Yerushalayim, Moza, Qalonie, Saltus Muratus) (**no. 167**), 12, 13, 83, map 8

Qaqun (Caco, Cacho, Yikon) (**no. 168**), 7, 11, 13, 83–4, figs. 1, 45, pl. LXXXV, tables 1, 3, map 5

Qaratiya (Galatia, Galatidis, la Galatie, Qeratya, *Qaratayyā*) (**no. 169**), 10, 84, table 3, map 7

Qarawat Bani Hassan (including Badd Bunduq) (**no. 170**), 13, 14, 85, map 5
Burj al-Yaqur, 85, fig. 2e, table 3

Qarhata, Kh. (Mezad Qarha) (**no. 171**), 85, table 3, map 3

Qarta, H. *see* Dustray, Kh. (**no. 90**)

Qaryat Sa'ida *see* Su'aida, Kh. (**no. 206**)

Qasale Imbert/Siph *see* az-Zib (**no. 237**)

Qasila, Tall (al-Khirba, Tel Qasile) (**no. 172**), 13, 85, map 7

Qasr, Kh. al- (H. Qazra) (**no. 173**), 10, 85, map 8

Qasr al-'Atra (le Chastelez, Mezad 'Ateret, Vadum Iacob) (**no. 174**), 10, 85, pl. LXXXVI, map 4

Qasr al-Faifa *see* al-Faifa al-Gharbiya (**no. 91**)

Qasr al-Mantara (Franche Garde?) (**no. 175**), 10, 11, 86, map 2

Qasr ash-Shaikh Raba (Ard al-Qasr, Raba) (**no. 176**), 86, table 3, map 6

Qasr at-Tuba *see* Tawahin as-Sukkar (**no. 220**)

Qasr az-Zuwaira (Mezad Zohar, Lower Zohar) (**no. P21**), 114, map 10

Qasr Bardawil (al-Bardawil) (**no. R14**), 117

Qastal (Belveer, Beauverium, Ma'oz Ziyyon) (**no. R15**), 118

*al-Qaymūn* see Qaimun, Tall (**no. 159**)

Qazra, H. *see* Qasr, Kh. al- (**no. 173**)

Qeratya *see* Qaratiya (**no. 169**)

Qesari, H. *see* Caesarea (**no. 76**)

Qibya (**no. P22**), 115, map 8

Qila' ar-Rahib *see* Qal'at Rahib (**no. 166**)

Qiri, Tall, 1

Qiryat Frostig (**no. 177**), 13, 86, map 3

Qiryat Moshe, 113

Qison, Tel *see* Kaisan, Tall (**no. 123**)

Quarantena *see* Jabal Quruntul

al-Qubaiba (Parva Mahomaria, Mahomeriola) (**no. 178**), 6, 11, 12, 13, 14, 86–7, 113, figs. 1, 46, pls. LXXXVII–LXXXVIII, tables 1, 4, map 8

al-Qubaiba (Deirelcobebe, H. Kefar Lakhish), 119

Qu'da, Kh. al- (H. 'Aqdim) (**no. 179**), 12, 87, map 3

al-Quds ash-Sharif *see* Jerusalem (**no. 115**)

Qula (Cola) (**no. 180**), 7, 87, fig. 47, table 3, map 8

al-Quraiya *see* Jazirat Fara'un (**no. R9**)

al-Qurnaifa *see* Jifna (**no. 118**)

Raba *see* Qasr ash-Shaikh Raba (**no. 176**)

Raheb *see* Qal'at Rahib (**no. 166**)

Rafidiya (**no. 181**), 12, 87–8, map 5

ar-Ram (Aram, Nova Villa, Rama, Ramatha, Ramathes) (**no. 182**), 7, 11, 14, 18, 88, figs. 1, 48, pls. LXXXIX–XCI, tables 1, 3, map 8

Ramalie *see* Ramallah (**no. 183**)

Ramallah (Ramalie?; including al-Burj) (**no. 183**), 12, 90, map 8

Ramatha (Ramathes) *see* ar-Ram (**no. 182**)

Ramla, 67, fig. 1, table 1

Ramot *see* Bait Kika, Kh. (**no. 34**), *and* Burj, Kh. al- (**no. 61**)

Rantiya (Nofekh, Rantia, Rentia, Rentie) (**no. 184**), 12, 90, map 8
al-Baubariya, 90

Ras, Tall ar- *see* Ras Kikis (**no. 187**)

Ras ad-Diyar, Kh. (near Bait Dajan) (**no. P23**), 115, map 6

Ras al-'Ain (Derina, Rasalme) (**no. 185**), 13, 90, map 3

Ras al-Qantara (Sarepta, Sarphen) (**no. 186**), 10, 90, map 2

Ras Kikis (on Mount Garizim, near Tall ar-Ras) (**no. 187**), 10, 12, 90, map 5

Rasalame *see* Ras al-'Ain (**no. 185**)

Recordana (Recordane) *see* Kurdana, Kh. (**no. 133**)

Red Tower *see* Burj al-Ahmar (**no. 63**)
Regba *see* as-Sumairiya (**no. 208**)
Rentia (Rentie) *see* Rantiya (**no. 184**)
Reonde Cisterne *see* Bir Khuwailifa (**no. 52**)
ar-Riha *see* Jericho (**no. 114**)
Roma (Rome) *see* Ruma, Kh. al-
Rosh ha-Niqra, Tel *see* Mushairifa, Kh. al-
Rosh Maya, H. *see* Ryshmiya, Kh. (**no. 190**)
Rotunda Cisterna *see* Bir Khuwailifa (**no. 52**)
Rouge Cisterne *see* Qal'at ad-Damm (**no. 162**)
Rujm as-Sayigh (**no. 188**), 90, table 3, map 9
Rujum az-Zuwaira (Zuwaira al-Fauqa, Mizpe Zohar, Upper Zohar) (**no. R16**), 114, 118
ar-Rujum *see* as-Safi (**no. 193**)
Ruma, Kh. al- (Roma, Rome, H. Ruma), 119
Rumaida, Tall ar- (Hebron), 50
Rumaila, Kh. (Tall ar-Rumaila, Bethsames, Bethsame Iudae, Tel Bet Shemesh; near 'Ain Shams, Aineseins?, Ainesens?) (**no. 189**), 12, 20, 90, map 8
Rushmiya, Kh. (Francheville?, Haifa-Romena, H. Rosh Maya, Rūshmīya) (**no. 190**), 11, 90–1, fig. 49, pl. xcii, table 3, map 3

Sabastiya (Sebaste), 5, fig. 1, table 1
Saboach, Castrum *see* Montreal (**no. 157**)
Safad (Saphet, Zefat) (**no. 191**), 7, 10, 11, 13, 91, figs. 1, 50, pl. xciii, table 1, map 4
le Saffran (Safran) *see* Shafa 'Amr (**no. P25**)
Saffuriya (le Saforie, Sephoris, Sepphoris, Zippori) (**no. 192**), 11, 18, 91, fig. 2c, pl. xciv, table 3, map 5
as-Safi (ar-Rujum, Kh. as-Safia, Kh. Shaikh 'Ali) (**no. 193**), 13, 92, map 1
Safi, Tall as- (Blanchegarde, Blanca Guarda, Tall as- Safiya, Tel Zafit) (**no. 194**), 10, 93, fig. 51, map 7
Safia, Kh. as- *see* as-Safi (**no. 193**)
Safitha (Chastel Blanc), 7
Saforie, le *see* Saffuriya (**no. 192**)
Saget (Sagitta) *see* Sidon (**no. 201**)
Sahl as-Sarabat, Tall (**no. 195**), 14, 93, map 9
Saida (Saiete) *see* Sidon (**no. 201**)
Sa'ida, Qaryat *see* Su'aida, Kh. (**no. 206**)
Sailun (*Saylūn*, Seylon, Shiloh) (**no. R17**), 118
S. Abacuc de Cancie (s. Abaccu de Cantie, s. Abacuch de Quantie) *see* Kafr Jinnis (**no. 120**)
S. Abraham *see* Hebron (**no. 101**)
S. Egidii, casale *see* Sinjil (**no. 203**)
S. Elyes, castiaus/castiel *see* at-Taiyiba (**no. 215**)
S. Georgii, casale *see* al-Ba'ina (**no. 25**)
S. Helye, castrum *see* at-Taiyiba (**no. 215**)
S. Iohan de Tire/Tyr *see* at-Tira (**no. 224**)
S, Job chastiau *see* Bal'ama, Kh. (**no. 41**)
S. Jorge Labane/de la Baene *see* al-Ba'ina (**no. 25**)
S. Lazarus *see* Bethany (**no. 47**)
St Margaret's Castle (Cava Templi, S. Margareta cast., Mount Carmel) (**no.**

196), 10, 11, 93, map 3
St Mary of Carmel, 14
*al-Sala'* *see* Sila', Kh. as- (**no. 202**)
Salamiya, Kh. *see* Burj, Kh. al- (**no. 62**)
Salman, Kh. *see* 'Ain Salman al-'Anid (**no. 14**)
Salome *see* Burj, Kh. al- (**no. 62**)
as-Salt, 2
Salt Island *see* Bait al-Milh (**no. 28**)
Saltus Muratus *see* Qaluniya (**no. 167**)
Samahete *see* Suhmata (**no. R19**)
*al-Samiriyah al-Bayda'* *see* Sumairiya, as- (**no. 208**)
Samiya, Kh. *see* 'Ain Samiya (**no. P3**)
as-Samu' (Samoe, Semoa, Eshtemoa) (**no. R18**), 118
Samueth *see* Suhmata (**no. R19**)
Sangeor *see* al-Ba'ina (**no. 25**)
Saphar castrum (Sapharanum) *see* Shafa 'Amr (**no. P25**)
Saphet *see* Safad (**no. 191**)
Sarafand al-Kharab (Sarafand as-Sughra, al-Babariyya, Yad Eli'ezer) (**no. 197**), 12, 93, map 7
Sarepta (Sarphen) *see* Ras al-Qantara (**no. 186**)
*Saydā* (Sayette) *see* Sidon (**no. 201**)
*Saylūn* *see* Sailun (**no. R17**)
Scandalion (Scandalium) *see* Iskandaruna (**no. 106**)
Scobach *see* Montreal (**no. 157**)
Sea Castle *see* Sidon
Se'adim, H. *see* Su'aida, Kh. (**no. 206**)
Seete *see* Sidon (**no. 201**)
Segor *see* Tawahin as-Sukkar (**no. 220**)
la Semerrie *see* as-Sumairiya (**no. 208**)
Semoa *see* as-Samu' (**no. R18**)
Sephoris (Sepphoris) *see* Saffuriya (**no. 192**)
Seylon *see* Sailun (**no. R17**)
Shabatin, Kh. (**no. P24**), 115, map 8
Shafa 'Amr (Cafram, Castrum Zafetanum, Safran, le Saffran, Saphar castrum, Sapharanum, *Shafra'amm*, Shefar'am) (**no. P25**), 10, 115, map 3
Shaikh Abu Talal, wely *see* Biddu (**no. 49**)
Shaikh 'Ali, Kh. *see* as-Safi (**no. 193**)
Shaikh 'Isa, Kh. ash- *see* Tawahin as-Sukkar (**no. 220**)
Shaikh Musafar, Maqam ash- *see* Kafr Sum (**no. 122**)
ash-Shaikh Sha'ala (al-Baubariya) (**no. 198**), 12, 94, map 5
Shama', Kh. (H. Shema') (**no. 199**), 12, 94, map 4
*Shaqīf Tīrūn* *see* Tirun an-Niha (**no. 225**)
Shaubak (*al-Shawbak*) *see* Montreal (**no. 157**)
Shefar'am *see* Shafa 'Amr (**no. P25**)
Shelomi *see* al-Bassa (**no. R2**)
Shema', H. *see* Shama', Kh. (**no. 199**)
Shiloh *see* Sailun (**no. R17**)
Shu'fat (Dersophath) (**no. 200**), 12, 94, map 8
Sidon (Saget, Sagitta, Saida, Saiete, *Saydā*, Sayette, Seete, Sydon) (**no. 201**), 5, 6, 10, 11, 86, 94–5, figs. 1, 52, pls. xcv–xcvi, tables 1–2, map 2
Land Castle (Qal'at al-Mu'azzam), 94, fig. 52, pl. xcv.
Sea Castle (Qal'at al-Bahr), fig. 52, 95

as-Sila' (Celle, *al-Sala'*, *al-Sila'*) (**no. 202**), 10, 95, map 1
Siloam *see* Jerusalem (**no. 115**)
Sinjil (Casale S. Egidii) (**no. 203**), 95, table 3, map 8
Sira, Kh. as- (H. Zir) (**no. 204**), 12, 95, map 6
Sirin (Losserin) (**no. 205**), 12, 95, map 6
Somelaria *see* as-Sumairiya (**no. 208**)
Spring of the Brigands/Templars *see* 'Ain al-Haramiya (**no. 11**)
Starkenberg *see* Montfort Castle (**no. 156**)
Su'aida, Kh. (Qaryat Sa'ida, H. Se'adim) (**no. 206**), 12, 95, map 6
Suba (Belmont, Zova) (**no. 207**), xvii, 7, 11, 12, 13, 14, figs. 53, 96, map 8
Subaiba *see* Qal'at Subaiba
Suet, Cava de *see* 'Ain al-Habis (**no. 10**)
Suhmata (Samueth, Samahete, Zomet Hosen) (**no. R19**), 118
Suita (Suhite), praesidium in regione *see* 'Ain al-Habis (**no. 10**)
as-Sumairiya (Regba, *al-Samiriyyah al-Bayda'*, la Semerrie, Somelaria) (**no. 208**), 12, 14, 96, fig. 54, pl. xcvii, map 3
Summail (including Bir Summail) (**no. 209**), 7, 10, 13, 97, table 3, map 7
Summaqa, Kh. (H. Sumaq) (**no. 210**), 12, 97, map 5
Sur *see* Tyre (**no. 227**)
Susiya, Kh. (**no. 211**), 13, 97, map 10
Sydon *see* Sidon (**no. 201**)

at-Taba'iq *see* Mushairifa, Kh. al-
Tabaliya, Kh. (Tablie, Tyberie, Bait Yunan an-Nabi) (**no. 212**), 12, 97, map 8
Tabarie (Tabariya) *see* Tiberias (**no. 222**)
at-Tabgha ('En Sheva', Mensa Domini/Ihesus Christi, Tabula, Tabula Domini, la Table Nostre Seigneur) (**no. 213**), 6, 97, table 3, map 4
Tablie *see* Tabaliya, Kh. (**no. 212**)
Tabula (Tabula Domini) *see* at-Tabgha (**no. 213**)
Tadun, Kh. *see* Faris, Kh. (**no. 94**)
Tafat, H. *see* Mazra'a, Kh. al- (**no. 151**)
Tafila (Taphila, Taphilia, Traphyla) (**no. 214**), 10, 98, map 1
Tahunat al-Hawa *see* Jabal Quruntul (**no. 109**)
at-Taiyiba ('Afra, Effraon, castiel/castiaus … Saint Elyes, Castle of St Elias, castrum S. Helyae) (**no. 215**), 7, 12, 98–9, fig. 55, pl. xcviii, table 3, map 8
at-Taiyiba *see* Umm at-Taiyiba (**no. 228**)
Talhum *see* Capernaum (**no. 77**)
Tall al-Akhdar, 2
Tall al-Fukhkhar (Tel 'Akko, Toron, *Tall al-Mµallīyīn*) (**no. 216**), 10, 12, 99, table 3, map 3
Tall as-Safiya *see* Safi, Tall as- (**no. 194**)
Tancred's Tower *see* Jerusalem (**no. 115**)
Tanninim, Tel *see* Burj al-Malih (**no. 67**)
Tantur, Kh. at- (Jabal at-Tantur, *Tall al'Ayadīya*, H. Turit, Turon de Saladin) (**no. 217**), 10, 99, map 3
Tantura (al-Burj, Dor, Merle) (**no. 218**), 1, 10, 99, fig. 1, table 1, map 5
Taphila (Taphilia) *see* Tafila (**no. 214**)

Tarenta *see* al-Burj (**no. 57**)
Tarphile *see* Manhata, Kh. (**no. 146**)
Tawahin as-Sukkar (Jardinz Abraham,
   Campi Abraham, Abrahe Ortus,
   below Jabal Quruntul) (**nos. 219a/b**),
   xvii, 13, 99–100, figs. 56–7, pl. xcix,
   map 9
Tawahin as-Sukkar (Qasr at-Tuba,
   Palmaria, Palmer, Segor; near Kh.
   ash-Shaikh 'Isa, Soara) (**no. 220**), 13,
   101, map 1
Tawahin as-Sukkar, Kh. (**no. 221**), 13, 101,
   map 1
Tekoa *see* Tuqu', Kh. at- (**no. 226**)
Tertille *see* Manhata, Kh. (**no. 146**)
Teverya *see* Tiberias (**no. 222**)
*Thamanin see* Tibnin (**no. 223**)
Tharenta *see* al-Burj (**no. 57**)
Tharfila, Kh. (Tharthilla) *see* Manhata, Kh.
   (**no. 146**)
Thecua *see* Tuqu', Kh. al- (**no. 226**)
Tiberias (Tabariya, Tabarie, Teverya,
   Tyberias) (**no. 222**), 5, 6, 10, 11, 101,
   fig. 1, pl. c, tables 1–2, map 4
Tibnin (*Thamanin*, Toron, Toronum,
   Tinenim, *Tibnin*) (**no. 223**), 10, 11, 79,
   102, 117, fig. 1, pl. ci, table 1, map 4
Tinenin *see* Tibnin (**no. 223**)
at-Tira (St Iohan de Tire/Tyr, Tirat
   ha-Karmel) (**no. 224**), 102–3, pl. cii,
   table 3, map 3
Tire *see* at-Tira (**no. 224**)
Tirun an-Niha (Cave de Tyron, Qal'at
   an-Niha, *Shaqif Tīrūn*) (**no. 225**), 10, 11,
   103, map 2
Tittora, H. *see* al-Burj (**no. 57**)
Tolma *see* Bait Tulma, Kh. (**no. 38**)
Tolonum Rohardi de Chabor *see* Kaisan,
   Tall al- (**no. 123**)
Tor de l'Opital, le *see* Burj ash-Shamali
   (**no. 69**)
Toron *see* Tall al-Fukhkhar (**no. 216**)
Toron *see* Tibnin (**no. 223**)
Toron des Chevaliers/de los Caballeros *see*
   Latrun (**no. 136**)
Toronum *see* Tibnin (**no. 223**)
Toronum in sabulo *see* Damietta
Toronum Militum *see* Latrun (**no. 136**)
Tourre-Rouge *see* Burj al-Ahmar (**no. 63**)
Tower of the Flies *see* Acre (**no. 5**)
Tower of the Unbelievers *see* Kufriya, Kh.
   (**no. 132**)
Traphyla *see* Tafila (**no. 214**)

Trefile *see* Manhata, Kh. (**no. 146**)
Tres Pontes *see* al-Haddar (**no. 98**)
Tuqu', Kh. al- (Tekoa, Thecua) (**no. 226**),
   10, 103, map 8
Turit, H. *see* Tantur, Kh. al- (**no. 217**)
Turon Dame Joiette *see* Kaisan, Tall (**no.
   123**)
Turon de Saladin *see* Tantur, Kh. al- (**no.
   217**)
Turricles *see* Burj al-Ahmar (**no. 63**)
Turris Latinae *see* Burj al-Ahmar (**no. 63**)
Turris Rubea *see* Burj al-Ahmar (**no. 63**)
Turris Rubea *see* Qal'at ad-Damm (**no. 162**)
turris Salinarum *see* Burj al-Malih (**no. 67**)
Tyberias *see* Tiberias (**no. 222**)
Tyberie *see* Tabaliya, Kh. (**no. 212**)
Tyr *see* Tira, at- (**no. 224**)
Tyre (Tyr, Tyrus, Sur) (**no. 227**), 5, 6, 13,
   70, 90, 103–4, figs. 1, 58, tables 1–2,
   map

Umm Baghag ('En Boqeq) (**no. R21**), 114,
   119
Umm Dar, Kh. *see* Khuljan, Kh. al- (**no.
   129**)
Umm ar-Ras ash-Shamaliya, Kh. (H. Bet
   Bad) (**no. R20**), 118
Umm at-Taiyiba, ('Afrabala, Borgelet,
   at-Taiyiba) (**no. 228**), 7, 104, fig. 2f, pl.
   ciii, table 3, map 6
Umm Khalid (Castellare Rogerii
   Longobardi, Mukhalid, Nathanya)
   (**no. 229**), 12, 104–5, fig. 59, pl. civ,
   table 4, map 5
Upper Zohar *see* Rujm az-Zuwaira (**no.
   R16**)
Urniet *see* Baituniya (**no. 40**)
Uza, H. *see* 'Ayadiya, Kh. al- (**no. 23**)

Vadum Iacob *see* Qasr al-'Atra (**no. 174**)
Valdecurs *see* 'Ain Siniya (**no. 15**)
Vallis Moysis, Castellum (li Vaux Moysi)
   *see* al-Wu'aira (**no. 230**)
Vetus Bethor *see* Bait 'Ur al-Fauqa (**no. 39**)

Wadi al-Makkuk, 99
Wadi Musa, 95; *see also* al-Wu'aira
al-Wu'aira (Castellum Vallis Moysis, li
   Vaux Maysi) (**no. 230**), 10, 11, 105–6,
   fig. 60, pls. cv–cvii, map 1

Yad Eli'ezer *see* Sarafand al-Kharab (**no.
   197**)

Yafa (Yafo) *see* Jaffa (**no. 110**)
Yalu (Castellum Arnaldi/Arnulfi, Chastel
   Arnoul/Arnold/Hernaut) (**no. 231**),
   10, 106–7, fig. 61, pls. cviii–cix, map 8
al-Yanuhiya (Lanahie, Lanoye, Lanahiam,
   Noie, *al-Yānuīyah*) (**no. 232**), 13, 107,
   map 3
Yanun, Kh. (**no. P26**), 115, map 6
Yarin (**no. P27**), 115, map 3
Yarmuq, river, 18
Yarqon, river *see* Nahr al-'Auja
Yavne *see* Yibna (**no. 235**)
Yazdūd *see* Isdud (**no. R8**)
Yazur ('Azor, Casellum de Planis, Casel des
   Plains, Casale/Casellum Balneorum,
   Casellum de Templo) (**no. 233**), 7, 108,
   fig. 62, pls. cx–cxiii, table 3, map 7
Ybelin *see* Yibna (**no. 235**)
Ybelin Hospitalariorum *see* Bait Jibrin (**no.
   32**)
Yehi'am *see* Qal'at Jiddin (**no. 165**)
Yerushalayim *see* Jerusalem (**no. 115**)
Yesod ha-Ma'ala (near Mallaha, Lacus
   Meleha) (**no. 234**), 13, 108–9, map 4
Yibna (Gibelim, Ibelin, Yavne, Ybelin) (**no.
   235**), 10, 12, 109, fig. 1, table 1, map 7
Yikon *see* Qaqun (**no. 168**)
Yizra'el, Tel *see* Jezreel (**no. 116**)
Yoqne'am, Tel *see* Qaimun, Tall (**no. 159**)

az-Zababida (Zababda; including
   al-Baubariyya) (**no. 236**), 7, 109–10,
   table 3, map 6
Zafit, Tel *see* Safi, Tall as- (**no. 194**)
Zahran, Kh. az- (**no. P28**), 115, map 5
Zarain *see* Jezreel (**no. 116**)
Zefat *see* Safad (**no. 191**)
Zeror, Tel *see* Durur, Kh. Tall ad- (**no. 89**)
az-Zib (Akhziv, Casel Imbert, Casale
   Huberti de Paci, Casale Lamberti,
   Castellum Ziph, Qasale Imbert/Siph)
   (**no. 237**), 110, fig. 1, tables 1, 3, map 3
Zippori *see* Saffuriya (**no. 192**)
Zir, H. *see* Sira, Kh. al- (**no. 204**)
Zir'in *see* Jezreel (**no. 116**)
Zoara *see* Tawahin as-Sukkar (**no. 220**)
Zoenita *see* Zuwainita, Kh. (**no. 238**)
Zomet Hosen *see* Suhmata (**no. R19**)
Zova *see* Suba (**no. 207**)
Zuwainita, Kh. (H. Bet Zeneita, Zoenita)
   (**no. 238**), 12–13, 110, map 3
Zuwaira al-Fauqa *see* Rujm az-Zuwaira
   (**no. R16**)

For EU product safety concerns, contact us at Calle de José Abascal, 56–1°,
28003 Madrid, Spain or eugpsr@cambridge.org.

www.ingramcontent.com/pod-product-compliance
Ingram Content Group UK Ltd.
Pitfield, Milton Keynes, MK11 3LW, UK
UKHW030904150625
459647UK00025B/2884